£6 £1.80

D1337106

WITHDRAWN FROM
THE LIBRARY

UNIVERSITY OF
WINCHESTER

KA 0059751 1

Borough Politics

Borough Politics

A STUDY OF THE WOLVERHAMPTON
TOWN COUNCIL, 1888–1964

G. W. JONES

MACMILLAN

© G. W. Jones 1969

First published 1969 by
MACMILLAN AND CO LTD
Little Essex Street London WC2
and also at Bombay Calcutta and Madras
Macmillan South Africa (Publishers) Pty Ltd Johannesburg
The Macmillan Company of Australia Pty Ltd Melbourne
The Macmillan Company of Canada Ltd Toronto

Printed in Great Britain by
ROBERT MACLEHOSE AND CO LTD
The University Press, Glasgow

KING ALFRED'S COLLEGE
WINCHESTER

b 6907860

352· 04249
JON   101109

To my Mother and Father

Contents

Tables

MAPS

The wards of Wolverhampton:

Preface

ACKNOWLEDGEMENTS

I WISH to thank the Warden and Fellows of Nuffield College, Oxford, for awarding me a Studentship which enabled me to conduct the research on which this book is based. The Warden, Mr D. N. Chester, Professor Bryan Keith-Lucas, and Mr P. M. Williams read and commented on the work as it progressed, and gave me most valuable advice, some of which I took. I wish to thank also those people of Wolverhampton who answered my queries with such candour and allowed me to examine documents in their possession. Without their co-operation this book could never have been written. And finally I wish to thank my wife Diana for spending the first year of marriage typing the whole book from my execrable handwriting. It could only have been a labour of love.

DESCRIPTION OF THE BOOK

This study examines the elected members of the Wolverhampton Borough Council from around 1888 to 1964; who they were, why they went on to the Council, how they were organised and what they did. After an introduction to the town, Chapters 2 and 3 consider the political background, the growth of the involvement of political parties in local government, the interaction between their Parliamentary activities and their municipal interests and the changing role of municipal elections. Chapter 4 surveys the wards over the period and relates the types of Councillor elected to the social and economic characteristics of the wards and to the different methods used by the parties to select their candidates. Chapter 5 examines the changing occupational composition of the

Council over the period, and relates it to the changes in the parties' strength in the Council. Chapter 6 looks at the various associations to which the elected members were attached. Chapter 7 considers whether the calibre of the elected members declined over the period. Chapter 8 examines the origins, development and working of the Labour Group, Chapter 9 looks at the Conservative Group, while Chapter 10 considers the other parties which fought municipal elections and had Councillors. Chapter 11 examines the role of the Chairmen of the Council committees, their relationship with their parties, other elected members and the officials, and the rise to pre-eminence of the Finance Committee and its Chairman. Chapter 12 considers the functions of the Mayors and Aldermen over the period, and Chapter 13 looks at the Town Clerks, their personalities, their conceptions of their roles and their changing relationships with the elected members and other chief officers of the Corporation. Chapters 14 and 15 discuss the conflicts which divided the Council, and what each group of Councillors was trying to make the Council do, what the political battle was about and what the contestants were aiming at. Chapter 16 tells the story of the controversy of 1961–2, which bitterly split the Council, provoked a High Court action and almost paralysed the work of the Council for a year. This episode shows the political process under strain.

This study is therefore a political study of the elected members. It treats the Town Council as a political institution and examines its political process. It is not a legal or an administrative study, nor is it a sociological study, but a work of political history. It does not deal with the growth of services, the administrative history of the Corporation, central–local relations, or the relations of the Council with surrounding authorities. Each of these topics would require a separate book, if the same time-scale were to be adhered to.

The 1890s were the last years of a traditional style of politics on the Council, which reached back to its foundation in 1848, but they also saw the beginnings of new developments, particularly the growth of the Labour Party, bringing with it on to the Council new techniques, new aims and a new style. The roots of the modern political process on the Council lie in the years at the turn of the century.

PROBLEMS OF LOCAL STUDIES

This study asks the same questions as one would of the central political process. But to study local politics presents certain difficulties not encountered by students of national politics. The student of national politics has a general framework about his subject. Certain dates have significance, like 1906, 1931 and 1945. He has an opinion about statesmen like Ramsay MacDonald or Lloyd George or Harold Macmillan. He knows roughly who were the leading men, when they were decisive and what they did. Certain important statutes are well known. And he also has similar studies to guide his researches. There is some type of accepted conceptual framework to guide his studies. The student of the politics of a local authority has no such guides. His subject has not been written about extensively by local people. There are no clear significant dates, or people, or events, or Council decisions, until he has unearthed them. And since there are no comparable studies, he has no conceptual framework to follow or attack.

His source material too presents difficulties not experienced by the student of national politics. The people involved in local politics rarely keep full diaries, do not write memoirs of their activities, produce no autobiographies, have no biographies written about them, and keep no papers and letters which would assist scholars to gauge their work. The institutions in the process, the Council itself, the parties, and the interest groups rarely hoard their past records; they are too much concerned with their present activities to store what they regard as the jumble of the past, especially when space is so short. The Council and committee minutes which have been saved record only the decisions reached, the resolutions, motions and amendments, their movers and seconders and who voted for and against, when a division was called for. The arguments used are not recorded. There is no official local authority *Hansard*. No records of the Liberal Party survive in Wolverhampton; they vanished when the party collapsed after 1945. But the Labour and Conservative Parties saved some of their records back to the 1900s, although they were not expertly written and kept. To rely therefore on written original material would deter one from ever embarking on a study of local politics. But two sources remain which can supplement the original material

-- personal interviews and the press. This study depends to a great extent on a large number of interviews and conversations with people who were involved in the Council and its political process. Human recollection, however, is not infallible, so these interviews have to be treated with caution; faulty memory, special pleading and self-justification have to be taken into account. Their statements can be checked to some extent against the Council and party records which remain, but especially against the local press, particularly for the early years of the period.

THE PRESS

At the turn of the century the daily evening paper, the *Express and Star*, devoted a large amount of space to local politics; Council meetings were extensively reported, speeches were printed verbatim, and the proceedings were covered in one slab of long unbroken paragraphs with few cross-headings. Party and election meetings were similarly fully covered. Committee reports were often printed in full; much background material about particular schemes was given, and detailed biographies appeared about the local politicians. The face of the paper in the 1950s and 1960s is quite different. The print is larger; cross-headings and headlines are more prominent; more national news is carried; photographs are frequent. Council meetings are not fully covered nor speeches produced verbatim. The topics which come up at a Council meeting are broken up into separate 'newsy' stories of a few lines, and fragments of speeches are reported only if some scandal or row has broken out. Hardly ever is much background material given, or an interview with, or a biography of, a member of the Council. Once a week the local government correspondent is allowed a few paragraphs to talk about a local government topic, usually from an administrative and rarely from a political angle, and he often deals with authorities other than Wolverhampton. An editorial occasionally considers a project of the Council's and some letters to the editor will show that a few members of the public follow the work of the Council.

The two World Wars appear to have been important factors in the decline of the coverage of Council affairs. Then newsprint was short; the size of the paper was reduced; reporters were not easily available; the Council did little of note and the press got out of the habit of reporting fully Council affairs. But other developments have been of greater significance. In 1900 the *Express and Star* was truly a local Wolverhampton paper concentrating on the affairs of Wolverhampton. But the quest for increased circulation encouraged the paper to cater for an audience in an area wider than the town itself. Its daily circulation in 1900 was 41,287 and in 1963 232,208,[1] but the majority of its sales, 61·22 per cent, were made beyond the boundaries of Wolverhampton, in the Black Country at Bilston, Walsall and Dudley, and in Staffordshire and Shropshire at Stafford, Wellington and Bridgnorth. The local government correspondent is not responsible for covering solely the Wolverhampton Council, as he was sixty years ago, but he has to cover the County, District and other Councils in the wide area where the paper sells. The reporting of Wolverhampton news has been crowded out.

In addition the local government correspondents of the 1950s and 1960s have not been of the standing of the reporters of sixty years ago. The position is not an important one in the newspaper world, but is regarded as a jumping-off point for a comparative newcomer to a better position in the paper or other papers. Recent correspondents have not been natives of the town, or lived for a long time there, nor have they stayed above two years as the local government correspondents. But for most of the period from the 1900s to the 1950s one reporter, William Small, concentrated completely on the affairs of the Town Council and got to know intimately the local officials and politicians. It is little wonder that today's coverage of the Town Council is sparse, sometimes inaccurate and usually dull.

The local political correspondent suffers from certain disadvantages not experienced by his national counterparts. The latter deal with men who often want to appear in the press, who seek publicity, and who are used to the press intruding into their activities and discussing them. But local politicians are suspicious

---

[1] From July to December 1963 its circulation was 235,347, which enabled it to claim that it was 'the fastest growing evening newspaper in the country other than those which have been merged'. *Express & Star*, 7.1.1964. From January to June 1964 the circulation was 243,297 and it was calculated that it served over 620,000 readers every evening. *E. & S.*, 8.7.1964. (See p. 18 for abbreviations used in the footnotes.)

of the press and shun publicity.[1] Where the national correspondent
is able to personalise politics, the local man is inhibited. He has to
live with the Councillors in a small community. If politics were
personalised in the press, it is likely that life for the Councillors
would be difficult, so close are they to their constituents, while
the reporter would see his sources and contacts become very
reluctant to talk to him at all. In carrying out his very limited task
as it is he depends to a great extent on the goodwill of the local
officials and politicians. If he were to rub them up the wrong way,
he would be unable to present what news he does. Further, the
reporter of sixty years ago was not so dependent on the Council for
official handouts and press releases as he is today. Then he would
have to do much digging out of stories himself, but today, with the
pressure of work so much more intense, he is grateful to the
Council for predigesting so much of his material. For all these
reasons, therefore, the local paper is a much more valuable source
for the study of local politics before the First World War than it is
for the study of contemporary events.

Despite the difficulties of finding reliable source material, it is
still a worthwhile task to make use of what is available in order for
the first time to present a survey of the political structure and
process of a town Council over a period of more than sixty years.

I conducted my research between 1961 and 1963, and this
means that two big issues, which provoked considerable controversy in the town and Council after 1963, are not discussed.
A large number of Asians and West Indians settled in the town in
the late 1950s and early 1960s. Up to 1964 politicians paid little
attention to the problems which these immigrants posed, although
in the areas where they had congregated there was a simmering of
discontent. It was not until 1964, however, that local politicians
began to talk openly about the issues involved, when they felt that
electoral advantages could be gained; the result was that a
racialist was elected to the Council in 1965, standing as an
Independent, the first real Independent for twenty years to be
elected to the Council.

The second issue was the reorganisation of local government in

---

[1] This factor was quite apparent from the many interviews with members of
the Council of both parties. Only one Councillor regularly gave the press
complete versions of his speeches, and he was not a leading member.

the West Midlands. The Local Government Commission had recommended a large extension of the boundaries of Wolverhampton to take in many neighbouring authorities who were reluctant to be amalgamated. The Government accepted the Commission's advice, and in 1966 a new Wolverhampton County Borough came into being with a population of 267,000 and an area of 17,000 acres. The old Wolverhampton had had a population of 150,000 and an acreage of 9126. This book is about the old Wolverhampton which ceased to exist in 1966. Nothing in this book refers to the present Council.[1] This book is history.

[1] Except the opening section of the Conclusion.

ABBREVIATIONS USED IN FOOTNOTES

C.M.	*Council Minutes*
E. & S.	*Express and Star*
M.C.G.	*Minutes of the Conservative Caucus or Conservative Group*
M.L.G.	*Minutes of the Labour Group*
M.L.L.P.	*Minutes of the Local Labour Party*
M.M.C.	*Minutes of the Management Committee of the West Wolverhampton Conservative Association*
M.R.S.	*Minutes of the Wolverhampton (Penn Ward) Ratepayers' Society*
W.C.	*Wolverhampton Chronicle*

1 The Town

THE GEOGRAPHICAL SETTING

WOLVERHAMPTON is a county borough in the West Midlands in the south-west of Staffordshire. It lies thirteen miles from Birmingham, on the north-west extremity of the Black Country. The town centre is 530 feet above sea level on the top of the north-west end of a sandstone ridge which runs north to south and divides the watersheds of the Severn and the Trent. To the east the ridge slopes down to the conurbation of the Black Country, an industrial area built up all the way to Birmingham, while to the west it spreads out to the lush farming country of the Shropshire plain. Geology and geography have put the town half in and half out of the Black Country, for its south-eastern part rests on coal, ironstone and limestone, while in the north and west the earth is rich fertile clay.

ECONOMIC HISTORY

In 1750 the town's population was 7454, rising by 1801 to 12,565.[1] Around the turn of the century it was already an industrial manufacturing town and no longer merely a centre for marketing rural produce, especially wool, which it had been in the Middle Ages. Its chief products were small metal goods[2] and japanned iron and papiermâché ware,[3] which all demanded a high degree of skill and were made either in the homes of craftsmen or in small workshops. From the 1820s the exploitation of the coal and iron deposits around the town began on a more massive scale and the population of the town soared, from 18,380 in 1821 to 49,985 in

[1] See Table I. (See pp. 351 ff. for tables.)
[2] e.g., locks, buckles, screws, thimbles, watch chains, whistles, metal toys, jewellery and buttons.
[3] e.g., snuffboxes and coal scuttles.

1851. From the 1820s to the 1860s the town flourished as a
manufacturer of iron sheets and bars and of heavy crude-iron
products.[1] It also turned out finished articles of metal, a variety of
cast- and wrought-iron household goods, and it was famed as the
centre for the manufacture of the highly decorated japanned tinplate ware.[2] The blast furnaces, forges, foundries, mills, factories
and workshops belched out the flames and smoke which gave the
Black Country its name.

By the 1870s the coal and iron seams were largely exhausted or
difficult to tackle because of flooding and subsidence. Foreign
competition and tariffs, and competition from other parts of
Britain, particularly the new steel areas, hit hard the ironmasters
of the town. Firms closed; some moved away to more convenient
sites. The town concentrated less on the heavier products and
more on finished metal goods, like edge tools,[3] hollow-ware[4] and
brassware.[5] It made a wide variety of metalware and ironmongery,
cast, wrought, turned, enamelled or galvanised, and household,
industrial and agricultural implements for use both at home and
abroad.[6]

In 1871 the population was 68,291; in 1891 it had risen to
82,662, a slower increase than had taken place in the early and
middle years of the century. But the old pace revived in the 1890s,
for by 1901 the population was 94,187. The 1890s were boom years
again for the town; buildings rose at an unprecedented rate;
suburbia emerged as the tramways pushed out from the town
centre, especially to the western part of town; new industries took
root and the older industries once again adapted themselves to
changed economic conditions. Change was forced on them by
dwindling markets due to increased foreign competition and

[1] e.g., bridges, girders, rails, axles, spikes, pulleys, anchors, cables, chains,
wheels, tubes, gates and fences.
[2] e.g., trays, caddies, dishcovers, boxes for bread, cake, jewellery and cards,
workboxes and inkstands, vases, tea urns and coffee pots.
[3] e.g., hoes, axes, spades, shovels, picks, trowels.
[4] e.g., pots and pans, kettles, baths, buckets, watering cans, troughs, churns.
[5] e.g., taps, pipes, washers, pumps, engine fittings.
[6] e.g., anvils, hammers, rivets, bolts, nuts, hooks, hinges, latches, files, springs,
pins, nails, door-knockers and -scrapers, wire netting, grates, fenders, fire irons,
bedsteads, screwdrivers, locks, keys, safes and strongrooms, chests, corrugated-
iron roofing, enamelled signs for railways, streets and notice boards, boilers and
tubes for gas, water and steam, tanks and gasometers.

tariffs, and by the increased difficulties and expense of obtaining raw materials. Wolverhampton became a town making electrical apparatus,[1] vehicles of all kinds,[2] the accessories and components of vehicles, engineering equipment and the machine tools needed to produce the finished articles.[3] The town became an engineering centre. In 1901 16 per cent of the male workforce was occupied in the manufacture of metal goods, 11 per cent in engineering and 9·5 per cent in the building industry. The rest were scattered among other industries; the railways, particularly the G.W.R., which had a works for the manufacture and servicing of loco-motives in the town; the chemical industries, producing the acids for the metal trades, the paints, oils and varnishes for the finished articles and fertilisers and artificial manure; the boot and shoe industry, the rope, twine and sacking industry and the breweries. Wolverhampton had a very diversified economy.

From 1901 to the First World War the growth of the town slackened. The 1900s were not so dynamic as the 1890s. By 1911 the population had risen only to 95,328. During the war the town's engineering and metalware industries were of great significance in the war effort, especially for the manufacture of munitions and tanks. In the inter-war years the car industries vanished, bankrupt and overtaken by other towns like Oxford and Coventry, but new industries established themselves too; the manufacture of artificial fibres, rubber tyres, aluminium foil, aircraft and their components. Engineering enterprises expanded as did those industries con-cerned with the making of composite articles demanding skilled labour. The older industries making cruder products contracted. In 1921 the population of the town was 102,342; by 1933, following two extensions of the borough boundaries, it was 138,622. The Census of 1951 showed the town at its peak of 162,672; how-ever, during the 1950s as the slums were cleared and the people rehoused beyond the boundary, the population fell, to 150,825 in 1961.

The town in the 1950s as in 1900 was not dependent on a single industry. Seventeen per cent of the workforce was engaged in the manufacture of metal goods, 13 per cent in making electrical

---

[1] e.g., switchgear, generators, motors, conduits, fans, batteries.
[2] e.g., cars (Sunbeam, Star, Clyno), cycles and motor-cycles.
[3] e.g., presses, lathes, drills, dies.

apparatus and in the engineering industry and 10·5 per cent in the manufacture of vehicles and their accessories and components. The rest were spread over the rayon and nylon industry, the rubber tyre, chemicals and building industries and the railways. Wolverhampton is reputed to be a town of over 150 trades. This diversified economy enabled the town to weather the depression years without large-scale unemployment. In the 1920s and 1930s it attracted workers from the depressed areas of the North and Wales; in the late 1940s many East Europeans came to the town, and in the 1950s and 1960s it was a magnet for West Indians, Indians and Pakistanis. The economic variety of the town and the possession of a large source of skilled labour have enabled Wolverhampton to adapt itself successfully to changing economic conditions throughout its history.

At the end of the nineteenth century the heavier and cruder products were manufactured in the eastern part of the town, where coal and iron had been mined and through which three railway companies had driven their lines and two canals flowed to bring to the town its raw materials and to take away its finished products. The lighter and smaller articles were made in this area too, but more so in an industrial ring which encircled the town centre and contained a large number of small factories. Most of the working men of the town lived in the courts and alleys of the east, and among the workshops of the inner industrial circle. The more skilled workmen, the artisans and the middle classes lived in the west; the more prosperous living further from the centre and the industrial area than the less well-off. The most prosperous men of the town, the manufacturers, professional and commercial men, lived in the far west of the town among the trees, fields and parks at Penn Fields, Goldthorn Hill, Merridale and along the Tettenhall Road.

The east remained an industrial area, although in the course of the 1950s and 1960s the Council pulled down many of the old factories and slums, reclaimed the land left derelict by the mines and furnaces, and levelled the pit mounds and slag heaps to provide municipal housing estates. In the north-east, close to the railways and canals, the new industries of the 1920s sited themselves and were followed by numerous engineering and electrical apparatus firms. Here also the Council built huge housing estates at Low

Hill and Bushbury in the 1930s, 1940s and 1950s. The west remained less industrialised than the east, but more residential than in 1900. The fingers of suburban terraced housing, which pushed out to the western countryside of the 1890s, were in the 1920s and 1930s surrounded and then in the 1950s and 1960s extended both by Council estates and, preponderantly in Penn and Merridale, by private estates. In the industrial ring around the town centre the slums were cleared away in the 1930s and 1950s, and in the 1960s the factories were removed, relocated and concentrated in a zone in the south-west at Blakenhall, while on the reclaimed land, high blocks of Council flats were built, together with offices, shops and a new Retail Market Hall.

The town centre to 1964 was largely a creation of the 1880s, following the acquisition by the Corporation of the decaying medieval centre, its demolition and rebuilding and the re-designing of its street patterns. Between then and the 1960s the centre was little altered save for some street widenings in the 1920s. But in the 1960s its face is being drastically renovated as urban renewal and redevelopment get under way. This area is still, as it was sixty years ago, the administrative, judicial, business, commercial, professional, shopping, religious, cultural and enter-tainment centre of the town.

In 1964 the town was still divided into a western and an eastern half, but the split was not so glaring as in 1900. The west was mainly a residential area, chiefly of private owner-occupied estates, with occasional Council estates and a pocket of industrial activity. The east was basically an industrial area, containing larger enter-prises than in the west, with growing Council house estates and very little private housing.

THE POLITICAL SETTING

This economic and social division has had political consequences. From 1832 to 1885 the borough returned two M.P.s, usually Liberals of the Radical type. In 1885 the borough was divided into two constituencies, East and West Wolverhampton.[1] The former

---

[1] South Wolverhampton contained no part of the municipal borough. It was later renamed the Bilston division. It comprised Bilston and Sedgley.

returned Liberal M.P.s to 1945, while the latter returned Conservatives, except when Labour was successful in 1906, 1929 and
1945.[1] The Parliamentary boundaries did not coincide with
municipal boundaries until 1948. Before then the East Division
comprised only three of the fifteen wards of the borough plus a
large area beyond the boundaries at Wednesfield and Willenhall.
The West Division contained nine wards and a little area at
Ettingshall. The other three wards lay in the Cannock division of
Staffordshire. In 1948, however, the whole municipal borough
was divided between the North-East and the South-West constituencies. Since then the former has returned a Labour M.P.
and the latter a Conservative.

Thus the whole of the borough of Wolverhampton has never
been within the boundaries of one Parliamentary constituency.
This factor has had important consequences for the organisations
of the major political parties of the town, which will be examined
later. The Liberals and Conservatives have had a similar pattern
of organisation. Their basic unit was the ward party which sent
delegates to the constituency association, one for each constituency.
The Labour Party is the same, but in addition it has had an
organisation covering the municipal borough to deal with municipal
affairs, which has been called at various times the Central, the
Municipal or the Borough Labour Party. It comprised delegates
from all the wards into which the borough was divided and from
the constituency organisations. In the Conservative and Liberal
Parties municipal affairs were the responsibility not of a special
organisation but of the constituency associations. Further, both
the Labour and Conservative Parties have Groups, i.e. the meetings
of their members of the Town Council to plan the policy and
tactics of the parties on the Council. Labour introduced this
system and it was later adopted by the Conservative Party.

THE TOWN'S GOVERNMENT

For local government an Act of 1777 created Town Commissioners
to be responsible for the good order and government of the town.
In 1848 Wolverhampton received a royal charter of incorporation

[1] See Table II.

as a Municipal Borough; and in 1888 it was one of the original
county boroughs. From 1848 to 1927 the Council numbered
forty-eight members, twelve Aldermen and thirty-six Councillors.
Increases in the area of the borough in 1927 and 1933 resulted
in a Council numbering sixty; fifteen Aldermen and forty-five
Councillors. From 1848 to 1896 the town was divided into eight
wards; twelve from 1896 to 1927; thirteen from 1927 to 1933, and
fifteen from 1933.

The Council was divided into committees, each responsible for
administering a particular service and each reporting to the full
Council about its activities. In 1900 there were fifteen standing
committees of the Council and fifteen sub-committees with two
special temporary committees.[1] The normal size of a committee
was thirteen, and each member of the Council sat on between
three and five committees; three members sat on over five committees, two on six and one on seven. In 1963 there were twenty-
six standing committees and twenty-three sub-committees.[2] The
normal size of a committee was ten and each member sat on
between three and five committees; a few members sat on six,
although some of these committees were minor like Rating and
Payments. A comparison of the lists of Council committees in
1900 and 1963 shows the great increase which took place in the
Council's activities over the period, and that, although the Council
lost some functions,[3] it gained far more.[4] To meet this increase in
responsibilities without increasing proportionately the number of
Councillors, the size of the committees was reduced; they met
less often and many were amalgamated.[5] The number of full-time
servants of the Corporation increased. Tables VA and VB show
the chief officials of the Corporation and their departments in 1900
and 1963, and a comparison of these two lists shows the great
increase both in the functions of the Council and in the Chief
Officers of the Council. In 1900 the Corporation employed around
100 to 200 people, but in March 1963 it employed 7183 including
1147 teachers.

[1] Lists of the committees in 1900 and in 1963 are given in Tables III and IV.

[2] The Council also nominated to 31 positions on 19 other bodies.

[3] e.g., electricity and hospitals.

[4] e.g., care of children, education, welfare services, housing, town and country
planning.

[5] e.g., Free Library and Art Gallery into Cultural and Entertainments.

HISTORY OF THE COUNCIL'S SERVICES

In the middle of the nineteenth century the main functions of the Council were to provide services to property and to enable trade to flow freely. The town was paved, lighted, cleaned and drained. A police force gave law and order. The fire brigade gave protection, and the markets were regulated. In the 1860s the Corporation bought out the Water Company to ensure that the water of the town was pure, and it undertook a great scheme of deep drainage and sewage disposal to make the town more healthy; at the same time it established a Free Library. In the 1870s a new Town Hall was built and the Corporation purchased the baths to be run as a municipal concern. The 1860s and 1870s were the years when H. H. Fowler, later Lord Wolverhampton, was the great municipal leader, urging Corporation enterprise before Joseph Chamberlain at Birmingham.[1] In the 1880s an Improvement Scheme was adopted, which resulted in the modernising of the town centre. The race-course was converted into a public park and an Art Gallery and Museum was established. The latter came about through the generosity of a leading citizen, Philip Horseman, who gave the land and money to set up the Gallery and Museum.[2] The 1890s saw another large public park formed out of some derelict land in the east.[3] Municipal enterprise was extended to the manufacture of electricity which was used to light the town, and the tramways were purchased and then electrified by the Corporation with a revolutionary new system.[4] A new covered Wholesale Market, Cold Stores and Abattoirs were constructed. Existing services were improved and extended to the growing suburbs.[5] In 1903 the Council took over the elementary schools from the School Board and later a School Medical Service was set up. The 1900s and up to the war saw little new activity by the Council, other than consolidating existing functions, improving Queen's Square, laying out anew St Peter's Churchyard and erecting a new refuse destructor. After the war the Council became deeply

---

[1] E. H. Fowler, *The Life of Henry Hartley Fowler*, London, 1912.

[2] In the late nineteenth century many wealthy citizens donated money to establish various institutions in the town. It was a great era of municipal patriotism. See W. H. Jones, *The Story of the Municipal Life of Wolverhampton*, London, 1903.

[3] A donation of Alfred Hickman.

[4] See Chapter 2, pp. 40–2.   [5] e.g., libraries, sewers, water, electricity.

involved in slum clearance and the building of houses. A drive was made to substitute the water-carriage system of excrement disposal for the pan system.[1] Personal welfare services grew, a midwifery service was introduced, maternity and child welfare clinics set up and the Council became responsible for the care of the blind and the mentally defective. From 1930 the responsibilities of the Board of Guardians were transferred to the Corporation, and, although in 1934 unemployment relief became a government responsibility, the duty of providing general relief to the needy remained with the Council and was the foundation on which was later laid the Welfare Services Committee. The boundaries of the borough were extended twice. The streets of the centre were widened. Trolley buses replaced trams. A new public hall, the Civic Hall, was built next to the old Town Hall. A municipal aerodrome was opened. The Cemetery Company was bought by the Council. Existing services were further improved and extended to the new housing estates and to the recently acquired areas. After the Second World War the Council's tasks increased further. Slum clearance and the building of new estates sped on quickly. Under Town and Country Planning legislation the Council formulated a town development plan; urban renewal began to make its impact; an inner ring road was started; the old Retail Market Hall was demolished and a new one built on a new site. The Council's responsibilities for welfare services increased. It had to care for children in need, old people, the handicapped and the mentally ill. Home Helps, Health Visitors and a Municipal Chiropody Service were under the wing of the Council. The education system was expanded; new schools were built on the new estates and new types of educational institutions opened, bilateral schools, the Wulfrun College and the Day Teachers' Training College. A fine sports stadium was erected. All the time existing services were being carried out, improved and extended. Many of the activities of the Council were forced on it by government legislation, or stimulated by government grants, particularly the percentage grant, but many, too, were undertaken on the initiative of the Council itself.

[1] With the pan system the human waste products remained in containers in the house, until collected by Corporation officials and their carts. With the water closet the wastes were flushed from the lavatory into the Corporation sewers.

Thus the Council of 1963 had far more responsibilities than the Council of 1900. There was far more work for the Councillors. The area of the borough had grown from 3525 acres to 9126. Its population had risen from 94,187 to 150,825. Its rateable value in 1900 was £362,592; in 1963 £7,343,693. The Corporation's rate raised in 1900 £79,188 and in 1963 £2,844,727. Government grants in 1900 totalled £8994; in 1963 £2,203,105. The Council in 1963 had responsibility over a greater area, a larger number of people and a more varied range of services than in 1900. It raised and spent more money and employed more staff, and yet the number of its elected members had increased by only twelve.

2 The Political Background 1888-1919

In 1900 the forty-eight members of the Wolverhampton Town Council, except the four Labour Councillors, called themselves Independents. They did not owe their seats to the support of any national or local political party.[1] Nor inside the Council did they vote together in permanent groups. Their election addresses rarely mentioned their national party allegiances. Newspaper reports of nominations for Council seats gave more prominence to the candidates' occupations, religion and places of residence than to their national party loyalties. Councillors and candidates agreed that national political parties were inappropriate in municipal affairs, since their purpose was to gain and sustain support for a Member of Parliament and not to promote municipal candidates and to advocate and implement policies for the town. There were, therefore, strictly no Conservative nor Liberal members of the Council and no Conservative nor Liberal municipal policies. Even the Labour members represented only in a vague way the working classes and in particular some local trades unions; there was as yet no national Labour Party. Municipal and Parliamentary affairs were separate.

But all the non-Labour members of the Council supported either the Liberal or the Conservative Parties, as voters and members, and many indeed held official positions in the local constituency and ward organisations of their parties. When these connections are taken into account, it can be said that in 1900 the Wolverhampton Town Council consisted of twenty-five Conservatives, fifteen Liberals, four Labour and only four whose allegiances are unknown.[2] A comparison of this analysis with that

[1] There was no 'Independents'' association.
[2] See Table VI. Details of the political affiliations of members of the Council are taken from newspaper sources, mainly obituaries, reports of election contests

of the Council in 1889 shows that during the course of the 1890s
the Conservatives gained two seats, the Liberals lost six and Labour
made its first appearance.[1]

ELECTIONEERING

The way in which these Councillors entered the Council was quite
different from that of the 1950s and 1960s. To become a member
of the Council the aspirant has to win an election, as does every
Councillor after having served for a period of three years. These
elections took place annually in November,[2] and in Wolverhampton
at this time twelve seats became vacant each year. Actual contests
between competing individuals, however, were exceptional.
Between 1849 and 1902 only one or two contests took place each
November. The greatest number of seats contested in a November
election was four, and these occurred only in the two years 1878
and 1897. During the 1880s there were three years when
there were no November contested elections. Many wards
never witnessed a contest, for example between 1896 and 1902
six wards had no November fights. Competition, therefore,
both for nominations to and for a seat on the Council was not
intense.[3]

Only a small proportion of the town's population were given
the chance to participate in electing Councillors. In 1900, when
one seat was fought, 959 people voted, a mere 1 per cent of the
town's inhabitants. In 1897 there were four contests in which
4 per cent of the population voted, and in 1903, when there were
nine fights, 10 per cent of the population was engaged. These low
figures are explained by the small number of actual contests and
by the small number of those eligible to vote: in 1897 only 15

---

and Council debates, and occasional articles and letters. The 'unknowns' were
insignificant men who made no mark on the Council nor in the town generally,
and thus never merited much newspaper attention.

[1] Table VI. In 1889 the Council comprised 23 Conservatives, 21 Liberals
and 4 unknown.

[2] From 1949 May was the election month.

[3] Between 1888 and 1902 there were 27 contested elections in November:
unopposed returns totalled 153. During the same period there were 54 new
members of the Council.

per cent of the town's population was eligible and in 1903 18 per cent. These percentages of the town's population are a more realistic measurement of the amount of public participation in the elections than the percentages of the actual electorate of the particular ward who voted. In 1897 and 1903 there were turnouts of between 70 per cent and 80 per cent in the contested wards, but these large figures conceal the fact that only a small proportion of the population was eligible to vote. The years 1897 and 1903 were chosen deliberately, because more contests occurred then than was usual, yet even at these high peaks of electoral activity very few of the inhabitants of Wolverhampton took part in choosing their town's governors.[1]

Fighting an election contest was not the typical means by which a Councillor gained or retained his seat. Usually he was nominated by a group of colleagues, sometimes business or professional acquaintances, neighbours from the same area as his home or work, fellow worshippers at his chapel or church, or members of his political party and club. Teams of canvassers would tour the ward urging the electors to support their candidate; rivals might attempt to discover if another candidate stood any chance. If his cause appeared hopeless, he would withdraw, and thus the first in the field would enter the Council unopposed. The small size of the electorate would enable the canvassers to discover what support their candidate could command far more easily than when the electorate has grown larger. This factor may partly explain the paucity of contests, since the early soundings would give a more accurate picture of the electorate's opinions than would be possible today.

If, however, the rival did not withdraw, then the canvassers pressed all the harder the claims of their candidates. Committee rooms and canvass headquarters were established in private houses, in commercial premises[2] especially public houses, and in the political clubs. Clergy of all persuasions, Anglican, Nonconformist and Catholic, urged their flocks to support a particular candidate, and the churches and chapels provided bands of eager helpers. Business and professional men spurred their employees to support the man of their choice. The drink trade, brewers and

[1] See Table VII.
[2] An undertaker put his premises at the disposal of the Radical Liberals.

licensed victuallers, rallied to the publicans' candidate; lawyers and their clerks turned out to help the solicitors' candidate.

Public meetings were held in the ward for the candidate to explain his policy and for his supporters to praise his qualities.[1] Their speeches were reported almost verbatim in the press: its correspondence columns were full of letters about the election, and the paper itself often took sides, advocating from its leader columns the return of a specific individual. Finally on election day the canvassers called on the voters to fulfil their promises; anything 'from a milk float to a carriage and pair'[2] were used to transport the electors to the polling booths. To depart from this style of campaigning invited comment. In 1894 one candidate proclaimed his contempt for his opponent by refusing either to canvass or to hold public meetings, but he took care on polling day to have forty vehicles at his disposal. Labour found itself hampered in its early contests by its lack of committee rooms and vehicles.

This style of campaigning is perhaps a partial explanation of the high percentage turnout of the electorate in the individual wards. Since so few contests were fought each November, attention would be concentrated on those few where the battles were taking place. Eager helpers of a particular candidate would converge on the ward from all over the town. That an election was soon to take place could not be missed in this atmosphere of drama. These factors, plus the fact that the electorate was restricted to the more wealthy, better educated, more politically conscious and civic-minded groups in society, go far to explain the high turnout figures for the few wards where contests did occur.

All the candidates used these similar campaign methods, and their appeals to the electorate in their election addresses and at public meetings were also similar. First, the personal qualities and special experience of the candidate were displayed as fitting him to serve on the Council. For the sitting member seeking re-election service on the Council itself was deemed an adequate qualification. But the experience which was most constantly stressed was knowledge of business. The businessman, it was claimed, was

---

[1] These meetings were invariably held in halls attached to schools or places of worship. *Wolverhampton Chronicle*, 22.10.1890, and *Express and Star*, 13.3.1890.
[2] *E. & S.*, 1.11.1890.

skilled in management and finance, accustomed to looking five years ahead, possessed of the ability to make a good bargain and the opportunity to assist the working man far more than could the working man himself; he had the time to devote to the Council and was a man of integrity and straightforwardness. The second desirable attribute was a close connection between the candidate and the ward which he sought to represent. A long residence in the ward, even a lifelong residence, and being a large ratepayer or an employer of labour there enabled the candidate, it was said, to promote more effectively the interests of the ward. Promises to advance the welfare of the ward constituted the third part of the appeal, especially in the wards of the east end of the town, which many candidates claimed were neglected by the Council composed chiefly of 'West-End swells'.[1] Branch libraries, reading-rooms, baths, laundries, improved lighting, cleansing and road-mending were the amenities sought for what was called the 'worst-lighted and worst-cared-for area in the town'.[2] The fourth element of the appeal was to take up a position over some current topic of controversy, the issue of the moment, which varied from year to year. Candidates would be for or against the Lorain system of tramway propulsion, the construction of the Municipal Cold Stores, a Municipal Tram Service, compulsory vaccination, the pan system of excrement disposal, or the Corporation's devices to treat sewage effluent. The final part of the appeal was to denigrate the opponent as lacking the requisite personal qualities and experience, as being out of touch with the ward and neglectful of its interests, and as proposing the wrong policies.

The leading characteristics of the appeal to the electorate were its highly personal nature and its concentration on the interests of the ward. Noticeably absent were any references to political parties and any comprehensive municipal programme. The specific policies advocated varied from candidate to candidate, from year to year and from ward to ward. During the early 1890s the nearest approach to a consistent policy came from the Radical Liberal temperance reformers. In five of the annual elections between 1885 and 1897 the teetotallers campaigned to reduce the numbers of licensed houses; drink, they argued, was the cause of the

---

[1] *E. & S.*, 27.10.1893.   [2] *E. & S.*, 31.10.1890.

appalling social conditions in the east end of the town. This cause was promoted by a group of Radical Nonconformists and can be called the earliest example of a municipal programme. But the Labour candidates were responsible for the first comprehensive municipal programme, covering numerous aspects of the Council's work. During the 1890s a Labour policy was gradually evolved which all Labour candidates advocated in whatever ward and at whatever election they stood. They pressed for a municipal cemetery, municipal tramway service and a municipal gasworks, the construction of low-rent Council houses for artisans, the speedier abolition of the pan system and improved wages and conditions for the Corporation employees.

Thus, with these two exceptions, elections were not contested by local organised groups which over a period of time were seeking to promote distinctive sets of policies. In this sense then the elections were 'non-political'. But the most common meaning of 'non-political' was that national political parties did not put forward candidates bearing the label of the national party, backed by the organisation of that party and championing the particular policies of that party. It is true that a candidate who supported one national party might be nominated by a sup- porter of another party, even to fight against a member of the nominator's party.[1] Members of one party might appear on the public platform as supporters of a candidate who belonged to the other party, and occasionally in by-elections members of the same party might fight each other for a seat on the Council. Candidates stressed the non-political nature of their campaigns, proclaimed their refusal of the help of political parties and criticised any candidate who tried to introduce politics into a campaign. And once on the Council they asserted that in local affairs, as far as Council work was concerned, they did not recognise political parties. Despite all this there was covert party political influence at work; for example in general a candidate was nominated, supported on the public platform and assisted in his campaign by colleagues of the same political persuasion as himself.[2] His

[1] e.g., in 1892 the Liberal, S. T. Mander, nominated W. G. Allen, a Conserva- tive, who was opposing a Liberal, S. Larkinson.

[2] In 1927 a correspondent to the local paper looked back on forty-five years as a voter in the borough and said: 'There have always been cliques of Liberals

campaign headquarters was most often a political club; for the Liberals the Liberal Club was a centre; the Conservatives used their Deanery Club and their working-men's clubs; and the Labour Party, too, had its base in its clubs. Never in a November election did members of the same party compete for office. The candidates, sitting members and aspirants save for the most insignificant, had well-known national party allegiances, and very often held high office within the constituency organisations. It is clear that those people who took an active interest in national politics tended also to be active in municipal affairs and Council politics. Thus it could always be argued that one side or the other had introduced party politics into an election, for a well-known political figure had only to seek election and receive the help of his colleagues, and he would meet this kind of criticism, whether or not he had put his national politics on his election address. To do that was regarded as making an open bid for party support and was deprecated by the opposition. One election during the years 1888 to 1902 stands out as being the most openly political. In 1892 'the Liberals have asked the Irish electors to vote for Phillips and Larkinson who are supporters of Gladstone and Home Rule; Stanton and Gough Allen being put down as supporters of Balfour and coercion',[1] and local Conservative M.P.s lent their carriages to the Conservative candidates. Such a blatant political campaign was exceptional; most of the elections for the Town Council at the turn of the century, compared with those of the 1950s and 1960s, were non-partisan, personal battles more than party conflicts. Parties based locally or nationally did not fight municipal elections in a systematic and organised manner. The contestants were individuals or informal and unofficial groups without permanent organisations behind them.

That party politics, as regards the Council, were comparatively in the background during this period has numerous explanations. One is that neither the Liberal nor the Conservative Party possessed a distinctive and coherent municipal policy which it wished to implement through the Council; the parties opposed each other

---

and cliques of Tories fighting each other for seats on the Council.' *E. & S.*, 14.3.1927.

[1] *E. & S.*, 1.11.1892.

over issues other than municipal affairs, and the work of the Council did not give rise to the kinds of issues which divided Conservatives from Liberals. There were no opportunities for solid groups of party adherents to face each other, and thus there was no constantly recurring cleavage. The Councillors, of roughly the same social standing, whose families intermarried, were members of similar associations, possessed of a common ethos and were not divided in the context of the Council by any ideological or political differences. In Council they voted not with a group with whom they always voted, but now with some members and now with others. On each division, over each issue, there was a new combination of Councillors.

THE M.P.S

There was also little incentive for the parties to organise for and fight local elections in order to improve their positions at the General Elections, for on the Parliamentary level at the turn of the century very little divided the bulk of the Liberals from the Conservative Party. They shared the Parliamentary representation of the town.[1] In East Wolverhampton the Liberal M.P. was Sir H. H. Fowler, a solicitor, who had married into the family of a leading local ironmaster. In the West the Conservative M.P. was Sir Alfred Hickman, himself a prominent local ironmaster.[2] These similar substantial men worked in harmony; indeed Fowler was closer in many respects to Hickman than to the Radical members of his own party. These Radical Liberals were temperance reformers, opposed to the Boer War, idolising Lloyd George, and their religious persuasion was extreme Nonconformity, Primitive Methodism and Baptism in particular. Fowler, however, was not an extreme temperance reformer; he was a foremost Liberal Imperialist, a Wesleyan Methodist of conservative inclinations, and he lived in a large house to the west of the town. He was not the ideal M.P. for the Radical Liberals who lived in the squalid

---

[1] See Table II. In 1900 both candidates were returned unopposed.
[2] Fowler was M.P. 1880–1908 and Hickman 1885–6, 1892–1906. For Fowler see E. H. Fowler, *The Life of Henry Hartley Fowler*, London, 1912.
There is no biography of Hickman, but see *Wolverhampton Journal*, Mar 1902, and *W.C.*, 16.3.1910, for newspaper sketches of his life.

eastern parts of the town and earned their living from grocery. But he was well suited to appeal to the more wealthy Liberals, especially the manufacturers who were not teetotal, extreme Nonconformists or worried about social conditions in the eastern wards. Religion alone divided these men from their Conservative counterparts. The former were on the whole Nonconformists and the latter Anglicans. There was no other significant difference between these manufacturers, industrialists, merchants and businessmen. Since the late 1880s some of them had slipped over to the Conservative Party, disillusioned with the Liberal Party's adherence to Home Rule, disliking the raucous Radical element in the Party, but above all believing that Protection for the depressed Midland iron and metal industries would more likely come from the Conservative than the Free Trade Liberal Party. That the transference of support was not large before, say, 1908 can be laid at the feet of Fowler, who was not associated with Home Rule, Radicalism or Free Trade to any extent. It is noticeable that after 1908, when the Radical G. R. Thorne replaced Fowler as M.P., the Liberal Party became primarily the party of the shopkeepers; the industrialists had gone over to the Conservatives.

This sketch of the Parliamentary situation in the town has revealed factors which had important implications for the development of party politics on the Council. The M.P.s were similar; the leading elements in their local parties were not really divided socially and economically; both sides were in a position of power and influence in the Council and in the town. The present position was to their liking. Such an atmosphere was not conducive to party political activity in municipal elections. There was no incentive to upset the balance either at the Parliamentary or municipal levels.[1]

CONFLICTS

Two groups, however, were dissatisfied with this harmony and wished to break the monopoly. The Radical Liberals and Labour

---

[1] It is significant that the most 'political' of the municipal elections of this period, that of 1892, occurred in the same year as the election of Hickman for West Wolverhampton, when he defeated the Liberal Plowden. The intensity of the Parliamentary campaign spilled over into the municipal.

Party were disruptive forces seeking to end the easy-going alliance
of Conservatives and conservative-Liberals. These two groups
initiated the majority of the electoral contests for the Council
between 1888 and 1902. From 1888 to 1894 eight of the election
fights were between Conservatives and Radical Liberals: two were
between Conservatives and Labour and only one was between the
Liberals and Labour. But from 1895 to 1902 Conservative *v.*
Labour contests rose to eight, while Conservative *v.* Radical
Liberal fights fell to three, and there was still only one Liberal *v.*
Labour contest. Thus in the early 1890s the political battles at the
municipal elections were mainly between the Conservatives and
Radical Liberals, while in the late 1890s the chief contests were
between the Conservatives and Labour. The issues in the elections
of the early 1890s were the plans of the temperance reformers and
their efficacy in improving the social conditions of the eastern
wards; while those of the later 1890s were Labour's schemes of
municipalisation and most of all its proposals to improve the wages
and conditions of the Corporation employees. But in this period
before 1903 the battles were sparse and spasmodic. There were
few contests and little consistent sustained pressure to advance any
particular municipal policy. Then in 1903 the tempo of Council
politics suddenly quickened.

In the November municipal election of 1903 nine wards were
contested, the highest number since the incorporation of the town
in 1848, never to be surpassed until 1927, and after that not until
1945 and the years following. After 1903 more seats were fought
each November than before. Education was the topic which
sparked off the conflagration. In 1902 the Liberal Nonconformist
members of the Council protested against the Education Bill.
They proclaimed that education should be 'national, free, un-
sectarian, efficient and under direct popular control'; they objected
to the composition of the proposed Education Committee and to
'the use of public funds for the maintenance of schools over which
they will not have full control'.[1] In the following year they attacked
the composition of the committee responsible for drawing up
Wolverhampton's scheme on the grounds that there were on it too
many Anglicans and that the Nonconformists were unrepresenta-

---

[1] *Council Minutes*, 13.10.1902. *W.C.*, 15.10.1902.

tive of the views of their congregations. One, it was said, 'out-heroded Herod in his views'. Bantock, the leader of the objectors, said that if the Church Party would not come to terms, 'it meant war in the town.'[1] When the scheme had been completed the Nonconformists attacked the system of co-opting on to the committee individuals nominated by the Voluntary Schools. It was claimed that they would watch over the interests of their own schools and not of education in general, and that what was required was for the Council 'to obtain the best men and women from the standpoint of Education'.[2] The Nonconformists, defeated at every stage, accused the Catholic and Anglican leaders in the Council of dragooning their supporters into voting by the 'use of whips' and of concocting their schemes in the Deanery Club.[3]

In the election of 1903 education was the main issue. In November 'the real fight was between the ill-assorted union of the forces of the Protestant Church of England with those of what is alleged to be the elder branch of the Christian faith whose foundations are laid in Rome, aided by the equally strong, ever dominant power of the "trade" – These were pitched against what is termed the "Chapel influence".'[4] Feelings ran so high that one Councillor refused to pay his rates for the upkeep of denomina-tional schools and had his goods distrained.

The education issue, though new to the Council, was an old topic in the town. Sectarian and party conflict over the composition of the School Board and its policy went back to the days of the first School Board of 1870. Elections for the School Board were always contested by parties. All candidates had a sectarian label; Liberal Nonconformists stood against Anglican Conservatives, while the Catholics hovered in a state of independence, though leaning to the Anglican position. School Board elections were fought more bitterly than Town Council elections; there was no lack of candidates and there was more public participation in these elections than for the Council elections. In 1894, 1897 and 1900 around 10 per cent of the population voted, compared with 3 per

[1] *C.M.*, 9.2.1903. *W.C.*, 11.2.1903.
[2] *C.M.*, 16.3.1903. *W.C.*, 19.3.1903.
[3] *W.C.*, 29.4.1903.
[4] *E. & S.*, 2.11.1903. In two by-elections earlier in the year the Nonconformist candidates had fulminated against the Anglican and Catholic alliance. *W.C.*, 27.5.1903, 8.7.1903.

cent, 4 per cent and 1 per cent for the corresponding Council elections.[1] Many factors explain this greater interest. Education was an issue which touched off violent passions and religious prejudices and aroused public interest. The electoral procedures had important consequences. School Board elections were not annual but triennial, and all the seats on the Board were declared vacant; thus every three years there was an opportunity to elect a fresh Board, which would be in control for three years. More was at stake (the work of the Board for three years ahead could be decided at one election) than in the Council elections, when each year the electorate chose only one-third of the Councillors who composed only one-quarter of the Council, since the Aldermen comprised also one-third of the Council. Also for the Board election the town voted at large and not by wards, thus everyone qualified to vote, could vote and was not disqualified because a particular ward was not contested, as happened with the Council elections. And, finally, since each voter for the Board had as many votes as there were vacancies, the parties had an incentive to organise the voting so that their supporters would concentrate their votes on their candidates and not spread them. Thus it is not surprising that there was more public interest in the Board elections than in the Council elections.[2] In 1903 the explosive subject of education became the responsibility of the Council, which then became rent by the divisions which had once split the School Board.[3]

Education was not the only issue, however, which inflamed the passions of the Councillors and split them into competing blocks. In 1902 and 1903, at the same time as the debates on education were taking place, the Councillors were quarrelling over the method to be adopted by the Corporation for propelling the municipal trams. The division-lists on this topic reveal an almost identical voting pattern to that on education, but with some significant exceptions. The Chairman of the Transport Committee, the Conservative varnish manufacturer Sir Charles T. Mander, was

---

[1] See Table VIII.

[2] *Wolverhampton Journal* of October 1903 noted that before 1903 a Council contest had sunk to the level of a purely personal nature.

[3] It is significant that in the 1903 Council elections 10 per cent of the population voted; a similar figure to that voting in the Board elections. See Tables VII and VIII. Thus for the first time Council elections produced the same degree of participation as had the School Board elections of the 1890s.

an advocate of the American Lorain system of surface contact. This system propelled the trams by means of electrical impulses picked up by the tram through an arm fixed to its underneath, which came into contact with plates set in the middle of the tramway tracks. The champions of this method proclaimed that it would avoid the unaesthetic cluttering of the streets with over-head wires; it would be safer, since there were no wires to fall down; it was the latest development, whose adoption would make Wolverhampton a renowned pioneer; and this system would enable the town to escape from the monopoly of the British Electric Traction Company which controlled the tramways of the surrounding areas. Mander persuaded the Council to give the system a trial. If it fulfilled certain stipulations the Corporation bound itself to adopt it. After a trial period Mander argued that, although all the conditions had not been precisely fulfilled, it was a success. But the opposition alleged that the system was too costly to install and maintain, and that it would burden the ratepayers far more than would the overhead method. It was dangerous, too, they claimed, since humans and animals received shocks from the plates, and cyclists and carriages found them a nuisance. It was feared that, since no other town in the country had adopted the system, it might be a costly and risky experiment, soon to fall obsolete; far better, they said, to rely on the tried and trusted British methods and not on American gambles. And, most important of all, they complained that Wolverhampton would be isolated from her neighbours who possessed the overhead method: intercommunication would be impossible and fewer people would come to Wolverhampton, whose trade would languish. The trial period, they claimed, had proved all their fears. But Mander stated that, if the Council refused to adopt the system, the Lorain Company would take the case to arbitration, which would involve the Corporation and ratepayers in expensive litigation. The verdict was likely to be in favour of the Company, and the Corporation would still have to accept the system. His view eventually pre-vailed, and the Lorain system was adopted, but a substantial minority was very embittered at what they regarded as the devious way in which they had been tricked into adopting the system.

The Lorain question 'keenly divided the Council and the Town'[1]

[1] *W.C.*, 14.10.1903.

and was 'one of the most momentous public questions which they had ever considered in Wolverhampton'.[1] Although on the surface it was not an issue which would produce a division along party lines, yet it did. In the final vote on whether or not to accept the system, twenty-five were in favour and fifteen against. Of those for, only three were Liberals; the other twenty-two were Conservatives: of those against, only two were Conservatives, the other thirteen were Liberals and Labour. This analysis is similar to the divisions on the education issue which were taking place at the same time. For instance, when a vote was taken on whether or not to accept the scheme for the composition of the Education Committee, twenty-nine were in favour and sixteen against. All the sixteen were Liberals and Labour, all Nonconformists: twenty-seven of the others were Conservatives and Anglicans; the remaining two were Liberals but Roman Catholics. Never before 1903 had men of the same political party voted together so consistently. Never had the Council been divided on such political lines.

The explanation why the Lorain question became a party political issue is perhaps twofold. The division on the School Board was transferred to the Council, and the polarisation on this issue remained for other issues. Men accustomed to work together for one cause quickly found themselves involved in others. And secondly, Mander was the leading Conservative of the town[2] and this factor was likely to encourage fellow Conservatives to accept his judgement on the tramway question, especially when his main opponents were such leading Liberals as A. B. Bantock and P. Lewis; while the Liberal rank and file would be likely to follow their leaders also. Since the issue was concerned with technical detail, the ordinary Councillors, those who were not members of the Transport Committee, had to rely on their estimates of the judgements of the main contestants. Unable to judge the issues themselves, they followed their leaders.

At elections the quarrels continued. The Liberals formed a Progressive Association, really the radical Liberals organised for

---

[1] *W.C.*, 15.5.1903. One Councillor said: 'I never remember being present at a meeting of this Council at which I have heard language so strong.'

[2] It can be argued that he was the leading man in the town, since his Mayoralty, 1892–6, was the longest in the history of the town. In 1896 he was said to have surpassed all other Mayors.

municipal purposes, whose aims were to 'check extravagance, achieve efficiency in municipal government and to fight for a fair free national system of education'.[1] More seats were contested in the November elections than before 1903, seven in 1904 and five in 1905. The Party agents, S. Bowers the Conservative and W. Meggit the Liberal, organised the campaigns of their respective municipal candidates. In 1908 it was reported that 'the office of the local Conservative Association has apparently directed the Tory candidates', and that Sir Alfred Hickman 'after the manner of a political chief' sent an encouraging telegram to the Conservative candidates.[2] But by 1909–10 the force of the Progressives was spent. They were never able to gain a majority on the Council, their leader, Bantock, had become part of the 'Establishment', a Committee Chairman and a Mayor, and was no longer a driving force behind the Radicals. As a party they had never possessed a positive municipal policy; they were a negative defensive group defending Nonconformist education against Anglicans and vaguely opposing municipal expenditure. Thus as the education controversy evaporated and since the Council entered upon no more large enterprises,[3] there was nothing to keep the momentum of the Progressives in being. They were also finding that they had much more in common with the Conservatives than with the Labour Party, which was growing and asserting itself.

Thus ended the Liberal Revival, a temporary phenomenon stimulated by the education controversy of 1902–3. But for this issue, the Liberals might have declined much more quickly as a political force than they did. In 1902 it was widely expected that the Liberal Club would close through lack of support. After the Liberal-Unionists had left the Club in the 1880s; 'its fortunes have been on the wane'.[4] The education issue, however, although provoking a revival of Liberalism, also showed that the Liberal Party was eventually doomed. The only topic capable of raising

[1] *E. & S.*, 30.10.1906.

[2] *E. & S.*, 2.11.1908.

[3] From 1898 the Corporation had undertaken some costly schemes, the construction of a new Sewage Disposal Unit, extensions to the Waterworks, a new Wholesale Market, Cold Stores and Abattoir. After 1903 the Council embarked on no more such enterprises. The prosperity of the late 1890s gave way to the depression of the middle and late 1900s.

[4] *Wolverhampton Journal*, Aug 1902.

Liberal fortunes was a sectarian issue. Such religious issues were anachronistic in an age when social questions were coming to the fore. It was clear that a party whose *raison d'être* was the defence of the interests of a sect or group of sects would not remain for long as a significant force when the main battle was between capital and labour. Between 1903 and 1913 forty-five seats were contested at the November elections. From 1903 to 1908 the majority of the fights had been between the Conservatives and the Liberals, twenty-one out of twenty-five. But from 1908 to 1913 most were between the Conservatives and Labour, twelve out of twenty.

THE EMERGENCE OF LABOUR

The call for Labour representation on the Town Council was first heard in the 1890s, when both Liberals and Conservatives wooed the working man. In 1890 the Chairman of the East Wolverhampton Liberal Association, Councillor W. M. Fuller, an artificial-manure manufacturer, urged the need for Labour representation. The Conservative licensed victualler, Councillor Levi Johnson, was instrumental in getting the Council to adopt a 'fair wages clause' to prevent sweating by Corporation contractors, and he was keen to denounce breaches of the clause. Indeed the first working man to enter the Council was a Conservative, Abiathar Weaver, a clicker,[1] who was elected in 1891. He was, however, not regarded as a genuine working man by the Trades Council and Labour Representation Committee, since he refused to join a trade union. Wolverhampton's Labour Party had its origins in the trade union movement, in the Labour Representation Committee established by the Trades Council to achieve Labour representation on the Council.[2] In 1890 the Trades Council first attempted to obtain seats on the Council when it financed the campaigns of two trade union candidates, both Liberals in national politics, against Conservative opposition. Its first success came in

---

[1] A foreman shoemaker who cuts out the leather and gives out the work.

[2] The Trades Council in 1890 comprised 40 delegates representing 3000–4000 trade unionists. Its objects were 'to bring all trade disputes to an amicable settlement, by bringing the contending parties together for the purposes of deliberation and to advance the social position of the working men by legislation, whether Imperial or local'. *E. & S.*, 3.11.1890.

1891 one month after Weaver had entered the Council, when James Stevenson, a boot finisher, was elected, independent of either party – representing Labour alone. By 1898 their numbers had increased to five, and remained around four or five until 1908 when the Conservatives mounted an attack on the Labour seats and reduced their representation to two. By the outbreak of the First World War they had regained only one seat.

THE CONSERVATIVE COUNTER-ATTACK

The reason for the Conservative attack on Labour was not because of any issue of Council policy but because of Parliamentary considerations. In 1900 the Trades Council had tried to find a Parliamentary Labour candidate, but had failed since it had not the money to finance his campaign. In 1903 the Trades Council selected T. F. Richards of the Boot and Shoe Operatives' Union as 'the trade unionist candidate for one of the Parliamentary constituencies of Wolverhampton'.[1] His union promised to pay his election expenses and to continue to pay him a salary if elected. His official position in the union was as 'Parliamentary Agent', for which he was paid £300 a year. Hickman's seat was chosen as the battleground; no Liberal candidate came forward, and in 1906 Richards defeated Hickman by a majority of 168. The loss of the seat spurred the Conservatives to fight hard to regain it. They realised that their enemy was not the Liberal Party but Labour. The Conservative Association was reorganised, new rules devised, new officers chosen and a new candidate selected. He was Alfred Bird, the head of the Birmingham custard-powder concern. His money kept the Conservative Association in being: he paid the full-time agent's salary and expenses, the rent of the headquarters and its maintenance; he financed the renovation of the Conservative Clubs in the town and helped to keep going the Conservative newspaper the *Midland Evening News*, and at the end of each year made up any deficiencies in the Association's accounts. The Subscription Book of the Conservative Association shows that he gave £150 in 1908, £200 in 1909 and 1910, and £326 in 1911,

---

[1] *W.C.*, 18.2.1903. A biographical sketch of Richards appeared in *Wolverhampton Journal*, Feb 1903.

1912 and 1913. This was in addition to the 'abnormal expenditure' of the Association which he paid off.

With a Parliamentary candidate and a revitalised organisation the Conservatives began to use municipal elections as part of their strategy to regain the Parliamentary seat and then to retain it afterwards. Their new attitude was shown in a resolution passed by their Management Committee in 1908: 'It is desirable in the interests of the Conservative and Unionist Party in West Wolverhampton that Municipal Elections be fought politically unless there be some special reasons to the contrary.'[1] What this cryptic resolution meant was explained by the President of the Association in 1913: 'the policy of contesting Municipal Seats has to be considered purely with relation to the effect that may be produced upon our Parliamentary prospects and nothing else.'[2] In practice this policy meant that in one ward in June 1912 it 'was better to leave it to the Liberal and Labour to oppose one another, thus still further widening the breach between these two parties, which from a Parliamentary standpoint operates to our advantage'.[3] In October 1912 in one ward no candidate was adopted, since to do so, it was feared, 'would be the means of bringing the Liberal and Labour Parties together'.[4] In 1913 the Liberal prospective Parliamentary candidate withdrew, and therefore the Conservatives expected that they would be engaged in a straight fight with Labour. The Conservative agent calculated that 'we shall possibly receive a certain amount of support with votes from the Liberal Party, therefore it is inadvisable to oppose either Pincock (Park Ward) or Henn (Dunstall Ward),[5] both Liberals. The Association decided 'whenever possible to oppose the retiring Socialist Councillors'.[6] The supremacy of Parliamentary considerations had the full support of Bird, whose attitude is illustrated in a letter

[1] Minutes of the Management Committee of the West Wolverhampton Conservative Association, February 1908.

[2] Ibid., 16.9.13. Between 1908 and 1913 the Association had been divided over the question as to whether or not they should oppose sitting Councillors' re-election. Generally sitting Conservatives were hostile to the idea since it might provoke opposition to their re-election. By 1913 Parliamentary considerations were deemed more important than the anxieties of Conservative Councillors about their seats.

[3] Ibid., 11.6.1912.   [4] Ibid., 14.10.1912.

[5] Ibid., 16.9.1913.   [6] Ibid.

which he wrote to the President of the Association, and which deserves to be quoted in full.

12th October 1912

My dear Marston,

With respect to our conversation on Monday evening, whilst maintaining the attitude of neutrality I have always observed in municipal politics, I may say that it seems to me the policy of contesting seats has to be considered with relation to the effect that may be produced upon our Parliamentary prospects, and nothing else.

As a broad principle, attack is generally the truest strategy, even in defence. Municipal elections in politics are the equivalent of Autumn manœuvres in military affairs; they are the best means we possess of keeping our fighting forces in the highest efficiency.

Therefore, when certain ward Committees are keen on a contest, have a good candidate, and are able to produce satisfactory evidence of probable success, to deprive them of a chance of a fight must have a disastrous influence upon our forces and bring about certain discouragement and slackness when a Parliamentary election comes along.

On the other hand it would be unwise to countenance futile contests, where there was only a remote possibility of success either from the unsuitability of the candidate or other causes.

As to the question of finance: that is not a difficulty which need weigh in the matter.

Yours sincerely,
Alfred Bird[1]

The Conservatives struck first in the Municipal Elections of 1908. Their plan was seen as a 'preliminary canter to ascertain in some degree the prospect of the Unionist candidate for Parliamentary honours'.[1] In Graiseley Ward the brother of the President of the Conservative Association challenged a Labour Councillor who had represented the ward for twelve years, while in a neighbouring ward a Conservative publican was run against

---

[1] Preserved in *M.M.C.* The underlining is Bird's. It is significant that Bird came from Birmingham, and that the new agent, Sam Bowers, had worked with Joseph Chamberlain. Chamberlain had from the 1870s fought Council and School Board elections not only to promote his particular policies but also to assist his Parliamentary position.

[2] *E. & S.*, 2.11.1908.

another sitting Labour Councillor in order to disperse the energies of the Labour supporters. Labour not only lost seats on the Council, but the Parliamentary seat too, for in 1910 Bird defeated Richards. For the second General Election of 1910 Labour was unable to obtain a candidate: Richards refused to stand again and the Osborne judgment restricted the flow of Union funds to the party. Not until 1913 did the party recover – with the reversal of the Osborne judgment by the Trade Union Act, with the adoption of a new Parliamentary candidate and with the emergence in the town of some local issues which enabled the Labour Party to head a movement of protest against both Conservative and Liberal Parties.

THE LABOUR REVIVAL

In the early months of 1912 Labour adopted as prospective Parliamentary candidate A. G. Walkden, the General Secretary of the Railway Clerks' Association.[1] This union took over 'the financial responsibility of working and fighting the Constituency'.[2] By 1913 £500 had been spent on Walkden's candidature, only one-tenth of which had to be raised by the local party. An agent was appointed for the first time on a full-time basis; a Labour monthly journal, the *Wolverhampton Worker*, was established; offices were rented in the town centre. Walkden visited the Labour organisations of the town, brought national figures to speak, over-hauled the organisation, appointing street captains for each street and setting up a Ladies' Labour League. Walkden provided for the Labour Party a similar kind of support and stimulus to that provided for the Conservative Party by Bird. Its renewed vigour was shown in 1913 when it contested five seats in the November municipal elections, the highest number ever fought by Labour, and its candidates stood against both Conservatives and Liberals.

Two local issues, in addition, helped to galvanise the Labour Party. In 1913 many landlords who were members of the Wolver-hampton Property Owners' Association increased the rents of all their properties. In opposition to these simultaneous and dramatic

---

[1] A biographical sketch appears in *W.C.*, 14.2.1912.
[2] *Minutes of the Local Labour Party*, 12.2.1912.

increases the Labour Party formed a Tenants' Defence League, whose leaders were prominent Labour Councillors, J. Whittaker and J. Walsh. Walkden himself spoke at two great mass protest meetings in the Market Place. The second controversy in which the Labour Party was to the fore concerned the minimum wage of Corporation employees. At a Council meeting in June 1912 the Labour members pressed that the minimum wage of all Corporation employees should be 25s a week. The matter was referred to the Finance Committee, which six months later recommended that the wage be 24s, but only for those actually working within the borough. Again Labour pressed for a 25s wage for all employees, including those working beyond the borough in the sewage farm and waterworks, but they were defeated. These two controversies, although ending in defeats for the Labour Party, encouraged in the party a great sense of confidence. As an independent body it was now of age. It had been pitted against the industrialists, shopkeepers, *rentiers*, landlords and solicitors, and it had shown itself as the champion of organised labour, of the wage-earner and of the tenants in the town against both Conservatives and Liberals, who had been seen as accomplices in the 'minimum wages fraud' and of increasing the rents of working men's houses.

THE COUNCIL IN 1914

The political composition of the Town Council at the outbreak of the First World War resembled that of 1900.[1] The Conservatives still had fifteen members; the Liberals had increased their representatives by one to sixteen, while Labour had lost one to total three. This straight comparison, however, neglects the large shifts in the party strengths during the intervening years, and secondly it is not an accurate reflection of the trends as revealed at the elections. The framers of the Municipal Corporations Act of 1835 wished to insulate Town Councils from sudden changes of opinion by the electorate. For this reason only a third of the Councillors were to seek election each year; thus it would take three years before all Councillors had come before the electorate. In addition the creation of the Aldermanic bench to be elected

[1] See Table VI.

every six years not by the electorate but by the Councillors was a
further defence against what was expected to be the dangerous
Radical views of the electorate. These devices served to buttress
the *status quo* and prevented the views of the electorate from
drastically reshaping the composition of the Council in any one
year. Thus the composition of the Council in 1914 does not really
reflect the trends of the years 1910–11 to 1914. An examination,
however, of the changes in the political composition of the Council
during the years 1900–14 does confirm the general movements
outlined above.

The Liberals. The Liberal figure of fifteen in 1900 represents a
decline in Liberal membership from the late 1880s when, for
instance, in 1888 they possessed twenty-one. They were revived
by the clash over education, which brought them by 1906 to
twenty-two members, the peak of their strength. The education
issue rallied together both the radical and conservative elements
in the Liberal Party, who were divided about social questions. But
when this controversy died, so did the binding force of the party.
Its only distinctive policy seemed to be the defence of Nonconformity, an anachronistic position for a party to be in at a time
when social questions were becoming more prominent. From 1907
their numbers dropped steadily year by year to the sixteen of 1914.
   Other local factors contributed to the Liberal decline before the
First World War. Their very success in the East Wolverhampton
constituency assisted their fall. In that seat they were safe from
being unseated by either Conservatives or Labour, none of whom
ever represented the seat or ever really came close to doing so.
Facing no significant opposition they had little incentive to
organise and fight municipal elections to safeguard their Parliamentary position. The East Wolverhampton constituency, in
addition, comprised only three of the twelve wards of the
municipal borough; it stretched beyond the town to take in places
like Willenhall, Heath Town and Wednesfield. This meant that
the Liberal Party's attentions were not solely concentrated on
Wolverhampton, and thus its Town Council and its elections were
not for the Liberals such a key factor as for their opponents. In
the West Wolverhampton constituency the Liberals had really
abdicated at the turn of the century to the Conservatives, and they

were unable to regain a strong foothold later when Conservatives and Labour fought each other. The competition between these two parties kept their organisations keen, especially since they were so evenly balanced and victory seemed near. For these the Town Council and its elections were important factors in their battle for Parliamentary supremacy, since the West Wolverhampton constituency comprised nothing but the borough, the remaining nine wards.[1] Thus the attention of these two parties, unlike that of the Liberals, was concentrated on the town. Parliamentary and municipal interests converged in the West but not in the East. And, finally, a most important cause of the Liberals' decline was that they never received anything like the stimulus and support which the Conservatives received from Bird and his custard-powder profits or which the Labour Party received from Walkden and his union contributions. Thus the Liberal Party was weaker than the other parties; it lacked the incentives which they had to fight municipal elections, and its attention was dispersed and not focused on the town. Also its basic unifying theme, the defence of Nonconformity, was increasingly inappropriate at a time when politics were being polarised into a fight between capital and labour, and when the parties representing these groups began to develop a distinctive policy at municipal as well as Parliamentary levels.

The Labour Party. The Labour Party's period of growth was from 1891 to 1899, when it increased from one to five members of the Council. Between 1899 and 1908 it marked time, maintaining its position, but was pushed into the background by the controversy between the Liberals and Conservatives. From 1908 to 1911 its fortunes slipped as the Conservatives mounted their attack, but from 1912 Labour began to advance again, only to be checked by the First World War. Once that barrier was removed Labour surged ahead. The reason for Labour's rise was that it was voicing the real grievances of wage-earners and tenants against two parties who increasingly represented the opinion of employers and landlords. It was encouraged in its efforts by winning the seat in the West in 1906 and later by the assistance of Walkden and his union. The basis of the Labour Party was organised labour, i.e. members

[1] Except for a very small area called Ettingshall beyond the borough boundary.

of trade unions, who tended to be skilled men. Non-unionised
workers, mostly unskilled, tended either to maintain their
traditional loyalties to the Liberals or else to vote Conservative.
The latter was attractive because it advocated Protection, which
meant jobs and high wages, and supported the drink trade which
meant solace after work.

The Conservatives. The Conservatives in this period maintained
their position, save for their temporary setback in the middle years
when they lost the seat in the West and when their membership of
the Council dropped to only nineteen in 1906, as against twenty-
five in 1900. Their quick recovery after 1908 was due not only to
the assistance of Bird, but also to the fact that the Conservative
Party was being seen as the main opposition to Labour. In
addition, the Conservative Party in the town was strongly Protec-
tionist, and this appeal attracted from the Liberal Party many
manufacturers who had lost faith in Free Trade as foreign competitors cut into their markets at home and overseas.

Between 1903 and 1914 parties came to be involved in the
Town Council to an extent to which they had not been in the
1890s. The first explanation is that the Education Act of 1902
transferred to the Council the controversies which had previously
divided the School Board. Secondly, the Conservatives began after
1908 to fight municipal elections, not to promote a particular
Conservative municipal policy, but to assist their Parliamentary
campaign. And thirdly, the Labour Party was evolving a distinctive municipal policy which provoked Conservative and
Liberal opposition. These three factors changed the style of Town
Council politics.

3 The Political Background, 1919-64

THE trends observable on the outbreak of the war in 1914 – the revival of the Labour Party, the decline of the Liberal Party and the consolidation of the Conservative Party – continued after the end of the war with greater intensity. By 1926, the date of the last Council before the extension of the Borough boundaries, Labour had increased its membership of the Council from three to thirteen, the Liberals had fallen from sixteen to nine, and the Conservatives had fallen slightly from twenty-five to twenty-one.[1] Labour was clearly gaining at the expense of the Liberals, and the most dramatic illustration of this development occurred in the November election of 1919, when a Labour candidate, fighting his first municipal election, defeated a Liberal Councillor who had represented the ward for twenty-five years. Other wards, which previously had returned Liberal members, increasingly in the 1920s sent Labour members to the Council.

THE LIBERAL–CONSERVATIVE PACT

Liberals and Conservatives drew closer together. Between 1919 and the 1950s no Conservative ever fought a Liberal in a municipal election. In October 1919 the minutes of the Management Committee of the West Wolverhampton Conservative Association record that 'The Secretary intimated that Alderman Bantock, on behalf of the Liberals, and the Secretary on behalf of the Association had agreed not to oppose one another's Candidates, but to work as a coalition to assist each other's candidates.' His action was approved.[2] Their alliance was more positively cemented for

[1] See Table VI.   [1] *M.M.C.*, 22.10.1919.

the municipal 'general' election of 1927. For the first time in the history of the Borough its boundaries had been extended; the size of the Council was increased from forty-eight to fifty-two; and elections were held for all the seats on the Council in March 1927. The Labour Party decided to contest every seat, thus making a bid to gain control of the Council, which the *Express and Star* called an attempt at 'political dictatorship'.[1] Opposing the Labour Party were what were called the 'anti-Socialist' candidates, an amalgamation of Conservatives and Liberals, who had pooled their resources, planned their election campaigns together and issued a common election address. In November 1926 the Management Committee of the West Wolverhampton Conservative Association had appointed a sub-committee of three members of the Council to confer with the agent and the Liberal Party about the election.[2] They reported to the next meeting, 'indicating agreement between Alderman Bantock (Liberal Leader) and ourselves, in regard to the general position and as to individual Conservative, Liberal and Independent members of the present Town Council, contesting wards in the West Division.'[3] Final arrangements were made at a meeting of the Management Committee in January 1927, when the Liberal Municipal Committee, comprising four Liberal members of the Council, arrived to confer about the individual candidates and to draw up the election address.[4] They partitioned the town into spheres of interest. In the West Division the Conservative organisation sustained the campaigns of the anti-Socialist candidates, while the Liberals concentrated their activities in the East.

This division of the town suggests that Parliamentary considerations were to the fore in the Conservatives' strategy. They accepted that the Eastern Division would be represented by a Liberal. Indeed the Conservatives have never represented the Eastern Division of the town. Their organisation there was almost non-existent. L. S. Amery, who in 1908 fought the seat as a Conservative, said of the organisation: 'I hardly expected so little as I found . . . beyond the score or so who had adopted me, there were very few traces.'[5] The only function of the Conservative

[1] 14.3.1927.   [2] *M.M.C.*, 5.11.1926.   [3] Ibid., 10.12.1926.   [4] Ibid., 31.1.1927.
[5] L. S. Amery, *My Political Life*, vol. i, 1953, pp. 276–7.

Association there was to select a Parliamentary candidate, which it did with difficulty only very close to the elections. What little organisation there was was maintained by the donations of the pump manufacturer J. O. Evans. In 1929 there was a move to close down the Association, it being explained that 'ours was an industrial division and our subscribers in the past simply consisted of about 25–30 and were not spread over the division'.[1] It was thus to the Conservative interests in the West to admit the hopelessness of the East and to leave it to the Liberals, who would thus be obliged not to intervene in the West and present the Conservatives with a fight against both Labour and Liberals.

In the West the Liberals honoured their part of the bargain. For the 1924 General Election no Liberal candidate opposed the Conservative candidate, and Bantock, the Leader of the Liberals, wrote to the Conservative candidate: 'As a Liberal I have no hesitation in saying that my views are much more in accordance with those expressed in your address than the views which are being expounded by the Labour candidate. I shall record my vote at the election in your favour, and I do not hesitate to advise all Liberals in the division to do likewise.'[2] But in 1929 the Liberals were divided; a group of younger Liberals rebelled against the leadership[3] and invited a Liberal candidate to stand at the General Election.[4] The Liberal members of the Council urged Liberals to vote for the Conservative candidate in order to keep out the Labour man. But the anti-Socialist vote was split and in 1929 the Labour Party for the second time provided an M.P. for the Western Division. Thus the Conservative strategy had been proved correct. It could only maintain its hold on the Western half by keeping the Liberals out of the contest and involved in the East. But for the revolt of the Young Liberals the defeat of the Conservatives in 1929 might not have occurred.

---

[1] *Minutes of the East Wolverhampton Conservative Association*, 27.6.1929.
[2] *E. & S.*, 17.10.1924.
[3] The Young Liberal Association in the town sent the following resolution to the Head Office: 'That under no circumstance should any pact be entered into between the Liberal and other parties in either Parliamentary or Local Government elections.' *Minutes of the Young Liberal Association*, 24.1.1928.
[4] *E. & S.*, 26.1.1929.

CONSERVATIVES AND LABOUR

As Alfred Bird before 1914 had encouraged the Conservative Association to contest municipal elections as part of a general Parliamentary strategy, so did his son, Sir Robert Bird, who on his father's death in 1922 replaced him as M.P. for West Wolverhampton.[1] Like his father, Sir Robert was the financial mainstay of the Association, promising on his adoption to contribute £500 per annum to the Association,[2] and at the end of each year clearing up the debts of the Association and its clubs. Just as Bird and his custard profits spurred the Conservatives to fight municipal elections with the Parliamentary struggle in mind, so was the Labour Party encouraged in the same policy by its Parliamentary candidates. A. G. Walkden retired as the candidate in 1923 and was replaced by W. J. Brown, General Secretary of the Civil Service Clerical Union, which financed the running of the local party.[3] Thus the two main contestants in the Western Division of the town possessed party machines backed by substantial resources. And they were further stimulated by the prospect of victory, since the election contests were very close, Brown managing in 1929 to defeat Bird. Every incentive therefore was present for the Conservative and Labour Parties to organise to their fullest extent and contest municipal elections in order to strengthen their position in the Parliamentary elections.

Parliamentary considerations were not the only factors which spurred the Labour Party to contest municipal elections on party lines. Alone of all the parties it had a distinctive municipal policy, a comprehensive programme for the town as a whole. To implement this programme it had sought to gain control of the Council in 1927. Labour's policy had been advocated by all Labour candidates in all the elections since 1918. It had been revised in readiness for the 1927 election; to sub-committees, each of two party members, had been delegated the task of drafting policy for such topics as municipal trading, public health, housing, municipal

---

[1] There is no biography of Sir Robert Bird, but for a sketch of his life see *E. & S.*, 29.10.1935.

[2] *M.M.C.*, 19.6.1922.

[3] For Brown's career see *E. & S.*, 25.5.1923, 5.2.1931, 17.4.1936, and his autobiography *So far . . .*, London, 1943.

banking and insurance, electricity development and care of the mentally defective.[1] These groups reported to the party, which sent the programme to the ward parties for affirmation. Thus the party possessed a programme for Wolverhampton. Labour's attitude was that 'municipal affairs could only be successful when there was a united party to carry forward a pronounced programme'.[2]

THE ANTI-SOCIALIST VIEWS

The anti-Socialist groups, however, possessed no distinctive policy. Neither the Liberals nor the Conservatives had a municipal programme, and even in 1927 their joint election address proposed no positive anti-Socialist alternative policy. It contained general statements about the need to resist Socialist dictation and to oppose 'wild and extravagant schemes', which might have the effect of gaining for Wolverhampton a reputation similar to that of West Ham and Poplar.[3] The anti-Socialist *Express and Star* complained of the vagueness of the anti-Socialist case: 'it might have been more precisely stated what particular policies as related to Wolverhampton are regarded as wild and extravagant.'[4] Each candidate was left free to campaign for his own pet scheme. A. E. Beardmore, a dentist, wanted a further demolition of slum property; a solicitor, F. R. W. Hayward, wanted more branch libraries, street improvements and economy; J. Haddock, a publican, wanted 'the right eye on efficiency, the left eye on efficiency and both eyes on economy'. R. E. Probert, a butcher, said he would make no rash promises, keep an open mind and adopt a business attitude; and A. E. Wood, a commercial traveller, called for 'sound economic government on progressive lines unhampered by the party spirit'.[5]

These representative attitudes illustrate the nature of the anti-Socialist appeal. It was not a municipal programme which they were advocating. They relied on the traditional individual approach, pressing for the interests of the wards and making general remarks about the running of the town. In policy they were concerned to keep the rates low and were opposed to

[1] *M.L.L.P.*, 24.1.1926.
[2] *E. & S.*, 14.3.1927.
[3] *E. & S.*, 4.3.1927.
[4] Ibid.
[5] *E. & S.*, 9.3.1927, 10.3.1927.

municipal expenditure for social services especially if they had a redistributive effect. They opposed 'Party', particularly party discipline on members of the Council, and its attempts to control the Council. They still believed that the source of policy was the Council, its committees especially, and not a party. They were defending a traditional style of politics. Since they had a safe majority they had no incentive to organise as a block inside the Council to resist Labour policies; since also they had no programme to implement, they had no stimulus to act as a solid group and maintain discipline; and thus they had no reason to think in terms of 'controlling' the Council. Against this traditional and secure system Labour was bringing jarring policies, disturbing techniques and new concepts. Labour had a municipal programme especially designed to favour the less well-off sections of society, and it believed that the programme could be carried out only by a party which acted as a solid group and gained control of the Council.

THE GROWTH OF LABOUR

The growth of Labour representation on the Council is due largely to the extension of the franchise in 1918, when the local government vote was extended to all men or women who had occupied any property in the borough for six months and to the wife of an occupier if she was over thirty years of age. The Act also abolished the disqualification of those in receipt of poor relief.[1] These extensions doubled the Burgess roll, which increased from 18,987 in 1914 to 37,512 in 1919. In 1912 19 per cent of the town's population were eligible to vote; in 1921 the figure was 38 per cent.[2] The newly enfranchised were the heads of working-class households and their wives, who mostly supported the Labour Party, whose policies were designed to win their support. The extension of the franchise increased not only the number of voters but also the number of those qualified to be elected to the Council, since the qualification for election was being on the Burgess roll. Thus not only were Labour supporters enfranchised in 1918, but they were given opportunities to join the Council itself.

Labour also benefited from the extensions of the borough

[1] 7 & 8 Geo. V, c. 64.　　　　　[2] See Table VII.

boundaries in 1926 and 1932, which added to the area of the town 5601 acres and to the population about 30,000, to make by 1933 the acreage of the town 9126 and its population 138,000. By 1933 the total membership of the Council was sixty. Five new wards had been produced out of the reorganisation of the boundaries following these expansions. Two, Bushbury and Low Hill, were predominantly Labour. They were situated to the north-east of the town, largely estates of Council houses for those who had moved from the slums of the centre of the town and worked at the near-by railway yards, rubber factory and engineering enterprises. Low Hill from 1933 to 1945 elected but one Independent: the rest were Labour. From 1945 only Labour Councillors represented the ward. Bushbury from 1927 returned only Labour members. Heath Town Ward, also in the east, was a former Urban District, an industrial village incorporated wholesale into the town in 1927. From then to 1938 it returned Independents who had been members of the U.D.C.: in 1938 it returned its first Labour Councillor who had been a member of the U.D.C. Only from 1955 was it solidly Labour. But in the west of the town Penn and St Philip's Wards returned Ratepayer Councillors up to the 1950s and from then Conservative members. These preserves of the middle-class owner-occupier never sent a Labour representative to the Council. The extensions to the franchise and to the boundaries worked to the advantage of the Labour Party, for by 1939 they had nineteen members, an increase of six on 1926.[1]

THE COUNCIL IN 1939

The composition of the Council in 1939 presents a different picture from that of 1926. The Conservatives seem to have fallen slightly from twenty-one to eighteen; the Liberals to have dropped from eleven to eight; and the Independents to have made a great increase from three to fifteen. These crude comparisons, however, conceal some significant developments and do not reflect the rhythm of the leading trends of the period.

Labour and the Independent Labour Association. Labour's rise from thirteen in 1926 to nineteen in 1939 was mainly a phenomenon of

[1] See Table VI.

the late 1930s, since even with the extension of the boundaries Labour in 1933 possessed only one more member than in 1926. Only after 1935 did Labour again increase steadily. The early 1930s, then, were a setback to the rapid progress which the Labour Party had made in the early 1920s. This poor showing is explained by events which had their origin at Westminster. There W. J. Brown supported Mosley and his New Party. His resignation from the Parliamentary Labour Party was treated by the local Labour Party 'as a resignation from the Labour Party', and it was resolved that 'we cannot have any further communication with him'.[1] But the local Party was split; although a majority decided to 'stand firm' to our National Party,[2] ten members of the Executive Committee resigned to follow Brown.[3] He founded the Independent Labour Association financed by his Union; he fought the 1931 General Election under its banner and lost to Bird. After the election Brown still thought he might regain the seat and announced that the I.L.A. was going to carry on as a 'political body financially self-supported'.[4] This latter word was not strictly accurate, for his Union assured him of £1,000 for his campaign.[5] In the General Election of 1935 Brown again fought and lost as an I.L.A. candidate, and this time he faced an official Labour candidate, whom he comfortably defeated; one of the few occasions when a rebel has been able to get more votes than an official candidate. After this defeat Brown severed his connections with the town, and the I.L.A., deprived of its head and financial support, and indeed of its *raison d'être* (since its function was to act as an electoral organisation to get Brown into Parliament) disbanded, and its individual members slowly returned to the official Labour Party.[6]

These splits and upheavals severely disrupted the local Labour Party. It had lost its dynamic M.P. and candidate, a number of its energetic though extremist members and its financial support. Thus weakened, it could not, even in the 1935 election, run a candidate to beat Brown. In Council politics, too, the repercussions

---

[1] *M.L.L.P.*, 25.3.1931.   [2] Ibid., 2.3.1931.   [3] Ibid., 7.5.1931.
[4] *E. & S.*, 5.1.1932.   [5] *E. & S.*, 20.9.1933.
[6] The *E. & S.*, 20.1.1938 reported that the I.L.A. had ceased to exist and that the members had transferred themselves to the Co-operative Party, thereby returning to the Labour fold.

were felt, since the I.L.A. and Labour Party fought each other for representation on the Council. In 1932, for instance, the I.L.A. opposed the official Labour candidates in three wards, and in one ward defeated the sitting Labour member. The I.L.A. in the period of its existence managed to send four of its members to the Council from the two wards of St James' and St Matthew's in the eastern half of the town. Here the main efforts of the I.L.A. had been concentrated with regards to Council affairs. Especially assiduous in this local campaign had been William Lawley, who was unemployed and thus had time to devote to nursing three wards. He had appreciated that these were the areas of the town most hit by unemployment, where social conditions were at their most unpleasant. Almost daily he appeared in the wards, offering help and representing people in their appeals against the meagre amount of Unemployment Relief paid to them. His work in these wards was the foundation of the I.L.A. membership on the Council, for the other three I.L.A. Councillors were on the whole insignificant individuals, who gained membership of the Council only through being associated with Lawley and his work.[1] Lawley's energies in these eastern wards worked in the long run to the advantage of the official Labour Party. It had never been able to establish a firm foothold in these wards, which were the centres of Liberal strength in the town. Where the official Labour Party had failed, Lawley's unorthodox Association succeeded, and for the first time the Liberal strongholds were captured. They were retained for Labour when the I.L.A. members returned to the Labour Party. Thus Lawley and the I.L.A. achieved the first Labour breakthrough in the Liberal wards in the east of the town.

In the short run, however, the squabbles between the I.L.A. and the Labour Party impeded the cause of Labour representation and halted the advance of the 1920s. The quarrels, however, took place only in respect to Parliamentary and national affairs, at Parliamentary and municipal elections, but not in the Council.[2]

---

[1] One later joined the Fascist Party, another the Conservative Party and the other remained in the Labour Party, but his only contribution to the Council was in connection with the Small Holdings and Allotments Committee.

[2] Although they fought each other for Council seats, there was little difference in their programmes.

There it was impossible to distinguish I.L.A. from Labour members. They voted together; they spoke for the same motions; one from one side would second a motion proposed by one from the other side. A common alliance on the Council in the 1930s was between Lawley and H. E. Lane, who contested the East Wolverhampton seat as official Labour candidate in 1935. These two proposed and seconded motions and amendments together on the Council during the same time as the I.L.A. and the Labour Party were at variance over Brown. Lane said, 'Lawley loaded the gun and I fired the bullets.' Thus over municipal policy there was no divergence between the I.L.A. and the Labour Party; their only bone of contention was W. J. Brown. Once he had abandoned the town, unification was quite simple. Then Labour began to advance again.

Conservatives and Independents. The Conservatives, consisting of twenty-five in 1919, had apparently lost support in the 1920s and 1930s, since in 1939 they possessed only eighteen members of the Council.[1] Their decline, however, is illusory, since the group called Ratepayers and Independents comprised individuals whose national allegiance was to the Conservative Party, but in local affairs they preferred not to bear openly the party label and to receive open assistance from the party machine. This group, six in 1919, consisted of fifteen in 1939; thus making the true Conservative total not eighteen but thirty-three.

These Independents represented three types of ward: first the wards in the west, Penn and St Philip's, where there grew up a flourishing Ratepayers' Association in the 1930s, narrowly confined to promoting amenities for the wards; secondly, Heath Town Ward, members of whose U.D.C. came on to the Council as Independents. They were mainly concerned with protecting the interests of Heath Town. And, thirdly, various other wards usually returning Labour members, but which occasionally sent to the Council a well-known ward figure such as a priest or a publican. For instance St Mary's Ward, which in 1927 had elected three Labour Councillors, returned T. Brady, a publican, and F. Lockett, a Catholic priest, as Independent Councillors

[1] See Table VI.

from 1928 and from 1930 respectively until 1945 when the ward again sent Labour men to the Council. 'Independent' in these cases can be seen as an electoral device, since a candidate standing openly as a Conservative would have had little opportunity of victory; it allowed anti-Socialist individuals to insinuate themselves into what were normally Labour strongholds. The Independents therefore were either Councillors concerned particularly with the interests of their wards or else people infiltrated into safish Labour seats to reduce Labour membership of the Council.

There was no organisation for the 'Independents'; they were not a coherent party with an electoral machine covering the town, nor did the Independent Councillors meet as a caucus for planning their activities in the Council. In national politics they were Conservative supporters and in municipal elections they never faced official Conservative opposition. In Council affairs they voted with the Conservatives and were indistinguishable from them.

A leading feature of the appeal of the Independents was that they were not connected to a political party; a position which they contrasted with the situation in the Labour Party. Conservatives too criticised the Labour Party for bringing party politics into municipal affairs, and explained that they, though fighting elections openly as Conservatives, dropped their political affiliations once on the Council and in an Independent manner judged each issue on its merits. The Labour Party was accused of demanding from its Councillors a rigid adherence to a party line. For instance in 1930 the Conservative agent, Sam Bowers, said: 'In Wolverhampton the Socialist Party candidates had to subscribe to the Socialist Party programme. If they deviated from it when elected they were subject to party discipline. The Conservative Association supported its nominees for election to the Town Council, but with this difference – that if elected they were not subject to any party discipline or interference by the Conservative Association. They are there solely to exercise their judgement in the best interests of the ratepayers.'[1] Hostility to Labour united the Conservatives and Independents, and the Liberals too.

The Liberals. The Liberals in the inter-war years were indistinguishable as regards voting in the Council from other anti-

---

[1] *E. & S.*, 23.12.1930.

Socialist Councillors. They, too, stressed their objection to party politics and their desire to judge issues on their merits. Although their national affiliation was well-known, at municipal election time it was not emphasised. They never stood openly as Liberals, but called themselves Independents. More and more they came to be limited to two wards in the eastern half of the town, which the Conservatives allowed them to keep and which Labour did not really invade until the I.L.A. and Lawley made the breakthrough. In crude terms their decline does not appear all that sharp, a fall from eleven in 1919 to eight in 1939, but of the eight in 1939 five were Aldermen of long standing and only three were Councillors. Thus it was clear that the Liberals had not been recruiting fresh support; for example the Young Liberals wound up their Association in 1929 through lack of interest. The decline of the Liberals was due to their irrelevance at a time when the main battle was between the Labour and Conservative Parties. The Liberals were not an adequate opposition against either. Squeezed between the two, they merged with the Conservatives, at first through electoral pacts which then led to closer connections. As an independent body the Liberals let their organisation run down, and relying on Conservative sufferance and assistance they faded away.

All these anti-Socialist groups, Conservatives, Liberals, Independents and Ratepayers possessed a common ethos – hostility to the Labour programme and to Labour's means of implementing its proposals. Even as late as 1939 none of these groups had a distinctive, positive, constructive and comprehensive programme for the town as a whole, nor did the anti-Socialists as a group possess one. Their *raison d'être* was essentially negative and defensive, a protection of the *status quo* and the methods of the 1890s. Their ethos was that electors should choose not measures but men; not a policy and programme but individuals who would tackle each problem as it arose on the Council in the best interests of the town.

THE COUNCIL IN 1945

In 1945 Labour gained for the first time an overall majority, holding thirty-two seats against the Conservatives' thirteen and the Independents' fifteen. In the Parliamentary sphere too Labour triumphed with John Baird's victory in East Wolverhampton over the Liberal Geoffrey Mander, who had held the seat since 1929; and in the West H. D. Hughes defeated the Conservative candidate J. Beattie, who had been chosen as candidate after Bird had declared his intention not to seek re-election. Labour was in command of both the Parliamentary and municipal representation of the town.

The Liberals were a spent force: they had run only two candidates in the November elections as Independents and both had lost. The Conservatives did not campaign openly as Conservatives but as Progressives. Before the election the anti-Socialist members of the Council had met to plan their election strategy. They decided to drop the label 'Conservative' since they reckoned that it was very unpopular with the electorate, having regard to their large Parliamentary defeat in June. Such a move was also in accord with their opposition to partisanship over Council affairs. Their election address, similar to that of 1927, stressed hostility to Socialist measures which they called ill-considered and liable to raise the rates. As in the past, they made no distinctive and positive proposals. They were soundly defeated;[1] only eight of their twenty-six candidates were elected.

The Conservative come-back. The Conservatives in Wolverhampton were stunned by the defeats, but only temporarily; a new agent was appointed in the West; a new Parliamentary candidate, Enoch Powell, was chosen and the organisation was overhauled for the first time since the defeat in 1906. One of the main changes was that the Constituency Association was no longer dependent on financial contributions from its candidate to maintain the organisation. The agent reported in 1946 that 'in the past this Association has relied on the generosity of its former M.P. Sir Robert Bird: now it is the members themselves who are responsible for the financial obligations of the up-keep of the Constituency H.Q. and for maintaining and furthering the Conservative Party throughout the District. This followed

[1] In 1950 Sir Robert Bird said: 'after the 1945 election, the party in West Wolverhampton was in disarray and it was not easy to see how it could be restored'. *E. & S.*, 20.4.1950.

               J.B.P.

the remodelling of the Constituency on democratic lines as laid down by Central Office.'[1] Money was sought primarily by appealing to local businesses; a circular was sent to local firms asking for assistance.

Not only had the Party to go out to find money, it had to persuade people to vote for the Conservative candidate, and to Powell's mind that meant, as it had to Alfred Bird in 1912, using the municipal elections as the 'autumn manœuvres' for the Parliamentary battle.[2] He urged that all non-Socialist candidates for the Council should stand openly as Conservatives, and that the titles of Progressive, Ratepayer and Independent should be dropped, so that all anti-Socialists could rally behind the Conservatives and the Party could know where Conservative support really lay. He also argued that this change would redound to the benefit of the Council, for the Independent, he said, with no party machine to guide and help him, had no possible chance of representing his electorate satisfactorily in the increasing intricacies of local government. Party labels were a great help. They enabled the electorate to understand what line a candidate would take on the point at issue.[3] Most of the Councillors followed his advice. The only resistance came from Penn Ward, where the Ratepayers' Association possessed a genuine Independent existence, distinct from the local Conservative Association. Bitterness between the two bodies was so intense that in the municipal election of 1950 the Ratepayers' Councillor of Penn had to face not only a Labour but also a Conservative candidate, and he defeated them both. By 1955, however, the Conservatives had won; in the election of that year the Ratepayers' candidate came bottom of the poll. They could find no other candidate prepared to finance his own campaign; their former Councillors had accepted the Conservative label; support dwindled and the Association was dissolved. Most of the other Independents accepted the Conservative label, although a few preferred to retire from the Council. From then on all anti-Socialist members of the Council attended the Conservative 'caucus', the group

---

[1] *The Agents Report* for 1946.
[2] He said that local elections should be used as 'a public platform on which the party's national policy can be expounded'. *E. & S.*, 17.4.1950.
[3] Report of a speech at the town's Wulfrun Hall. *E. & S.*, 2.5.1950.

which conferred before a Council meeting to concert action there. At the height of the crisis over the position of the Independents, an Independent caucus had almost been formed, but such a split had been avoided by the diplomacy of the Conservative leader, J. Beattie, and by the recognition of the harsh political reality that the Labour Party could only be kept out of control by common action by the Conservatives and Independents. Thus Parliamentary considerations had once again intervened in the politics of the Council, this time to cause the elimination of the Independents.

Labour in power. Labour's victory in 1945 heralded a new style of political process on the Town Council. Party became more significant than before in the actual work of the Council. When Labour had been in opposition, its Group meetings of Councillors had been informal and irregular, called to deal with specific items, and they were not a permanent feature. In power, however, frequent and regular Group meetings were held to concert policy and tactics in the Council chamber. The Labour Party in Wolverhampton tried to act with regard to the Council as the Labour Party did nationally with Parliament; namely a governing party with a majority facing a minority opposition party; one party in office and responsible for policy, the other without any office. This situation was not finally reached until 1955 for at first, from 1945 to 1949, Labour did not take all the Chairmanships of the Council committees; in opposition from 1949 to 1952 they refused to accept any offered to them by the Conservatives; from 1952 to 1955 again they shared them, then from 1955 they took them all. Labour regarded the Chairmen as analagous to Ministers; and to allow members of different and opposing parties to share these offices, it was felt, would detract from the concept of the collective responsibility of a single party for the policy of the whole Council. Conservatives at first protested at the imposition on local government of Parliamentary techniques which, they argued, were inappropriate in the context of a Town Council with a Committee structure. Yet by the late 1950s, realising that they could not defeat Labour or indeed run the Council along the traditional lines of sharing office and responsibility, the Conservatives had adopted these very techniques and had even perfected them more effectively than the Labour Party. Regular Group meetings were held at the same time as Labour's; shadow Chairmen watched their opposite numbers in the Labour Party, and a policy committee was established to act as a kind of Shadow Cabinet. The Conservatives had become an alternative government poised to take over from Labour when a majority was won. The traditional style of running the Council, which was in operation at the turn of the century, finally vanished in the 1950s.

In the 1950s partisanship in the Council was far more rife than it had been in the inter-war years, mainly because the parties were so evenly balanced. Labour had a majority of never more than ten in 1945–9; the Conservatives were in a majority during 1949–52; then Labour regained control, which it kept into the 1960s. In 1961–3, however, the parties were equal with thirty members of the Council apiece. This balance was a feature of the Parliamentary representation too. J. Baird maintained his seat in the East, while J. E. Powell in 1950 defeated the Labour member, H. D. Hughes, and retained the seat, increasing his majority at each election, until 1964. This pattern of representation was not accepted by the Labour and Conservative Parties with such equanimity as the Liberal and Conservative Parties had accepted the division of the town's Parliamentary representation at the turn of the century. In each Division both parties created strong organisations. None abdicated, as the Liberal had done.

ELECTIONEERING

Municipal elections reflected the antagonism between the two competing parties. Independents stood no chance, whether it was a Ratepayer challenging a Conservative or an ex-Labour Councillor expelled from the Labour Party challenging her former party. The Liberals began to make a tentative reappearance, fighting safe Conservative wards in the 1960s. The Communists fought some safe Labour wards too. But the main clash at the elections was between the Conservative and Labour Parties. This partisan conflict has, so it is sometimes argued, produced apathy among the public and is responsible for low polls at municipal elections since the voters cannot see the relevance of this kind of political struggle for the Town Council. In Wolverhampton, however, there was no evidence that party politics contributed to an increase in public apathy; rather it pointed to the opposite tendency.

There were more contested elections after parties took an interest in municipal politics, and especially since the Labour Party entered the scene. During the 1920s at the November elections never fewer than four seats were fought, and in three years eight seats were contested. In the 1930s when the Labour Party was somewhat weaker there were slightly fewer fights each year, but after 1945 there were never fewer than eight contests at each election. In one year all fifteen seats were fought; in three years fourteen and in four years thirteen. More contests meant that more people had the opportunity to participate in the elections than in the days when contests were few. Their opportunities were further widened because of the extensions of the franchise, not merely in 1918 but also in 1945 when the municipal franchise was made as good as equal to the Parliamentary franchise.[1] In 1939 the Burgess roll totalled 73,222; in 1945 106,245. In 1932 46 per cent of the town's population were eligible to vote; in 1952 68 per cent, the same percentage as in 1960. In 1932 10 per cent of the town's inhabitants voted in the election; in 1952 29 per cent. Thus just under one-third of the population participated, whereas at the turn of the century it rarely rose above 3 per cent or 4 per cent; and in the inter-war years it was about 10 per cent.[2]

As the percentage of the *population* voting rose, so the percentage of the *electorate* voting fell. Before 1914 polls of 60–80 per cent were typical; in the 1920s 50–60 per cent polls were common; in the 1930s 30–40 per cent became usual. After 1945 polls of 30–40 per cent remained normal. These figures, relating to the individual wards, are more meaningful than figures for the town as a whole which level out the large variations between wards. The reasons for the drop in the percentage of the electorate voting are mainly two; first, the extension of the franchise to people not owning property and possessing little wealth and little education, lacking knowledge, awareness and interest in politics and local government. The narrower electorate of the 1890s was more concerned with the Town Council and its policies than

[1] 8 & 9 Geo. VI, c. 5.
[2] See Table VII.

the wider, basically working-class, electorate after 1918. And second, the parties' habit of contesting hopeless seats has pulled down the figures for the turnout, since the safe seats have the lowest polls.

Three related factors determine whether turnout will be large or small: the socio-economic composition of the ward, the safeness of the seat and the intensity of party activity. Between 1958 and 1964 turnouts of under 30 per cent were recorded for twenty-four contests. All took place in safe Labour wards. Turnouts of under 20 per cent occurred in five fights and four of these were straight fights between Labour and Communist candidates. The highest turnouts took place in marginal wards. In this period eleven contests produced turnouts of over 50 per cent; eight were in marginal wards and the other three were in safe Conservative wards, where three-cornered contests were held between Conservative, Labour and Liberal candidates. Safe Conservative wards witnessing straight fights between Labour and Conservatives had larger turnouts than safe Labour wards where there were straight fights between Labour and Conservative candidates.

Therefore the working class who predominate in safe Labour wards have not the same inclination to vote as the middle class who predominate in safe Conservative wards. The latter group, better educated, more civic-minded and politically conscious, perhaps feels more intensely than the former that it has a duty to vote. The level of party activity is a significant factor, too, for the Conservative Party in safe Conservative wards is much more active on election day than the Labour Party in safe Labour wards. Further, the Conservatives are apt to stay in their ward and not go out to help in the marginal seats, while the Labour members make only a token showing in their safe wards and concentrate on the marginals, especially when they face only Communist opponents in their safe wards. In addition, low polls here are easily explained by the lack of Conservative candidates; without a candidate to support, the Conservative voters stay at home. This factor explains the high polls in Conservative seats when the Liberals entered the fray against both Conservatives and Labour. Previously the Liberal voters had had no candidate to support. When they had, they turned out. The importance of party in influencing the turnout can be seen in the marginal wards; here party activity is concentrated, for these wards hold the key to control of the Council. More intense party activity produces a higher poll.

If the parties were solely concerned with the Town Council, they would fight no other seats but the marginals; however, since they have Parliamentary aspirations too, they have fought hopeless seats to keep in trim their Parliamentary organisation and to activate their supporters. Because these hopeless seats are fought, the percentage of the turnout for the town has been reduced. Therefore the entry of party politics into local government elections has given more people than before the opportunity to cast a vote; it has enabled a higher proportion of the inhabitants of the town to take part in choosing the town's governors; but the price paid for this has been a lower percentage turnout of those eligible to vote.

The appeal of the candidates at elections since 1945 differed sharply from the style around 1900. Now each candidate is a party candidate. His name is not as important as the party behind him. His helpers are party workers, more committed to the party than to him personally. His committee rooms are festooned with party posters and literature. The Parliamentary agents manage the campaigns. The election address is common for all candidates drawn up by the party to emphasise party policy, with only a small space for the candidate to make a personal appeal, calling attention to his experience, connections with the ward, personal interest and adherence to the proposals of his party. The parts of the address written by the parties possess a similarity of approach. When in power it justifies and praises its record, seeks support to carry on its sound programme and attacks the opposition for negative obstruction and for advocating misguided proposals. In its election addresses for 1961 and 1962 the Labour Party listed its achievements and future plans for health, education, housing, welfare, town development, care of children and open spaces. It attacked the Conservative Government's high interest rates and the Conservative Group's policy of 'selling out Wolverhampton to the private speculator'. In opposition the party condemns the failure of the Administration, which it accuses of pursuing unnecessary and expensive schemes, which have raised the rates and produced no public benefit. It urges the adoption of alternative proposals, more economical and efficient than those of the majority party. In its election addresses for 1961 and 1962 the Conservative Party complained of lavish expenditure which had increased the rates: it attacked Socialist Party puppets who badgered and interfered. It called for consultation with people affected by slum clearance and not dictation. It opposed what it called Labour's plans to municipalise 'taxis, laundries, printing, catering and petrol stations', and its plans for Comprehensive Schools which would injure the town's Grammar School. It called for a differential rent scheme, the sale of Council houses to tenants, and encouragement to private builders and developers, and it attacked Labour's hostility to these proposals. The election has become a clash, not of personalities, but of parties, and the Conservatives during the course of the 1950s evolved a distinct municipal policy, an alternative to Labour's. As the Labour Party in opposition formed its alternative to the traditional *status quo*, so the Conservatives in opposition, yet on the brink of taking control, were stimulated to propose their own alternative to the Labour *status quo*. Before 1945 there was no Conservative municipal policy; afterwards they produced one.

The financing of the election campaigns differs slightly from party to party. In the Labour Party the election expenses are borne by the party; whereas in the Conservative Party, if a candidate can afford it, he pays for his own campaign. In one Conservative ward, West Park, in the early 1960s the financing and the actual election campaign were in the hands of two families who acted under the name of the Conservative Association. The Guys, father and son, and the Fullwoods, father and son, all represented the ward as Councillors or Aldermen. They provided the money, organised the canvassing and the arrangement of cars for polling day: an easy task for them, since the Guys owned a motor-car-servicing business and the Fullwoods a tyre-selling concern; therefore they had many contacts with leading businesses in the town. This situation in West Park Ward represented a blending of the old and the new; on the one hand it appeared as a personal fief of two closely linked families, and on the other these families operated under the banner of a political party. Within the Labour Party on the Council there were no members to compare with the Guys and Fullwoods in wealth and range of business contacts. Their candidates were more dependent on the party for financing and organising their campaigns.

The style of the campaigns pursued by the parties is similar. Each candidate is nominated by members of his party, residing in the ward he seeks to represent. For a number of evenings before the actual poll, the candidate and his canvassers will tour the ward, posting literature and talking to voters on their doorsteps. The efforts of both parties are concentrated on known party supporters who have previously indicated loyalty to the party; or else on doubtfuls or new arrivals to the ward. No attempts at conversion are made. Often a loudspeaker will be used by the candidate on the streets or outside a factory gate. Posters are put up in windows or on boards in gardens. There is little excitement until election day itself. Then all attention is paid to getting out supporters. Canvassers knock up voters, cars hurry them to the polling station: school children run from the polling station to committee rooms to keep the organisers informed of those who have voted. Canvassers go from the committee rooms to pull out those who have not yet been to vote. The time of most activity is between 7.00 and 8.30 p.m., when the largest number of party workers are engaged in the fight and when the majority of people are at home after work.[1]

Compared with the elections of the turn of the century two features are significant. Party is now uppermost; the candidate himself stands first and foremost as a party man; and, secondly, there are now few public meetings. It is most rare for a candidate to hold a public meeting. If one is held, then it is sparsely attended and usually by loyal party workers only. Both parties have come to the conclusion that the public meeting as a means of putting a candidate before an electorate is inappropriate, and that, since the people won't come to the candidate, the candidate must go to them.

This decline of the public meeting has reduced the opportunities for the press to report the election. Often the only signs in the local newspaper that an election is to take place are a series of letters in the correspondence columns praising or attacking a

---

[1] The author has contributed a case study of the municipal elections of 1964 in Wolverhampton to a symposium edited by L. J. Sharpe, *Voting in Cities*, London, 1967, pp. 262–89.

particular candidate, or taking up points raised in the election addresses. On the day of the election the leader columns exhort the electorate to vote and not to kill democracy through apathy. The press does not report the activities of the parties and candidates, nor do the parties inform the press of their doings. It could therefore be argued that the press has contributed to a decline of interest in local government, since it no longer gives such prominence as it did to the elections. In reply the press would say that they have cut down their coverage because of lack of public demand. If the public wanted to read such news, they would demand and receive it.

In 1900 political parties played little part in municipal elections and there were no party groups on the Council. In 1964 only party candidates stood for election to the Council and two party groups, one the governing and the other the opposition party, faced each other in the Council chamber. The introduction of party politics into local government is often thought to have been a cause of increasing apathy. But in Wolverhampton there was no evidence of growing apathy. Just the opposite – because of the introduction of party politics more people have been given the opportunity to vote for their Councillors than in 1900 and more people have the opportunity to stand as candidates. Today there are more contests and more people seeking to be Councillors than sixty years ago. Now more people are eligible both to vote and to be elected; party has enabled them to make use of these opportunities. It has increased public participation in the municipal political process.

4 The Political Background: a Survey of the Wards

BETWEEN 1896 and 1964 the boundaries of the wards were altered twice, in 1927 and 1958, but on both occasions most of the wards retained their essential characteristics. Thus it is possible to examine each ward over the whole period to reveal its economic and social composition, its voting behaviour and the types of Councillor it sent to the Town Hall.[1] The reorganisation in 1966 completely altered the wards, and the description which follows deals with the wards only up to their demise in 1966.

ST PETER'S WARD

The town centre has since 1848 been in St Peter's Ward, the commercial and professional centre of the town. It is the smallest ward in area and population, but the richest in rateable value. It has also contained a working-class area in the northern part in shabby narrow streets of nineteenth-century terraced houses.

[1] *Sources* (*a*) The details of the economic and social composition of the wards come from the author's personal observations, based on 25 years' residence in the town and a tour of every ward between 1963 and 1964. Wide use was also made of descriptions in the press of the wards over the period. Assistance was received from Mr A. J. Robbins, the Chief Electoral Registration Assistant of Wolverhampton, also a native of the town, who discussed with the author the returns made by the canvassers who compiled the electoral register. There are no surveys, for example, of the rateable value of property in each ward, because the wards have not been used as administrative units. The Census returns have not presented their material by wards.

(*b*) Details about election results have been taken from the local press, and the size of the electorate, from 1896 to 1913, from the press and the *Wolverhampton Directories*, and from 1919 to 1964 from lists supplied by Mr Robbins.

(*c*) Details about the Councillors, i.e. their occupations, religions, etc., are taken from *Council Yearbooks*, the press interviews and replies to a questionnaire.

(*d*) The boundaries of the wards from 1896 are shown on the maps on pp. 405–7.

During the 1950s and 1960s these have been demolished and Council flats have begun to rise in their place. The business vote has declined since 1945 as private owners have been replaced by limited liability companies whose directors do not qualify for a vote. The population of the ward fell until 1958, when a re-drawing of the boundaries added to it a working-class area in the north-east which was formerly part of St Mary's Ward. This part has continually lost population as the older properties have been cleared.

From 1896 to 1945 the ward was a Conservative stronghold. Only one Liberal was elected, a prominent businessman in the ward. There were few contests in the ward until Labour candidates began to contest seats in the middle 1920s,[1] but they never gained more than 40 per cent of the vote. In 1945 Labour won a seat with 52 per cent of the vote, but the ward remained basically Conservative until the revision of the boundaries in 1958 made it highly marginal.

Before 1945 its Councillors had three main characteristics. They were either professional men who had offices in the town centre, businessmen with factories in the ward, or traders with premises there. The latter element remained constant, while the former dwindled. Since 1945 the Conservative Councillors were usually shop-keepers with establishments in the ward.

The Labour Councillors had fewer links with the ward. None ever lived or worked there. Their occupations were various, trade union officials, housewives, a boilersmith and a machinery inspector.

Before 1914 one attachment of the representatives to the ward was far more noticeable than later. Many Councillors worshipped at the parish church of St Peter and held such lay offices as sidesman and churchwarden. This connection was not apparent after 1914.

ST MARY'S WARD

Adjoining St Peter's Ward on its north-east side was St Mary's Ward, which vanished as a separate ward in the reorganisation of 1958, part going to St Peter's and part to Eastfield. It was an industrial and working-class area, of large and small factories and

[1] Three contests between 1896 and 1924.

streets of terraced houses. In the 1920s it contained some of the worst slums of the town and had one of the earliest of the Council's slum clearance areas. By 1958 its population had dwindled as its people had been moved to new estates.

It saw only one contest between 1896 and 1914. Conservatives, Liberals and Independents peaceably shared the representation of the ward. After 1920 no Conservative or Liberal who stood openly as such was elected. Labour first won the ward in 1920 with 59 per cent of the vote. Its hold was shaken in the 1930s by two independents who were well-known local figures, the Catholic parish priest and a publican. Between 1945 and 1957 it was a safe Labour seat.

Its Councillors were often Catholics, for the ward contained the Irish quarter dominated by St Patrick's Church, whose priest at the turn of the century, Father Darmody, was an influential figure who 'controlled the vote'. A Liberal manufacturer and a shopkeeper who represented the ward were both Catholics; Labour's representatives have included two Catholics; one Independent was a Catholic and this ward is the only ward to have returned a priest, the Catholic Father Lockett, to the Council. Four of its Catholic Councillors were also Irish.

Many of its Councillors were connected with Butler's Brewery, whose Springfield works was situated in the ward. The managing director was a Councillor in 1895–1903; one Councillor was the steward at the brewery's sports and social club, one was a licensed victualler of a Butler's house and another became a Butler's publican after retiring from the coal trade.

Between 1945 and 1958 its Labour Councillors were all working men except the wife of a working man and the owner of a small bakery. Only one of them lived in the ward.

DUNSTALL WARD

To the north and north-east of the town centre lay Dunstall Ward. In 1964 it was an industrial area, containing the Electrical Construction Company, which was established in the 1890s; Courtaulds, which came to the town in the 1920s; and many small engineering firms. The large railway sheds and workshops, which used to be the main employers in the ward, were closed down in

1964. Most of the housing dated from the late nineteenth century, both working-class and lower-middle-class terraced houses. Much was scheduled for demolition. There were small pockets of inter-war semi-detached houses, but hardly any were built after 1939. Before the Second World War it used to be a ward of mixed working- and middle-class social composition. After 1945 its status declined, especially after many West Indian and Indian immigrants flocked into the ward in the early 1960s.

No Labour member won a contested election in the ward before 1919. When Labour candidates fought a straight fight with the Conservatives, Labour gained just over 40 per cent of the vote, but when Liberals fought straight fights with the Conservatives the Liberals got over 60 per cent. Labour and Liberals fought each other only once before 1919, in 1913 when the Liberals gained 55 per cent of the vote. After 1919 Labour won some seats in the ward; the most dramatic election being that of 1919 when a Labour candidate fighting for the first time defeated a Liberal Councillor who had represented the ward for twenty-five years. When all the seats were fought in the municipal 'general' election of 1927, each of the three successful candidates belonged to a different party; one was Labour, another a Conservative and the last a Liberal.

After 1945 it became a fairly safe Labour seat, being lost only twice, in 1947 and in 1960, and on the last time by only nine votes. As the social composition of the ward became more homogeneous, so its political allegiance hardened and was no longer spread widely over the three major parties.

Its Councillors were as varied in occupation as in politics, a mixture of Labour working men, Liberal shopkeepers and Conservative industrialists and professional men. It had the distinction of being the first ward to return a female Councillor, the Labour Mrs E. Sproson, in 1921. The one striking characteristic of its Labour representatives in particular was their connection with the railways: four of its Labour Councillors were railwaymen between 1919 and 1964.

GRAISELEY WARD

To the south and south-west of the town centre was Graiseley Ward. It was always a ward with a very varied social composition.

Until the early 1960s it contained an area of very old and poor slums tightly packed in alleys and courts. Some of the worst were cleared in the inter-war years and most went in the 1950s. At the turn of the century it had a number of small factories, now removed elsewhere. On the cleared land were erected the Council's first multi-storey flats in the 1950s, while in the corner furthest from the town centre was one of the Council's first housing estates of the 1920s. The ward also had a large number of private houses of different kinds, ranging from terraced lower-middle-class housing of the period 1890–1914, through more substantial villas of the same period, to some large houses of the inter-war years. Many of the larger houses were flatted or, if near the town centre, taken over by West Indians. Thus from 1896 it was a far from homogeneous ward; in 1900 in the area nearest the town centre were ugly slums, while at the other end were the large houses of the well-off. In 1964 a select area of the well-to-do still existed, while at the other end was a West Indian community.

Over the whole period this ward was eagerly contested by the Conservative and Labour Parties. Labour's first Councillors were from this ward in the 1890s. From this time right up to the 1960s it was a marginal ward returning both Labour and Conservative Councillors. A seat in Graiseley was never safe. No Liberal was ever elected for the ward.

The Conservative Councillors for the ward before 1945 were mainly manufacturers and businessmen, with an occasional professional man or a local publican. After 1945 their occupations were more varied: an estate agent, a chemist, a sales promotion manager and the owner of a large store. The Labour members, too, produced no significant occupational type: they were a newsagent, a housewife, a travel club agent, and a trade union official.

BLAKENHALL WARD, FORMERLY BLAKENHALL AND ST JOHN'S WARD

To the south of the town centre lay Blakenhall Ward. From 1848 to 1896 this area was in St. John's Ward. In 1896 it was divided into two: Blakenhall and St John's Wards. In 1927 they were largely combined, becoming known as Blakenhall and St John's Ward, until in 1958 it became merely Blakenhall Ward.

The Blakenhall and St John's sections could always be distinguished. The latter was nearest the town centre and consisted of numerous nineteenth-century factories and very slummy working-class housing. The former was to the south of St John's, more residential and middle-class. The industries it contained were newer, the Sunbeam Motor Car Company, the Villiers Engineering concern, Star Aluminium and some engineering and electrical concerns, mostly of twentieth-century origin. Over the period the shift of population was away from the St John's part, which by 1964 was cleared of houses and had become a factory zone. The Blakenhall area, too, in the late 1950s witnessed considerable clearance, but it was intended to be a residential area. Council flats would be erected on the cleared ground. At the end of the ward farthest from the town centre was a select residential area of large inter-war detached houses. West Indian and Indian immigrants settled in a small part of the ward. Thus like Graiseley Ward it had a very mixed social composition.

No Liberal ever stood for election in St John's Ward between 1896 and 1925, nor was any Liberal ever a representative of the ward. The contests which took place were between Conservatives and Labour. The former usually won. Other Labour members became Councillors for the ward by being elected unopposed. This ward was one of the earliest wards to send Labour men to the Council, between 1898 and 1903, like a decorator, a carpenter, a spectacle-maker and a plumber. The Conservative Councillors had one striking characteristic: four between 1891 and 1908 were publicans in the ward. They were likely to be the only Conservatives who were well-known and liked by the working-class population of St John's. No employer with a factory in the ward ever became its representative.

Blakenhall was quite different. Conservatives rarely got over 48 per cent of the vote: only once between 1896 and 1925, in 1913, did they win a contested election. Liberals did well in this ward before 1913; Labour won seats in 1897 and 1911, but not until after 1918 did they have a long run of successes. The Conservative and Liberal representatives had similar occupations, manufacturers and professional men; the publican element was not so prominent among the Conservatives as in St John's Ward. The Labour members were mainly workmen.

The combination of the two wards in 1927 and the splits in the Labour Party injured Labour's chances in the ward and made it largely a Conservative ward until the increase in the electorate of 1945, when it became very marginal, often changing hands. But the slum clearance and removal of the population in the course of the 1950s turned it by 1960 into a safe Conservative ward. Its Conservative Councillors since 1945 were shopkeepers and small businessmen; its Labour Councillors were mixed; a shopkeeper, salesman, sheet-metal worker and trade union official.

PARKFIELD WARD, FORMERLY ST GEORGE'S WARD

To the south and south-east of the town centre lay Parkfield Ward, which before 1958 was called St George's. In 1958 it lost an area of working-class terraced housing at its northern end to East Park Ward. It was predominantly an industrial and working-class area, with some large and small engineering enterprises and builders' yards. Half of its housing consisted of Council estates, both pre- and post-war, mainly pre-1939, and half was nineteenth-century terraced housing, which at the turn of the century was occupied by the middle and lower middle class and by the 1950s by the working class.

It witnessed few contests between 1896 and 1910. Those which took place were straight fights between the Conservatives and Liberals, with the latter winning. Labour won in 1910 and 1913. Between 1919 and 1927 Conservatives and Liberals combined to defeat Labour candidates, but after a redrawing of the boundaries in 1927 it became a safe Labour seat, never to be won by any other party afterwards. Conservatives rarely gained over 30 per cent of the vote. In the 1950s the Communists ran candidates but they won only about 6 per cent of the vote.

Before 1914 its Liberal and Conservative representatives were of similar occupations, manufacturers with their factories in the ward or an occasional professional man like a doctor or an accountant. Labour's Councillors were working men. Between 1919 and 1927 the representatives remained manufacturers, but after 1927 the Labour representatives were of mixed occupations: housewives, grocers, a commissionaire, a trade union official and a tool-maker.

This ward is unique in that it sent three Labour grocers to the Council. Considering that shopkeepers are not a high proportion of the Labour membership of the Council, it is odd that most should have come from the same ward. This suggests that there was a powerful personal influence at work in the Ward Labour Party. The influence was that of Alderman H. E. Lane, once the Councillor for the ward (1930–45), Chairman of Housing Committee (1945–9, 1952–60, 1962–7), and a most dominant individual, who was credited with pushing forward as candidates those he liked and of pushing out those he disliked.

WEST PARK WARD, FORMERLY PARK WARD

To the west and north-west of the town centre lay West Park Ward, which contained some of the most attractive parts of the town around the West Park and astride the Tettenhall and Compton Roads. It was an area of tree-shaded avenues, squares and culs-de-sac, with large Regency and Victorian houses (many converted into flats), inter-war detached houses and modern luxury flats. It was once, and to some extent remained, the most select residential area of the town. The ward also contained valuable retail property in Chapel Ash and a sizeable area of terraced housing, which, at the turn of the century, was of middle- and lower middle-class status. In the 1950s they housed many of the workers at Courtaulds in the adjacent ward of Dunstall. This area also held a considerable number of immigrants: East Europeans who came to the town after 1945, and Indians and West Indians who entered in the 1960s. A cluster of multi-storeyed Council flats was erected in the ward. It had no industry. It was also the educational centre of the town, containing the town's three grammar schools and the Wulfrun College of Further Education. Symbolically perhaps, the South-West Wolverhampton Conservative Association had its headquarters in the ward.

Since 1896 it saw few electoral contests. When there were fights the Conservatives won. Only two Liberals represented the ward: one defeated a Conservative in the education battle of 1904, but the other in the 1920s had Conservative support against Labour opposition. Since 1945 Labour never got over 29 per cent of the vote; in 1960 it sunk to 10 per cent. In 1963 the Liberals fought the seat for the first time since 1906 and obtained 30 per cent of the vote. It was indeed a Conservative stronghold.

Up to 1945 its Councillors were very similar to those elected by St Peter's Ward, business and professional men with their premises in the town centre but their homes in Park Ward. Its representatives were some of the leading figures in the business life of the town. After the war it was dominated by two families, the Guys and the Fullwoods. L. R. Guy was elected in 1939; H. T. Fullwood was co-opted in 1942. Their sons came on later, E. Y. Fullwood in 1955 and G. A. Guy in 1960. These two families – particularly the Guys – ran the ward organisation with great efficiency. Because of their contacts with garages and motorists they were able to produce for an election the highest number of cars of any party in any ward. Although their organisation bears the label Conservative, it looks like a personal family machine, against which the Conservative Group and Association have been occasionally powerless. For example, in 1958 the Conservative Group was displeased at the way the Fullwoods and Guys had voted over the choice of Mayor. A resolution was passed deploring their attitude and complaining of their non-attendance at Group meetings. An attempt was made to have the South-West Conservative Association withdraw the official Conservative label from them, but nothing happened. They remained inviolate in their ward, too important to antagonise. Among some progressive Conservatives these two families, 'alike as two peas', and always a solid block, were regarded as an obstructive force.

MERRIDALE WARD, FORMERLY ST MARK'S AND MERRIDALE WARD

To the west and south-west of the town centre and adjoining the southern part of West Park Ward was Merridale Ward. From 1896 to 1927 this area comprised two wards, St Mark's and Merridale; they were combined in 1927 and renamed in 1958 Merridale Ward. Then it lost the land between the Compton and Tettenhall Roads to West Park Ward, but gained from St Philip's the area around Finchfield.

In 1964 it was, on the whole, a large private housing estate of inter-war and post-war detached houses and luxury flats. It was

one of the most desirable residential areas in the town. Nearer
the town centre – around St Mark's Church – was a nineteenth-
century area of very poor terraced housing and larger villas,
which in the 1960s were being demolished or else taken over by
West Indian immigrants. But this area, which was once the hub
of the ward, became rapidly empty and formed only a small
proportion of the ward. In 1900 those parts of each ward nearest
the town centre – around St Mark's Church and near to Brickkiln
Street – contained some small factories and working-class housing.
But as one moved out to the boundaries of the borough the wards
became more middle class until one reached the substantial
houses of the business and professional men, set in a rural area
to the west of the town.

Between 1896 and 1925 St Mark's Ward saw two contests – in
1903 and 1905 – when the Conservative candidates got 60 per cent
of the vote in straight fights with the Liberals. No Liberal ever
represented this ward. Merridale saw more contests and a few
Liberal victories. In 1919 a Labour Councillor was elected, a
surprise result to the agent, who put the victory down to a thorough
campaign to bring out every Labour vote. No Labour man ever
won the seat again, nor was Labour ever successful in the area
between 1927 and 1964. It gained 36 per cent of the vote in
1945; by 1960 its share had fallen to 12 per cent. Liberals began
to fight the ward again in 1962, reaching a peak of 36 per cent of
the vote in 1963. Thus this area throughout the period was a
Conservative stronghold.

Its Councillors were over the period people of similar types:
manufacturers, professional men and shopkeepers. These Conservative shopkeepers were quite different from the Liberal
shopkeepers. The former, like those who represented St Peter's,
had establishments in the town centre and often many branches in
the suburbs. They were high-class traders, often in the wholesale
business too. The Liberal shopkeepers, in St James' and St
Matthew's Wards especially, tended to have a single shop only
and that in a working-class district. The Conservative shopkeepers
were of a higher social status than their Liberal counterparts.

Merridale had the distinction of being the first ward to return
a working man to the Council. In 1891 A. Weaver, a Conservative
and a clicker, was elected, before the Liberal or Trade Union

Parties could get one of their men in. The Conservatives appear to have chosen Weaver as their candidate as a deliberate attempt to woo the working-class vote and to get one step ahead of the other parties. Weaver was fiercely opposed by the trade unions of the town, since he ostentatiously refused to join a trade union, one of his attractions to the Conservatives. They put him up in Merridale Ward not only because he lived there but also because he might have been defeated if he had stood in a working-class ward.

Like Park Ward, Merridale Ward was influenced by two families who ran the Conservative Party machine in the ward. The sweet manufacturer, H. Bowdler, and his wife were Councillors for the ward from 1930 to 1955, while A. H. Windridge, a manufacturer and retailer of perambulators, was its Councillor from 1946 to 1962; his son-in-law, an accountant, H. R. Elliston, was its Councillor after 1957, and another accountant, G. C. Millichamp, represented the ward from 1958 to 1961. But no one in this ward had the reputation as a boss as had the Guys and the Fullwoods.

EASTFIELD WARD, FORMERLY ST JAMES' WARD

To the east of the town centre was Eastfield Ward, which from 1896 to 1958 was called St James' Ward. At the turn of the century the ward was an industrial and working-class ward. At the west end of the ward was the shopping area of Horseley Fields, a cluster of small shops of low status, serving the working class who lived in the ward. To the east of the shops and out to the borough boundary was the area where the Industrial Revolution began in Wolverhampton. In 1900 the mines were no longer working and their machinery and mounds had left large tracts of the area derelict. Here also were the large iron works and metal-trade factories. The canals and railways cut through the ward. The houses dated from the middle of the nineteenth century and were some of the worst and most unhealthy slums of the town. During the twentieth century these were cleared, the last going in the 1950s; the derelict land was reclaimed and huge post-war Council house estates covered the old industrial sites. Industry still flourished in the ward; the iron and metal trades, the chemical industry and some small engineering concerns. In 1958 the Horseley Fields shopping area was put in St Peter's Ward, and the new Eastfield Ward gained the new Council house estates in the east from Heath Town Ward and some early-twentieth-century working-class housing from St Mary's Ward, including the area around Butler's brewery. Thus in 1964 the ward was, as it was in 1900, an industrial and working-class ward, but shorn of its shopping centre.

To 1945 it was a Liberal stronghold. From 1896 to 1919 it saw two electoral contests, when the Liberal got 53 per cent of the vote against Conservative opposition. After 1919 Conservatives no longer stood against Liberals, who now faced Labour opposition. But until 1945 Labour could never gain over 38 per cent of the vote. It was left to groups other than the Conservative and Labour Parties to upset the Liberal hold. The Ex-Servicemen's candidate won in 1919; an I.L.A. candidate won in 1932 and then turned Fascist; in 1945 the Communist candidate won and then turned Conservative. These groups, the Ex-Servicemen, the I.L.A., the Fascists and the Communists, received the bulk of their support from the unemployed, of whom there were many in this ward during the 1920s and 1930s.[1] Between 1946 and 1952 Labour battled against Independents to represent the ward, and by 1952 had dislodged them. Afterwards only Labour members were elected, and their hold was strengthened by the reorganisation of 1958. The Independents of the late 1940s and early 1950s were really the old Liberals under a new guise, but their strength was eroded as the shopping area was cleared and the slums demolished.

The Liberal Councillors for the ward before 1945 were mainly traders and shopkeepers with establishments in the ward. They were of a lower social status than the Conservative shopkeepers of Merridale and St Peter's Wards, and they were all Nonconformists, Congregationalists, Wesleyan or Primitive Methodists, whereas the Conservative shopkeepers were Anglicans.[2] One shopkeeper who represented the ward at the turn of the century was a butcher whose house and shop were in the ward. Socially he was identical with the Liberal shopkeeper Councillors, but politically he was a Conservative and by religion an Anglican, a Warden at the parish

[1] See John Yates, *Lifting Timber for the King*, London, 1939.
[2] One was a Catholic.

church of St James'. Opposite this church was the Mount Zion Primitive Methodist Chapel at which many of the Liberal Councillors worshipped. Before 1945 religion rather than class was the determinant of political allegiance. The Labour Councillors since 1945 were of various occupations: a housewife, grocer, electrician and a stores clerk; religion was no longer significant.

To 1952 this ward presented many features which made it unique. Liberalism persisted longer than elsewhere; Labour was slow to take hold of working-class loyalty and minor parties did well. The inspiration provided by Mount Zion Chapel is a partial explanation of the strength of the Liberals, but some aspects of the ward's social structure are significant. The working class of this ward lived in the oldest and worst slums of the town and they worked in the oldest and largest factories of the town. These enterprises made iron and steel products, heavy and crude manufactures in no way comparable to the more finished and composite goods made in wards like St John's, Graiseley or Blakenhall. Here labour was skilled and unionised, but in the larger concerns of the east labour was unskilled and not unionised. The trade unions of Wolverhampton created the Labour Party and naturally the working class in these western wards turned to it as their party of protest against employers both Liberal and Conservative. But the working class in the east, without any trade union tradition and facing employers who were mainly Conservatives,[1] turned not to the Labour Party, which had put down no roots in the area, but to the Liberal Party, which was associated not with the employers but with small shopkeepers who lived close among them in the ward. These shopkeepers, Radical Liberals, became the leaders of the working class. After the First World War, however, the working class became disillusioned with Liberalism as unemployment mounted in the depressed heavy metal industries. Still without any tradition of trade unionism and loyalty to the Labour Party, many of them turned to the Ex-Servicemen, the I.L.A., the Fascists and the Communists, who championed the unemployed and offered easy panaceas for their plight. By the late 1940s these groups had disappeared, and it was only then that the

[1] The need for protection against German and Belgian competition in the production of iron and steel had turned these large industrialists against the Liberal Party and its doctrine of Free Trade.

working class became firmly linked to the Labour Party and no different from the working class of other wards. Liberalism persisted as long as there remained a sizeable number of small shopkeepers in the ward and as long as religion was a potent influence. Both had declined by 1945; they had been on the wane since 1914, but old habits persist until a new generation comes to the fore.

EAST PARK WARD, FORMERLY ST MATTHEW'S WARD

To the south-east of the town centre and adjacent to the southern boundary of Eastfield Ward was East Park Ward, which before 1958 was called St Matthew's. Like St James' Ward, it was the scene of the first industrial activity in the town. The mines and ironworks were situated here too. In the 1960s it was still an industrial area of small engineering firms and larger metal-trade enterprises. In 1900 it contained a basically working-class population housed in mid-nineteenth-century terraced houses squashed together in alleys and courts. These slums were cleared in the 1950s and the population rehoused on land reclaimed from the old industries of the ward. In 1964 it contained a basically working-class population housed in Council flats and estates which were erected in the 1950s and 1960s.

In the 1890s this ward was the battleground for the Radical Liberal temperance reformers and the drink trade. Between 1885 and 1897 it could be called marginal, between these two groups. The Liberal Councillors were mainly shopkeepers, all Non-conformists, while the Conservatives were licensed victuallers and wine and spirit merchants. As this conflict subsided, Labour made its challenge and succeeded here far more than in St James'. Many of the working class in this ward worked at the John Thompson boilerworks in near-by Ettingshall. The first Labour Councillor for the ward, elected in 1901, was William Sharrocks, a full-time organiser for the Boilermakers' Union. From then to 1932 it can be called a marginal ward between Labour and the Liberals. In the 1930s the I.L.A. made its most impressive advances in this ward. By 1936 it had all the three Councillors, with nearly 60 per cent of the vote. Its success was due to the fact that the official Labour Party did not oppose it and because the leading local figure in the I.L.A., W. Lawley, nursed the ward with great thoroughness. After 1936 no Liberal nor Conservative ever represented the ward. It was a solid Labour seat, with Labour gaining over 70 per cent of the vote in straight fights with the Conservatives and 90 per cent against the Communists. In 1960 and 1961 the Liberals fought the ward for the first time since 1934 and got 27 per cent of the vote.

The occupations of the Labour Councillors were very varied: a trade union official, railwaymen, a housewife, a grocer and a sheet-metal worker.

This ward, so like St James', had a different political history. The explanations for its different development are the absence of a considerable shopocracy, the absence of a strong focus of Nonconformity and the presence of the trade union tradition among the working class.

HEATH TOWN WARD

Heath Town was an Urban District acquired by Wolverhampton in 1927. Up to the 1950s it retained a strong sense of independence from Wolverhampton. Its community feeling was intensified because it had its own centre for shopping, commerce and culture. During the 1950s this centre was demolished and the ward became as closely integrated with the town as its other wards. The majority of its housing was by then working-class. Most of the low-value nineteenth-century terraced houses were pulled down in the 1950s, but many remained. The bulk of the working-class housing consisted of pre-war Council estates, although some new estates were built in the 1960s. There was also some pre-war private development in the ward and some substantial Victorian houses. It contained an industrial area too, of large and small engineering firms, and vehicle and electrical apparatus enterprises. In the reorganisation of 1958 it lost an area of new Council houses to Eastfield and some terraced Victorian houses to St Peter's, but gained some inter-war Council houses from Low Hill Ward.

Up to 1945 the Labour Party never got over 40 per cent of the vote in the annual elections, whether its opponents were Independents with Liberal or Conservative support. In 1945 the

proportions were reversed, although until 1952 the ward was
highly marginal between Labour and the Independents. After 1952
it was a safe Labour seat.

Its Councillors in the 1920s and 1930s were mainly former
members of the U.D.C.; even the first Labour Councillor, elected
in a by-election in 1938, had been a member of the U.D.C.
Most of them were also retired men: a former brewer, boot
manufacturer, doctor and railwayman. The Independents, who
represented the ward in the late 1940s and early 1950s, were all
people who lived in the ward, but they differed significantly from
the Independents of the 1930s. The latter had well-known national
party allegiances and at election time they were assisted by their
parties, but the former sought to be genuine Independents,
eschewing the support of any party. They regarded themselves
as spokesmen for their ward and not as party men.[1] The Labour
Councillors since 1952 were rarely working-class; they included a
teacher, a press relations officer and an insurance agent. At first
they tended to be inhabitants of the ward, but in 1964 two of the
three representatives lived outside the ward.

BUSHBURY WARD

In 1927 north of the town centre was Bushbury Ward; in 1933 it
was divided into Bushbury and Low Hill Wards and in 1958 it
was divided again into Bushbury and Oxley Wards. Both divisions
were caused by the great increase in the population of the area. In
1957 the ward was basically a large housing estate, containing an
area of inter-war private development and some post-war private
development, but most of it consisted of pre- and post-war
Council houses. Many of the inhabitants worked on the railways,
in Goodyears or in some engineering and chemical works which
were in the ward. In 1958 the ward lost the bulk of the private
development to the new Oxley Ward.

Only Labour representatives were elected to the Council. Since
its foundation in 1927 it was a safe Labour seat, and it became
more so after 1958. Many of the Labour Councillors were railwaymen, particularly active members of the railway unions A.S.L.E.F.
and N.U.R. Two brothers were elected in 1945, Norman and

[1] They resented being pressed to join the Conservative Group.

Harry Bagley, who were the leading figures in the ward party. They produced an organisation comparable to Lane's in Parkfield Ward or to a lesser extent to the Guys' and Fullwoods' in West Park Ward.

OXLEY WARD

Oxley Ward, formed out of the north-west part of Bushbury Ward in 1958, was varied in social composition, a mixture of private development, both pre- and mostly post-war, and of Council development, about equally pre- and post-war. It also contained a considerable industrial area in the north, consisting of a number of engineering and chemicals works. The largest open spaces in the borough lie in this ward, the airport, golf course, sewage farm and sports stadium.

It was a very marginal ward, frequently changi ng hands between Labour and Conservative Parties. The Conservative Councillors were in the superior white-collar group: a works manager, a director of an advertising agency and a buyer for an iron foundry. The Labour representatives had diverse occupations: a housewife, toolmaker, salesman and turner.

LOW HILL WARD

Cut out of the north-east part of Bushbury Ward in 1933, Low Hill Ward was a huge Council estate, the first major estate constructed by the Corporation in the inter-war years, to which was added much post-war Council housing. It contained hardly any private development. It was predominantly a working-class area and was regarded as holding the 'roughest' elements of the town's population.

Since 1933 it was a safe Labour seat except when an Independent was elected in 1935 and again in 1938. He was T. W. Glynn, a clerk at Butler's Brewery and a Catholic. The reason why he broke Labour's dominance was that the ward contained many Catholics who had moved from St Mary's Ward, but who still worked at the brewery. He was thus a well-known personality to the voters of Low Hill, where, in addition, he lived. The Conservatives rarely fought in Low Hill, only four times in thirty-one years, and they never gained over 26 per cent of the vote. The Communists began to fight the ward in 1960 and they increased their share of the vote from 6 per cent to 17 per cent, in 1964 although the turnout fell to 18 per cent.

Many of the Labour Councillors, like those of Bushbury, were railwaymen or the wives of railwaymen, keenly interested in the unions' activities. One, A. E. Griffiths, became General Secretary of A.S.L.E.F.

OXBARN WARD, FORMERLY ST PHILIP'S WARD

This area in the far south-west of the borough was taken into the town in 1927 when it was called Upper Penn Ward; in 1933 it was renamed St Philip's Ward and in 1958, after a readjustment of its boundaries, Oxbarn Ward.

From 1927 to 1958 it was a private housing estate, of very select housing in the Finchfield area built in the inter- and post-war years, and around St Philip's church, of late-nineteenth-century middle-class terraced housing. In 1958 it lost the Finch-field area to Merridale Ward, but gained the Council houses and private development at Warstones from Penn. This area was built in the pre-war years and in the late 1940s. The ward contained no industry.

To 1947 it was represented by Independents or Ratepayers, all of whom then adopted the Conservative label. Their share of the vote remained the same whatever the label. Labour did not get over 20 per cent of the vote after 1945 until 1958, following the reorganisation which gave the Council houses to the ward. In 1962 and 1963 the Liberals fought the ward and pushed Labour into third place, although in 1964 Labour pushed the Liberals into third place. Never was a Labour or Liberal candidate elected.

Its Councillors were largely shopkeepers or minor businessmen resident in the ward.

PENN WARD

This area was taken into the borough in 1933. It lay to the south of Oxbarn Ward and at the far south of the borough. Like Oxbarn it was non-industrial, and contained only private housing, ranging from some semi-detached to a considerable number of large detached houses. It contained no Council houses; it lost the Warstones estate to Oxbarn in 1958. It was a very select residential area with less of the nineteenth-century terraced housing than Oxbarn.

From 1933 to 1945 its Councillors were elected unopposed and all were candidates of the Penn Ratepayers' Association. From 1945 to 1950 Labour opposed them, usually gaining around 25 per cent of the vote. The Conservative Party in 1950 ran an official candidate against both the Ratepayers' nominee and a Labour man. The Ratepayer pushed the Conservative into second place. When the Conservatives stood again in 1954 and 1955, the Ratepayers came bottom of the poll with only 20 per cent of the vote. From then the Conservatives became the Councillors and the Ratepayers' Association disappeared. After the loss of the Council houses in 1958 Labour rarely fought the seat. In 1960 in a straight fight with the Conservatives it had only 10 per cent of the vote, and in 1964 it was pushed to the bottom of the poll with 11 per cent when a Liberal stood too. He gained 18 per cent of the vote against the Conservative's 71 per cent. From 1933 to 1954 it was a safe Ratepayers' seat; after 1954 it was a safe Conservative seat.

Its Councillors were mainly men who resided in the ward and were small businessmen, especially shopkeepers. They were of a very similar type to the representatives of St Philip's Ward.

ANALYSIS AND EXPLANATION

This survey shows that social class is an important factor correlating with voting behaviour and party membership. Safe Conservative wards contain predominantly a middle- and upper-middle-class population, living in private houses usually owner-occupied. Safe Labour wards contain predominantly a working- and lower-middle-class population, living in Council houses or late-nineteenth-century privately rented property. Marginal wards are those of mixed social composition. Conservative Councillors have consisted in the main of manufacturers, professional men, shopkeepers and white-collar workers in supervisory positions, while

Labour Councillors have been working men, the wives of working men, retired working men, trade union officials and white-collar workers, like clerks and insurance agents.

But class has not been the sole determinant of party loyalty. At the turn of the century religion played a significant role, deciding whether individuals of similar occupation would be Liberals or Conservatives. Generally a manufacturer or a shop-keeper who was an Anglican would be a Conservative while, if they were Nonconformists, they would tend to be Liberal. Other factors cut across class solidarity. Shopkeepers with premises in the town centre, who were of a higher social status than those who had establishments only in the suburbs serving working-class areas, tended to be Conservatives against the latter who were apt to be Liberals. Indeed the Liberals in 1900 were regarded as being between the working class at the bottom of the social scale and the manufacturers and professional men at the top. The Liberals in the 1960s did not consist of shopkeepers, whose loyalty was mainly to the Conservatives, but of white-collar supervisors, who were neither independent businessmen nor working class. Thus even in 1964 the Liberals come 'in between'. The working class was not a homogeneous block, but was divided into a skilled and unionised group who tended to support the Labour Party, and an unskilled and non-unionised group who tended to support any party but the Labour Party.

The survey also showed that in the 1950s and 1960s fewer Councillors lived or had business interests in the wards they represented than before the Second World War. In 1903–4 the majority of Councillors did not live in the wards they represented (22:14), but at least ten of those who did not live in them had business interests there. In 1929–30 more lived in the wards than not (21:18) and of those who did not at least seven had business interests there. In 1945–6 and 1962–3 the business connection had fallen away, and those who lived in the wards were outnumbered by those who did not (24:21 in 1945–6 and 25:20 in 1962–3).

Party has played an influential part in this process. Before 1945 it is hard to correlate party allegiance with ward connections. In 1929–30, for example, eight Conservatives lived in and nine did not; three Liberals did and four did not; eight Labour did and four did not. This does show that Labour members had the strongest residential links with their wards. After 1945 this position was reversed. In 1945–6 more Conservatives lived in their wards than Labour Councillors; eleven Conservatives did and eight did not; ten Labour Councillors did and thirteen did not. The difference by 1962–3 was very pronounced. Then fourteen Conservatives lived in their wards and eight did not, but only six Labour did and seventeen did not. In safe seats the difference was even more marked. In 1962–3 in Conservative safe seats eleven lived in and four[1] did not; in Labour safe seats only five lived in and thirteen did not.

THE SELECTION OF CANDIDATES

(i) *The Labour Party.* The explanation for this variation lies with the different procedures used by the two parties for selecting municipal candidates. In the Labour Party between June and September each year each organisation affiliated to the Borough Labour Party – that is, each ward party, constituency party and trade union branch, the Women's section, the Co-operative Party and the Fabian Society – was entitled to nominate individuals for the 'panel' of approved municipal candidates. Each year a new 'panel' was drawn up, consisting of retiring Aldermen and Councillors seeking re-election, former members of the 'panel' wishing to stand again, and those wanting to be candidates for the first time. For the panel of 1963–4 thirty were nominated, seven retiring Aldermen, seven retiring Councillors, three former members of the Council, eight former members of the 'panel' and five seeking to be put on the panel for the first time. Nominations were received from all ward parties but two, the North-East Constituency Party, the Women's Section, the Co-operative Party and six trade union branches, A.E.U. numbers 1 and 3, A.S.L.E.F., D.A.T.A., N.U.P.E., and U.S.D.A.W. The nomination form required the name and address of the nominee, his age, years lived in the borough, years as an individual member of the Labour Party, years as an affiliated member, his trade union, years in the trade union and general information about offices held in the party and in public life.

In October the Executive Committee of the Borough Labour

[1] Two of these four were related to Councillors who did live in the wards.

Party scrutinised the qualifications of the nominees. It was entitled to interview any it wished, normally only those nominated for the first time or sitting members of the Council who deviated in some way from party policy. The latter were usually asked to give assurances to abide by party decisions in the future. The Executive then recommended to the full Borough Party meeting in November which names should be accepted or rejected. At this session nominees could be interviewed again. For the panel of 1963–4 the Executive advised the acceptance of all and the Borough Party placed all 30 on the 'panel'.

From December the ward parties began to select their candidates for the May elections. They requested from the Borough Party the 'panel'. It was examined by the ward party, which drew a short list, usually never more than three. By the rules of the party the actual selection should take place at a joint meeting of the ward party and the Executive Committee of the Borough Party, but in practice the Borough Party asked two of its Executive to attend the ward party meeting. They had the right to speak and vote, but usually forgo to exercise the latter. At this meeting the qualifications of the nominees were examined, the record of sitting members reviewed and they could be asked to speak and answer questions. Then ballots were taken until the one with an absolute majority was selected as the candidate. Some of the more active wards chose their candidates in December so as to have the pick of the bunch; some selected at the last minute around mid-April; but most did so in February or March. Sitting members of the Council were usually readopted automatically at a very late date.

(ii) *The Conservative Party*. The Conservative Party, unlike the Labour Party, had no Borough Party devoted solely to municipal matters and to drawing up a list of approved municipal candidates. The two Constituency Associations were responsible for both Parliamentary and municipal affairs. The two Associations, and not a single Borough Party, dealt with the ward parties over the selection of candidates. The choice of the candidate was made at a selection meeting of the ward party, to which all its members were entitled to attend. It did not have to nominate an individual to be scrutinised by any other body in the party, nor was it restricted to adopting only candidates on an approved list. The ward party was solely responsible for its choice, usually made from among names raised at the ward meeting.

Before a candidate has been selected the party rules say that the name should be submitted to the Executive Council of the Constituency Association for approval.[1] This was a mere formality, for it was unlikely that the Executive at this stage would want to incur the wrath of a ward party, particularly if that party were wealthy and strong, by rejecting its nominee. The agent for the North-East Association said that if a ward did choose someone who was not 'a good Conservative' then his Executive would veto the candidature; this situation was unlikely to occur. In the South-West the autonomy of the ward parties was forcefully asserted, and its agent regarded the Executive's approval of a ward's choice as automatic.

Conflict between the Executive and the ward parties was unlikely to arise because the Executive consisted mainly of people who were themselves the officers of the ward parties. This interlocking membership tended to promote harmony as it did in the Labour Party, since there, too, the same individuals were likely to be officers of their ward parties, Constituency Parties and the Borough Party. Overlapping personnel overcame institutional separation.

DIFFERENCES BETWEEN CANDIDATES

The Conservative Party's lack of a list of approved candidates, lack of a Borough Party, and lack of limitations on ward independence had consequences which made its candidates differ in significant respects from those of the Labour Party. The prime qualification to be a Labour candidate was service to the party and a trade union. This enabled him to be nominated to the panel in the first place, to pass the scrutiny of the Borough Party and to

---

[1] Wolverhampton's practice was not that suggested by the Conservative Central Office's model rules, which advised, but did not direct, that if a ward party wished to fight a seat its Executive should send the name to the Executive of the Constituency Association for its approval before the name is submitted to the general meeting of the ward party. (*Model Rules No. 3*, Conservative and Unionist Central Office, 1956, p. 14.) A Central Office official wrote: 'the attitude of the Associations towards local elections is entirely for local decisions, hence the varying attitudes in different parts of the country.'

D

gain the favour of the ward party when it selected. This concentration on party service was reinforced by the fact that Labour
members had less social activities outside the party than Conservatives, who engaged in a wider range of social activities which
had no connection with party politics.[1] Thus when Labour
members came to select a candidate, both the party rules and the
narrow range of their social contacts limited them to choosing
known party stalwarts. Party activity was not such an important
factor in choosing a Conservative candidate. Many had not been
active in the party, indeed many were not even members of the
party, when they were selected to fight their first contests. They
had made reputations in non-party activities, which had brought
them to the attention of the officers of ward parties, who asked
them if they would like to stand for the Council. If they agreed,
then the leaders of the ward parties had little difficulty in persuading their wards to adopt them. Thus in the Conservative Party
the way to become a candidate was not so much to have been a
loyal party worker as to have come to the notice of a ward officer,
and since party activities did not loom so large in the life of the
Conservatives as for Labour members, other activities than party
work brought the individuals to the notice of the key officers.
A reputation as a suitable candidate could be made in business,
trade, or in a profession, in a trade or professional association, at a
social club, in Rotary or the Round Table. D. H. Haselock, a
hairdresser, was asked to stand by a confectioner, M. G. Evans,
whose shop was near his; the solicitor, S. Brindley, was asked
by the estate agent, A. B. Kennard, with whom he came into
professional contact; the accountant, A. E. Lacon, was asked by
F. Jennings, an undertaker, at a meeting of the Rotary Club.
None of them had been active party men. In the Conservative
Group of members of the Council, members were asked to seek
out possible candidates and secure their adoption by their ward
parties, of which they were usually officers. Circulars were sent
from the Group to industries and to the Chamber of Commerce
asking if they could recommend suitable candidates. In the
Labour Group, however, there was no discussion about candidates.
That was regarded as the preserve of the Borough Party.

[1] See Chapter 6.

The Conservative means of selecting candidates put a premium on informal and personal contacts, and allowed the leaders of ward parties great scope to make their friends candidates and even Councillors. As shown above in West Park Ward the clans of the Guys and Fullwoods held sway and in Merridale Ward family influence was significant. In Graiseley Ward in 1958 J. Beattie and W. G. Morrison were Councillors, the former the managing director of a large store and the latter his sales promotion manager.[1]

In addition, the Borough Labour Party enabled members of the two constituency associations to meet each other, and thus members of wards in the south-west got to know members in the north-east. Further, in the numerous committees of the Labour Party there were many opportunities for Labour members to meet other Labour members from other wards. Thus when selecting a candidate the ward party was not so tied to choosing a candidate from that particular ward. But the Conservative Party had no Borough Party where members from the two halves of the town could mingle. This explains why in 1964 fifteen Conservative Councillors sat for wards in the constituency in which they resided and only three did not; while fourteen Labour Councillors sat for wards in the constituency in which they resided and eleven did not. Further, since the ward parties of the Conservative Association were more autonomous than those of the Labour Party and since the Conservative Party had fewer committees where members of the various wards could meet each other, there was a strong tendency for ward parties to select candidates who resided in the wards. This explains why in May 1963 ten Conservatives represented the wards where they lived and eight did not; but only five Labour Councillors lived in the wards they represented and twenty did not.[2] Thus institutional and social

---

[1] Informal and personal contacts are of importance in the Labour Party too, though less so than in the Conservative Party. The brothers Harry and Norman Bagley were Councillors for Bushbury Ward in the 1950s, and the grocers H. Preece and F. V. Law represented Parkfield Ward.

[2] These figures are distorted because of the revision of ward boundaries in 1958. It would be fairer to give the figures for the Councillors as if the boundaries had not been reorganised. In that case 11 Conservatives would have represented wards they lived in and 7 would not; while 9 Labour would and 16 would not. The main generalisation, however, still remains true.

factors explain why the Conservative members had closer connections with their wards than the Labour representatives. Labour
candidates were chosen by a rigorous selection process which
favoured those who served the party. Conservatives were 'co-opted'
on the basis of informal and personal contacts usually made outside
the context of the party.

ATTITUDES TO PARTY

These different selection processes go far to explain the different
attitudes of each party to the role of party politics in local government. The Labour Councillor owed his seat to his party; work for
it was rewarded with Council membership. The Conservatives
tended to have come on to the Council not through party activity
and thus they did not owe so much to the party. Further, the
Labour Councillor had fewer non-party leisure pursuits than his
Conservative counterpart, who had a wider range of social, business
and professional connections. He thus did not devote so much
time to his party as did the Labour member. For the Labour
Councillor party was essential, beneficial and loomed large in his
life, but for many Conservatives party was a harmful intrusion, one
factor in his life among many and not of crucial importance. In
addition, the Conservative Councillor tended to see himself more
as a representative of his ward than as a representative of a party.
This is a partial explanation why the Conservatives only recently
adopted a specifically Conservative municipal policy for the town
as a whole, whereas the Labour Party from its earliest years
continuously advocated a policy for the town and not for specific
wards only. Before 1950 each Conservative Councillor and candidate had his own line which stressed the advantages he could
bring to the ward. Labour representatives never made such strong
ward appeals.

The businessmen. Another significant development was the decline
of the Councillor's business interest in his ward. Before 1930 many
Councillors, although not living in the ward, owned a shop or a
factory there, in a personal capacity and not as a member of a
board of directors. Many of these Councillors lived out of the
borough in the rural areas at Compton, Tettenhall, Pattingham,

Oaken, Palmers Cross, Shifnal, Seisdon or the Wergs. Such men were often the leading men on the Council. But after the 1930s they did not come onto the Council, because with the spread of limited liability they no longer qualified for membership of the Council; in addition, the increasing demands on the time of professional and executive types made membership of the Council not so attractive as it once was. Members of the Council lived within the boundaries of the borough and did not qualify for membership through a business interest.

The ward connection. Since the attachment of a Councillor to his ward declined over the period, so have the occasions when Councillors press in open Council the interests of their wards. At the turn of the century many divisions in the Council were about the claims of wards for special attention, either for them to have some particular amenity provided or else to be protected against some nuisance. Claims were made for baths and wash-houses and footbridges over canals, or for some wasteground to be laid out as an open space. Objections were made against the changing of old street names and the erection of cab stands, knackers' yards or a urinal for females. In their election addresses candidates stressed their attachment to their wards and the benefits they would gain for them. After 1919 divisions in open Council about ward affairs declined, but in the 1930s Penn Ward established a Ratepayers' Society, whose chief purpose was to improve the amenities of Penn Ward. In the 1950s and 1960s, although battles over ward claims no longer rent the Council, Councillors still promoted the welfare of their wards, but behind the scenes, like the Ratepayers' candidates who, when they wanted something for Penn Ward, would first lobby the officials, then the committee concerned, and only if they did not have satisfaction would they air the matter in open Council. In the 1960s occasionally a ward claim produced a division which cut across party lines. In 1962, for example, the Councillors of Graiseley Ward sought to allow children to play on some open land from which children were debarred, and the Councillors of St Peter's urged the Council to refuse permission to a fair company to have its entertainment booths erected on a piece of waste ground in the ward. After 1945 the battle between the parties superseded the battle between the wards, except in the

general sense that the Labour Party promoted the interests of its
safe wards as the Conservatives promoted the interests of their
wards. In 1962, for example, the Conservatives opposed the
Labour proposal to build a large swimming-bath in Bushbury
Ward, arguing that a smaller bath there would enable a bath to be
built in Penn Ward too. Thus the battle between the wards was
itself contained within the battle between the parties.

In 1900 the wards of the borough were much more separate
communities than in 1964. Over the period they became more
integrated into the town, as transport improved and enabled
people of one ward to cross more easily to another, and to work
even at the opposite side of the town from where they lived.
Building also joined up areas which had previously been cut off
from each other. In 1900 the distinctive social characteristics of
each ward gave an individuality to its voting behaviour, but after
1945 the wards became moulded into three political types, safe
Conservative, safe Labour, and marginal, each reflecting a
different type of social and economic structure. The previous
variations were wiped away.

ELECTION RESULTS

Before 1945 the municipal election results in each ward showed
generally little uniformity; the swing was not the same for all
wards nor was it even in the same direction, although occasionally
a clear pattern emerged, like a swing to the Liberals in 1905 or a
swing away from Labour in 1920. After 1945, however, both the
general direction of the swing and its size became more uniform,
especially in the keenly fought marginal wards. There were clear
swings in all wards to Labour in 1952, 1956 and 1962 and to the
Conservatives in 1946, 1951, 1955 and 1960.[1] The occasional
disparities were not as large as those before 1945, and can be
explained by numerous factors. A popular well-known candidate,
especially a sitting member, could arrest slightly a swing against
his party or encourage one for it. Conservatives, with more cars
at their disposal than the Labour Party, could produce more
favourable results for their candidates in their safe wards, where

[1] It is difficult to calculate swings before 1945 since all parties did not contest
all wards every year.

their cars were concentrated, than where they did not have so many vehicles. Bad weather between 7.00 and 8.30 p.m. on polling day could reduce a swing to Labour, for the majority of its vote came out then. Conservatives seemed not to be so inhibited from voting by bad weather as the Labour voters. The sex of the candidate had a significant effect on the swing; generally females did less well than males.

Since the swing was more uniform in the marginal wards, it was usual for one party to take all the marginals in any one election. This movement of the seats in Wolverhampton was very similar to the general trend over the whole country. A comparison of the parties' gains and losses of seats in Wolverhampton with the gains and losses published in *The Times* after each bout of municipal elections shows that even from the 1870s[1] the movement in Wolverhampton corresponded to national trends, especially since 1945. There were Liberal gains in 1904, Conservative gains in 1908 and Labour gains in 1919. Conservatives had good years in 1947, 1949, 1955, 1960 and 1961, while Labour did well in 1945, 1952, 1956, 1957, 1958, 1962 and 1963. The gains and losses usually took place in marginal wards where party activity was concentrated. Thus the figures suggest that in these wards the key factor determining the result was not so much the individual candidate or any local issue but the national fortunes of the parties. And since psephological studies and opinion polls have shown that voting for a particular party is a habit which few ever change, the factor which decides the election is whether the national party can inspire its supporters to get out to the poll in sufficient numbers to defeat the opposition.

Voting behaviour in municipal elections in Wolverhampton was very similar to that in Parliamentary elections. Before 1945 it was hard to correlate the two, since the franchises were different, municipal and Parliamentary boundaries did not coincide and all the parties did not fight all the wards close to a General Election. Since 1948 the franchises have been equal, the boundaries the same and all wards are fought in order to keep the party machine in trim for the Parliamentary fight. Table IX shows that, although

---

[1] In 1872, after the introduction of the secret ballot, *The Times* first began publishing surveys of the results.

the municipal poll was half that at a General Election,[1] the parties' shares of the vote were almost identical; especially in 1959. Municipal election results seem a clear reflection of Parliamentary results, despite the far lower turnout in the former. This correlation is further evidence that local issues and policies are not particularly decisive in municipal elections. The popularity of the national party is the determining factor.

[1] The mass media give far more publicity to a General Election than to a municipal election. The parties spend more money and are more active, and voters feel they have more of a duty to vote and that their votes will be more significant than in a municipal election. Also in Parliamentary elections each candidate is allowed one free postal delivery of literature, but not in local elections.

5 The Occupational Composition of the Council[1]

THE occupational as well as the political composition of the Council changed during this period, and these two developments were closely connected. The pattern of occupational change is depicted in Tables X–XII. Table X presents the occupational composition of the Council at seven dates in the period 1888–1963; Table XI shows the occupational composition of the new entrants to the Council for the years between the dates of those Councils selected for particular analysis, while Table XII shows the occupational break-down of all members of the Council over roughly decennial periods. This triple approach provides snapshots of individual Councils over the period, the changing composition of the new recruits to the Council, and a wider view of the types of people who composed the Council during each decade of the period. Table XIII then analyses the party affiliations of the occupational groups for the new entrants to the Council over three periods, and Table XIV does the same for two specific Councils, 1903–4 and 1962–3.

For the new entrants, the period 1888–1903 was a time when party was not prominent; from 1903 to 1919 party became more significant; the periods 1919–29 and 1929–45 witnessed the growing importance of parties: 1945–53 and 1953–62 show the trends following Labour's first victory, before party had really hardened, and then in the 1950s when party was very significant. The dates of the specific Councils and periods were chosen to present typical examples of the Council membership at various times throughout the period. The occupational descriptions used are not the usual ones of sociologists, but they do conveniently cover the occupations of the members of the Wolverhampton

[1] See Appendix, at p. 350, for a note about the sources used for discovering the occupations of members of the Council.

D2

Council and provide a useful tool for analysing the composition of the Wolverhampton Town Council.

THE COUNCIL 1888–9

In the Council of 1888–9 the largest single occupational group was the manufacturers, comprising 38 per cent of the Council. The bulk of these, seven-ninths, were connected to the main industry of the Black Country at that time, iron and metalware production, as ironmasters, manufacturers of hardware, hollow-ware, edge-tools, tubes, corrugated iron, locks and doorsprings, or as the manufacturers of chemicals used in the processing of the metals or of the varnish and paint to adorn the finished articles. Closely associated with these men was the small 'administrative' group, composed of two metal brokers and a carrying agent for the Great Western Railway. Thus over a third of the Council were engaged in the basic Midland industries, as the owners and controllers of substantial enterprises. The second-largest single group was the 'professional' element of 21 per cent, six solicitors and four doctors. Following closely behind these were the shopkeepers, 19 per cent of the Council, comprising two grocers, a butcher, fruit merchant, chemist and tailor.[1] Socially akin to these retailers were the licensed victuallers, but they have been itemised separately as the 'liquor' interest, since people involved in the 'drink' trade were regarded as a distinct group both by themselves and by others. As publicans or wine and spirit merchants they formed 10 per cent of the Council. Finally there were three members of the Council who claimed to be 'retired' or 'gentlemen', a former farmer, baker and antique dealer. Thus just over two-fifths of the Council were industrialists, just over a fifth were professional men and just under a fifth were shopkeepers, while a tenth were engaged in the drink trade.

THE COUNCIL 1962–3

The Council of 1962–3 bore little occupational resemblance to that of 1888–9. The manufacturers had fallen to 7 per cent and no longer represented the leading industries of the locality. Only one was connected with metal manufacture, and he was the

[1] Also a 'photographer' and a 'merchant'.

director of a minor welding concern. Another made and sold perambulators and two were building contractors. The professional group, too, had diminished to 8 per cent, but had broadened its scope to include not only a doctor and a solicitor but also an accountant, a surveyor and estate agent and an advertising agent. The shopkeepers, however, had increased to 27 per cent and had remained retailers of a similar kind to those in 1888–9, comprising three grocers, a butcher, jeweller, ironmonger, tobacconist and a stationer.[1] The 'administrative' group had grown, and can be conveniently divided into the 'superior white-collar' section, all employees yet with much responsibility, like two chief buyers, a press officer for an engineering firm, a projects engineer, a sales production manager and a works director, and an 'inferior white-collar' section, employees with little status and responsibility, like clerks and insurance agents.[2] Each of these two sections formed 10 per cent of the Council. The largest single group in the Council was the 'working-class' members; none of this category was present on the Council in 1888, but in 1962 it formed 30 per cent of the Council. Of these, half were male active workers, mostly skilled, like a coppersmith, boilersmith, master printer, engineer, turner and fitter;[3] the other half comprised two retired workers, an electrician and a trade union official; and seven wives of workers, four of whom were the wives of railwaymen. No women had been in the Council of 1888, but they now composed 13 per cent of the Council and were all but one the wives of workmen. Retired persons made up 8 per cent of the Council and consisted, in addition to the two working men, of a brewer, a hairdresser and a railway official. The drink trade had dwindled to one licensed victualler. Thus the working class formed just under a third of the Council, followed by the shopkeepers with just over a quarter. In 1888–9 all members of the Council were independent, responsible for their own enterprises as manufacturers, shopkeepers or professional men. But in 1962–3 just over 40 per cent of the Council were or had been employees or were the wives of

[1] This group also included two motor-car traders, two tyre traders, a milliner, a hairdresser, a timber merchant and the proprietor of a shop selling electrical apparatus.

[2] This section comprised two clerks, an insurance agent, a Friendly Society agent and an Admiralty examiner.

[3] Also a trade union official, a sheet-metal worker and a railwayman.

employees, lacking occupational experience of executive and administrative responsibility. Few of the working men, however, were unskilled; these formed a mere fraction of the working men. Just under 60 per cent of the Council were men of independence, experienced in business or holding positions of professional responsibility. The Council of 1962–3 was certainly not dominated by the workmen and their wives.

The trends which emerge from a crude comparison of these two Councils are clear: the decline of the manufacturing and professional groups, an invasion by the working class and a slight advancement of the shopkeepers. But such a comparison reveals neither the rhythm and timing of these trends nor the significant periods affecting the changing occupational composition of the Council. A crude comparison suggests that the development was straightforward and even. Closer examination is needed.

THE MANUFACTURERS

The number of new entrants to the Council who were manufacturers did not fall sharply until after 1929; before then they had composed about a quarter of the new Councillors in each of the three periods, 1888–1903, 1903–19, and 1919–29, but in 1929–45 only about 9 per cent of the newly elected members were manufacturers. They rose a little in 1945–53, but fell back to 9 per cent in 1953–62. Two further sets of figures indicate that the 1930s were the years when the industrialists fell away from the Council. In the Council of 1929–30 they comprised 21 per cent; but in that of 1945–6 only 12 per cent, and over the period 1919–30 they comprised 25 per cent of Council members, while in 1930–40 only 16 per cent; this represents their largest fall during any of the decennial periods. The second-largest fall occurred in the 1890s and 1900s, since in the period 1888–1900 the manufacturers had formed 33 per cent of the members of the Council, but from 1900 to 1910 they comprised 27 per cent. Thus the manufacturing element on the Council was falling from 1888; the biggest falls occurred around the turn of the century and in the 1930s. Up to the 1930s they had been the biggest single occupational group on the Council. During the 1930s they were overtaken by the shopkeepers and then after 1945 by the working class.

As well as falling away in numbers the manufacturers changed in kind, and this process was also a feature of the 1930s. The great ironmasters and metalware manufacturers, who had formed the majority of the industrialists, no longer joined the Council; the new men were the manufacturers of dairy produce, sweets, confectionery, clothing, perambulators, builders and men in charge of light engineering businesses. The great ironmasters, employers of large labour forces, producing metalware for export to world markets, gave way to lesser men in charge of smaller enterprises, catering for a mainly local market, and manufacturing lighter products.

THE PROFESSIONAL MEN

The professional men, mainly doctors and solicitors, had increased their proportion of the new entrants in the early years of the twentieth century before the First World War; during the period 1903–19 they formed the largest single occupational group of the new members of the Council with 30 per cent, and they had steadily increased their proportion of all members of the Council, from the period 1888–1900 when they were 16 per cent of the members, to 1910–19 when they formed 27 per cent. But after the First World War they slumped to comprise a mere 8 per cent of the new entrants from 1919 to 1929. The 1920s and the late 1940s were poor years for the professional element; they only began to pick up in the late 1950s, when they comprised 13 per cent of the new entrants. Taking the decennial periods, however, the picture is one of a steep decrease in the 1920s and a continual decline from the 1930s onwards, with them forming 13 per cent of the members in 1919–30, 8 per cent in the years 1930–40 and 1940–50 and 7 per cent in 1950–60. Looking at the particular Councils, it is seen that the professional men formed about a fifth of the Council in 1888–9, 1903–4 and 1919–20, and then they never rose above 8 per cent.

The kinds of professional men on the Council changed somewhat too. Solicitors and men involved in land and real estate have remained a significant proportion of the professionals, but the doctors have dwindled; only one was a member of the Council in the 1950s, and he had been elected way back in 1930. No doctor had been elected to the Council after his entry, except one female doctor co-opted to the Council during the war.

THE SHOPKEEPERS

The shopkeepers have been a significant and constant element on the Council throughout the whole period, except for a temporary falling away in the 1920s. Of new entrants they formed between a fifth and just over a quarter except for the years 1919–29 when they composed only 9 per cent. This decline did not make itself felt all that sharply in the actual composition of the Council, since although in the period 1919–30 they were at their lowest with 13 per cent of all members, they still counted as the second-largest single occupational group. Their proportion of the members of the Council in the 1940s was exactly what it had been in the 1890s, 23 per cent, while in the 1950s they comprised 25 per cent of the Council. Thus, except for the 1920s, the shopkeepers have formed a consistently high proportion of the Council. Their consistency is marked in another direction too, for the kinds of shopkeeper elected have throughout the period remained of the same type. This emerges not only from comparing those of 1888–9 with those of 1962–3; any year will yield a similar result. For instance in 1929–30 they comprised two greengrocers, a butcher, a chemist, a tailor, undertaker, stationer, jeweller, furniture dealer and a milliner. Such occupations could have been typical of the Council members for any year in the period.

THE 'DRINK' TRADE

The number of Councillors connected with the drink trade – that is, licensed victuallers, wine and spirit merchants and brewers – has declined since the turn of the century. Just before 1900 they contributed 11 per cent of all members of the Council, which they did again in the 1930s. But apart from these peaks of representation, their proportion of new entrants fell from 9 per cent in 1888–1903 to 2 per cent in 1929–45. The last man to enter the Council as a publican was elected in 1936 and he retired in 1951. The only other member of the Council in the 1950s who was a publican, had been elected in 1935 as a railwayman, but later became a publican.

The first working man to enter the Council was elected in 1891, and from then to 1903 the working class formed 15 per cent of the new entrants, the third-largest single occupational group of the new members. This initial impetus was lost in the years before the First World War; they comprised only 8 per cent of the members elected from 1903 to 1919. But in the 1920s, 1930s and 1940s they greatly increased their proportion of the new members, 23 per cent in 1919–29, 24 per cent in 1929–45 and 31 per cent in 1945–53. In the 1950s they declined again. Up to the First World War they comprised about 10 per cent of the Council members and afterwards just under 20 per cent for the decennial periods. In addition, besides the male workers and those actually engaged in a job, women and the retired formed a significant part of the working-class element. In 1919–30 all the four female Councillors were working-class; and in 1950–60 of the eleven female Councillors, eight were working-class. Of the retired group, in 1930–40 five were retired workers; in 1940–50 nine and in 1950–60 seven out of eleven. These two groups boost the working-class representatives from 1919 to be the largest single occupational group of members of the Council, comprising around a third and just over a quarter both of new entrants and the actual membership of the Council.

Among the working-class members two groups stand out as being particularly numerous, the railwaymen and engineers. Between 1891 and 1962 there were twenty-two railwaymen and twenty-one engineers who were members of the Council. In 1919–30 there were ten active or retired railwaymen on the Council, eleven in 1930–40 and eight in 1950–60. Three wards in the town provided the railway representatives. Dunstall Ward, where the railway sheds and workshops were situated, was described in 1923 as 'the railwayman's ward'. Low Hill and Bushbury Wards were described as the 'pocket' wards of the railway unions, whose members provided the bulk of the membership and finance for the ward Labour Parties there. On the establishment of Bushbury Ward in 1927 it returned to the Council three members of A.S.L.E.F. and, when these retired, they were replaced by railwaymen. Low Hill exhibited a similar pattern. Many of the female members of the Council have been the wives of railwaymen and members of the women's section of their husbands' trade union. The engineers were the second leading group within the working-class representatives, and eleven of the twenty-one engineers who have been Councillors in this period worked at one time or another at one factory, the Sunbeam Motor Car Company, where trade unionism was particularly strong.

Trade union officials have provided an important group of Councillors. The first was William Sharrocks, agent for the Boiler-makers' Society, a Councillor from 1901 to 1921; then followed J. Whittaker, an official of the Plumbers Union and Secretary of the Building Trades' Federation, a member of the Council 1903–12 and 1924–40. Between 1945 and 1962 five Labour members of the Council were trades union officials, agents for N.U.P.E., N.F.B.T.O., A.E.U., N.U.F.W., and the Trades Council.

A distinctive feature about the working-men Councillors was that they were mostly skilled men; rarely did an unskilled labourer become a Councillor. Less than a dozen unskilled men were members of the Council over the period 1891–1962.

THE WOMEN AND THE RETIRED

The first woman elected to the Council was the Labour representative Mrs E. Sproson in 1921. In the Council of 1929–30 they formed 4 per cent of the membership and in the Council of 1962–3 13 per cent. Of the new entrants to the Council in the periods 1945–53 and 1953–62 they formed 11 per cent. Throughout the period the women have been mainly of working-class background; of the seventeen women who were members of the Council from 1921, twelve were working-class: the others were a doctor, a teacher, and wives of businessmen. The women therefore gradually increased their membership of the Council.

The retired group does not exhibit such a steady rise. As a proportion of new entrants, they rose from about 4 per cent from 1888 to 1919 to about 9 per cent in the inter-war years, falling back to about 5 per cent after 1945. This pattern is reflected in the figures for the specific Councils. Both in 1903–4 and 1919–20

4 per cent of the members were retired persons; in 1929–30 and 1945–6 the proportion was in the 13 per cent range, while 1953–4 and 1962–3 saw a fall to 10 per cent and then 8 per cent. Men of various occupational groups have comprised the retired element, but since the 1930s the working-class element has been in the majority among them, half in 1939–40, two-thirds in 1940–50 and four-fifths in 1950–60. Railwaymen again formed a large part of the retired group: five in 1930–40, eight in 1940–50 and five in 1950–60.

ADMINISTRATIVE

The final group is the administrative, divided into, first, the managerial and supervisory element, and, secondly, the clerical. The former were, until the 1950s, not at all significant, providing a handful of members, never above 6 per cent of the Council between 1888 and 1940. They were 9 per cent of all members in 1950–60, 10 per cent of the Council in 1962–3, and 9 per cent of new entrants in 1953–62. Their increase is clearly a phenomenon of the 1950s; but that of the clerical group was earlier, in the years after the First World War. Before 1919 they had been 4 per cent of the new entrants; then from 1919 to 1929 they were 11 per cent and in 1929–45 10 per cent, reaching a peak of 13 per cent in 1945–53, and then falling away slightly in the late 1950s. These, too, were never a large part of the Council; never above the 6 per cent of all members in 1919–30; but they increased a little in the 1950s to form 10 per cent of the Council in 1962–3.

In the 1920s a significant element in this group was the insurance agents, three of whom were Labour members; while there was also a Labour Friendly Society agent who did similar work to that of the insurance agents. Their occupations fitted them ideally to become Councillors. Their door-to-door visits would make them known to a large number of people. They would become very close to their clients and get to know their personal problems. They would act as advisers. In addition, they had the time to give to Council and committee meetings, since they could arrange their collecting work for any time of the day, and when they did call at their customers they could keep them informed about the Council and receive complaints which they could channel up to the Council.

Thus they had support and the time to give to Council work. They were invariably Labour, since their occupation was not regarded as of high status, save by the working class, and the bulk of their clients were working-class. Thus they could conveniently represent the working class. The peak of their representation was in the 1920s, when the Labour Councillors consisted mainly of railwaymen, engineers and insurance agents. In 1962, however, only one Labour member was an insurance agent.

Looking at the occupational composition of the Council chronologically, it is possible to say that, in the years before the First World War, 1888–1914, the Council was mainly composed of manufacturers, professional men and shopkeepers; in the inter-war years the manufacturers and professional men dwindled as the working class invaded the Council; this process continued after the Second World War, when, in addition, the administrative group began to rise, until in the early 1960s the Council became composed of shopkeepers, the working class – that is, men, women and retired, and the administrative groups.

EXPLANATIONS

The reasons for the changing occupational composition of the Council are many and complicated. Actual proof is hard to come by and suggestions advanced here are largely tentative. A crude Marxist view would argue that the rise and fall of the various occupational groups is related to the benefits which these groups could obtain from Council membership for their own members. Later chapters examine what each section could and did get out of the Council over the period and discuss the motives for seeking membership. Here other explanations will be put forward.

The Manufacturers. The incursion of the working-class members clearly reduced the number of manufacturers and professional men on the Council. The extension of the franchise, the reduction of the property qualifications for membership, the introduction of loss of earnings allowances and the growth of party, all contributed to enabling working men to enter the Council. The initial decline of the manufacturers in the 1880s and 1890s can be ascribed partly to the abolition of the property qualification for Council membership. By the Municipal Corporations Act of 1835 the qualification for membership of the Council of a large borough like Wolverhampton was the ownership of real or personal property worth £1,000 or the occupation of property rated at £30 per annum.[1] This was a device to prevent public funds from falling into the hands of poor people, who would profit from lavish municipal expenditure. It was not repealed until 1880, when any person on the Burgess roll became eligible for election.[2] Broadly, this Act enabled all householders living within or up to seven miles beyond the borough and who had paid rates for the previous twelve months to qualify for membership. On the Council of 1888–9 twenty-two of the forty-eight members had been elected before 1881, and thus just under half of the Council had had to conform to the high property qualification. It was not until the 1880s and 1890s that lesser men could get into the Council. The actual franchise remained full of anomalies until tidied up in 1948, but by 1884 virtually household suffrage had been attained. No further extensions took place until 1918, when the vote was granted to all men or women who occupied any property in the borough for six months prior to the coming into operation of the list, and to the wife of an occupier, if she was over the age of thirty. In addition, those receiving poor-relief were no longer dis-franchised.[3] In 1926 the qualifying period was reduced to three months,[4] and in 1928 the female franchise was made equal to that of males.[5] In 1945 a temporary Act enabled all who had the Parliamentary vote to have a municipal vote[6] and in 1948 this provision was firmly enacted: thus those people over the age of twenty-one and in residence on the qualifying date had both a municipal and Parliamentary vote; while to the former were added those who owned or rented rateable land or premises in the borough to the annual value of not less than £10.[7] These Acts greatly extended the franchise. In 1914 Wolverhampton's Burgess roll totalled 18,987; in 1919 37,512. In 1939 it was 73,222 and in 1945 106,245. Following these extensions of the franchise came the Labour advances of 1919 and 1945. The composition of the

[1] 5 & 6 Wm IV, c. 76.
[2] 43 Vic. c. 17.
[3] 7 & 8 Geo. V, c. 64.
[4] 16 & 17 Geo. V, c. 9.
[5] 19 & 20 Geo. V, c. 12.
[6] 8 & 9 Geo. VI, c. 5.
[7] 11 & 12 Geo. VI, c. 65.

Labour representatives was predominantly working-class. Labour was the party of the working class, formed by it to advance its interests. The growth of the number of Labour Party Councillors reduced the proportion of the seats held by other occupational groups.

The political allegiances of the occupational groups is given in Table XIII. It shows that in the period 1919–45 the anti-Socialist new Councillors were the manufacturers, shopkeepers, professional and managerial men, while of the thirty-eight new Labour entrants thirty-one were working-class.[1] Thus the decline of the occupational groups of manufacturer, professional and managerial Councillors had to a large extent a political cause, the rise of the Labour Party.

This is a general trend applicable to the whole period, but beginning in the 1890s. About the same time two other trends manifested themselves and acted to reduce the number of manufacturers returned to the Council. Many family businesses in these years were converted into limited liability companies and many firms grew in size by reason of amalgamations.[2] Within these more impersonal undertakings the head of the firm exerted less personal dominance and had to have regard to his board of directors. No longer could he easily arrange his business life so that he could devote a great part of his time to local government; his company and fellow directors made more demands on his time and it was seen that too great a preoccupation with the Town Council would impede his success within his business, against competitors and among his directors.[3]

Family concerns were being further reduced by the expansions, amalgamations and take-overs in Midland industry which became evident at the turn of the century. Small local firms were merged into nationwide combines, and the directors and managers who controlled what were now local branches were no longer pre-

[1] This includes 21 men, 6 women and 4 retired.

[2] For the economic background see G. C. Allen, *The Industrial Development of Birmingham and the Black Country 1860–1927*, London, 1929.

[3] Ex-Councillor J. Beattie, managing director of the town's leading store, said that fewer businessmen than in the past owned their own businesses, and as members of boards they could not afford to give up time to local government, since 'the board might hit back'. Ex-Councillor T. W. Phillipson, who ran a chain of tobacconists' shops, said that young business executives were too involved in building up their own businesses and forwarding their careers to engage in Council work.

dominantly local men, brought up in the town, but newcomers without deep attachment to Wolverhampton, often staying there but a short time before moving up the ladder of promotion in the business to other parts of the country.[1] Such men owed their primary loyalty to the firm; the town came low on their scale of concern. They were not likely to join the Council since a pre-requisite for membership of the Council appears to be an attach-ment to the town springing either from birth or long residence there. Table XV shows that very few Councillors had lived in the town for under ten years before they first entered the Council. Although in many cases the length of residence in the town is unknown, especially in the earlier years of the period, it is clear that well over half and nearer three-quarters of the Council have been either natives or long residents in the town.

A further trend helped to loosen the connection between the industrial executives and the town. Although they worked in the town, they made their homes increasingly beyond the borough boundaries in the more rural, pleasant and spacious western surrounds, in places like Tettenhall and Pattingham, whence they would commute to work. The big houses which the manufacturers used to inhabit within the borough were often converted into flats or offices, or were demolished. This evacuation of the town was greatly stimulated by the development of the motor car, which enabled people to live at some distance from the town and yet be able to reach it conveniently for work. For these people the town was a work place: they lacked the wider interest in the town's affairs which might have encouraged them to have joined the Council.[2] A further consequence of the move out of the town as well as of the conversion of private businesses into limited liability companies was that many businessmen failed to qualify for the municipal franchise or for election to the Council. They did not reside in the borough, and as directors of a limited company they

[1] A similar phenomenon was noted in Glossop. See A. H. Birch, *Small Town Politics*, London, 1959, and in Banbury see M. Stacey, *Tradition and Change – A Study of Banbury*, London, 1960.

[2] The Local Government Commission, in its final proposals for the *West Midlands Special Review Area*, 1961, p. 19, noted that the movement of popula-tion from the county boroughs of the Black Country to the outer areas had reduced the supply of voluntary leadership available to the county boroughs, which found it difficult to recruit Councillors of sufficient calibre.

did not qualify for a vote, as they could if they had been in charge of a personally owned enterprise or were partners in a private non-limited firm.

All these factors help to explain the gradual falling off of the manufacturers over the whole period, but not the spectacular dwindling of the 1930s. It is easy to find statements of the business-men as to why they sought entry to the Council, but it is more difficult to find statements as to why they no longer came on; the positive is easier to assert and find evidence for than the negative. In default of firm explanations for the fall in the 1930s, two tenta-tive suggestions will be advanced. The Local Government Act of 1929, which derated industry by 75 per cent,[1] and in 1932 the adoption of the policy of Industrial Protection, provided relief for Midland industry, which ever since the 1880s had been relatively depressed. The depression had been an incentive to businessmen to enter the Council in order to keep the rates low, to oppose any policy injurious or burdensome to industry, and to promote any policy which would help trade. In the 1930s this stimulus was much reduced and the incentive which had propelled businessmen to enter the Council was removed.

The 1930s then saw a large reduction in the numbers of manu-facturers gaining entry to the Council, because they were no longer heavily rated and a measure of Protection had been introduced. Compared with the North, the Midlands was a prosperous area in the 1930s: there was relatively little unemployment and trade flourished. These years, in addition, saw a change in the type of manufacturer who entered the Council, but these new men shared important characteristics with the manufacturers of old. Both were personally responsible for the running of their enterprises, which were often family concerns, untrammelled by boards of directors and limited liability, or else were very small limited companies. Both had often been born in the town, or had lived there for a long time, and had acquired local roots. Their work and their homes were within the town, in whose life they took an active part, not just by entering the Council, but also by participating in many of the town's associations and clubs. The businessmen who were the Councillors of the 1950s and 1960s although not engaged in the manufacture of the same products as those made by the in-

[1] 19 Geo. V, c. 17.

dustrialists at the turn of the century, in many ways were like the old-style manufacturers, particularly in being closely linked to the town. Their closeness to the town's life was perhaps the major factor making for their participation in local government.

The Professional Men. Many of the trends affecting the decline of the manufacturers apply also to the professional men. They were predominantly Conservative throughout the period (indeed only one Labour Councillor was a solicitor) and lost ground to the Labour advance after the First World War. The decline of the family venture and the moving out of town to live in more pleasant surroundings have affected solicitors and doctors too. Foremost in the reasons given for the disappearance of the professional man is the time factor. A chartered accountant, an ex-Councillor, said that it was no good for a professional businessman to go into public life, 'since it consumed so much of his time'. A solicitor, a Councillor, bemoaned that his partners were complaining that the practice was suffering because of the long hours he devoted to local government. Demands on the time of professional as well as businessmen were far greater in 1960 than in 1900. For instance, legal aid and the increase in property transactions for the solicitors, and the introduction of the Health Service with the need to keep abreast of the latest developments in medical science and technology for the doctors, have meant that they have less time to give to the Council.

Local government itself has increased in scope and complexity, making more demands on those involved in it. No longer can it be a hobby to be indulged in by leisured gentlemen. There are fewer leisured gentlemen now and local government work can no longer be dispatched without much energy, effort and time being devoted to it. Thus it is no wonder that most professional men, caught between the increasing demands made upon them by their careers and by the Council, decided to opt out of local government.

The Shopkeepers. Explanations are required for the steadiness in the proportion of shopkeepers on the Council and for their sudden temporary decline in the 1920s. They possess many advantages enabling them to take a seat on the Council. Their daily contact with customers gives them a knowledge of local gossip and events, anxieties and hopes, a channel for their own opinions, an unrivalled opportunity for meeting and influencing people and a fund of electoral support. An establishment in the centre of the town involves them closely in the property dealings in the borough, makes them sensitive to movements of rateable values, the burden of the rate, the prosperity of the town, and therefore arouses their interest in Council policies. If they own a number of shops in the suburbs, they have further centres and sources of information and points of concern. Also they can fairly easily find the time to devote to Council work, since they can leave their premises in the hands of assistants, especially as most Council and Committee work is conducted in the afternoon when trade is somewhat slacker than in the morning. Thus, having the time and possessing notable means to obtain local knowledge, an influential base from which to command local backing and a number of incentives to watch local administration, it is no wonder that shopkeepers have been an important element in the Council.

The reason for the fall of the shopkeepers in the 1920s is political, and is illustrated from the municipal elections of 1919. In Dunstall Ward the Labour candidate, Alan Davies, a railwayman, defeated the Liberal Councillor, Fred Evans, a fish and fruit merchant. Evans had sat for this ward since 1894; he had been Mayor in 1907–8, chairman of Markets Committee 1897–1917 and of Water Committee from 1917; yet, influential though Evans was, a Labour candidate in his first fight defeated him in the ward he had held for a quarter of a century. This defeat illustrates the plight of the shopkeeper in the 1920s. His party was the Liberal Party. Of twenty-one shopkeeper new entrants to the Council from 1888 to 1919, thirteen were Liberals, only eight were Conservatives and one Labour. Of the eleven shopkeepers who were members of the Council in 1903–4, seven were Liberals. H. G. Wells precisely described the appeal of the Liberal Party for the shopkeepers. It was, he said, 'a gathering together of all the smaller interests which find themselves at a disadvantage against the big established classes', yet it was also set against the collectivist state sought by Labour since 'the small dealer is doomed to absorption in that just as much as the large owner'.[1] Two quotations from

[1] H. G. Wells, *The New Machiavelli*, 1911 (Penguin edition, 1946), p. 238.

Liberal Councillors in Wolverhampton will illustrate the uneasy in-between position occupied by the shopkeepers. In 1903 T. Reade attacked the Lorain system because it imposed a heavy burden on the ratepayer. 'It frequently happened that when matters of this kind were taken in hand by men of easy circumstances and in possession of great wealth they could not find that consideration for struggling tradesmen and shopkeepers and hardworking artisans, who had to get their living and reside in the town, that was desirable.'[1] In 1905 the other enemy was revealed when P. Lewis attacked the Labour opposition to a grant for the independent Wolverhampton Grammar School. 'While he was in profound sympathy with labouring people and the struggles of the poor, there were people in other walks of life who, to maintain respectability, had an equally hard time.'[2] The fortunes of the Liberal Party, hit by the Unionist split and then revived by the controversy over education, were ebbing away. Before the war they had flirted with Labour, but afterwards they linked themselves to the Conservative Party. They decided to ally themselves with the 'established classes' against the growing strength of the 'labouring people'. The 1920s were the difficult years when the shopkeepers were in the process of reorienting their political allegiance. As Liberals they were being defeated by Labour and they had not yet made their commitment to the Conservative Party. By the 1930s they had cemented themselves to the Conservative Party. In the years 1919–45 of fifteen shopkeeper new entrants to the Council, only one was a Liberal and eleven were Conservatives. Thus the reason for the dearth of shopkeepers on the Council in the 1920s was that, as Liberals, they had been squeezed out between the Labour and Conservative Parties. But once they were committed to the Conservative Party, they returned to the Council in their old numbers and more.

The 'Drink' Interest. The 1890s and 1930s were the years when the drink trade was represented at its peak in the Council; and the causes for the high representation differ for each period. In the first, the publicans, wine and spirit merchants and brewers primarily sought to defend their trade against the atacks of the temperance reformers. This clash was, in addition, a political battle,

[1] *W.C.*, 14.10.1903. [2] *W.C.*, 24.5.1905.

since the drink trade was Conservative; of eight new entrants to the Council in 1888–1919 who were connected with the liquor business, seven were Conservatives and one an Independent. The temperance reformers were Radical Liberals. In the early 1890s the municipal elections were largely fought between the trade and temperance. An Alderman and a former brewer said that publicans were eager to get on the Council in order to be in a position to influence the licensing bench. This was a defensive move to obstruct the efforts of the temperance reformers, who were seeking to close down, and refuse licences to, as many public houses as possible, regarding them as causing the evil social conditions, particularly in the east end of the town. In an election in 1890 a temperance reformer claimed that 'the move of the publicans was to get on the Council, to get on the Bench, to get anywhere where the licensing system could be controlled.'[1] 'The drink traffic was at the bottom of all the social evils of the town.'[2] By the end of the 1890s temperance reform lost its impetus. No longer was it the main issue of elections. It flared up for the last time in 1903, when the 'trade' was described as a 'strong, ever-dominant power.'[3] Factors other than drink were now recognised as causing social distress: bad housing, for instance, and inadequate wages. Thus as the attack of the temperance reformers subsided there was less incentive for the publicans to join the Council.

Although the publican element among the new entrants declined, the actual publican element among the Councillors did not, and in the 1930s it was as high as in the 1890s. This is explained by the fact that some Councillors became licensed victuallers after joining the Council, like J. Haddock, a former Friendly Society agent, and G. J. Williams, a former engineer. Once on the Council these men became very friendly with the brewer Alderman J. F. Myatt, who put them in charge of his public houses. Some Labour members claimed that this process was not because Myatt wished to help his Council colleagues at a time when employment was short, but because he wished to buy their support for his property deals; indeed one Alderman claimed that Myatt offered him a public house if he would cease attacking him. With

[1] *E. & S.*, 31.10.1890.   [2] *E. & S.*, 23.10.1890.
[3] *E. & S.*, 2.11.1903.

Myatt's death in 1937 the trend stopped, and the publican element continued its decline.

There is an additional factor explaining the demise of the Councillors who were publicans. The early publicans were not the employees of a brewery, operating a tied house, but the independent masters of their own establishments, even brewing their own beer in their backyards, like Levi Johnson, Jeremiah Mason and William Moseley. They were similar to the shop-keepers and the small businessmen, but the publicans of the 1950s and 1960s were employees of breweries, not independent men. This loss of independence and status has perhaps removed an incentive to join the Council.

The Working Class. The increase in the number of the working-class Councillors has been shown to be related to the lowering of the property qualifications for membership and to the extensions of the franchise. They have been overwhelmingly members of the Labour Party, and it is the foundation of that party, and its activity in training people in the arts of, for instance, Committee work and in financing and organising election campaigns, which has enabled people of more humble circumstances than before to enter the Council. The Labour Party's policy, too, was designed to appeal to the newly enfranchised, promising to advance the social position of the working class; and, in its early days particu-larly, its policy was aimed at promoting specific trade union objectives.

The trade union connection explains the high proportion of railwaymen and engineers among the working-class Councillors; these two groups were highly unionised. We have shown above (p. 59) that Low Hill and Bushbury Wards were almost 'pocket wards' of the railway unions; while the engineers, especially those who worked at the Sunbeam Company, were highly unionised in the A.S.E. This union, now the A.E.U., had offices in the town and full-time staff and officials there. Its district officer was a Town Councillor, the Chairman of Town Planning Committee in 1964. Participation in union activities – indeed being an active member of a union – would bring the member close to politics and to the Lab-our Party, for the unions used the Labour Party as their political wing. The Trades Council was the first Labour organisation to run candidates at municipal elections; the unions formed the local Labour Representation Committee as the organisation to get Labour members elected in municipal and Parliamentary elections; trade union money financed the local Labour Party, paid for the election campaigns and gave out-of-pocket expenses to the early Labour Councillors, while the programme of the Labour Party contained policies to assist the unions. An active trade unionist could easily become an active Labour Party member and through the Party gain entry to the Council.

It was the strong trade union connection which prevented the Liberal Party from containing the working class. This party, predominantly of shopkeepers, showed, for instance, by its attitude in the minimum wages controversy that it was not the friend of organised Labour. Although in the 1890s many working men, indeed some active trades unionists, had been Liberals, by 1914 the Liberals had lost this element which had formed its own party. Thus the increase in working-class membership of the Council was due to the development of the Labour Party, backed by trade union support in terms of manpower and money and producing a programme designed to attract the newly enfranchised working men.

The Women and the Retired. The growth of the Labour Party also explains the increase in the number of female Councillors. Not until 1908 could women become members of Town Councils;[1] and not until 1921 did the first woman enter Wolverhampton's Council, following the enfranchisement in 1918 of women over thirty. Only after 1945 did the women come more and more on to the Council, as the Labour Party grew in strength. They were predominantly Labour, often members of the women's section of their husbands' trade unions, working-class and entering the Council often in their forties and fifties, after their children were sufficiently grown up for them to have time on their hands to devote to local government work. Thus the rise of the number of female Councillors is due to the growth of the Labour Party.

The number of Councillors who were retired has risen, albeit slightly; and, as we have seen, they were, since the 1930s, composed mainly of working-class men, and thus members of the Labour

[1] 7 Edw. VII, c. 33.

Party. Like the women after their children had grown up, they found that after retirement they had time to devote to politics and Council work. They had often been active in their trade union before retirement, but had been unable to find the time to give to local government. The advent of old-age pensions was also a factor enabling men to enter the Council, since no longer would they be compelled to keep on working well into their seventies. Thus earlier retirement, a more secure retirement – indeed the release from work altogether – allowed retired working men to enter the Council more than in the past.

Managers and Clerks. The small increase in the number of Councillors of administrative occupations, both managerial and clerical, can be explained by the increase of these groups as a proportion of the population. As the number of manual workers in the population declined, so the managerial, clerical and service occupations rose. As their numbers grew, so one would expect the number of Councillors to grow. This change in the population is also perhaps the explanation for the slight fall in the 1950s of the number of manual workers who were members of the Council. Despite these population changes the managerial and clerical groups appeared in the 1960s to be a small proportion of the Council as compared with their proportion of the population. The apparent reluctance of these groups to enter the Council can be put down to the nature of their work. Compelled to work set daytime hours, and not shifts which allow many working men to come to Council and committee meetings in the day, they have little opportunity to join the Council. And these groups are likely to be concerned about their prospects of promotion and therefore not keen to jeopardise their chances by appearing to neglect their jobs for local government. Like the professional men and the industrial executives, these newer occupational groups put their jobs first, and since both their jobs and local government have increased the demands on their time, local government has been given second and even lower placing.

Occupation has correlated closely with party allegiance during the whole period. Professional men throughout the period have been predominantly Conservatives. The shopkeepers up to 1919

were Liberals and later turned to the Conservatives. The manufacturers changed their loyalty too. In the Council of 1888–9 there
were eleven Liberal manufacturers and seven Conservatives. The
balance soon changed. Between 1888 and 1919 Conservatives
were the largest proportion of the new Councillors who were manufacturers,[1] and their share increased greatly from 1919 to 1945.[2]
Their change in allegiance had an economic cause; their desire for
Protection and their opposition to Free Trade. The Conservatives
in Wolverhampton advocated the former, while the Liberals
extolled Free Trade. The working class were consistently Labour,
as were the women members of the Council, and since 1919 the
retired and the clerical workers were mainly supporters of the
Labour Party. Managerial and administrative types were chiefly
Conservative, but during the 1950s a growing number of Labour
members fell into this category, through promotion inside their
firms.

The Council of 1903–4 presented a picture of Conservative
and Liberal manufacturers, Conservative professional men, Conservative publicans and Liberal shopkeepers, together with Conservative and Liberal administrative and retired individuals, all
accepting in a general way the *status quo*, opposed by a small
group of Labour working men. But the Council of 1962–3 presented a picture of Conservative shopkeepers, with a few Conservative professional men, small manufacturers, managers and
retired men facing Labour working men and women, retired
working men, clerical workers and some managerial types. These
two groups were evenly balanced.

[1] 14 Conservative and 9 Liberal.   [2] 14 Conservatives and 2 Liberals.

6 The Associations of the members of the Council

THROUGHOUT the period one aspect of the Council members' extra-Council activities is strikingly constant, their 'clubbability'. They were always inveterate joiners of Associations, and not merely in a passive role, but as active members, sitting on Executive Committees, and as officers. Initially membership of an Association would assist an individual to obtain a seat on the Council, in that he would be provided with an arena in which to make a reputation, to show his competence at administration and committee work, and to display his powers of persuasion. Success in this field might bring him to the attention of a sitting member of the Council, who would suggest that he too might become a Councillor. During the subsequent election campaign the Association would most likely be a valuable source of help for the candidate. Once elected, he would be drawn into other Associations, either as a result of his own initiative in the quest for further support, or as a result of approaches made to him by the Associations seeking his aid and patronage. A skilful Councillor could capitalise on small initial assets, augmenting them to provide an ever-growing fund of backers. Thus being in an Association helped the man into the Council, and then being in the Council helped him to become a member of more Associations, which in turn further consolidated his position on the Council.

Ward-based Associations. Over the whole period Councillors of all parties played a part in Associations, based in the wards which they represented. Sports clubs, hobby clubs, amenity associations, charitable and social welfare organisations, associations to defend particular interests, were all cultivated by the Councillors. Allotment Societies, Tenants' Associations, Parent--Teacher

Associations, Community Associations, Nursing Associations, Social Clubs, Bowling Clubs, Old Folks' Christmas Clubs, the list is huge of the various organisations centred in the wards, which have claimed Councillors as representatives.[1] Out of this welter of Associations four points emerge. First, the publican members of the Council seem to have been particularly good in obtaining membership and offices in Sports Associations, for example Bowling Clubs, Football Clubs, Dominoes Clubs, Darts Clubs, which were based on their licensed houses. Clearly this trend is evidence of the publican's attempts to widen his custom and to maintain the loyalty of his customers to his establishment. It would also make him more popular and better known, and thus of advantage when he came to seek a seat on the Council.

Secondly, there is no evidence of these ward-based Associations being active in putting pressure on the Council for particular policies. The only exception is the Allotments Associations, whose voices are heard on the Small Holdings and Allotments Committee of the Council. They were particularly vocal after the Second World War, when Councillors who were in these Associations opposed the return to public parks and children's playgrounds of land which had been converted into allotments during the war as part of the 'Dig for Victory' campaign. Even then the Allotments Associations had to fight hard against those who wished to keep the parks for recreation.

Thirdly, there is no correlation between party affiliation and membership of such Associations. Labour, Conservative and Liberal Councillors have been active in Sports Clubs, Parent–Teacher Associations, Allotment Societies and in the various local welfare and amenity organisations. The only exception here is that Labour members have predominated in the Municipal Tenants' Associations.[2]

Fourthly, these local Associations often had links with similar organisations for the town as a whole, and in these too the Council-

---

[1] Details about the Associations and their connections with members of the Council have been obtained from:
(a) Newspaper biographies or obituaries of Councillors.
(b) Newspaper reports of functions of the Associations.
(c) *Wolverhampton Red Book and Directory*, issues from 1900 to 1960.
(d) Interviews and questionnaires.
[2] No Conservative member of the Council has been a Council house tenant.

lors played a prominent part. The *Wolverhampton Red Book and Directory* in its issues between 1900 and 1960, listed the major Associations of the town, and their officials; amongst these names there always cropped up those of Councillors.

Trade Unions. Correlation between party affiliation and Association is very clear with regard to those Associations connected with occupations. With the Labour members trade unionism has been a significant force. We have already observed that the railway and engineering unions have been a fruitful source for providing members of the Council, and that trade union full-time officials formed a sizeable section on the Council. Every member of the Labour Party is constitutionally bound to join his appropriate trade union, and thus it is only to be expected that the majority of the Labour Councillors were members of trade unions. Their role within the unions, however, was not passive; often they filled the leading part-time official positions within their local branches. Indeed their work here was a factor commending them to the Labour Party as suitable candidates for Council membership. The trade union activities of such men did not end at the branch level; they were often delegates to the local Trades Council; and many Town Council members acted as officials of the Trades Council. Association with a trade union was a distinctively Labour phenomenon; never was a Conservative or Liberal member of the Council a trade unionist.

For the non-Socialist members of the Council the nearest equivalents to trade unions were their trade and professional associations. Here too the Council members were not passive, but active in their organisations. Throughout the period Town Councillors have been members and officials of a wide variety of trade and professional associations, for example the Law Society, the Master Printers' Association, the Grocers' and Provision Dealers' Association, the Chemists' Association, the Society of Chartered Accountants, the Confectionery Trades Council, the Tyre Distributors' Association, the Hardware Association, the Retail Fruit Trade Federation, the Ford Dealers' Association, the Licensed Trade Association, the Federation of Sub-Postmasters, the Master Bakers' and Confectioners' Association, the Retail

E

Market Hall Tenants' Association, the Butchers' Association, the Pawnbrokers' Association, and the Perambulator Manufacturers' Association. These types of connections were constant between 1888 and the 1960s and never slackened. Generally Conservative and Liberal members of the Council have been the majority of such individuals, but whenever there were Labour members of the Council who were not able to join a trade union, they too joined their appropriate trade or professional association.

Later chapters examine the activities of the trade unions and the trade and professional Associations in relation to the Council, and investigate the advantages of membership to the various occupational groups.

Chamber of Commerce. The number of members of the Council who were members of the Council of the Chamber of Commerce declined significantly over the period.[1] Eleven members of the Town Council of 1888–9 were members of the Chamber; in 1962–3 only one was in both. Between 1886 and 1933 members of the Town Council provided thirteen Presidents of the Chamber of Commerce.[2] Since 1933 not one member of the Town Council has been President of the Chamber. This decline is related to the decline of the number of industrialists on the Town Council. The one member in 1962 was himself not a representative of a manufacturing enterprise but of a retailing concern. No Labour member was ever a member of the Chamber of Commerce, and the Chamber itself was very closely connected with the Conservative Group of Councillors. For a long time the Conservative Group used to hold their pre-Council meetings in the Chamber's premises. When seeking candidates the Conservative Group circulated the Chamber to discover if it knew of anyone suitable.[3] In the 1920s the Chamber issued public statements about Council policy, usually to attack items in Labour's programme. In 1927, for

[1] See Table XVI.
[2] V. B. Beaumont, *Record of the Wolverhampton Chamber of Commerce 1856–1956,* 1956.
[3] *Minutes of the Conservative Group,* 28.12.1956, 10.3.1961. In 1925 the Management Committee of the Conservative Association in the West met three representatives from the Chamber to discuss the candidates for the municipal election. *M.M.C.,* 14.9.1925.

example, it claimed that Labour's policies would result in an 'enormous increase in the rates with the consequent depression in local industries and an increase in the number of unemployed.[1]' Similar statements did not emanate from the Chamber in the 1950s and 60s.

The Property Owners' Association. Another Association which has had links and influence with the Council was the Wolverhampton Property Owners' Association. It comprised the owners of rented property, Conservatives and Liberals, but no Labour Councillors. In 1901 its President and Vice-President were both Councillors, C. H. Cousins and W. Shepherd. It was particularly active before 1914; and it impinged on the Council mainly over four issues. It first became prominent in the late 1890s, when it defended the interests of the property-owners against those who wished them to bear the main burden of the expense of substituting the water-carriage system for the pan system of excrement disposal in the houses which they owned. It pressed that the Council should pay a substantial subsidy towards the conversions: one Councillor in 1895 bemoaned the plight of the property-owners absolutely dependent on their property for their livings. In 1897 another Councillor, angry at the delay in abolishing the pan system, exclaimed that 'one great difficulty in dealing with the insanitary property of the town was that a large proportion of them belonged to members of the Council'.[2]

Secondly, in the early 1900s it protested at what it regarded as the Council's grandiose schemes, particularly its plans to construct a new Cold Store and Abattoir. The Association feared that the rates would rise to an excessive level; and that the noise of the machinery and the nuisances created would reduce the value of the property in the vicinity.

Thirdly it delayed the building of Council houses. A Councillor said that the delay in the building of the first Council house was due to 'the pressure that is being brought to bear on the committee (Housing of the Working Classes Committee) by the Property Owners' and Ratepayers' Association'.[3] Indeed many of the

[1] *E. & S.*, 23.3.1927.   [2] *W.C.*, 15.9.1897.
[3] *E. & S.*, 14.4.1900.

Committee were themselves 'large owners of small house property',[1] and thus resented competition from the rate-subsidised
Council houses. In 1913 Labour members tabled a motion 'that
in the opinion of this Council it is detrimental to the speedy
solution of the housing question for members to hold interest in
any property which comes under the category of slums'.[2] The
other side maintained that there was no need to build Council
houses since 'private enterprise would come along and solve the
difficulty, if only speculators were allowed to get a fair remuneration on their outlay.'[3]

The attempts to get 'a fair remuneration' had led members of
the Association in 1912–13 to raise the rents of their properties,
which provoked the formation of the Tenants' Defence League
and thus assisted the advance of Labour.

Building Societies. After the First World War the Property
Owners' Association was no longer such a significant force on the
Council as it had been. In the inter-war years the Associations
which were prominent in the property market, and which had
very close connections with the Council, were the Building
Societies of the town. There were three: the Wolverhampton
Freeholders' Permanent Building Society, founded in 1849; the
Wolverhampton and District Permanent Building Society, founded
in 1877; and the South Staffordshire Building Society, founded
in 1902. Table XVII shows that in 1903–4 seven members of the
Council were directors of these Building Societies; the peak year
was 1929–30 when there were seventeen; by 1962–3 there was
only one. The 1920s and 1930s were the years when the Council
and the Building Societies were linked most closely. It was at this
period that much building was taking place in the town; slums
were being demolished near the centre; new estates, both public
and private, were being built; the Corporation was engaged in
improvements, street widening and laying essential services to the
new estates. Opportunities were available for expansion by the
Building Societies. The Labour Party, none of whose Councillors
were ever directors of the Building Societies, were not without

[1] *E. & S.*, 21.3.1900.   [2] *C.M.*, 8.12.1913. *W.C.*, 10.12.1913.
[3] *W.C.*, 11.12.1914.

explanations of the close tie-up between the Councillors and the Societies. Labour Councillors accused directors of the Societies of buying valuable land from the Corporation cheaply and of selling poor land to the Corporation dearly, and of arranging for the Corporation to lay essential services to their new estates at low cost. A typical 'incident' of the 1930s occurred in 1936 when Councillor Lane asked a question in Council as to whether Building Society directors came within section 76 of the Local Government Act of 1933 about the declaration of financial interests. The Mayor said that he would take no action, as they did not have full information of the financial interests of members of the Council. Lane retorted, 'I can give it to you.' The Mayor replied, 'I am not inviting it.' 'You are afraid,' said Lane. Then Councillor T. W. Simpson, Chairman of the Town Planning Committee and a director of the Permanent Building Society, spoke up that this was a serious affair, and if accusations were made he would take Counsel's advice. Lane retorted, 'If the cap fits, wear it.'[1] Another instance of Labour suspicion was in 1934 when Councillor A. Dallow opposed the sale of a piece of land by the Education Committee to private owners, and argued that it should be transferred to the Small Holdings and Allotments Committee. He said: 'the general public knowing that members of the Council were interested in various ways in building – building societies and speculative building – were asking why the 10 acres were being let go so easily.'[2] Nothing ever came of Labour's accusations: no one was ever prosecuted. One Alderman often accused by Labour said that the Labour members were merely consumed by envy and could not see how a man could do well for himself without being crooked. He claimed that there was no truth in Labour's accusations. After the Second World War the Building Societies severed their links with the Council; and the Labour Party made no more accusations about their activities.

Table XVII shows not only that Labour never got a foothold on the boards of directors, but also that at times the Societies had definite party biases, for example the Permanent in 1903 was Liberal, and the Freeholders in 1929 was Conservative. This

---

[1] *E. & S.*, 10.3.1936.   [2] *E. & S.*, 14.5.1934.

phenomenon is perhaps due to the way directors were recruited. Invariably a Councillor became a director only after being on the Council for some time. A director did not usually become a Councillor: it was the other way round. The way to the board was by making a good showing in Council, impressing a director, who would then invite one on to the board. Thus the Council was for some a means of advancement.

The Co-operative Movement. The anti-Socialists in turn accused the Labour Party of seeking to advance the interests of the Co-operative Society. It was a specifically Labour Society. No Conservative or Liberal has been prominent in the Wolverhampton Co-operative Society. In 1958 during a Council debate on whether the Society should be granted the lease of some shops on a new estate, twenty-five members of the Council declared an interest in the Society, all Labour members, about three-quarters of the total Labour membership of the Council. The interest which they declared was the possession of a share number; only one member of the Council over the whole period was really active in the Society, and she was an exceptional figure. Councillor Mrs M. Dale, member of the Council 1945–7 and 1949–65, held many official positions within the Co-operative Movement at both local and national levels, for example as a director of the Wolverhampton and District Co-operative Society and as President of the Co-operative Women's Guild. For her the Co-operative Movement contained the 'essence of Socialism'. No other Labour member ever came close to her involvement in the Co-operative Society. Normally each merely had a share number. The influence of the Co-operative Society on the Labour Party and on the Council will be examined later.

Except for religious Associations we have really exhausted the range of organisations with which the Labour Councillors have been connected, ward-based Associations, trade unions and the Co-operative Society. In the early part of the period they often held positions within Friendly Societies, like the Rechabites and Hearts of Oak, but with the advent of state social services, the need for such simple voluntary services declined. For social contacts, the Labour members have preferred to be members of the working men's clubs of the town, the Cannock Road and the West End mainly, or to frequent particular public houses. This range of contacts, compared with those of the anti-Socialist Councillors, is narrow. The Labour members, compared with the Conservatives, were 'socially undernourished'; they devoted more time to party than to social activities. They found and made social contacts within the party; and attended party functions, jumble sales, dances; indeed, the numerous committee meetings which occur in the party were really social functions for them.

Rotary and Round Table. The anti-Socialists had a far wider range of contacts, particularly in the social field, and were not so exclusively concentrated on their political parties to satisfy their needs for social contacts. Rotary and Round Table were, since their foundation in the 1920s, represented on the Council by a fairly constant number of anti-Socialist Councillors, twelve in 1929–30, eleven in 1945–6 and eleven in 1962–3.[1] No Labour members ever penetrated their ranks, except when a Labour member was Mayor and became an honorary member for his term of office. The high peak of Rotarian and Round Table membership of the Council came just before the 1945 election; sixteen were counted in 1944.[2] This was because these bodies had become recruiting centres for co-opting anti-Socialists on to the Council.[3] During the same period of the 1940s these Associations were exceptionally strong among the chief officers of the Corporation: the Town Clerk, the Treasurer, the Chief Constable, the Medical Officer of Health were all members, and the Director of Education, T. A. Warren, became a President of Rotary International. His activities for Rotary took him on a $2\frac{1}{2}$-months' visit to the U.S.A., which angered the Labour Party, who tabled a motion deploring his absence. However, a majority supported his visit as a service for the war effort and as bringing honour to the town. By 1961–2 the number of chief officers in Rotary had declined: in 1961 the Chief Librarian, the Borough Engineer, the

---

[1] See Table XVIII.

[2] *E. & S.*, 13.3.1944.

[3] During the election campaign of 1945 a letter in the *Express and Star* attacked the Progressive Party as 'guided and controlled by Masonic and Rotarian influences'; 'the same that co-opted members to the Town Council'. 4.9.1945.

Housing Manager and the Water Engineer were listed. The leading officials were not evident.

There was no evidence that Rotary or Round Table had particular policies to advocate. Their influence was not so specific. In 1943 the President of the Wolverhampton Rotary claimed that 'the quiet and pervading influence of the Rotary movement was making itself felt. In towns where Rotary had a footing there was a better spirit of tolerance, forbearance, mutual understanding and help.'[1] Its social exclusiveness, however, made it suspect in the eyes of the Labour Party, which viewed it as a sinister body where Council policies were formed on an informal basis between groups of Councillors and Chief Officers. Whether this was so is hard to prove, but the fact that Councillors did meet informally with officials here is a significant factor. Labour members did not attend social functions at which they were likely to meet the officials on such an equal basis. Anti-Socialist Councillors attended such functions, and were therefore more likely to be on better terms with the officials, or at least they could understand each other's position better than could the Labour members and the officials, who never really came into contact with each other save on official business. This difference goes far to explain the reason for the view often expressed by Labour Councillors that the officials were really 'Tories at heart' and 'not one of us'. Thus Rotary provided means to get harmony between officials and one group of Councillors and was a recruiting centre for new Councillors. Its influence was at its highest during the Second World War. Afterwards Labour came to power; yet the number of Councillors who were Rotarians was still significantly high in 1964.

Freemasons. It is most difficult to discover if an individual is a Freemason, since the very basis of this Society is secrecy. An attempt has been made to discover which members of the Council were Freemasons, by examining the lists of mourners at the funeral of particularly prominent Freemasons, and newspaper accounts of dinners and dances at lodges, and by making discreet inquiries.[2] The figures given below are not exhaustive: they should

[1] *E. & S.*, 6.7.1943.
[2] See T. J. Barnett, *A History of the Lodge of Honour No. 526 holden at Wolverhampton*, 1896, and F. W. Willmore, *A History of Freemasonry in the Province of Staffordshire*, 1905.

be regarded as merely suggestive. The figures for 1888–9 and for 1903–4 are exceptionally hazy since at such a distance it is hard to discover such personal information.

Council members being Freemasons

Council	Conservative	Liberal	Labour	Total
1888–9	2	1	0	3
1903–4	4	1	0	5
1919–20	9	1	0	10
1945–6	7	2	0	9
1953–4	5	0	0	5
1962–3	4	0	0	4

It is clear that Conservatives have predominated in the ranks of the Freemason members of the Council, that Labour was never represented and that since the 1920s there was a decline in the number of Freemasons on the Council. This fall is related to the fall in the number of industrialists and professional men on the Council, since the Freemason members of the Council in the 1920s were predominantly of that type.

It is hard to find any proof that the Freemasons had a distinctive policy to press upon the Council. Their main function, like that of Round Table and Rotary, would be social; providing opportunities for people to meet and forging social links between individuals which might help them to unite on matters of Council business. A former committee clerk said that in the 1920s and 1930s Free-masonry was strong among both Council members and officials, and that they tended to 'help each other up' and to 'stick together'.

Thus the Council became polarised, not only politically into the Labour and Conservative Parties, and not only occupationally into those economic groups represented by the Conservative and Labour Parties, but also socially, since the Conservative and Labour Party members of the Council had their own distinctive sets of Asso-ciations. At the turn of the century, in contrast, this polarisation was not so sharp; then the Councillors were more socially homo-geneous, and the main divisive factor was religion.

Religion. In 1900 there were three significant religious groupings on the Council: first an Anglican Conservative group of Council-lors, whose place of worship was the town's parish church of

St Peter's. Men of high social status in the town, like the manufacturer Sir Charles T. Mander, and the solicitors W. G. Allen, F. T. Langley and F. A. Willcock worshipped there and held such lay offices in the church as sidesmen and churchwardens. Their businesses were in the ward, and on the Council they represented the ward. Anglicanism and Conservatism went together. The Church Party was the Conservative Party. Table XIX shows the close correlation between Conservatism and Anglicanism among the Councillors. In 1903–4 seventeen Conservatives were Anglicans; but no Liberals.

The second group were those who worshipped at the Queen Street Congregational Church; manufacturers like S. T. Mander, J. Jones, W. H. Jones and A. B. Bantock, who held such offices in the church as deacons, Sunday School superintendents, patrons of mission churches and trustees of the Congregational School, Tettenhall College. They were of similar high social status to the St Peter's set, but different from them politically, since the Queen Street men were Liberals; all nine of them on the Council in 1888–9 and all eight in 1903–4. The Pastor of Queen Street from 1883 to 1899, the Rev. C. A. Berry, was a dominant personality who preached a civic gospel of the need to build 'the kingdom of God in the State'.[1] He was a partisan figure, eager 'to refute the exclusive claims of Anglicanism',[2] and often making political pronouncements, for instance publicly supporting particular candidates at municipal and Parliamentary elections.[3] He was an inspiration to many Liberals, and it was his influence perhaps that explains why 'Many of the members of Queen Street Church take an active part in municipal affairs, and are well known as esteemed public servants.'[4]

These two churches could be called the 'establishment churches' of the Council. There the leading Councillors worshipped. In 1900 of thirteen Chairmen of Council Committees, five came from Queen

---

[1] *The Congregationalist*, 28.10.1897, and C. A. Berry, *Municipal Patriotism. A Sermon*, November 1896.

[2] *The Congregationalist*, 28.10.1897.

[3] *E. & S.*, 20.10.1894. See J. S. Drummond, *Clarence A. Berry, A Memoir*, 1899, p. 186.

[4] W. H. Jones, *History of the Congregational Church of Wolverhampton*, 1894, p. 169, and see H. A. May, *Queen St Congregational Church. The Story of 100 years 1809–1909*, 1909.

Street and three from St Peter's. The other 'establishment' church was the Darlington Street Methodist Church, an imposing building like the other churches, situated also in the centre of the town, at which, for example, Sir Henry H. Fowler worshipped. Those members of the Council who worshipped here were not so committed to Liberalism as the other Nonconformists. These Wesleyan Methodists inclined in numerous cases to the Conservative Party.

At a lower level in the social scale were the shopkeepers who worshipped at the Waterloo Road Baptist Chapel and the Mount Zion Primitive Methodist Chapel. Those were the centres for the Radical Liberals, temperance reformers like T. G. Baker, P. Lewis and G. R. Thorne, who opposed the more moderate Liberalism and less severe Nonconformity of the Queen Street and Darlington Street sects. The members of the Council who were active in these two chapels, as lay preachers, organisers of the Pleasant Sunday Afternoon classes, and superintendents of Sunday Schools, were foremost in demanding reforms for the east end of the town, where Mount Zion was situated. Baptists and Primitive Methodists combined, speaking at each other's services and functions, and acting together in the Council and in municipal and Parliamentary elections. The wards of St James' and St Matthew's were their strongholds, and Mount Zion was regarded as the centre of their support. The alliance is symbolised by two men who worked closely together, Price Lewis[1] of Mount Zion, member of Council (1888–1914) and G. R. Thorne,[2] member of the Council (1888–91 and 1897–1920).[3] These two were regarded as the 'opposition', against the Chairmen from St Peter's and Queen Street. Indeed it is significant that despite their many years of service on the Council, neither of them ever became a prominent Chairman. Lewis was Chairman of Small Holdings and Allotments Committee (1907–8), and of the Free Library Committee (1912–14), while Thorne was Chairman of Health Committee (1903–9). They never became part of the town's 'Establishment'.

We have seen that sectarian issues were very divisive with regard

---

[1] For his life and work for Mount Zion see *Wolverhampton Journal*, May 1902 and *E. & S.*, 20.8.1943.

[2] For his life and work see *E. & S.*, 20.2.1934.

[3] Once a Councillor called Lewis 'Thorne's Lieutenant', *W.C.*, 13.12.1905. And Thorne called Lewis 'the most intimate friend he possessed', *W.C.*, 16.11.1898.

to the School Board at the turn of the century, and that Anglicans
and Nonconformists fought each other in 1902–5 over education
in the Town Council. But even before the clash over the Education
Bill religious bitterness spilled over into Council debates. In the
1890s Councillors fought over such topics as whether the Corporation should contribute to the provision of an illuminated clock in a
church tower (a Nonconformist Councillor objected 'to the ratepayers' money being given as a present to the vicar'); whether the
Corporation should buy, and then at what price, St Peter's burial
yard for conversion into a park; whether a ward of the town
should be named after the parish church or be given a secular
title; whether the Corporation should contribute to the laying out
of the front of St Peter's (a Councillor objected to having to pay
this 'Church rate'); whether to allow St Peter's to celebrate its
900th anniversary in the public park; and every year at the time
when the Council had to decide how to appropriate the assigned
revenues, a battle would rage over whether to grant some of the
money to a Church school. The objection of the Nonconformists
in all these debates was to having to contribute from their rates
towards the Anglican Church. This was the issue which really
irked them over the Education Act of 1902.

Another significant religious grouping on the Council and in
the town at the turn of the century was the Roman Catholics.
Their leader in the town was the Irishman Father Darmody,[1]
who was, for thirty-four years from 1890 to 1924, parish priest of
St Patrick's, in a part of the town where there was a substantial
Irish population – in St Mary's Ward. He dominated his flock;
they voted as he told them; first for the Liberals in the 1890s
because they supported Home Rule;[2] then for the Conservatives
over education, since Catholic schools would obtain more from the
rates under the Conservatives than under the Liberals,[3] then by
1908 he was urging them to vote Liberal, since, as Amery put it,
his 'educational zeal was much less ardent than his Irish national-
ism.' Amery indeed called Darmody 'the real controller of the vote'.[4]

By the 1920s St Mary's Ward was returning Labour members,

[1] *E. & S.*, 8.6.1942.
[2] *E. & S.*, 31.10.1892, 1.11.1892.
[3] *E. & S.*, 2.11.1903.
[4] L. S. Amery, *My Political Life*, vol. i, 1953, p. 333.

but they too were Catholics; in 1930 Darmody's successor, the Rev. F. Locket,[1] was elected to the Council, and he stayed for fifteen years. The Catholic tradition of the ward was evident even in the 1950s, since in 1955 C. M. Walsh, of Irish extraction and a Catholic, was elected to the Council.

Despite the above remarks the Roman Catholics on the Council have never really been completely connected to one particular party; in 1903–4 for example, they were equally divided into two Conservatives and two Liberals. But a general trend can be discerned: on the whole, the Catholics of Irish and working-class origin were in the earlier years Liberals and later Labour, while those of higher status and not Irish were Conservatives. The main concern of the Catholics (as such) on the Council was to ensure that the Catholic schools were not neglected by the Corporation. Even in the 1950s they watched with concern the Council's policy over their schools. In 1956 J. Cahill (Conservative) and C. M. Walsh (Labour) hoped that the congestion in the Catholic schools would be relieved.[2] But party loyalty sometimes conflicted with religious loyalty, and predominated, as when in 1953, before Labour took the Chairmanship of Education Committee, the Labour Catholic Councillor C. M. Walsh complained that the Education Committee had not stressed the needs of the Catholic community; and in answer the Conservative Catholic Alderman J. Cahill said that the committee had done all in its power to assist Catholics.[3] The other field of Catholic anxiety was birth control. They led the opposition in 1937 to a proposal that the Council should pay £50 to the Women's Welfare Centre, which taught family-planning techniques. A Catholic Councillor said that the birthrate should increase; the tradition of family life had to be maintained, and 'it was not a proper thing to support that kind of thing.'[4] That Wolverhampton had no Family Planning Clinic in 1964 could perhaps be ascribed to Catholic opposition.

During the 1920s and 1930s debates arose in Council which showed that Nonconformity was still a significant force. Nonconformists of all parties came together, for example, to prevent

---

[1] The only clergyman ever elected to the Council.
[2] *E. & S.*, 26.3.1956.
[3] *E. & S.*, 4.5.1953.
[4] *C.M.*, 8.3.1937. *E. & S.*, 8.3.1937.

the playing of games in the public parks on Sunday; one Catholic Councillor complained that the Nonconformists would stop the lambs skipping about on Sunday if they could. His kind of view was regarded by the Nonconformists as 'a deliberate attempt to undermine the Sabbath'. They sought to prevent mixed bathing from taking place in the public baths. They sought to prevent the opening of cinemas on Sunday and they assailed the Catholic Councillor who led this campaign as being in the pay of the cinema proprietors and as seeking 'to break down the barriers of our English Sunday'. The question of the nature of the Sabbath pitted Catholics against Nonconformists irrespective of party. They also battled over Council grants to Catholic schools; in 1928, for example, a grant of £400 to the Governors of St Chad's school was opposed by the Nonconformists as a 'sectarian grant'.

Since the Second World War these kinds of issues have not divided the Council. Only one Councillor, G. J. Costley, a Labour man, who was a Wesleyan Methodist lay preacher, really maintained the old Nonconformist tradition, inveighing against the evils of roller skating on Sunday or the opening of shops on Good Friday. He, however, was a lone voice. Religion was in 1964 no longer such a dominant force in the lives of the Councillors as in the past. Few played an active part in any church or chapel. At the turn of the century the religions of almost all the public figures in the town were known; that is why there are relatively so few 'unknowns' in Table XIX for the years 1888–9 and 1903–4. Afterwards religion was not such a key factor; the battle between Anglicans and Nonconformists no longer counted for anything on the Council. In 1900 to be a 'churchman' implied a political as well as a religious set of beliefs. In the 1960s the Councillor who put 'C. of E.' on his questionnaire was not making the affirmation of his political views that his predecessors did in espousing Anglicanism.

A final point about the correlation between religious and political affiliation emerges from Table XIX. There was quite clearly a connection between Liberalism and Nonconformity and between Conservatism and Anglicanism, and indeed within the range of Nonconformist sects there was a gradation from the moderate to the severe sects, corresponding to varying degrees of political Radicalism. With the Labour Party, however, the picture is not so clear-cut. In Wolverhampton the Labour Party was not associated with any religious group. Its secular policy won adherents from all: Anglicans like Thomas Frost[1] and Alan Davies,[2] Catholics like J. W. Kennedy[3] and H. E. Lane,[4] Nonconformists like J. Whittaker[5] and A. A. Beach[6] and agnostics like C. W. Hill.[7] Thus in another sphere Labour disrupted an existing pattern of relationships and conflicts, and substituted a new pattern.

Kinship. Another important Association for the members of the Council is kinship. A large proportion of the Councillors over the period was related to other members of the Council at one time or another.[8] It seems that once one member of a family joins the Council, other members of the same family are also encouraged to join. In addition there seemed to have been a tendency, especially around the turn of the century, for members of the Council to marry into the families of other members of the Council. Thus the family trees of many Councillors become intertwined.

From 1888 to 1952 two families spread the branches of their family tree over the Council; and these two families produced the two outstanding members of the Council, A. B. Bantock and Sir Charles A. Mander.

A. B. Bantock was a member of the Council from 1900 to 1937; he was Chairman of the Public Works Committee (1904–17) and of the Finance Committee (1917–37); three times Mayor 1905-6-7 and 1914–15), an Alderman for twenty-seven years, a J.P. and an Honorary Freeman of the Borough. He was the son of Thomas Bantock, himself a former Mayor (1869–70), Alderman (1868–93), and Chairman of the Team and Watch Committees (1890–3). Thomas Bantock had married the sister of Samuel Dickinson, also a Mayor (1876–7), Alderman (1876–97) and Chairman of the Parks and Baths Committee (1887–97). A. B. Bantock married the daughter of John Jones, who was Mayor (1878-9-1880-1) and an

[1] Member of the Council 1901–8, 1911–49.
[2] Member of the Council 1919–54.
[3] Member of the Council 1920–30.
[4] Member of the Council 1930—
[5] Member of the Council 1903–12, 1924–40.
[6] Member of the Council 1921–4, 1927–52.
[7] Member of the Council 1938–52.
[8] See Table XX.

Alderman (1877–88). Four of John Jones's brothers were members of the Council: W. H. Jones (Mayor 1873–4), Alderman (1874–1903) and Chairman of the Streets (1875–93) and Watch Committee (1893–1903); Joseph Jones, Mayor (1887–8), Alderman (1887–1912) and Chairman of the Free Library Committee (1883–1912); Harry Jones, a Councillor who died young in 1870, and Benjamin Jones, a Councillor (1871–88). One of John Jones's sons, H. B. Jones, was a Councillor (1904–10). Thus A. B. Bantock's father was on the Council, as were his uncle, father-in-law, brother-in-law and four of his wife's uncles. All were Liberals and Congregationalists: and all save H. B. Jones (a solicitor) were connected to the Midland metalware industries. They could be said to have formed a family power élite.

Sir Charles A. Mander succeeded A. B. Bantock as Chairman of Finance Committee in 1937 and remained there until his death in 1951. He was Mayor twice, in 1932–3 and in 1936–7; an Alderman for thirteen years, J.P. and an Honorary Freeman. His father, Sir Charles T. Mander, had been Mayor four times (1892–3–4–5–6), Alderman for thirty-four years, Chairman of Lighting Committee (1893–1902), Tramway Committee (1896–1920) and Watch Committee (1920–7). Sir Charles T. Mander's father had been a Councillor: and his great-grandfather and great-uncle had been members of the Board of Township Commissioners before the borough was incorporated in 1848. A cousin of Sir Charles T. Mander, S. T. Mander, was Mayor (1899–1900), Alderman (1891–1900) and Chairman of Art Committee (1885–1900). His son, Sir Geoffrey le Meseurier Mander, was a Councillor (1911–1920). The Manders were directors of a concern manufacturing varnish. All were on the board of directors. But over religion and politics the family was split.[1] Those on Sir Charles T. Mander's side were Anglicans and Conservatives, while those on his cousin's side were Liberals and Congregationalists.

Inside the Council these close family ties were not politically significant. The clan did not vote together as solid blocks on all issues. Sometimes relatives voted with each other; at other times they did not: they sometimes spoke against the policies advocated

[1] In 1911 Sir Charles T. Mander was prominently active for the Conservative candidate in St Peter's Ward against the Liberal Geoffrey Mander. *E. & S.*, 31.10.1911.

by their relatives, sometimes they spoke on their side. Family relationships were important as forces conducive to the social homogeneity of the Council, and had religious and national political correlations, but as far as the actual policies which were fought out in the Council were concerned, there is no close connection between voting and kinship.

An examination of the kinship connections in specific Councils will be helpful to illustrate the close ties between the Councillors. The Council of 1899–1900 contained both Sir Charles T. Mander and S. T. Mander, A. B. Bantock, Joseph and W. H. Jones out of those so far considered. It also held:

(*i*) *Alderman John Annan*, Mayor in 1884–5, whose daughter married T. W. Dickinson, Mayor (1911–12–13), and Alderman for twenty-eight years, Chairman of Sewerage Committee (1912–27) and of Watch Committee (1927–38) and an Honorary Freeman.

(*ii*) *Alderman F. D. Gibbons*, Mayor (1882–3), an Alderman for forty-three years, Chairman of Sewerage (1879–1903), Watch (1903–16) and Care of the Mentally Defective (1920–5) Committees; he married the sister of Alderman H. W. Ash, Chairman of Team Committee (1896–9).

(*iii*) *W. Edwards*, Councillor (1895–1900), whose father was Alderman W. H. Edwards, Mayor (1874–5), Alderman for fifteen years, Chairman of the Artisans Dwelling Improvement Committee (1875–87) and of Watch Committee (1887–90).

(*iv*) *Edwin Blakemore*, Councillor (1892–1905), Chairman of Team Committee (1899–1905), who was distantly related by marriage to James Cremonini, Councillor (1881–90).

(*v*) *J. W. Hamp*, Mayor (1900–1), Alderman for twenty-four years and Chairman of Health Committee (1909–11), whose son, L. W. Hamp, was a Councillor (1927–32).

(*vi*) *John Marston*, Mayor (1889–90–91), Alderman for twenty-seven years, Chairman of Finance Committee (1891–2) and of Waterworks Committee (1892–1917), who also had a son, R. Marston, who was a Councillor (1908–13).

(*vii*) *R. E. W. Berrington*, Mayor (1904–5), Alderman for ten years, Chairman of Health Committee (1898–1903), (1911–15) and of Sewerage Committee (1903–11), whose son, E. E. W. Berrington, was a Councillor (1906–12).

(*viii*) *R. A. Willcock*, Chairman of Markets Committee (1898–9), whose father had been an Alderman; his brother, F. A. Willcock, was Mayor (1925–6–7), Alderman for fourteen years and Chairman of Parks and Baths Committee (1917–38). Their sister married F. H. Skidmore, Mayor (1913–14), Alderman (1915–20) and Chairman of Housing Committee (1913–20), and his brother, A. C. Skidmore, was Mayor (1915–16–17), Alderman (1918–24), Chairman of Water Committee (1919–20) and of Care of the Blind Committee (1921–4).

The family connections of the Council in 1962 were not so varied and extensive as those of 1900; understandably since for the Councillors of 1962 we cannot have details about which of their relatives will be in the Council of the later 1960s, 1970s and 1980s. It contained:

(*i*) *Alderman Mrs A. A. Braybrook*, Mayor (1953–4), Alderman (1952–6), Chairman of Children's Committee (1948–9 and 1952–1967).

(*ii*) Her daughter-in-law was *Mrs M. H. Braybrook*, Councillor (1961–4), whose father, G. T. Challenor, was a Councillor (1937–46). This family group illustrates that party affiliations cannot be closely correlated to family connections, since Mrs A. A. Braybrook was Labour, Mrs M. H. Braybrook Conservative and G. T. Challenor a Liberal.

(*iii*) *Alderman H. T. Fullwood*, Mayor (1952–3), Chairman of Transport Committee (1949–52), whose son

(*iv*) *E. Y. Fullwood* had been a Councillor since 1955.

(*v*) *Alderman L. R. Guy*, Mayor (1950–1), Chairman of Fire and Ambulance Committee (1948–54), also had a son,

(*vi*) *G. A. Guy*, on the Council from 1960.

(*vii*) *Alderman A. H. Windridge*, Chairman of Small Holdings and Allotments Committee (1949–51) and of Water Committee (1951–2 and 1954–5) was father-in-law to

(*viii*) *H. R. Elliston*, a Councillor since 1957.

(*ix*) *H. Bagley*, Chairman of Cultural and Entertainments Committee (1952–65), was the brother of N. Bagley, Mayor (1959–60), Alderman (1954–61) and Chairman of Cleansing Committee (1955–61). N. Bagley's wife was formerly

(*x*) *Mrs G. Brazier*, a Councillor since 1957.

(*xi*) *P. Farmer*, Councillor since 1951, was the son of W. H. Farmer, Councillor (1934–52), Chairman of the Care of the

Mentally Defective Committee (1940–8) and of Public Relations and Development Committee (1950–3).

(*xii*) *C. Walsh*, Chairman of Civil Defence Committee (1955–61) and of Housing (1962–3), was the nephew of Alderman J. Walsh, Chairman of Education Committee (1918–22 and 1927–9).

In the Council of 1899–1900 eight members of the Council were related to previous members; in 1962–3 seven were. Thus since the Council as a whole has increased from 48 to 60 over the period, there has been a decline in the family tradition of Council membership.

This chapter has shown that members of the Council over the period have belonged to a wide range of Associations, catering for various kinds of activities. It has shown that the division between Labour and Conservative members is not merely a political or even an occupational division, but a social one too. They did not intermingle in the social associations. At the turn of the century, when Labour representation was small, the Council was a fairly homogeneous social unit and the main divisive factor was religion. During the course of time this factor receded from prominence, and a polarity emerged between Labour and Conservative members, each group inhabiting its own world and only coming together on the Council. Thus the Council served as a device to bring together the two groups; it was itself a force for socialising divergent interests. A further point of significance is that Labour members had fewer contacts with social associations than the Conservatives. Labour members were more closely involved in party and trade union work than the Conservatives were in the functions of their party and trade associations. Thus the Labour members could be said to be more like 'politicians' than the Conservatives. For the Labour member, the party, the trade union, and indeed the Council, loomed larger in his life than for the Conservative member, who had a range of other interests to occupy his attention. A conclusion from this is that Labour members were therefore more likely to make effective Councillors than the Conservatives, who were not so immersed in the business of the Council. The Conservatives, however, with a wider range of interests than the Labour members, might be able to bring a wiser sense of judgement to Council and committee deliberations. There is no means of testing if this was so beyond giving a purely personal assessment.

The Labour Councillors were likely to be more effective in opposition than the Conservatives. The former would stick to their Council work in opposition, since their life was so concentrated on the Council and their party. But the Conservatives, not so devoted and with a wider range of interests, would feel the state of opposition to be unrewarding. They would feel that their talents were being neglected and could be put to more fruitful use. Hence the exodus from the ranks of the Conservative Councillors in the 1950s of a number of men who had held Chairmanships before the Labour Party took them all.

7 The Calibre of the Council

CHANGES in the occupational composition of Town Councils have been regarded as indicating a decline in the quality of the elected representatives. Fewer people, it is said, with experience of administration and the responsibility for taking executive decisions have been coming on to the Councils, while an increasing number of middle-aged housewives, trade union officials and old-age pensioners has lowered the tone and the efficiency of local government. L. J. Sharpe has disputed this exclusive concentration on occupation as a measure of the ability of the Councillor: he has advocated the consideration of such intangibles as 'integrity, political *nous*, will power, judgement and local knowledge', but he still believes that 'a person's occupation can tell us something, but certainly not everything about his likely qualities as a councillor'.[1] Yet doubt can be cast on even his guarded claim by the experience of Wolverhampton.

In Wolverhampton, as on the national stage, the contention has been that the calibre of Councillors has shrunk, and the same reasons are given. Basically the main cause, so it is claimed, is the influence of party politics, and especially the advent of the Labour Party on the local scene. *The Economist* in 1960 bemoaned 'the new type' of Councillor who entered local government not to serve the community but because his party had asked him to stand, whose main concerns were not the burden of the rates but the work of his particular committees and the national fortunes of his party.[2] This charge was by no means new: eighty years earlier a leading article in *The Times* complained of the intrusion into local government elections of party politics, so that no longer

[1] L. J. Sharpe, 'Elected Representatives in Local Government', *British Journal of Sociology*, 1962, pp. 189–209.
[2] *The Economist*, 30.1.1960.

were the Councillors 'upright and thoughtful and courageous administrators', but 'docile tools of party politics'.[1] In Wolverhampton dismay at the low standard of Councillors is of long standing. After the municipal elections of 1885 the *Express and Star* deplored the apathy and called on the political parties to take part in municipal elections: 'There would be little difficulty in placing in and keeping in the Council men of a class all too few there now if only the political organisations of the town would bestir themselves in our Municipal as they do in the Parliamentary elections.'[2] The thirty years' experience of Alderman Craddock on the Council revealed that the problem of attracting able people to local government is not of recent origin. In 1897 he 'had to lament that so many of our leading townsmen refused to take their part in the government of the town to which they belonged';[3] and in 1923 he despaired that 'for many years he had tried to get men of that kind to come forward and take their part in the work of the Council, but the reply he sometimes got was "if you're fool enough to do it, I'm not!" '[4] These examples come from a period when party politics was not so pervasive in local government as it is today. In no case was party thought to be the cause of the failure of the able people to come forward. In 1944 a Conservative Councillor, W. H. Farmer, feared that the quality of the Councillors would not be sufficient to tackle the tasks of post-war reconstruction. To make them worthy of their new responsibilities, he proposed an age limit of seventy, a limitation of entry to those

[1] *The Times*, 3.11.1880.

[2] *E. & S.*, 3.11.1885. Two years later it again complained at the lack of contested seats. 'All the boroughs in the Kingdom are doing their best to improve the personnel of their Town Councils. Wolverhampton is doing nothing. . . .' And this was a time when the paper regarded the Council as 'a haughty, plutocratic, oppressive, supercilious, obnoxious body with horse-head proclivities'. *E. & S.*, 1.11.1887.

[3] *W.C.*, 26.5.1897.

[4] *E. & S.*, 29.10.1923. Alderman Craddock referred often to this topic. In 1898 at a dinner of the Ancient Order of Foresters he said he was 'depressed about the future of Wolverhampton chiefly because he found that the very best men of the town would not consecrate themselves to its service'. (*Midland Evening News*, 22.11.1898.) In 1900 he 'could not understand how it was that all the good men of Wolverhampton still remained outside that chamber'. (*W.C.*, 7.11.1900.) Before Craddock, Alderman Major had stated that 'there were many in the town who were well-cultivated and able to perform the duties in connection with the Corporation and other public offices, but who would not take upon themselves such duties.' (*E. & S.*, 9.11.1889.)

between twenty-one and fifty, free elocution lessons ('since some were forced to be yesmen because they lacked ability to express themselves'), refresher courses on local government, and payment of members.[1] Thus the inadequacy of the Councillors was not due to party but to their age, inarticulateness, ignorance and to the fact that service on the Council involved a serious diminution of their earnings.

Two former Councillors can illustrate the contemporary opinion. In his Mayoral speech of 1951 James Beattie said that he was disappointed at the failure of representatives from big industrial businesses in the town to enter the Council. Such men with special experience of large-scale management and administration he regarded as invaluable to the Council.[2] In 1957 he returned to this theme. Local government had failed to attract and hold a great number of those best qualified to serve on local authorities. He blamed the political parties, who had made it impossible for a candidate to stand as an Independent, and yet had failed to substitute from their own ranks candidates of similar or higher calibre.[3] Another ex-Councillor complained of 'deadbeats' on the Council, Council house dwellers who had never signed a four-figure cheque and who had never even possessed a cheque book. He was especially bitter about the appointment as Mayor of C. H. Davies, whom he castigated as an old-age pensioner, often on the dole, whose last job had been to open and close the gates of the gas works. Most Conservative Councillors when interviewed on this question were convinced of a fall in quality; that there was no one on the modern Council with the business acumen and social standing of Baldwin Bantock or Sir Charles Mander, and that the leading professional families of the town, like the Skidmores, no longer played their part in the Council chamber.[4] The former Town Clerk of 1919–29, Warbreck Howell, said that in his day substantial men entered the Council keen to serve the public

---

[1] *E. & S.*, 4.7.1944. In the 1920s and early 1930s the local paper considered that 'apathy' among the electorate meant that 'it becomes increasingly difficult to get representatives of the right type to offer themselves for public service.' *E. & S.*, 1.11.1924 and 25.10.1932.

[2] *E. & S.*, 21.5.1951.

[3] *E. & S.*, 27.9.1957.

[4] One said that when he was a member (1915–19) his colleagues were men of 'character, ability, wealth and a well-known name which entitled them to respect.'

and with no political axe to grind. But no one in Wolverhampton has stated that he personally had been deterred from standing for the Council because of the party political system. Further, the business and professional men who did enter the Council, even around the turn of the century, were very active within local political parties, and often held the leading official positions in their parties. Their political activities were well known and were not a deterrent to their becoming members of the Council.

Thus complaints that the quality of Councillors has declined are not recent, and party politics have not always been held to be responsible. This suggests that decline in quality did not set in about 1945, when the Labour Party first gained a majority on Wolverhampton's Council; indeed the antiquity of the complaints suggests that there may have been no decline at all.

Sharpe's opinion that occupation can reveal something of the potential of an individual to be a successful Councillor is based on the assumption that if a man holds a position of executive responsibility in private life, or is used to taking administrative decisions or has had professional training, he is thereby better equipped as a Councillor than someone who wholly lacks that kind of experience, notwithstanding the importance of the other less tangible variables that are not the prerogative of any one social class or occupation. One former Labour Councillor supported Sharpe's view because of his observations of a Conservative Councillor, who was the sales promotion manager of the town's largest departmental store. His position demanded that he took daily decisions of vital importance for the store. This experience had made him used to responsibility and authority, which earned him the leadership of the Conservative Group in 1962. On the other hand a Conservative Councillor praised the ability of the trade union officials on the Council, whom he regarded as making excellent Chairmen. Their experience in handling trade union committees, in drafting and presenting reports, and the training given to them by their unions, he considered as fitting them well for Council work. This opinion is relevant also for most of the Labour members of the Council. As the leading members of the party in the locality, they had great experience of committee work through their membership of the many committees which proliferated in the party; in addition as officers of their trade union branches they had further opportunities for becoming adept at committee work. Skill in this kind of work was likely to fit a man or woman better for Council work, which largely consists of committee work, than skill in running a business or a profession.

Tables XXI and XXII show the correlations between the occupations and the calibre of the members of the Council. The assessment of the member is based on a personal evaluation by the author, grading each into one of four classes.[1] The first-class members have come from the manufacturers, the 'drink' trade (really brewery owners), the superior white-collar group of administrators and working men. All groups have provided members who were of no consequence on the Council, but the 'drink' trade (really publicans), women, the inferior white-collar group, the retired and the shopkeepers have provided the majority of this bottom category. The administrative group produced most at the top and fewest at the bottom, while the professional group, the working men and women, have provided most of the solid competent types who have made a significant contribution to the Council. Those who have made a minor contribution of little distinction have been mostly shopkeepers, clerks and professional men. But there have been so many exceptions to any assertions correlating occupation with calibre that occupation is useless as a basis for a generalisation. Some examples of such exceptions follow.

Alderman W. M. Furniss was a highly successful businessman, the Managing Director of the Electrical Construction Company, and President of the Chamber of Commerce (1920–2). He was Chairman of the Council's Electricity Committee (1927–30). Furniss resigned from the Council in 1930, very hostile to his Committee. His letter of resignation[2] stated that 'while there was some small chance of my doing good work for the town of my adoption I was prepared to carry on, but it has been so plainly shown to me today that I have little knowledge of the profession in which I have made my living that I feel that to remain on the Council would be a pure waste of time'. Commenting on the resignation the Mayor said that 'it was indicative of the business-man who in the ordinary course found the procedure of Council

---

[1] This method is explained more fully on pp. 160–2.
[2] *E. & S.*, 10.2.1930.

work slower. Business people believed in getting on with the
job and they sometimes found the statutory limitations imposed on
municipalities irritating.'[1] Furniss was clearly not suited to the
exigencies of local government committee work, and his unfit-
ness was largely due to temperament and to his experience as a
businessman.

Other successful businessmen left the Council with poor reputations, while others, who made a relative failure of their private affairs,
gained great prestige for their public services. F. S. Thompson
was the Chairman of a large engineering firm, a member of
the Council (1925–45), Mayor (1943–4), Alderman (from 1939)
and Chairman of Water Committee (1930–41). Despite excellent
paper qualifications, he is remembered by some as a deplorable
Chairman, lacking purpose and direction, unable to control the
committee, always letting members ramble far from the point.
A similar case was G. E. J. Luce, Councillor (1927–45), Alderman
(from 1944), Mayor (1938–9) and Chairman of Parks and Cemeteries Committee (1942–5). Leaving school at the age of eleven, he
took his first job as a butcher's boy and rose to become the town's
leading baker and confectioner, with a café, shop and bakehouse in
the main square of the town. He was a prominent Freemason and
Chairman of the Wolverhampton Freeholders' Permanent Building
Society. He was a well-recognised personality in the town, always
sporting a white carnation and large diamond tiepin. Here clearly
was a successful businessman who had attained a leading social
position in the town. But many attested to his uselessness as a
Councillor. One said that he continually needed help. The other
said that he had little ability and he failed to understand how he
made so much money. A former Councillor described him as
illiterate and recalled how incoherently he had read his Mayoral
speech. Another member of the Council, J. H. Coleman, was
described by various colleagues as 'effete and helpless, without
initiative or brains', 'ineffective', 'decent, harmless and of no
influence', and as a man who 'never made a noise'. Out of fifty
years' membership of the Council he was Chairman of committees
for about only two years, and then only of minor committees.

---

[1] *E & S.*, 10.3.1930. A chief official said that Furniss had built up his company
by ability and drive: but he was a man who lived on his nerves, was used to
taking rapid decisions and therefore did not fit into Council work.

This obvious failure, however, was the first secretary and founder of the Wolverhampton and District Chemists' Association and for thirty-six years was a director of the Wolverhampton Freeholders' Permanent Building Society. He left in his will £53,415. Obviously outside the local authority he was effective.

On the other hand one of the most successful Chairmen was not successful in business. Joseph Clark was a Councillor (1912–54), Mayor for two terms (1923–5), Alderman (from 1925) and Chairman of Education Committee (1928–54). In 1952 his civic patriotism was praised: 'his enthusiasm, ability, wide experience in the work of education and in the general conduct of public affairs had earned for him the respect and esteem of the Council and the public'.[1] The Conservatives advocated that he be granted the Honorary Freedom of the Borough. So devoted was he to public service that he neglected his private business as a building contractor.

Eminent Chairmen have come from the ranks of trade union officials, the working class, old-age pensioners and women. Alan Davies was a Labour Councillor (1919–54), Mayor (1929–30), Alderman (from 1931) and Chairman of the Transport Committee (1925–49). Men of all parties acknowledged him as a most distinguished Chairman and Councillor, who had shaped the transport system of the town and had immensely improved the hospital service; 'first-class, able, charming' and 'most excellent' were some of his descriptions. He was a railwayman who had risen from a cleaner to be an inspector and had retired in 1938 at the age of sixty-five. He led the Labour Party during the war and for the first two years after, staying as Alderman until his death in 1954 at the age of eighty. Even at the close of his life he was influential and no one ever condemned him as senile. Thus a railwayman, an old-age pensioner and a man who left in his will only £9. 2s. 8d. could be a first-class Councillor.[2] Always linked with the name of Alan Davies as an able Councillor and leading figure in the Labour Party was C. W. Hill, who was secretary of the West

[1] *E.& S.*, 23.6.1952.
[2] In 1930 at a Mayoral Banquet a Conservative, R. A. Willcock, spoke of him – 'he has stuck to the line, has kept a good head of steam, has looked out for the signals and has never been known to miss the point'. *E. & S.*, 11.10.1930. Doctor Craig described him as an 'assiduous worker', 'a man of self control and quiet determination'. *E. & S.*, 11.11.1929.

Wolverhampton Labour Party for over forty years while Davies was Chairman. Hill entered the Council only after retiring from the railway, where he had been a clerk. He, too, died in harness at the age of seventy-six in 1952. He and Davies so arranged their membership of committees that they knew the policy of every important committee. 'A great figure of power', 'with all at his finger tips', 'a good organiser', 'sincere, able and firm' were some of the epithets applied to Hill, the old-age pensioner from a humble background who 'dominated the Labour Party' and together with Davies effectively ran the Council from 1945 to 1947. Harry Bagley, Labour Councillor (1945–65), and Chairman of the Cultural and Entertainments Committee (1952–65) was listed in the yearbook as an engineer; often he was unemployed through illness or at work provided by friends; he was clearly not of executive calibre and therefore, by Sharpe's theory, unlikely to be an effective Councillor. Yet officials regarded him as a powerful force in committee and Council, a man who knew what he wanted and with the skill to see it implemented. He was responsible for the speedy construction of the Aldersley Sports Stadium on its particular site. Bagley was especially disliked by the Conservative Party, which saw him as attempting to make his ward, Bushbury, the centre of Wolverhampton and as seeking to channel all improvements and amenities into this ward.[1]

The female members of the Council are not negligible. The first woman member, Mrs. E Sproson (1921–7), is remembered as being a most persistent questioner and critic of the financial administration of the Corporation. Ruby Ilsley, wife of a railwayman, Councillor since 1941, Alderman since 1952, Mayor (1957–8) and Chairman of Health Committee (1955–67) is regarded as a vigorous and able woman, skilled in achieving her aims. 'Intelligent', 'very forceful and dominant', and 'powerful' are some of the phrases used by her colleagues and officials to describe her.

The importance and significance of these sketches is to show

[1] In 1956 the Conservative leader J. Beattie led an attack on Bagley's Chairmanship, over the building of the stadium. 'We must stop a committee which having set its heart on an ambitious scheme intentionally or unintentionally, withholds the ultimate cost of it from the Council and then having got approval for part of the cost claws its way into far greater sums of money in such a manner with such indefinite reports and with such lapse of time between reports that no one knows what is really happening at all.' *E. & S.*, 8.5.1956.

that occupation is not necessarily a meaningful indicator of ability as a Councillor. Successful businessmen have failed in local government, while old-age pensioners, women, working-class individuals, all people with no executive experience have been outstandingly efficient. Sneers against this type of person are not warranted by the evidence. One reason why the businessmen failed and the others succeeded is perhaps a question of time. The businessmen were absorbed in their own private affairs, with little time or energy to spare for local government, while the others were able to devote themselves wholeheartedly to Council work. 'Time' is the aspect pointed out by one solicitor as being the most important. He stated that most professional people are deterred from public service not because of party politics but because of the lack of time to play a really full part in committee and Council. The housewives and old-age pensioners can be full-time Councillors, while the ordinary worker, shut off from responsibility during his daily work, can find an outlet for his organisational and administrative ability through work in the local authority.

Another reason for the success of the humble in origin and for the failure of the more socially elevated, is the training and experience gained by so many Labour Party members in the Party and in the trade union movement. In the committees and sub-committees at ward, borough and constituency level and in the trade unions at branch, district and area level, most of the Labour Councillors worked either as members or most often as Chairmen, or as some other officers, like Secretary or Treasurer. Such experience stood them in good stead for Council work which involved much committee work. Conservative Councillors seemed not to have so many opportunities; their committees were fewer and, most important of all, their progress to the Council did not depend on years of work within the party.

As we have shown above, the Conservative members of the Council were involved in many other than merely party-oriented activities. For this reason they did not make such devoted opposition members of the Council as did the Labour Councillors. Out of power, with no responsibility, they had little incentive to stay in the Council and pursue a negative critical role. Thus we can say that they were not such 'politicians' as were the Labour members.

After 1955 Labour took all Chairmanships and Vice-Chairmanships, and this policy, it can be argued, drove away such an outstandingly able man as James Beattie, who was Chairman of Finance Committee from 1951 to 1955. Without a Chairmanship such a man would have thought that his talents were wasted and his abilities could be better employed elsewhere.

Therefore it can be said that politics drove some able men out of local government; not only in the sense that the Labour Party, in gaining seats on the Council, therefore reduced the chances for a businessman to enter the Council, but also in the sense that the Labour Party, by introducing Parliamentary techniques into the Council in taking all the Chairmanships, deterred businessmen from joining the Council, since they felt that they would have nothing constructive to contribute.

The quality of the Councillor, his ability for Council work, cannot be assessed merely by his occupation. As we have seen, some businessmen were failures on the Council, and some workmen, women and old-age pensioners were generally recognised as first-class Councillors. This does not mean, however, that there were not able businessmen and useless workmen, women and retired members on the Council. Examples of such are as plentiful as the examples of the failures among the businessmen, and successes amongst the women, workmen and retired. The only assertion is that 'occupation' in itself is no guide to the calibre of a Councillor.

EDUCATION

One test of calibre could be perhaps the education of a Councillor: but details about the educational background of the Councillors are hard to uncover especially for the earlier years of the period. Hence the large number of 'unknowns' in Table XXIII, which relates the education received by members of the Council for specific Councils with their party allegiance. The figures tell very little, except that more Conservatives and Liberals had education beyond the elementary stage than Labour members, many of whom had little more than an elementary education, although their educational standard rose over the years, with more having a secondary, higher grade and grammar school education; however, they never really broke into the public school or university-educated categories. Table XXIII shows that since 1945 out of 60 Councillors about a third, between 20 and 22, received elementary education only, and most of these, 16–18, were Labour members. The next largest group were those who had a grammar school education, most of whom were Conservatives. In Wolverhampton after 1945 the higher grade school became known as the Municipal Grammar School; no pupils of this school after 1945 had joined the Council by 1964, but many of the years before had. It is more realistic to class these people with those who received a secondary education, which brings that group to above the grammar school block. Besides these groups, a handful had been to public schools and universities.

AGE

It could be argued that the age of the Councillors might indicate their ability, since the young might be considered vigorous, and the old sluggish – though it might be argued again that the young would be raw and inexperienced, while the old with their experience and wisdom might be able to make a more useful contribution. To the author's mind such qualities do not necessarily correlate with age. The young, too, can be sluggish and conservative; and the old can be energetic and radical. In any case, as far as Wolverhampton is concerned the age of the Councillors over the period is not a helpful indicator in any way as to calibre. The main point which emerges from a survey of the ages of the members of the Council over the period[1] is that little changed between 1888 and 1962. The average age of new entrants to the Council stayed in the mid-forties; the average age of all members of the Council stayed in the early and middle fifties, while the average of the Chairmen, the key figures, stayed in the middle to late fifties. There is also no evidence that the Chairmen have come very early or very late to their Chairmanships, since the average length of time in which they served on the Council stayed between thirteen and seventeen years.[2] Thus a consideration of the age structure of the Councils from 1888 to 1962 shows no evidence

[1] See Table XXIV.   [2] See Table XXV.

that the Council got either appreciably older or younger. It
stayed about the same.

Service on the Council is less a stepping-stone to Parliamentary
office since 1945 than before. Three members of the Council
became M.P.s, all Liberals and all for East Wolverhampton:
H. H. Fowler, 1880–1908, G. R. Thorne, 1908–29 and G. le M.
Mander, 1929–45. No other member of the Council was elected
to Parliament. The Council has, however, provided four un-
successful candidates: P. Lewis, Liberal for West Wolverhampton
in December 1910; H. E. Lane, Labour for East Wolverhampton
in 1935; J. Beattie, Conservative for West Wolverhampton in
1945, and G. J. Costley, Labour for Oswestry in 1964 and 1966.
Thus it might be argued that, since the Council was not such
fertile soil for M.P.s as before 1945, the calibre of the members
had declined. But on the other hand it could be said that being
an M.P. was not so attractive for the Councillors in 1960 as in
1900, particularly for one who was the Chairman of an important
committee. This latter position might give him more satisfaction
in being able to achieve something positive than being an M.P.,
responsible for nothing. The disadvantages of a Parliamentary
candidature might deter the Councillor from embarking on such
a course; he may not be able to accept the dislocation of his
family life, nor to afford the time from his work and his Council
activities. The more he is engrossed in and devoted to Council
duties, which have increased tremendously since 1900, the less
likely is he to wish to give them up to become an M.P.

AN ASSESSMENT OF CALIBRE

To assess the calibre of a Councillor is a complex process; so
much has to be taken into account, not merely the quality of the
Councillor but the demands made on him. More is demanded of
the Councillor in the 1960s than in 1900, and thus the standards we
expect and apply are stiffer. Table XXVI assesses for specific
Councils the quality of the Councillors. Marks have been awarded
to each one on the basis of appreciation by the author, taking into
account his performance in the Council and its committees, as
revealed by the Council minutes and newspaper reports, opinions
of colleagues, their letters or contributions to the press and their

activities outside the Council. Each individual would naturally award the marks in a different way, but this approach is the nearest possible we can get to finding out if the calibre declined. The Councillors' ratings have been divided into four. Class *A* is for those outstanding figures who made a mark on the Council as a whole, on many aspects of its work and not in just one committee. Class *B* is for those who made a significant contribution in more than one field on the Council, though more narrow in the range than Class *A*. Class *C* is for those who made some mark, though usually only in one committee. Class *D* is for those who made a little or no impact at all. The Table reveals a strikingly constant situation. The percentage of Class *D* has stayed within 37–44 per cent of the whole Council; and the variations for the other types are not tremendous. However it is clear that there was a decline in the first-class members of the Council; and an increase in those of Class *C* – that is, those who made a minor impact on the Council.

Two qualifications must be made about these figures; first the figures for 1962–3 are the least accurate, since many members of the Council had yet to make their marks; this fact pushed up the numbers in Classes *C* and *D*. In addition, when considering Class *A* it is important to acknowledge that time has enhanced the reputations of the great figures of the past Councils. Memories have perhaps increased the stature of these Councillors to an extent that they may be unrecognisable to their contemporaries. In fifty years' time some members in Class *B* may perhaps be firmly placed in Class *A* by historians who were not close to them.

Table XXVII correlates this calibre rating with party affiliation. Class *A* came from all parties; Class *B* also, except that from 1945 they came predominantly from Labour. The reason for this is that since Labour kept the Chairmanships for itself, non-Socialists were not given the opportunities to make a significant mark on the Council. Class *C* comprised more Conservatives than Labour, while Class *D* was composed largely of Labour members. Thus Labour produced more of the bottom category than the Conservatives. As for the Conservatives and Liberals, in the years before 1945 the various types were pretty evenly distributed between the parties. None was predominant in any category.

Table XXVI also presents cross-sections of the calibre contained in specific Councils over the whole period. At the top are two or

F

three outstanding figures, whose scope takes in the whole field of
Council activity; then a group of men, just under 30 per cent of the
Council, usually Chairmen of committees who are directing their
committees and leaving a definite mark on the policy of the
Council; then a group of Councillors, again just under 30 per cent,
perhaps Chairmen or long-serving Councillors who are competent
and leave a small imprint on the Council, and finally the largest
group of all, around 40 per cent of the Council, those who make
little or no contribution, either because they have just joined the
Council, or are too old or because they have no contribution to
make. This kind of picture has been typical for the Council over
this whole period.

But one should not cast scorn too eagerly on those members
who made little apparent contribution to the development of the
Council's policies. The function of the Councillor is to be a
representative, to speak on behalf of and to look after the interests
of his constituents, both individually and collectively. His job is
not simply to shape policy, but perhaps quietly and behind the
scenes, for example in talks to officials, to raise and seek the redress
of grievances expressed by his constituents, and to set at rest the
anxieties of those complaining to him. This representative function
is not susceptible to measurement, and it is likely that many of
those Councillors who played little part in forming policy did
perform this representative function. It should also be pointed out
that a representative body, if it is to be truly representative, should
not contain just the talented or the competent. It should represent
everyone, even the politically uninterested and apathetic, who
form the majority of the population. A Council consisting overwhelmingly of individuals in categories *A* and *B* would not be
representative.

8 The Labour Group

A LEADING contribution of the Labour Party to local government in Wolverhampton was the 'Group'; that is, the meeting of those members of the Council belonging to one party, held before the Council meeting in order to concert the action of party members in the Council. In the 1950s and 1960s both Conservative and Labour Parties held such meetings. But at the turn of the century no such institution existed. Liberals and Conservatives did not vote as party blocks, save on sectarian issues. Normally on each debate there was a fresh coalition for or against; alignments of the Councillors were in a continual state of flux. The Labour representatives, however, from their earliest days tried to act as a block, if not on all issues, at least on matters affecting Labour. The Labour Party tried many institutional devices to ensure unity of action by Labour Councillors, and they worked smoothly until the 1920s, when the party was rocked by recurring conflicts between some of its Councillors and a majority of the party. Only in the 1930s did peace return on the adoption of the Labour Party's model Standing Orders governing the relations between Labour Groups and the party outside the Council. However, not until 1945 was the Labour Group put on a regular and formal basis; before, it had met infrequently. The non-Socialists at first had strongly opposed the Group system, but in the 1940s they too, in order to be a more effective force against the Labour Party, perfected their 'caucus'. Thus by the 1950s each party, on the same night and often only a few yards from the other, held a Group meeting.

There are three reasons why Labour from the start sought unity from its representatives. Firstly, since the party financed the election campaigns and the out-of-pocket expenses of its representatives when they were engaged on Council work, it expected them to be loyal to party policy and to advance it in the Council. The constitution of Wolverhampton's Labour Representation Committee stated that 'the candidate selected shall have all printing, hire of halls and every expense incurred paid by the L.R.C.'[1] Once elected they were to be paid 9*d* per hour for 'all lost time from employment while engaged on representative duties', with an upper limit set at £6 in a year.[2] In return the representatives had to 'agree to abide by the decisions of the party in carrying out the aims of this Constitution'.[3]

Secondly, the Labour Party had a municipal policy to advocate. To achieve it required concerted action by Labour representatives, all the more important when they were not in a majority and when their only hope of success was to win over some non-Labour members of the Council to their proposals. Wavering by any member would injure the cause.

Thirdly, the Labour Party was infused with the trade union tradition of collective action. Most of the members of the L.R.C., and the Labour Councillors, were active trade unionists; local trade union branches financed the L.R.C. and the leading items of the Labour policy were to attain trade union objectives. Trade union experience taught the Labour Party the value of collective bargaining; only by presenting a united front could aims be realised.

Conservatives and Liberals, on the other hand, had no parties to finance their elections and expenses: these burdens individuals bore themselves. They had no municipal programme to propound; they had no tradition of trade unionism, and they did not face a hostile majority. Therefore they had no incentives to act as party blocks on the Council.

THE DEVELOPMENT OF THE GROUP

Before 1910 the activities of the Labour Councillors were supervised and co-ordinated by the L.R.C. There was no special institution for this function. The L.R.C. 'empowered', 'authorised', and 'requested' Labour representatives with regard to specific courses of action. It laid down their policy on workmen's cheap

---

[1] Rule 8, *M.L.L.P.*, May 1910.   [2] Ibid.   [3] Rule 3.

fares, the Girls' High School and the salary of the Electrical Engineer. Councillors reported to the L.R.C. about the work of committees they were on, and asked the L.R.C. what action they should take on the Council, for example 're. an application from the Borough Band re. engagements for the Parks'. Matters great and small were considered by the L.R.C. The Councillors were not regarded as possessing a corporate identity distinct from that of the party of which they were members. There were too few of them on the Council for such a divergence to emerge. Thus the L.R.C. considered municipal affairs in the Council, along with their other activities. It ran the elections, deciding which wards were to be fought and which candidates, nominated by the affiliated organisations, were to stand. It organised the campaigns and supervised the drawing up of the election addresses. It was also the body which was responsible for the Parliamentary campaigns.

Thus the L.R.C. combined the functions performed in the 1950s by the Group, the Borough Party and the Constituency General Management Committee; that is, it carried out Council, municipal and Parliamentary functions.

In 1910 an attempt was made to separate Council matters from the general work of the L.R.C. by establishing a Consultative Committee, comprising 'Labour members of governing bodies. and five elected members from the L.R.C. together with the Chairman and Secretary'. It was to meet once a month, and at its first meeting it decided to convene on the second Thursday of the month at 9.00 p.m.[1] These intentions, however, were never fully realised; between 1910 and 1913 the committee met only three times, the first meeting in the full flush of initiation to hear a report from Councillor Sharrocks on 'work to be done in Council', and the other two called specifically by the L.R.C. to consider particular items. Even at these the full complement of Councillors did not attend, three being absent in September 1910. The reason why the committee did not at first take root was that the L.R.C. continued to exercise its old functions. It still 'instructed' Councillors; it told them to watch 'the question of Corporation employees not being paid the standard rate of wages', to press for

[1] *M.L.L.P.*, 2.6.1910. It was thus not dovetailed in with Council work, since the Council met on the first Monday of each month.

the Land Acquisition Bill to be put into operation, and the representatives were asked to give reports about the work of their committees to the L.R.C.

Between 1914 and 1920 the Consultative Committee met more often than before. It was intended that it should meet on the Sunday night prior to the Council meeting next day,[1] and for the first time the committee systematically examined the agenda of the Council meeting for the following day, deciding the Labour attitude to the items on the agenda. The L.R.C., although allowing the committee to deal with more business, even referring some to it, such as the implementation of the Feeding of Necessitous Children Act, the Maternity and Child Welfare Centre and unemployment, retained supremacy. It told the Council members to vote against increases of salary for officials, to urge a municipal supply of coal and to support the establishment of a Building Guild.

As the number of Labour Councillors increased so did opportunities for division among them, and between them and the party outside the Council. In addition, changes in the Labour Party's constitution encouraged division within the party, since for the first time members could join the Labour Party as individuals and not, as previously, only as members of affiliated organisations. Previously the party had been predominantly a trade union pressure group, but now with the influx of people who were not primarily the spokesmen of trade unions it witnessed clashes between the two sides, which had earlier manifested themselves as conflicts between the trade unions and the I.L.P.[2] The conflicts which struck the party in the 1920s and disrupted the relationship between the Councillors and the party were mainly between the moderate trade-union-oriented Councillors and the extremist more doctrinaire Socialists whose home before 1918 had been the I.L.P.

This dichotomy is clear from the first big quarrel in the party in 1923 which provoked a revision in the local constitution. In the

---

[1] *M.L.L.P.*, 17.3.1914. Again a good intention, but not regularly carried out.

[2] e.g., *M.L.L.P.*, 1.10.1908. The I.L.P. wished to change the rule which allowed only trade unionists to stand as Labour candidates. Their request was rejected. The *Express and Star* commented that 'relations between the two sections have never been quite so cordial as could be desired'. 7.10.1908.

Town Council Mrs E. Sproson, a strong I.L.P. supporter, accused A. Davies, a railwayman and a trade unionist, of covering up mismanagement of the Borough Hospital.[1] After an inquiry by a Council committee she was severely rebuked.[2] The party divided 5:5 on a motion that she had not acted in the best interests of the party in that she had not consulted the party first.[3] The outcome of the dispute was a revision of the local rules. A new Consultative Committee was established, consisting of the elected Councillors,[4] two members from the Eastern Divisional Labour Party, five from the Western, one from the Trades Council, and the Trades Council's co-opted member on the Education Committee; all had full voting rights.[5] The new constitution stated that 'in all cases in which the policy and principles of the Party are affected a majority vote shall be binding on all members'.[6] 'No member shall make any resolution at a Council meeting until the same has been agreed upon by the Consultative Committee', and no question was to be asked before the opinions of the Labour members on the committee concerned had been consulted.

But a final settlement was still far away. From 1924 to 1930 the Wolverhampton Labour Party was torn by dissension over the voting behaviour of its Councillors in the Council chamber. Over these years some Councillors refused to accept the majority decisions of the Consultative Committee and failed to conform to demands made on them by the Labour Party to obey the decisions of the committee. In 1924 some voted to increase the Town Clerk's salary, against a decision of the committee; some refused to accept the committee's decision on Aldermanic vacancies; the Town Clerk's salary again provoked a split in 1926; and in 1928 some Councillors voted in favour of a grant of £400 to the Roman Catholic College of St Chad's against a committee decision.

These defections were followed by many meetings of the local Labour Party where recriminatory motions of censure were proposed against the rebels: their expulsion was demanded; threats to withdraw support were made and they were asked to

---

[1] *C.M.*, 14.5.1923. *E. & S.*, 14.5.1923.
[2] *C.M.*, 1.8.1923. *E. & S.*, 2.8.1923.
[3] *M.L.L.P.*, 10.8.1923.
[4] Labour had no Aldermen at this time.
[5] *M.L.L.P.*, 4.11.1923, 17.11.1923.
[6] *M.L.L.P.*, 4.11.1923, Clause v.

give undertakings to obey committee decisions in the future. The supporters of the rebels in their turn proposed that nothing be done, that the matter be dropped, that the Councillors be left to make up their own minds and that in any case the issues over which they had disagreed with the committee had not been questions involving the principles or policies of the party. No side was ever able to get the upper hand: they fought themselves to a deadlock and the party was paralysed. In 1924, for instance, the minutes from March to October were taken up with controversy about what should be done to the rebels.

Attempts to escape from the impasse were sought by convening joint meetings of the Executive Committees of the Constituency Labour Parties together with the Councillors to examine the constitution of the Consultative Committee in order to make it work effectively. The proposals went back and forth between the Executive Committee and the Party; new rules were devised for the Consultative Committee and its composition was altered again and again, to no avail, for as soon as a new system was arranged some Councillor or group of Councillors disobeyed a decision of the committee, and again the party was quarrelling. Typical of the views expressed by the anti-rebel group was a motion proposed by St George's Ward in 1926.[1] It said that 'it is about time that there was unity amongst our Town Councillors when in Council and less hobnobbing and pandering to the other party, and we call on the Executive Committee to discuss the agenda of all Town Council meetings (prior to Town Council meetings) and to arrive at a decision on every item of the agenda and to instruct our Councillors to vote and support every decision arrived at by the Executive Committee. Further any Councillor acting contrary to any decision arrived at by the Executive Committee should be dismissed from the party and forced to resign from the Town Council.' This motion expressed the views of those who wanted the Councillors to be completely the servants of the outside party. Their plan was to abolish the Consultative Committee, since it had failed to secure obedience, and to put control firmly in the hands of the Constituency Party.

It was clear that, in spite of the tinkering with the rules and composition of the Consultative Committee, it was a failure. In

[1] *M.L.L.P.*, 7.1.1926.

1928 a new solution was suggested for the first time, that 'the Committee be composed of Public Representatives only.'[1] This motion, like the St George's motion, was defeated, and the party limped on, crippled by dissension. Members were expelled; others resigned; the Consultative Committee failed to get a quorum; Councillors refused to turn up at party meetings. The moderates more and more urged that the solution was for the Councillors alone to decide their actions in the Council. A solution was in sight. At the Labour Party's annual conference at Llandudno in 1930 the National Executive Committee's draft model Standing Orders for Labour Groups were accepted. In Wolverhampton the Executive Committee examined them; the Council Group looked at them also, and the party then agreed to put them into operation.

The Group was to consist of members of the Council only, who alone were responsible for taking decisions on matters coming before the Council. The local Labour Party could send three representatives in a consultative capacity, able to speak but not to vote. The Labour Party could express its views by communicating to the Group secretary or through the three representatives, while the Group could appoint a representative to report from time to time on its work to the Constituency Labour Party.

Restrictions were placed on the actions of the members of the Group. Resolutions, motions or amendments could not be submitted to the Council meeting unless they had first been submitted to and received the approval of the Group meeting. Members, without consultation, could ask questions in Council, provided their tendency was not likely to be in conflict with the policy of the Labour Group. Members were not to speak or vote in opposition to a Group decision, unless it had been decided to leave the matter to a free vote. If a matter of conscience arose a member could abstain from voting, provided he first raised the matter at the Group meeting to ascertain its feeling. If any member violated the Standing Orders, the whip could be withdrawn, after due notice was given and after consultation with the local Labour Party. The outside party still possessed the ultimate deterrent of refusing to readopt a rebel as an official Labour candidate when the Councillor or Alderman came up for re-election.

The acceptance by the Wolverhampton Labour Party of these

[1] *M.L.L.P.*, 24.4.1928.

J.B.P.

model Standing Orders apparently ended the deadlocks which had paralysed the party in the 1920s. The 1930s witnessed no more expulsions. However, it was not the adoption of a formal set of rules which produced such harmony: indeed the full Group system did not come into its own until after 1945. Only then did the Group meet regularly and have its own minute book and its own formal procedures and officials. Other factors than Standing Orders brought consensus to the Labour Party.

Firstly, the division between the moderates and the extremists, who in the 1920s had been the protagonists, was no longer in the 1930s a feature of the Labour Party's internal affairs. The extremists left the party to follow W. J. Brown and his I.L.A., and they remained there until the I.L.A. disbanded in the late 1930s.[1] The people left in the Labour Party were of a similar outlook; they worked together harmoniously and were given an additional incentive to act together in unity by the presence of the I.L.A. intent on poaching their members.

Secondly, the leadership of the Labour Party in Wolverhampton fell into unquestionably able hands. One man, the railwayman A. Davies, was Chairman of both the West Wolverhampton Labour Party and the Wolverhampton Municipal Labour Party and he was also the leader of the Group; another railwayman, C. W. Hill, was Secretary of both the West Wolverhampton Labour Party and the Group. These two together ran the Labour Party in Wolverhampton until 1945, and remained a most significant influence until 1952. By all accounts by both Labour and anti-Labour, they were able, commanded the respect of their followers, kept their fingers on the pulse of all Council activities and exercised a moderate, tactful yet firm leadership. These personal qualities enabled the various bodies of the party to work together, as did their overlapping leadership of such bodies. Their hold over the party was such that when the I.L.A. group returned to the fold they were unable, and indeed unwilling after the fiasco of Brown, to challenge the well-established leadership.

Up to 1945 the Group met irregularly only when Davies and Hill called a meeting, and then often only half an hour before the

---

[1] Indeed their defection enabled the model Standing Orders to be accepted by the Labour Party; if they had been present they would have opposed the adoption of the orders.

Council meeting was due to start. At the Group meetings Davies and Hill really led the Councillors in the direction they wanted; they told the Councillors what the policy was to be and there was no question of leaving it to the meeting to decide after a rancorous and lengthy debate. They were the spokesmen of the Group, leading the party in Council debates and negotiations with the non-Socialist leaders and the officials. Their policies were not contested by the Constituency or Municipal Party since these two bodies were also under their firm management. The personal leadership of Davies and Hill did far more to harmonise the various institutions of the Labour Party than the adoption of the model Standing Orders. At the very moment in the early 1930s when at long last formal machinery had been devised to settle the quarrels over the spheres of interest of the Group and the Party, informal personal leadership rendered the formal rules irrelevant.

In 1945 the formal rules again came into prominence, as the informal leadership was challenged. The 1945 municipal elections increased the size of the Group from nineteen to thirty-two and for the first time the party had a majority. These two factors, the increase and the new responsibility, meant that the old system could not last; thus the working of the Group was formalised. It acquired a minute book, elected officials, devised rules for its procedure and arranged to meet regularly on the Friday night before the Monday Council meeting.[1] In addition, the rule of Davies and Hill was challenged. They were now ageing; Davies was seventy-two and Hill sixty-nine, while the majority of the new Councillors of 1945 were in their thirties and forties. In 1946 Davies retired as leader after the Group failed to follow his advice to oppose the campaign to hold Council meetings in the evenings. For three years three men acted as leaders of the Group, but none could give the kind of lead that Davies had done. Indeed it could be said that Davies and Hill continued until 1952 to be the informal leaders of the Group.[2] The official leader, F. Mansell, was a compromise figure for a party bitterly divided between the followers of two younger men, H. E. Lane and G. Rastall. Lane, an orator and an extremist, was scathing and sarcastic in speech and, far from

[1] *Minutes of the Labour Group,* 7.11.1945.
[2] Hill died in December 1952 and Davies in January 1954.

conciliating people, provoked quarrels. Rastall, a moderate right-winger, was slow and dull in speech, yet had a full command of Council work and was skilled in conciliating and managing people; he was greatly respected by the anti-Labour members of the Council, unlike Lane, who was detested or ridiculed. Lane and Rastall disliked each other, as did the followers of each; this situation opened the way for a compromise figure like F. Mansell, who had no firm views but was able to bring together the warring elements of the party. Lane had been chosen as leader in 1946, with Mansell as Vice-Chairman. When Lane was Mayor from 1947 to 1949, W. H. Hale was leader; in 1949 Mansell was elected leader. Mansell retained this position until he became Mayor in 1955; then Rastall defeated Lane for the leadership and in the following year Mansell returned, again defeating Lane. Thus after the departure of Hill and Davies the leadership of the Group was not so firmly based. From such an insecure position the leadership was not able to give a clear lead, nor was the leader personally able to do so; indeed that was why he was chosen. Those who were able to lead, it was feared by a significant number of the party, were likely to lead the party in the wrong direction; better, then, to have as little leadership as possible.

PARTY STRUCTURE

The formal organisation of the Labour Party after 1945 consisted of the basic units, the ward parties, and trade union branches, affiliated to the Labour Party. These were entitled to send delegates, first, to the organisation which was responsible for the running of the constituency, that is, Parliamentary affairs; this body was the General Management Committee, one for each constituency; and, secondly, to the organisation responsible for municipal affairs, the Borough Labour Party, one body for the town as a whole, on which sat representatives from the two constituencies into which the town was divided for Parliamentary purposes. Each of these two bodies elected annually an Executive Committee, which in practice executed nothing, since it reported everything back to the parent meeting, which was jealous of its powers as the ultimate authority and discussed most decisions of the Executive in great detail.

The Labour Group consisted of all Labour members of the

Council, and three representatives of the Borough Party, who could speak but not vote. Their role in theory was to co-ordinate the work of the Group with that of the Borough Party. In practice, however, they were superfluous, since co-ordination was achieved by overlapping membership. Councillors were usually members and officers of ward parties, Management Committees and of the Borough Labour Party. These connections enabled the bodies to work together in step. The Borough representatives on the Group were very poor attenders at Group meetings and only one, A. Cattell, was of significant influence.

The Borough Labour Party was responsible for laying down the general policy to be pursued by the Group; and the drawing up of the policy was the responsibility of the Policy Committee, consisting of twelve members of the Group and twelve from the Borough Labour Party. This body comprised the leading figures of the party in the town, the chief Councillors and officers of the other bodies. In theory it looked impressive; and annually the motions were gone through of electing it, though this consisted of re-electing *en bloc* the previous members. Its real function was not so much to initiate and formulate policy as to draw up an election address to be presented for the approval of the Borough Party.[1] The function of the Group was to implement this policy, though it alone determined how in the Council it should be implemented in detail. The Group was therefore solely responsible in theory for deciding what aspects of policy should be carried out, and for interpreting what the policy actually was. None of the other bodies could dictate to the Group; they could send resolutions to the Group requesting a particular course of action, but the Group alone decided whether or not to accept the advice. Possibilities of conflict between the Group and the party outside existed in theory, but in Wolverhampton clashes did not occur, because harmony was obtained by the interlocking leadership. In addition, since all Group members were members of the Labour Party and entered the Council through flying the Labour colours, discipline could be enforced on them individually by the withdrawal of the

[1] In 1957 and 1959 the election address was drawn up by a Committee of ten: 5 from the Group and 5 from the Borough Labour Party. In 1964 the election address for the Labour candidates in the North-East was drawn up by a leading Councillor, while that for the South-West was the creation of the South-West's agent.

party's support when their inclusion on the panel came up for review. This threat was used on those individuals in the Group who dissented from a Group decision. This type of conflict – that is, between individuals inside the Group – was more common than a conflict between the Group as a whole and the party outside.

THE WORK OF THE GROUP

The Labour Group met for its normal sessions eleven times a year: on the Friday evening before the Monday Council meeting. The Council agenda arrived at the Councillors' houses on the Wednesday before. In theory the Labour Councillor was supposed to examine the agenda and thus come primed to the Friday Group meeting, but complaints were frequent that Councillors opened their agenda envelopes only on arrival at the Group meeting. The place of meeting varied, since the Labour Party had no permanent place of residence after its premises were bombed in the war. The Group met in rooms hired from public houses or dance halls, in temporary party premises, in rooms hired from the Co-op, and in the 1960s it began to meet in the Committee rooms of the Town Hall; a symbol perhaps of a more respectable status, and a recognition that the functions it performed contributed usefully to the working of the Council. Indeed the Group had become in practice a Committee of the Council.

The main business of the Group meeting was to go through the agenda. The Chairman read out the page numbers and paused for contributions from the floor. At this stage questions were asked on the item reached; answers were given by the Chairman or spokesman of the appropriate Council committee; or else the Chairman of the committee on his own initiative explained the background to a resolution and its problems. Mansell said that his main aim was to get through the agenda quickly so that the meeting beginning at 7.45 p.m. would be over by 9.45 p.m., in time for members to get out to a public house. Since most of the items did not raise controversy, Mansell was often able to do this. If conflict arose, then a debate took place, followed by a vote, and the majority decision was binding on all members. If the issue was an important one then the item was often adjourned for a special Group meeting devoted wholly to that topic, for instance in the 1950s on housing finance, the rate for the year, civic catering and the Workshops for the Blind.

The Group planned the tactics of its members for the following Council meeting. The movers and seconders of motions were selected; speakers were designated; points to be made were rehearsed. It was decided whether or not to force an issue to a division. Replies to Conservative questions were planned, and sympathetic questions were organised from Group members. Permission was requested to move motions and ask questions. At each stage an eye was cast on the tactics of the opposition and means to outwit them were sought. If an election was near then consideration was paid to the effect a particular line might have on the result.

Another function of the Group was to arbitrate between committees and particularly between Chairmen; for instance in 1956 the Chairman of Watch Committee complained that the estimates of the Public Works Committee for the construction of police houses were too high. The Group had to rule on the matter. The Group also had to settle quarrels between the members of one committee.

Members of the Group claimed that the ordinary monthly Group meeting kept them informed of the activities of committees on which they did not serve and enabled them to see the work of the Council as a whole. Any queries or misunderstandings could be solved and disputes settled. It kept the members in touch, informed and educated them. It also facilitated the business of the full Council through holding a rehearsal. The unnecessary, trivial or ill-informed question could be eliminated. Debate could be concentrated on a few leading topics, and irrelevancy could be removed from the speeches. A certain order could be brought, therefore, to the Council proceedings. The Group also took decisions following debate on controversial issues by means of a majority vote, and the binding nature of a majority decision on all ensured that responsibility could be pinned publicly on a particular Group. A definite party could be held accountable by the public.

The Group did not initiate or formulate policy. It had not the time to go into detail. Normally after the agenda had been finished there was little time to deal with 'any other business' at any length or depth. Its function was to register or reject proposals drawn up elsewhere and to decide the Group's attitude to particular propositions. Therefore it did not look ahead and plan for the future; it was a 'hand to mouth affair' living from agenda to agenda. It was not a Cabinet but a miniature Council. The Group therefore waited on events, and, save for the occasional special meeting to consider a single item, it did not examine policy in depth; even the special meeting was a response to an immediately pressing problem. To overcome these drawbacks other towns instituted regular mid-monthly Group meetings, in addition to the agenda or epitome meeting, to discuss general policy, to look to the future and to consider particular items in detail. They also established sub-committees of the Group to be responsible for certain spheres of policy, and set up a policy sub-committee of the Group, comprising the leaders and the Chairmen of the main Council committees, to act as a Cabinet plotting future courses and co-ordinating the work of the various committees.[1] In Wolverhampton, however, there was no mid-monthly Group meeting, no policy sub-committee nor sub-committees charged with policy responsibilities.

In 1952 an attempt, the only one, was made to set up a kind of Cabinet of the Chairmen. The impetus for this development came from the return to power of the Labour Group, but this time without the leadership of Davies and Hill. Two men, G. Rastall and A. Cattell, felt that, with their grip relaxed, there was little co-ordination, that committees were going off on their own without regard to a general policy and that, particularly in the field of finance, estimates were being drawn up without regard to overall resources and policy.[2] They suggested that a meeting of the Chairmen should alternate with Group meetings. Bi-monthly meetings were accepted, to be attended by both Chairmen and Vice-Chairmen. Three meetings were held, which discussed the financial implications of the policies of certain committees. Then it was decided not to meet regularly, but only when called by the Chairman and Secretary. At the December Group meeting a

---

[1] L. J. Sharpe, 'The Politics of Local Government in Greater London', *Public Administration*, 1960, pp. 157–72. H. V. Wiseman, 'The Working of Local Government in Leeds', *Public Administration*, 1963, pp. 51–69, 137–55.

[2] *M.L.G.*, 3.6.1952. Rastall said, 'unfortunately the Group is not aware of what is happening until it is on the agenda'. *M.L.G.*, 22.8.1952.

number of complaints were made against the system, the main objections being that members of the Group were kept in ignorance about decisions taken by the Chairmen. They never met again. Reasons for the failure of this experiment were not limited to the resentment of those excluded from the meeting that decisions were being taken over their heads; the Chairmen themselves did not want to be more effectively controlled, especially over their estimates. They preferred the weak supervision exercised by the full Group to control by a smaller, more experienced body. Mansell, the leader, did not like the system, which detracted from his leadership and elevated the position of Rastall. Mansell preferred to deal individually with each of the Chairmen and not to be submerged in a type of collective leadership, where he would be overshadowed by more forceful colleagues. He claimed that the system never really worked well and that he and the majority of the Chairmen preferred the informal means of co-ordination through personal contact.

Paradoxically an additional reason for the failure was the very factor which gave rise to the demand for the system, namely the accession to power of the Labour Group. If it had remained in opposition, without the firm leadership of Davies and Hill, it would have been forced, as the Conservatives were later,[1] to turn to its own resources, to obtain information, plan ahead and concert its activities more effectively. But since the Group was in power, the Chairmen settled quickly into their committees and got on good terms with their officials, who kept them supplied with information and policy ideas. By their Chairmanships they were exalted above the Group and had no incentive to defer to Group control. They put the interests of their committees before the interests of effective Group control.

The implication of the failure of Rastall's plan was that the Group did not initiate policy or plot out the forward lines of advance. It was relegated to saying 'for' or 'against' to policies devised elsewhere. And the place where policy was devised and formulated was in the committees of the Council, or more accurately in most cases it was thought up by the officials, who then planted the policy inside the minds of the Chairmen, who in their turn guided the committees. Some towns, recognising that this was

---

[1] See below, Chapter 9.

so, set up Group meetings for members of the same party on each committee on a permanent basis. In 1952 Rastall proposed the establishment of such 'advisory committees' for the Education and Health Committees. None materialised. Only the Education Committee had very occasional Group meetings for its members, for instance to discuss comprehensive schools. Normally the members huddled together for a few minutes before the committee or its sub-committees met.

Since there was no formal Group supervision of the Council committees, people sometimes complained that a policy decided by the committee would be rejected by the full Group and then in open Council members would have to speak against their previous position and the committee would have to withdraw its agreed policy. In practice, however, this did not happen. On most issues Group policy was known, or at least its general tenor was, and this was a sufficient guide to the position to be adopted. If an item arose on which Group policy was unclear or unknown, the Chairman would find an excuse to defer a decision until the next meeting so that consultations could be had with the leader and perhaps a special Group meeting was called. In most cases the officials were not likely to spring on a committee an item of importance requiring an immediate decision.

Another objection laid against the Group system was that decisions were often taken without adequate knowledge, since the officials of the Corporation could not be present to advise. If they were to attend, it was argued, their neutrality would be compromised, since they were the servants not of one party, even if it had a majority, but of a committee and of the Council consisting of members of all parties. No official ever attended a full Group meeting: none was ever asked. If asked it is not certain that they would have refused, since the Director of Education attended an Education Committee Group meeting when invited to talk on comprehensive education. Even if they did not attend, their views were known and discussed at the Group meetings.[1] The Chairman of a committee was usually very close to his chief officer and was able to explain his position to the Group. If an official's views were not known or his advice was needed, then the Group would defer a decision until he had been sounded out. There is no

---

[1] An argument for holding the Group meetings in secret.

evidence that decisions were made without adequate official advice: indeed a criticism often made is that the officials were too influential, that the Chairmen were their mouthpieces and that the Groups did not effectively tell the officials what the public would not stand.

The officers of the Group consisted of the Chairman (the leader), the Vice-Chairman, the Secretary and the Whip. After 1949 the leader was F. Mansell, the Chairman of Transport Committee. This committee required little attention, and thus he was free to overlook many aspects of Council work. In some towns the leader has no committee to Chair and acts as a Prime Minister, but in Wolverhampton it was felt that the leader should have a Chairmanship to keep him in contact with the problems of a Chairman and the running of a department. In any case it was a minor committee. Mansell, as we have seen, was a compromise choice without the personality of a leader. Many are the complaints that he failed to give a lead; he was described as a voice or a spokesman of the Group. He issued statements on behalf of the Group; he discussed with the Town Clerk and other officials; he negotiated with the leader of the opposition, for example over Aldermanic vacancies, or discussed with him the estimates for the year. He informed the Mayor before the Council meeting of those members wishing to speak in the debate. He was consulted by the Chairmen of the committees about problems of their committees; if the item was minor he would give a quick decision, if more important he would call a special Group meeting to consider the matter. Ordinary members of the Council consulted him about difficulties and brought queries to him. His forte was personal relations; he had the skill to conciliate, but he had not the inclination to give a decisive lead in any particular direction. He wanted the machine to keep ticking over, and therefore angered the more forceful of both the right and the left, but since these could not agree on an alternative leader, Mansell remained as the lesser evil.

The Secretary after C. W. Hill was A. Cattell (1953–6). He was not a member of the Council, but was the representative of the Borough Labour Party to the Group; the only one to make a significant mark on the Group. He was a highly intelligent and articulate school teacher, whose occupation as an employee of the Council prevented him from standing for the Council. He was chosen as Secretary, so he said, because he had no ambitions to be a Chairman or Alderman or Mayor. Although not a member of the Council, he said that he could always see the minutes of any committee he wished; and on his appointment as Secretary he went to see the Town Clerk to tell him that in future they would have to work together. The job of the Secretary as carried out by both Cattell and his successor, F. Smith, was to record the minutes of the Group, especially its decisions, and to write letters from the Group. He was not a mere scribe. He drafted the schemes of committee membership; he interpreted and explained Group policy to those seeking guidance. As an officer, he was a leading member of the Group and Cattell said that since Mansell failed to give a lead, he found himself on many occasions acting as virtual leader. Complaints were also made that Smith was usurping the functions of the leader.

The office of Whip was abolished in 1960 in an attempt to wipe away the image of the Group as a coercive body whipping its members into submission. The Whip's job has been to inform members of Group decisions if they had been absent, and in Council to tell them which way to vote, a necessary function given the long-winded obscurity of some motions and amendments. He had to encourage attendance at both Group and Council meetings. He helped to 'straighten out problems' for Councillors, listen to their grievances, explain the Group policy and persuade them to follow Group decisions. Most attention has usually been paid to his disciplinary functions, reporting to the Group anyone who did not vote in accordance with a Group decision. In 1960 the Secretary took over the task of informing and encouraging the members.

These three officers, together with the Vice-Chairman, who had no specific task, were the formal leaders of the Group: but informal leaders were significant too. Able individuals with a following, whose voices were listened to with respect by the Group, could sway a meeting, particularly on an issue within the purview of their committees. Such on the right of the party were Mrs R. F. Ilsley, Chairman of Health, and D. A. Birch,

Chairman of Finance Committees;[1] and, on the left, H. E. Lane, Chairman of Housing. These were often angry at Mansell's lack of leadership, but since they could serve under no other, he was tolerated.

PATRONAGE

A function of the Group which took up much of its time and caused general furore was the distribution of patronage. Who was to be Alderman, Chairman of a committee or Mayor – indeed, who was to be a member of which committee – were the questions which continuously disturbed the Group. The allocation of members to committees was relatively easy. At the start of each municipal year, informal talks with the opposition leaders attempted to establish a balance of party members on each committee to reflect the parties' positions in the Council. Once that had been agreed or once the Group had decided on the proportion, the Secretary called for the wishes of the members about the committees on which they wished to serve. He produced a draft scheme, trying to accommodate their views, and, after consultation with the other officers, submitted it to the Group; then individuals voiced complaints and explanations were given. Normally this process caused little trouble.

The Chairmen in theory were elected by their committees each year. In practice the Group decided and the party members on the committees then voted them in. In 1945 the Group decided not to take all the Chairmanships: it decided which to take and who was to take them. When Labour lost the majority in 1949, the Group decided that none was to be accepted. In 1952, on regaining their majority, they decided not to take all, and settled which to take and who was to take them. The Group was divided at this time: one set wished to take them all; others, fearing that the Labour Group had no able people to replace particularly the Conservative Chairmen of Education and Finance, succeeded in persuading the Group to share the Chairmanships with the opposition. In 1955 this set was defeated and all the Chairmanships

[1] Birch thought that he should have been the leader of the Group since, as Chairman of Finance, he had connections with all other committees and since finance was the most important factor in any policy decision.

and Vice-Chairmanships were taken. The one side advocated that
all Chairmanships should be taken so that one party could be seen
to accept responsibility for the whole range of Council policy; it
was crazy, they argued, to have a Conservative as the Chancellor of
the Exchequer or the Minister of Education in a Labour Government. They said that such Chairmen without a majority in their
committees could not take day-to-day decisions with the confidence
of their committees' backing, nor could they really speak for their
committees in Council. The other side argued that it was doctrinaire to throw out able Chairmen, whom Labour could not
adequately replace. The difficulties of sharing, they claimed, had
been exaggerated: in practice no problems arose from sharing. But
after 1955 the Group decided who should be Chairmen of all
committees of the Council; and the Chairmen of School Governors.

The Mayor in theory was chosen by a Mayoral committee
comprising ex-Mayors, who recommended to a full Council meeting
a name, which was adopted. In practice when the Labour Party
was in a majority, the Group decided whether to take the Mayoralty and, if so, who was to be Mayor. In some towns arrangements
were made between the parties to share the Mayoralty; for
example, one party is to have it for one year, the other for the
next.[1] In Wolverhampton the Conservatives during the 1940s,
1950s and 1960s repeatedly tried to get the Labour Group to
agree to a set of rules governing the sharing of the Mayoralty. But
the Labour Party refused to have an agreement, chiefly because
the Mayor might have been a vital element in deciding who should
control the Council, since the majority of one party was never
overwhelming. Also the Labour Party contained many people
who aspired to the Mayoralty, powerful people at that, who had
entered the Council about the same time and who therefore
believed they had a right to the office. The Conservatives were
allowed to nominate for the Mayoralty only when the outcry
against the Labour monopoly of the office had become too loud
and might have adversely affected the position of the party.[2] Hence,
as with the choice of Chairmen, the Group decided by voting
who was to occupy the position.

[1] See W. Thornhill, 'Agreements between Local Parties in Local Government
Matters', *Political Studies*, 1957, pp. 83–8.
[2] 1958 and 1962.

The same voting process took place with regard to the Aldermen. Again the Conservatives sought to reach an arrangement with the Labour Group over the allocation of Aldermanic seats in proportion to the party majority. The Group was divided over this issue. Some favoured an agreement; others advocated that the Group should take all vacancies, when they arose, because the Aldermen could have been the key to control. The compromise position reached between these two views was that each vacancy was to be considered as and when it arose in the interests of expediency. The Group adopted delaying tactics to make the Conservatives think an agreement would be reached, but none ever was. The Labour Group wished to maintain its freedom of action and to consider each case as it arose. When the Group decided to take an Aldermanic vacancy, as with the Mayoral vacancy, it voted; voting was necessary because there were so many contestants, because of the large number of Councillors who entered the Council in 1945 between whom it was hard to decide seniority, which was the criterion for election to the bench.

Thus over patronage two types of issue arose: first over relations with the Conservatives, over whether as a Group they should choose the Chairmen, the Aldermen and the Mayors; and, secondly, inside the Group, over which member of the Group should actually be elected as the Chairman, Alderman or Mayor in question.

DISCIPLINE

The aspect of the Group's work which attracted most attention is that of disciplining members as regards their voting in the Council chamber. We have seen that in the 1920s this was a contentious issue. In the 1930s it became less important, and since 1945 the minutes of the Group reveal numerous cases where Councillors did not vote in the Council in accordance with a Group decision. The common practice was for a deviant to be reported to the Group, when an explanation was invited and was usually accepted. Normally defection was rare, since party loyalty, common ties, personal relationships and adherence to a common programme and set of principles meant that the members were in harmony on general policy and direction. Therefore the contentious issues which arose were usually of minor significance and could be and were ignored and forgotten. Once or twice since 1945 members became so alienated from the party that they consistently voted against all Group decisions, eventually left the Group, were invited to attend the Conservative Group, stood as Independents or Conservatives at the following election and were defeated and vanished from the Council. Such were B. Dagnan in the late 1940s, and Mrs M. Cattell in the late 1950s. Such cases were rare, since they rebelled not merely over one issue, but over many and for a long period of time. Only when it was clear that they had become out of tune with the party were they expelled.

Therefore Councillors voted together not because they were coerced, but because in most cases they were in agreement with each other. The criticisms often made of the Group were twofold and unfair. If the members of the Group did not vote together, the opposition would accuse them of having not made up their minds; if they did vote together they would be condemned as servile. Since most business was uncontroversial, few issues of conflict arose, and on most of these all were in harmony. If one Councillor decided on a single issue not to vote with the Group, he would be put on the mat, and if that was his only deviation nothing would follow but a mild rebuke. If, however, he had a record of defection then in the end he could expect to be removed or to withdraw himself.

In the Group debate on issues was free: anything could be said in complete secrecy and security, since the press was not admitted. After a full debate, a vote was taken and the majority decision was binding on all members, unless permission was given for particular individuals to abstain. They could request permission to abstain; sometimes it was given, sometimes the Whips were put on. Sometimes free votes were allowed. By the standing orders they could abstain on matters of conscience like religion.

Another aspect of discipline was the attempt made to ensure that all members of the Group were present at the Group meetings, so that they could take part in the debate and vote on the decision, that is, so that they could share in the responsibility for decision-taking. The Group was always concerned about poor attendance. Officers were asked to contact and encourage absentees, or in serious cases the Group sent messages to poor attenders. In the

1950s the Group met 14 or 15 times a year, for agenda and special sessions. The leading figures had attendance records of 12 out of 15: then came the majority of around 9 out of 12 attendances and then the others tailed off below 8 because of illness, laziness, other activities or a temporary alienation from the Group. This pattern of attendance was typical after 1945.

One drawback of the Group system and its discipline is that the policy ultimately approved by the Council may not command the support of a majority of the Council. An example of this occurred in 1959 over Housing Finance. The Borough Labour Party was divided equally, 22 : 22, over whether to adopt a differential rent scheme. The Group divided 19 against and 10 in favour. Thus all the Labour members, 39 in all, were committed to oppose a differential scheme. All the Conservatives, 21 in all, were in favour. Thus in open Council the measure was lost. However, if, of the Council as a whole, all who were in favour of the scheme had voted for, they would have had a majority, since at least they would have had 31 votes against 29. Such an issue is rare. Only two rebelled against the Group's verdict: one expressed sorrow and promised to obey in future; the other, Mrs Cattell, voted with the Conservatives afterwards. The other Labour members who voted with the Group and yet privately wanted a differential scheme explained that they accepted the Group's decision because the issue was not one of such overriding importance that they were prepared to cut themselves off from their colleagues, with whom they agreed on most other items of policy. Very often the criticisms made of the Group system attach undue significance to features which occur only rarely, and in no way typify the functions of the Group.

The Group system came into being in Wolverhampton not just because the Labour Party happened to conduct its affairs in this way. It arose to enable the Town Council to fulfil its functions in the twentieth century. In structure the Council formally exhibited its origins in the nineteenth century, at a time when the franchise was narrow and the Council's functions were not extensive. The twentieth century witnessed the widening of the franchise and from this the growth of mass parties, notably the Labour Party with a distinctive local policy. To achieve this policy required co-ordinated action by its Councillors. The Group fulfilled this need, as well as enabling the larger electorate to hold their rulers responsible, since the Group system allowed the public to see which group of men was responsible for a particular policy. In addition, the growth in the duties of the Council made it vital to have a co-ordinating body to overlook all aspects of the Council's work and to harmonise the activities of the various committees. The Town Clerk and the Treasurer and the Finance Committee performed some of this work, but the Group system enabled it to be performed more effectively by the elected representatives. The Labour leader, Mansell, justified the Group system with the statement that through it a majority can obtain a mandate to direct the town's affairs and can be held responsible to the electorate.[1]

[1] *E. & S.*, 23.9.1955.

9 The Conservative Group[1]

DEVELOPMENT OF THE GROUP

IN 1900 the non-Socialist members of the Council had no formal organisation which met before the Council meeting to plan their course of action inside the Council. This was because neither the Conservative nor Liberal Parties professed distinctive municipal programmes, which they required their representatives to implement; they did not fight local elections formally as parties; they did not pay the election expenses of their members who contested seats, nor did they pay their Councillors any out-of-pocket expenses. Nor had they a tradition of collective action. On the Council the members of one party did not continually vote together as permanent groups, for on each issue there was a new combination of individuals.

However there were informal meetings of members of the Council to discuss Council affairs. These were 'get-togethers' to 'talk over' policy, held in the political clubs. The Conservatives met in their Deanery Club, which in 1902–4 the Liberals regarded as the centre from which the Anglican policies on education emanated.[2] The Liberals met at their Liberal Club, or else talked over Council matters after Chapel with their Methodist and Congregationalist friends. Informality was the keynote of these sessions: they were not organised; no summons to attend were issued; no officers were appointed. Councillors were not compelled to act as consistent voting blocks on all issues. These 'get-togethers' can hardly be called official party meetings: rather they were informal meetings of like-minded men, where they could discuss Council affairs, give and take advice and extract information.

If an important issue arose on the Council, the usual way to round up support or opposition was for individuals to canvass

[1] Up to 1960 it was called a 'Caucus'.
[2] *W.C.*, 29.4.1903.

their friends. For instance in June 1936 a motion came before the Council to increase the salaries of the chief officials. On hearing about this proposal Councillor W. J. Rawlins hurried around to his closest colleagues, urging them to oppose. They then pressed other Councillors close to them. The other side canvassed also. At the June meeting the voting was 25 for the increase and 25 against, and the Mayor gave his casting vote in favour. Canvassing began again, more fiercely. At the July meeting 26 voted to rescind the resolution, but 29 voted against. On both sides were members of all political parties.[1] This example is typical of the way in which support was gained for a particular measure; a small nucleus would canvass on a personal basis as many Councillors as possible. There was no attempt to impose a party line. Liberal Councillors claimed that the Liberal Constituency Association did not instruct them or give them advice; nor did they meet before the Council as an official Liberal Group to decide on a peculiarly Liberal position in the Council. As for the Conservatives, the minutes of the West Wolverhampton Conservative Association's Management Committee reveal between 1907 and 1945 only one occasion when the Association expressed any view about the activities of Conservative Councillors on the Council. In 1928 the minutes report 'considerable dissatisfaction amongst Members of our Committees at Conservative Town Councillors voting for the contract for the purchase of R.O.P.'.[2] These Councillors had voted that 40 per cent of the petrol used by the Corporation's Transport Committee should come from Russian Oil Products Ltd. Some Conservatives had opposed the purchase of Soviet petrol 'on principle' despite its cheapness and high standard, because the proceeds would go 'to foster the forces of revolution and anarchy'.[3] No further action was taken. The controversy died. The Conservative Councillors were not torn by such quarrels as divided the Labour Councillors in the 1920s: nor did their outside party Associations seek to instruct them as regards Council matters. The Associations did not regard their Councillors as their servants to implement a given programme.

The traditional means of obtaining support ended in the late

[1] *C.M.*, 8.6.1936 and 13.7.1936.
[2] *M.M.C.*, 20.3.1928.
[3] *C.M.*, 12.3.1928. *E. & S.*, 13.3.1928.

1930s, with the growth in the number of Labour representatives and with the deaths of two men who had led the Council for over twenty years. Before the 1930s the Labour members had been too few to force the non-Socialists to act together consistently as a united block. By 1939, however, the Labour Party formed the largest single group of Councillors,[1] and thus the non-Socialists had to act together or else, divided, they would let the Labour Party have its way.

In 1938 the two leading men on the Council both died: in February A. B. Bantock, Chairman of Finance Committee since 1917, a Liberal;[2] and in August J. F. Myatt, Chairman of Public Works Committee since 1917, a Conservative.[3] For over twenty years these two had been the leaders of the Council, the dominant influence. The Town Clerk from 1919 to 1929 said that if any policy was approved by the two, then it was guaranteed to get through. After their deaths no one was left on the Council with their stature to replace their personal leadership. To fill the void there emerged a collective leadership, which to rally support to its proposals had to adopt new methods, since individually each had not the prestige of Bantock or Myatt to influence followers. Thus to enable the non-Socialists more effectively to combat a growing Labour Group and to fill the vacuum left by the deaths of Bantock and Myatt arose the anti-Socialist 'Caucus'.

The Caucus was a meeting held before the Monday Council meeting, either half an hour before or else, for more important issues, on the Friday evening before, to which were invited all non-Socialist members of the Council. There was no compulsion to attend. Since it comprised Conservatives, Liberals, Ratepayers and Independents, the evening meeting could not be held at a political club, for fear it became associated with a particular party. Most often it was held in a room rented from the main hotel of the town or over the shop of one of the Councillors. Not all those invited attended; only a few came regularly, and these were the 'cornerstones' of the Council, mainly the Chairmen of the Council committees, like T. W. Simpson of Town Planning, J. Clark of Education, R. E. Probert of Health and W. J. Rawlins of Sewerage. From these were chosen the officers, Chairman and Secretary.

[1] See Table VI. [2] *E. & S.*, 9.2.1938. [3] *E. & S.*, 15.8.1938.

The form of the meeting was to go through the agenda; the Chairmen would explain their policies and answer questions, rank-and-file members would express their views. It was an opportunity for the leadership and 'backbenchers' to exchange opinions and to try to reach general agreement. The atmosphere was 'free and easy'; discipline and compulsion were not in evidence. One Councillor who had the opportunity to attend both the Caucus, as an Independent, and later the Labour Group after switching to that party, said that the only difference between the two bodies was that the Caucus was not so concerned with discipline and the need for all to vote the same way as was the Labour Group. Also since the Caucus was composed of members of more than one party, the discussion ranged not so much over what would benefit any one party, but over the merits of the case under discussion. Members voted later in the Council as their consciences dictated.

Conservatives claim that they adopted the Caucus system reluctantly, only to meet the Labour threat. Since Labour was organised, the anti-Socialists had also to organise or else they would let the Labour Group take over control by default. The ideal way of running a Council, in the Conservative and Liberal view, was for each ward to select a representative for his personal qualities; and on the Council and in committee this individual would judge each issue on its merits with only the good of the town as his objective. The Councillor should not be elected because of his party affiliation and should not vote in Council as a member of a party block. In the 1920s and early 1930s the non-Socialists frequently attacked the Labour Councillors for subservience to party decisions, pointing out that the Labour Party expelled Councillors 'because they wanted to use their own judgement in voting in the Council chamber'.[1] The ideal of the non-Socialists was inappropriate in the changed conditions of the twentieth century, with a widening of the franchise, the growth of a mass party with a particular local policy to implement, and the increase in local government functions. Thus the Conservatives had to adopt the very practices which they had once condemned, although many of their Councillors still express longings for the old system when party did not prevail.

[1] *E. & S.*, 31.10.1930.

The Conservative defeat in 1945 'shook up' the Conservative Association. With the Labour Party in a majority on the Council it was felt necessary for the Caucus to act more as a united block than it had in the past, and this meant that a majority decision should prevail. In addition the new Conservative candidate, Enoch Powell, was urging that the Independent and Ratepayer Councillors and candidates should stand openly as Conservatives in order to assist the party's Parliamentary prospects. He was aided in this task by Councillor T. G. Williams, Chairman of the South-West Wolverhampton Conservative Association, who pressed candidates to change their labels and urged the Caucus to act as a solid anti-Labour group. These developments upset some of the Ratepayer and Independent Councillors, who resented having to give up their labels and to conform to Caucus decisions. At one point in 1950 Councillor J. Ireland was about to establish a separate Independent Caucus, distinct from the Conservative Caucus, but he was prevented from doing so by the tactful per- suasion of the Chairman of the Caucus, J. Beattie, when he made it clear that only by combining the Conservatives and Independents in a united group could the Labour Group's control be prevented.[1] The crisis passed and the Caucus carried on as the Conservative and Independent Caucus.

In 1954 the Conservatives took stock of their position in the town. In the minutes of the Conservative Caucus is to be found a paper entitled 'An appreciation of the Wolverhampton Local Government party political situation as at July 1954'. It bemoaned that the years 1950–4 had been 'disastrous for all who opposed Socialism on the Wolverhampton Council, having lost 9 Council- lors' seats, 2 Aldermanic seats and control of the Council'. It reviewed the working of the Conservative and Independent Caucus.

'There never has been close co-operation between the Caucus and the two Conservative Organisations. This may partly be due to the fact that all 3 in the past wished to maintain their independence and were fearful of complications which might arise from closer co-operation.'

[1] *E. & S.*, 9.5.1950. In 1949 the Caucus had passed a resolution describing its role as 'purely an anti-Socialist co-ordinating body', saying that it bore 'no allegiance to *any* political or non-political body in the town'. *M.C.G.*, 25.11.1949.

The Caucus was also hampered by the absence of discipline within its ranks and the existence of several members who claimed independence from all parties. 'These members have given most valuable service to the Caucus, and as individuals, and because of their anti-Socialist support, they have been most welcome. In return they have shared in such honours and appointments as have been earned by the Caucus as a whole.

'Nevertheless they have in the past few years been the cause (sometimes quite unintentionally) of major crises, with the result that the Caucus and the Associations have sometimes found themselves as opponents.[1]

'The greater part of the work on the Council is still non-political and many members of the Caucus cling to the hope that party politics may find expression only to a limited degree. These members are perhaps a little frightened that closer co-ordination with the political associations, may cause them to beat the political drum rather more often and rather more loudly than they would wish.' The paper then stated the future responsibilities of the Caucus:

(i) to get its house in order and to do everything in its power to act as a single unit and with the strength and confidence which comes from unity.

(ii) to so conduct itself and develop its team spirit that would-be Councillors (especially those already in positions of responsibility in the town) will be attracted by it and by the privilege of becoming one of its members.

(iii) to do all in its power to assist the Associations to find candidates.

Despite this review little changed in the working of the Caucus although no new Independent or Ratepayer Councillors entered the Council, and those who remained adopted the Conservative label or else retired from the Council when their three years were over. The Independents who were Aldermen stayed on the Council until death removed them. They attended the Caucus, though not regularly, and they were inclined not to speak or vote with the Caucus over one or two matters, for example over the

---

[1] e.g., over the position of the Ratepayers in Penn. In 1954 a Conservative and Ratepayer candidate fought for the seat. See Chapter 10.

expansion of the boundaries. The Caucus opposed extension, while the old Independent Aldermen were in favour. Such an event was exceptional. In 1960 the Independent title was dropped and the Caucus was renamed 'The Conservative Group of the Wolverhampton Borough Council'.[1] Councillors wishing to be members had to be 'known Conservatives'.[2] Thus by 1960 the two parties had their Groups of Councillors who met to do very much the same thing at the same time before the Monday Council meeting.

The Caucus gradually came to meet more and more on the Friday evening before the Council meeting: in 1953 it was resolved to meet at 6.30 p.m. save when the Chairman would decide to transfer it to 2.15 p.m. on the Monday afternoon 'in the light of the Council Agenda and the probable amount of discussion arising therefrom'.[3] The use by the Chairman of his discretion provoked complaints that matters had arisen which needed to be considered by the Caucus, yet could not be thoroughly gone into in a quarter of an hour.[4] From 1955 the Caucus met regularly on the Friday evening.[5] The Monday afternoon session was abandoned ten years after the Labour Party had abandoned theirs.

Those who could attend were at first the anti-Socialist members of the Council and by 1960 only 'known Conservatives' who were members of the Council. From 1955 the agents of the two Associations were invited and they became regular attenders; they also received copies of the minutes of the Caucus. The Labour Group's standing orders did not allow the agents to attend; in any case the Labour Party in Wolverhampton in the 1950s and 1960s had no full-time paid agents. In 1957 the Chairmen and Vice-Chairmen of the two Conservative Associations were invited to the Caucus. The Labour Group had no provision for such *ex officio* attendances. In 1956 the Conservative M.P. was invited to attend the Caucus. He came and was invited to attend whenever possible. In fact he does not appear to have come again. In the Labour Group the Labour M.P.s were never invited; none ever attended and there was no discussion about inviting them to attend. The Conservative Terms of Reference also allowed to attend, by a

[1] Terms of Reference adopted 20.5.1960, clause 2.
[2] Ibid., clause 5(a).
[3] *M.C.G.*, 18.5.1953.
[4] *M.C.G.*, 29.10.1954.
[5] From 1959 at 6.15 p.m. *M.C.G.*, 22.5.1959.

majority vote, adopted municipal candidates, potential or prospective candidates and such other persons as were needed in an
advisory capacity.[1] But only members of the Council had a right
to vote at any Group meeting.[2] The Labour Group was restricted
to the members of the Council and three representatives of the
Borough Party only. The Conservatives did not regard their
Caucus as such a closed body reserved to the Councillors only, as
did the Labour Group. This difference probably arose from the
difficulties experienced by the Labour Group in the past in
obtaining autonomy from the party outside the Council. The
Conservatives, not having had to fight for the independence of
their Caucus, did not have such a strong sense of their Caucus as
an autonomous unit.

OFFICERS OF THE GROUP

The officers of the Caucus were the Chairman, Vice-Chairman
and Secretary, elected annually at the start of each municipal year.
Only once in the 1950s was there a contested election, in 1956
for the Chairmanship and Secretaryship. Their functions were the
same as those of the Labour officers: the Chairman presided at the
Caucus meeting, acted as the spokesman of the Caucus, negotiated
with the Labour leader and Town Clerk and advised members
about the policy of the Caucus. The Secretary kept the minutes,
dealt with Caucus correspondence, drafted members to committees and generally advised members about Caucus policy. The
Conservative Caucus never had a Whip, nor any officer charged
with the responsibility of watching how members voted: a sign
of the lesser importance attached by the Conservatives to discipline.

The leader of the Conservative Caucus, like the Labour leader
Mansell, was a compromise candidate. The Conservatives were as
divided as the Labour Party, but not so much over ideological
issues. A number of divisions could be detected in the 1950s and
1960s but they did not all coincide. There was the group of old
Ratepayer and Independent Councillors who had adopted the
Conservative label and could not be called keen partisans. They
did not play a prominent part in the Conservative Associations.

[1] Terms of Reference, clause 5(c) i, ii, iii.
[2] Ibid., clause 5(c) iv.

They invariably sat for the safest seats. The keen partisans who were active in the Conservative Party were often those who sat for marginal seats and who owed their positions to the party. They were often much younger than those who sat in the safer seats. There was a division between those who were active in the North-East Association and those in the South-West: the former resented the wealth and strength of the latter and felt that it should have made more efforts in the north-east to assist it regain seats. The leadership was divided so that no group predominated. Birch, the leader, was a Ratepayer who had changed his label. The Vice-Chairman, P. T. W. Farmer, was regarded as a leader of the younger, more partisan element, and the Secretary, E. Y. Fullwood, though young, was more inclined to vote with the traditional Conservative sections. Since the Caucus was so divided, Birch was unable to give a decisive lead, much to the annoyance of many, but at least he was safe and referred matters to the Caucus for decision.

WORK OF THE GROUP

The Caucus met less often than the Labour Group.[1] It had its normal monthly meetings before the Council meetings, but unlike the Labour Group it had very few special meetings to deal with particular issues. This difference arose because the Conservatives were in opposition and had therefore not the work, the responsibility nor the need to take as many decisions as had the Labour Group. Office meant more work for the Labour Group. Another result was that when the Conservative Caucus did meet it had less to discuss than the Labour Group. The latter never held a meeting at which nothing came up for discussion, but on many occasions the minutes of the Caucus report that 'no matters arose

[1] Number of meetings per annum:

	Con.	Lab.
1953–4	10	14
1954–5	11	14
1955–6	12	Unknown
1956–7	11	13
1957–8	14	16
1958–9	13	15
1959–60	12	15
1960–1	13	14

Sources: *M.C.G.* and *M.L.G.*
Attendance Registers

for special consideration'. The pattern of attendance at the Conservative Caucus meeting was similar to that at the Labour Group.
There was a core of regular attenders, a large number of moderate
attenders, and one or two who rarely attended. As in the Labour
Group concern was often expressed at poor attendance and the
officers were encouraged to urge members to turn up. The form
of the Conservative meeting was like that of the Labour Group.
The Chairman went through the agenda, reading out the subject
headings and drawing attention to noteworthy points, not merely
reading out the page numbers as did the Labour Chairman.
Members then stated their opinions, said what they thought
should be done, and commented on the Labour Party's actions.
When the Caucus decided on a line, whether to accept a resolution,
to refer it back or to amend it, the wording of motions and amendments were drafted, the movers and seconders were chosen,
speakers, questioners and questions were selected. As in the Labour
Group the tactics to be pursued in the Council were considered
and points to be made in debate were rehearsed. Members also
announced that they would ask a particular question in Council or
would speak on a certain topic.

The Caucus reached a decision on an issue either by the Chairman summarising the sense of the meeting or by a vote. The
minutes then recorded that it was decided that all should vote in a
particular way or that members should vote as they wished. The
main difference in this part of the proceedings compared with the
Labour Group lay in the role of the Chairman. The Conservative
Chairman gave the Caucus more guidance about problems, but
some of the younger members of the Caucus complained that he
was apt to give little decisive leadership, but merely waited on
events and followed the general sense of the meeting.

The Caucus meeting enabled Councillors to be put in touch
with developments in committees on which they did not serve;
they could acquire information on which to base their vote in
Council and could learn how their colleagues felt about a particular
issue. An ex-Councillor said that he found it useful to talk over the
agenda before the meeting in a secret session where 'steam could
be let off' and where they could 'kick the shit about'. A difference
in the style of the Conservative Caucus as compared with the
Labour Group arose because the Conservatives were in opposition.

Much of its work consisted of scrutinising Labour proposals and seeking out failings. For example, members announced that they had not been satisfied with the way tenders had been dealt with in the Parks Committee; it was decided to query some bad estimating and to ask for a detailed explanation; they decided to discover why no full report had been issued on a certain matter, and members of the various Council committees concerned with Compulsory Purchase Orders were asked to be extremely vigilant on this subject and to report back to the Caucus meeting regarding such orders. The Conservative Caucus acted as an opposition in the Council, continually subjecting Labour policy to criticism.

STRUCTURE OF THE GROUP

Being an opposition produced for the Conservatives a slightly different structure to their Caucus from that of the Labour Group. In 1955 the Caucus resolved that 'generally the caucus attempts to form a useful and constructvie opposition, carrying out its responsibilities in an efficient and dignified manner'.[1] To achieve this aim the Conservatives went further than the Labour Group in establishing a small policy-making body, a type of Cabinet, and policy study groups for particular topics. Since the Conservatives were in opposition, they held no Chairmanships, and were therefore not as close to the officials as were the Labour members. In Chapter 8 it was argued that the Labour experiment of a Cabinet of Chairmen failed because the Chairmen were closely bound up with their chief officials. The Conservatives, not being so tied up, were forced back on to their own resources. They therefore established a Policy Committee of the half-dozen leading members of the Council to think out policy and future lines of action, overlooking the work of the Council as a whole, and to report to the full Caucus meeting. Individuals were chosen as Shadow Chairmen to watch over the activities of particular committees and to report to the Caucus any matter likely to interest it. In 1955 W. J. Rawlins was called on to hold 'a watching brief' on the work of the Sewage Disposal Committee, of which he had been Chairman. In the following year Shadow Chairmen were allocated to all committees, and the practice was continued. At a meeting attended

[1] *M.C.G.*, 2.6.1955.

by the author it was suggested that the Shadow Chairmen should consult members of their committees half an hour before the committees met to get a 'more cogent policy'. In addition, the Caucus set up 'study groups', concerned with particular topics, to engage in research and to suggest future policy. In 1957 two were established, for education and housing. The housing study group was later asked 'to formulate a policy on slum clearance with particular reference to reallocation of commercial and shopping premises'. These study groups and the policy committee reported to the Caucus after the agenda of the Council had been examined.

PATRONAGE

As in the Labour Group the problems of 'patronage' took up much of the time of the Caucus. For a long time the Conservatives tried to reach an agreement with the Labour Group about appointments to the Aldermanic bench and to the Mayoralty. They wanted seats for the former to be allocated in proportion to the number of Councillors possessed by each party and for the latter they wished it to be granted to each party on a rota basis. On many occasions the Caucus thought that agreement had been reached with the Labour Group, but when the time came for an appointment to be made they found that the Labour Group would not be bound by an agreement. Labour's stalling tactics succeeded in confusing the Conservatives, for the Conservatives at one point were convinced that an agreement had been made, only to be disillusioned when the Labour Group would not convert a verbal agreement, a 'gentleman's agreement', into writing. The Conservative minutes show that the Labour leaders had said that they wanted an agreement to settle these disturbing quarrels but that they found it difficult to carry their rank and file with them on this issue. Thus they could only deal with each occasion as it arose.

When the Labour Group allowed the Conservative Caucus to appoint a Mayor or an Alderman, it was the Caucus who decided who exactly was to fill the vacancy. The choice was made on the basis of seniority. In 1958 the Caucus was deeply divided over the Mayoralty. They had not been allowed to nominate to it since 1952 and demand for the position was intense. Two claimants arose: J. C. Homer, who had joined the Council in January 1944, and

A. H. Windridge, who had come in July 1944. Homer was backed by the older Ratepayer and Independent groups, while Windridge was supported by the younger, more party-oriented Councillors. Windridge gained a slight majority in the Caucus meeting, but this vote was not final since the Conservatives at this time still chose their Mayor through the Council's Mayoral Committee, composed of ex-Mayors. On this committee the Labour members stayed silent while the Conservatives proposed Homer. At the full Council meeting his name was put forward; the Conservatives again split, but after a seventy-five-minute session, decided to accept Homer.[1] After this episode the Caucus decided that in future the Caucus would choose the Conservative Mayors, and not the Mayoral Committee. Thus the Conservatives followed the Labour Group's practice, and did not allow their representatives on the Mayoral Committee to disregard Caucus decisions.

The Caucus was concerned about the allocation of Chairmanships. In 1955 it protested against the Labour Group taking all the Chairmanships and claimed that they should be shared among the best qualified in the whole Council. When the Labour Group paid no attention to these complaints the Caucus declined to accept any Vice-Chairmanships or Chairmanships of Sub-Committees. Although the Conservatives made no pronouncement on this subject after 1955 it was likely that if they had got a majority, they would have taken all the Chairmanships without offering any to Labour, since each committee had its Shadow Chairman. In any case the Labour Group would not have accepted any if offered by the Conservatives, as in 1949.

The Caucus was also keen to ensure that its representation on committees was in proportion to its strength on the Council. After every election or by-election which produced a change in favour of the Conservatives, they pressed for extra representation on committees. The method of allocation to committees was similar to that used in the Labour Group. Members informed the Secretary of their preferences. He produced a draft scheme and then had talks with the Secretary of the Labour Group. It was made clear to Caucus members that the Labour Party really decided; their own people had 'not the final word in this matter'.[2] Contacts between the two leaderships were frequent. They could

---

[1] *E. & S.*, 13.3.1958 and 14.3.1958.   [2] *M.C.G.*, 27.4.1954.

be called the 'usual channels', and were not merely for discussing the composition of committees but for all aspects of policy.

DISCIPLINE

The Town Clerk said that he could detect no difference in the way the two parties operated. Their Group systems seemed to be the same and the effect on the behaviour of the Councillors was similar; they voted solidly as party blocks and spoke along the same lines. But the Conservatives claimed that on one matter at least they did differ radically from the Labour Group and that was over discipline. Their Caucus, they said, was a 'free and easy' meeting, with little or no discipline. No one was reported to the Caucus for voting against a Caucus decision; no one was 'put on the mat' or 'drummed out of the Brownies' for disobedience. Conservatives, it was said, had their own minds; if they disagreed and voted against their colleagues nothing happened. The Terms of Reference of the Caucus stated that 'any member conscientiously feeling he wishes to vote against a Group decision may do so; but should, if possible, by courtesy previously inform any member specifically concerned or the Chairman of the Group, of his intentions.'[1] But the Terms later stated that 'where the control of the Council by the Conservative Group is in jeopardy, the majority decision of the Group concerning Aldermanic Elections etc. shall be final'.[2] The minutes show no evidence of anyone being disciplined for voting against a Caucus decision, unlike the minutes of the Labour Group. In fact few voted or spoke against a Caucus decision in the 1950s, except for a few of the old Ratepayer and Independent types over, for example, the boundary extensions and the future of the sewage farm. Indeed so united was the Caucus that in October 1961 it discussed devices to create an artificial division in the Caucus to show the public that it was not a monolithic block and that it did allow its members to vote as they liked without any action being taken against them.

The minutes do reveal, however, in the way Caucus decisions were recorded, that it was expected that members would abide by the decisions. The minutes stated that all members would 'vote solidly against'; 'no member of the Caucus would take part in any

[1] Clause 6(a).   [2] Clause 6(b).

debate on the subject'; 'in future all members of the Group would vote in Committee and in the Council Chamber in favour of all contracts going out to tender'. And like the Labour Whip, the Secretary was asked to inform absent members of Caucus decisions. The implication of this form of wording is that a Caucus decision was binding. Indeed, although there was no formal and official discipline imposed, many Conservative and Independent Councillors and ex-Councillors said that 'they get back at you in other ways'. J. Ireland, a former Ratepayer Councillor, explained that the Conservative Association would threaten to refuse to help a candidate with election expenses, not to nominate him as official candidate and to run an official candidate against him.[1] In 1949 Sir Charles A. Mander, Chairman of Finance Committee and President of the South-West Wolverhampton Conservative Association, praised the work of the Direct Labour Building Department of the Corporation, which had been established by the Labour Group in 1947 in the face of fierce Conservative opposition.[2] The Caucus was angry at Mander. W. J. Rawlins was delegated to tell him that he had 'embarrassed' the Caucus. The Conservative Association was angry, too, and as a result of their hostility Mander resigned as President. Many Conservatives felt he had become too soft and mellow.

Other Councillors told of the 'moral pressure' to comply with a Caucus decision; how colleagues would cold-shoulder someone who had let the team down. One said that when he disagreed with a Caucus decision he found it convenient to be absent from the Council meeting when the matter arose. Such occasions were rare; for most of the time the Caucus was united: as an ex-Councillor said of his time on the Council, 'I found complete unity within the party's Council group, and I know this unity still prevails.'[3]

PARTY ORGANISATION

Another difference between the Conservative and Labour Groups lay in their relations to the outside party organisations. The basic unit of the Conservative Association was the ward association, or

[1] This was the fate suffered by the Ratepayer candidates of Penn Ward.
[2] *E. & S.*, 10.5.1949. He called it 'one of the show departments not only in this town but in the country'.
[3] *W.C.*, 18.4.1957.

branch, of the Constituency Association. To this body the individual paid his dues. There were no affiliated organisations.
Membership was on an individual basis. The branches, together
with the various organisations of the Association like the Young Conservatives, the Women's Section and the Conservative Clubs sent
representatives to an Executive Council, akin to the Labour Party's
General Management Committee, which elected a Management
Committee, akin to the Labour Party's Executive Committee. However, the Conservative's Executive Council did not meet as frequently
as Labour's General Management Committee, since it allowed its
Management Committee more scope than was given to Labour's
Executive Committee. This constituency organisation and the
Council Caucus was the total of the Conservative organisation.
It had nothing to correspond with Labour's Borough Party,
whose responsibility was municipal affairs only. This body in
practice consisted of members of both the General Management
Committees. It drew up the panel of candidates and discussed
Council policy; although it could not instruct the Group, three
of its members sat with the Group, with the right to speak but not
to vote. In the Conservative Organisation there was no Borough
Party, breathing down the necks of the Councillors. The ward
branch selected its own candidates, subject to the approval of the
Executive Council which was always automatic.[1] In practice members of the Caucus, who were the leading figures in their ward
branches, recommended to their branches suitable candidates.
The 1954 review of party organisation said that the Caucus should
'do all in its power to assist the Associations to find candidates'.
Thus the Conservative Caucus had a role which the Labour group
did not fulfil. Also the Conservative Caucus discussed electoral
plans, how to organise the campaign and which wards to contest;
in the Labour Party this was the function of the Borough Party.
The Labour constituency Associations were not responsible for

---

[1] In 1950 when the fight with the Ratepayers was taking place, the Executive
Council resolved: 'The right of each ward branch to elect its prospective candidate is indisputable and must remain intact.' It said that the names should be
submitted to the Executive Council so that it could express its views but,
'whatever the conclusion of the Executive Council it is repeated that ward
branches are entirely at liberty eventually to elect the candidate of their own
choice'. *Minutes of the Executive Council of the South-West Wolverhampton
Conservative Association*, 22.2.1950.

any aspect of municipal activity as the Conservatives' were. In practice, however, since the Borough Party consisted of the same people as manned the constituency organisation, it came to the same thing in the end. But since the Conservatives had no Borough Party, liaison between the Caucus and the constituency Associations was maintained by having the agents and the Chairmen and Vice-Chairmen of the Associations present at Caucus meetings, able to speak but not to vote; and in both parties liaison was further strengthened by the interlocking membership of the various organisations. The leading Councillors were prominent at the ward, the constituency and the Borough levels.

RELATION WITH THE NATIONAL PARTIES

There is no evidence that any party received instructions from its Head Office as to what municipal policy to pursue. Neither Transport House nor Central Office presumed to direct the Council Groups, although they sent a constant stream of advisory leaflets, for example, giving details of recent legislation. The Labour Group adopted the model Standing Orders for Labour Groups as recommended by the party: while the Conservative Caucus devised its own Terms of Reference without any guidance from above. Indeed the Conservatives had no model orders for Groups. A result of this lack of national direction of the Groups was that fears that the involvement of party in local government would cause national issues to take precedence over local issues did not materialise. Indeed since 1945 only in 1957 were detailed accusations made that the Council chamber was being used for national and not local objectives. In January 1957 the Labour Group attacked the Government's Rent Bill as a 'barefaced act of exploitation', 'hitting hard at the low-paid workers, pensioners and those about to be evicted', and requested its withdrawal. The Conservative leader stated that: 'it was the considered opinion of his fellow members that it was not an appropriate subject for discussion by the Council; the resolution being a matter purely of national party policy'.[1] In March 1957 the Labour Group protested against the decision to increase the price of school meals by 2*d* per day. The Conservative leader again deplored that 'a matter

[1] *E. & S.*, 28.1.1957. *C.M.*, 28.1.1957.

of purely national policy' had been brought to the Council. His colleagues 'refused to enter into discussion. They were there to administer the affairs of the town.'[1] The same charge was made whenever the Labour Group criticised the high interest rates for borrowing money. But for these events, the charge was not made. Both local Council Groups concentrated on local matters.

The Council had become, in the 1950s, like the House of Commons; a governing party with a majority facing an opposition with a minority. The fact of being in office and of being close to office caused both of them to adopt a similar system.

In the 1920s, the then Town Clerk has claimed, if Bantock and Myatt were in agreement over a matter, it would get through the Council. In the 1950s the present Town Clerk presented a different picture. Neither of the party leaders was strong enough to commit his followers to a line of action without consulting them. Neither could rely on the loyalty of his followers. Even if the two leaders agreed privately there was no guarantee that they could carry their colleagues with them. Thus the Group system has made the Council more democratic; the decision-making process was not limited to a knot of key leaders.

[1] *E. & S.*, 25.3.1957. *C.M.*, 25.3.1957.

10 Independents, Ratepayers and Other Parties

THE Labour and Conservative Parties did not always monopolise the municipal elections and the Council of Wolverhampton. Independents, Ratepayers, Liberals, Suffragists, Progressives, Communists, Fascists and Ex-Servicemen all contested wards, and some gained seats.

INDEPENDENTS

The word Independent had many connotations during the period. Around 1900 all save the Labour candidates would have ascribed themselves Independent, in the sense of not being official representatives of a political party. In the inter-war years, indeed from 1908, more and more Conservatives stood openly as Conservatives, save in those fairly safe Labour seats where the term Independent was likely to be more attractive. In the safer Conservative seats they would try to have the best of both worlds, for example in 1939 a candidate for Park Ward said: 'I am standing as an Independent candidate, free of all party politics in Municipal Administration, but nationally I wholeheartedly support the Conservative Party.'[1] During these years Liberals also used the term, as did the Councillors of those areas recently amalgamated with Wolverhampton such as Heath Town; here Independent signified not so much detachment from a particular party as attachment to a particular ward. In the late 1940s the word applied to those candidates who opposed the Conservatives' attempts to force all anti-Socialists into the Conservative mould, such as A. L. Kitching and Mrs Hayton in St James' Ward, where Liberalism flickered still. Indeed the hostility of such

[1] *E. & S.*, 9.2.1939.

Councillors was really a protest against the Conservative destruction of the last remnants of Liberalism. Also the term was adopted by Councillors who, like Mrs Cattell, stood against former colleagues.[1] Such cases are rare; as is also the use of the term which is most commonly attributed to it, the case of the lone individual seeking to represent his ward, basing his appeal not on a party but on the merits of his case and on the force of his own personality. Over the period of sixty years less than a dozen put themselves forward in this way. An example is W. A. Jones, who stood four times in the 1930s. His main proposal was to extend the Manchester Ship Canal to Birmingham, since the geographical position of the Midlands caused high transport charges and thus prevented the emergence of new industries in the area. The outcome in 1933 typifies his fate and that of other such Independent candidates who have stood without the backing of an organisation. He received 44 of 1937 votes cast.[2] There is no evidence that such candidates have been driven out by party politics, as is often argued, for example in the local press. In 1952 it was said that 'continued insistence on party labels is making it increasingly difficult for men and women interested in good local government and not deeply concerned with partisan politics to secure a seat on the local Council'.[3] Such individuals, both cranks and sound men, relying on no organised support, have but rarely come forward as candidates over the sixty years under survey, and when they did their results were miserable.

One group of candidates who did not stand as representatives of a political party between 1910 and 1920 were women. The first female candidate stood in 1910, a Miss Edridge, a Conservative nationally, who stood as an Independent.[4] In 1912 a suffragist and Independent, Miss Pearson, stood,[5] and in 1920 a Mrs Highfield-Jones, as a representative of the Women's Citizens' Committee.[6] After this date women no longer presented themselves for election just on the basis of their sex, but adopted the same kinds of labels as the male candidates. The first female

---

[1] *E. & S.*, 13.5.1960, and Mrs E. Sproson, *E. & S.*, 22.3.1927. G. J. Williams *E. & S.*, 2.11.1929. Miss M. L. Perry, *E. & S.*, 29.10.1930.

[2] *E. & S.*, 1.11.1933.

[3] *E. & S.*, 7.5.1952.

[4] *E. & S.*, 29.10.1910.

[5] *E. & S.*, 2.11.1912.

[6] *E. & S.*, 2.11.1920.

Councillor, Mrs E. Sproson, was elected as a Labour representative in 1921.[1]

THE RATEPAYERS' ASSOCIATION

The Penn Ward (Wolverhampton) Ratepayers' Society was founded in 1930, when Upper Penn was still a parish in the Seisdon Rural District of Staffordshire. Penn was originally a village on the outskirts of Wolverhampton three miles from the town centre, which in the course of the 1920s and 1930s became linked to Wolverhampton by a ribbon of houses. More and more were built until Penn became a huge housing estate of detached and semi-detached dwellings, middle-class, privately owned and owner-occupied. In the early 1930s it was a wasteland of houses, lacking proper amenities and with few social activities. The Ratepayers' Society expressed the grievances of the inhabitants of Penn, wanting to obtain for their area amenities up to the standard of their desirable residences and to provide for the area some social activities. Besides the usual whist drives and dances which the Society held,[2] it organised a flourishing Choral Society and Chess Club. Thus the Society was fulfilling its pledge as laid down on the membership card 'to provide facilities for the promotion of social activities for the bringing together of residents for the purpose of getting to know each other'.

The work of the Society was performed by a monthly meeting of the Central Committee, comprising the officers, Chairman, Secretary and Treasurer, and other members elected at an Annual General Meeting; this latter was very well attended: 140 in 1930[3] and 150 in 1932 were present.[4] The objects of the Society as outlined by the Chairman at the first general meeting were: to protect the interests of the ratepayers; to attack unduly high assessments; to give facilities for obtaining legal advice at cheap rates for fighting appeals against assessments; and to bring to the notice of the R.D.C. by concerted action the ratepayers' views concerning, among other things, the condition of the roads

---

[1] *E. & S.*, 2.11.1921.
[2] *Minutes of the Ratepayers' Society*, 11.2.1932.
[3] *M.R.S.*, 14.10.1930.
[4] *M.R.S.*, 26.1.1932.

in the parish compared with those in the Borough of Wolverhampton, and the removal of refuse.[1] The *Express and Star*[2] said that its primary aim was to attack the rateable value of premises in Wynn Road, part of which was in the borough and part in Upper Penn. Though the houses in the road were identical, those in the borough had a lower assessment than those in Upper Penn. The inhabitants felt that to appeal individually without legal advice was useless, but that by banding together they could be a more effective force and retain a solicitor. In addition, the part of the road in the borough was channelled and tarred, while that in the parish was not, and the resultant dust, so the householders complained, was a nuisance and a menace to health. Further, the dustbins in the borough were emptied each week, but those in Upper Penn were emptied once a fortnight and even at longer intervals;[3] also the Upper Penn refuse carts were pulled by horses, while Wolverhampton had lorries.[4]

The activities of the Society were therefore twofold. The first was to tackle the assessments. A solicitor was engaged; his services were paid for by a membership fee of 1s 6d and by charges levied on those houses whose assessments were to be contested at rates of 2s 6d on a rateable value up to £20, 5s up to £25 and 7s 6d up to £30. Appeals were made; those which failed before the Local Assessment Appeals Committee were taken to the Quarter Sessions at Stafford. Members were asked to pay an additional 5s towards the costs. The Society appealed against garden sheds being assessed as garages, and against garages being too highly assessed. They succeeded in having many assessments reduced.

The second function of the Society was to obtain better facilities for the area. It pressed the Parish Council and the Rural District Council for the more frequent removal of the dustbins and for a lorry to be used. It asked for footpaths to be improved, lighting to be brighter, a school bus to be provided and streets to have their houses numbered. The Society also sought to take over the Parish Council, which it regarded as dominated by a small clique with backward notions. The Society attacked the '3 years idleness in office'[5] of the 'old gang'. It packed the election meeting of the parish and took nine of the eleven seats.

[1] *M.R.S.*, 26.8.1930.   [2] 28.8.1930.
[3] *M.R.S.*, 12.11.1930.   [4] *E. & S.*, 21.1.1931.   [5] *M.R.S.*, 29.1.1931.

Almost at once the Society found a new objective to abolish the Parish Council and to have the area incorporated in the Wolverhampton Borough as a separate ward. It petitioned the Ministry and the local authorities involved. It attacked the R.D.C.'s opposition to the Bill providing for the amalgamation as 'an unwarranted spending of the ratepayers' money'. Penn would be better served and governed by Wolverhampton.[1] Their wishes were granted and Penn became a ward of the borough.

The three Councillors for the ward were all members of the Society and stood as the Society's candidates. Until 1945 they were returned each year unopposed. Then the Labour Party ran candidates against the Society's, but in vain. The manner of the functioning of the Society remained the same over its twenty-five years' existence. When a matter requiring action by the Council was raised at a meeting of the Society, the Secretary would write a letter to the appropriate official outlining the grievances and seeking redress. The Society's Councillors would see the official also, bring pressure to bear on the committee concerned, and, if need be, raise the matter in full Council. The Transport Manager was contacted about poor bus services and badly-sited bus stops, and the Borough Engineer about the need to make up some roads, to improve damaged pavements and to number some houses. The Chief Constable received protests about the diversion at night of heavy transport through the residential area of Penn, and about unsafe roads. The Town Clerk was informed of Penn's need for a branch library and for a Maternity and Child Welfare Clinic. For over twenty years the Society maintained a constant pressure on the Corporation for local amenities, waste-paper receptacles at bus stops or outside fish and chip shops, traffic signs at dangerous junctions, more conspicuous street name plates, wider footpaths, brighter lighting, pillar boxes, pedestrian crossings, bus shelters, and playing fields. A stream of complaints flowed to the Council about potholes, blind corners, dangerous cambers, overhanging hedges, flooding by storm water, unpleasant water courses and cesspools, unsightly air-raid shelters, smelly static water tanks, waste-food bins and dumping grounds, neglected traffic islands, noisy motor cyclists, flooded playing fields, missing lamps and stop-tap covers. The Society sought to

[1] *M.R.S.*, 26.1.1932.

preserve the middle-class residential character of the ward by opposing plans to establish a public house in the ward or the erection of cheap houses. Thus the Society was performing its function as laid down on its membership card 'to draw the attention of our Councillors to complaints of irregularities and to generally support them in their efforts to improve the amenities of Penn'.

Like the early Labour Representation Committee, the Ratepayers' Society was an organisation to promote the representation on the Council of a particular group, trade unionists for the L.R.C. and the householders of Penn for the Ratepayers' Society. Both organisations had a similar relationship with their Councillors. The Councillors were regarded as the servants of the organisation, bound to implement on the Council the wishes of the outside Association. But although the Ratepayer Councillors financed their own campaigns and received no expenses from their Society, they were as closely supervised by their Society as the Labour Councillors by their party. In 1938 the Society resolved that 'all Council nominees for this Association shall be expected to support any unanimous proposal, framed by this Committee and in the event of such unanimous proposal being in opposition to the Candidate's opinion, the Candidate should refrain from opposing such resolution before the Borough Council or any of its Committees'.[1] One of the Councillors was expected to be present at each meeting to give 'account of his Stewardship'.[2] One representative had to appear before the Society to answer charges that he had been drunk at civic functions. He denied that he had been 'in an unfit state to represent the interests of the people of Penn'.[3] But no Councillor was ever expelled or lost the Society's support for the way he acted in Council.

Before 1945 party politics had not impinged on the Society. Then a Labour candidate was run against its nominee. The Ratepayers' candidate, M. P. Birch, stated that the Society was 'composed of men and women of all shades of political opinion'. 'I am very strongly opposed to party politics entering into Municipal Affairs and consider that I should always be free of party pressure to enable me to work solely for the well-

[1] *M.R.S.*, 27.9.1938.
[2] *M.R.S.*, 18.10.1938.
[3] *M.R.S.*, 20.11.1934.

being of the whole of the electorate of Penn.'[1] The Labour Party complained that the Society was not representative of all opinions in Penn; in 1949 the Labour candidate, who lived in Penn, said that he had never been asked to a meeting nor had he any chance of assisting the Society to choose a candidate. He asked the Society 'how if you are non-political can you explain the fact that Conservative canvassers for Mr Birch are stressing almost exclusively the national policy of Toryism and neglecting local affairs'.[2]

But the non-political nature of the Society was not in any danger from the Labour Party, who could not muster any significant strength in Penn; it was the Conservative Party which was to disrupt and finally to destroy the Society. In 1948 Penn, which had been part of the Cannock Parliamentary division of Staffordshire, became part of the South-West Wolverhampton Constituency. Before 1948 there had been no Conservative organisation in Penn, but as soon as it became part of Wolverhampton, the South-West Conservative Association quickly organised a branch there. At the same time Enoch Powell, the new Conservative prospective Parliamentary candidate, was campaigning to have all non-Socialist Councillors sporting the Conservative colours. The Ratepayers resisted. Birch said to the Society in 1948 that 'there should be no party politics in Local Government'. A Councillor should 'not be tied down but be free to vote whichever way he pleased'.[3] He refused to adopt the Conservative label and the Chairman stressed the intention of the Society to remain 'non-political'.[4] No Conservative ran against Birch in 1949. But in 1950 when A. Baker, the Ratepayers' candidate, refused to adopt a Conservative label or attend the Conservative selection conference, the Conservative branch chose its own candidate, S. S. Tatem. The Ratepayers' Society regretted the Conservative action[5] and restated its intention to be non-political. The Conservative Association was attacked by the Ratepayers and Independents on the Council for opposing the sitting Ratepayer candidate, and the Association replied that it had no power

---

[1] *Election address of M.P. Birch.*
[2] Letter from A. E. Eaton to the Ratepayers' Society, 4.5.1949.
[3] *M.R.S.*, 7.12.1948.
[4] *M.R.S.*, 1.2.1949.   [5] *M.R.S.*, 7.2.1950.

over the choice of candidates by ward branches. It was their responsibility. The Ratepayers' Society had meetings with the Conservatives, but to no avail. The election went ahead and the Conservative candidate came second to the Ratepayer.

An agreement was reached after the election that the Conservatives would not oppose the re-election of any sitting Ratepayer Councillor. In 1954 J. Ireland retired and the Society discussed whether or not to promote a candidate. Birch argued that, in view of the agreement, in this instance it would be in the Society's interest to offer the seat to the Conservatives on the understanding that he and Baker would go forward in the future unopposed. A majority decided in favour of putting up a candidate.[1] The Conservatives were angry that, in view of their previous self-restraint, the Ratepayers had taken no steps to consult the Penn Branch of the Conservative Association. The Ratepayers stated that they were 'strictly non-political' and saw no reason why they should 'establish any precedent by consulting any organisation, political or otherwise'.[2] The Conservatives adopted a candidate and the Secretary of the Ratepayers wrote to the Conservative leader in the town:

This Society exists as a democratic body, maintained for the purpose, amongst other things, of giving the residents of Penn facilities for taking part, through its own representatives, in the administration of the affairs of the local Council; *without* reference to, or collusion with any political organisation whatsoever, and its first consideration has been and always will be, the residents of Penn and the effect its actions will have on them.

The Conservative Party in opposing our Candidate is obviously actuated by its desire to increase its numbers on the Borough Council and not necessarily therefore to reduce the balance of power as between Socialists and anti-Socialists.

On your own admission[3] our Candidates by their actions have always been anti-Socialist, so what can the party gain by winning the seat in Penn, particularly if by expending, as you put it, their time, thought and money in such a venture, seats are

[1] *M.R.S.*, 2.3.1954.
[2] Letter from the Society to J. Beattie, 8.4.1954.
[3] In a letter from Beattie to the Society, 12.4.1954, when he said, 'all your candidates have voted against the Socialists', and 'if you have a bias at all it is not on the side of Socialism'.

lost in other wards for the lack of the expenditure of those very things.[1]

Beattie replied that he had become very tired of 'all the argy-bargy'.[2]

The battle raged in the press; Conservatives claimed that the Ratepayers' Society was not representative of all Ratepayers and that it could not effectively fight against the No. 1 enemy, the Socialists.[3] Enoch Powell proclaimed that 'in national and local affairs there is room only for two parties'.[4] A Ratepayer complained that party politics in local government was a 'malignant disease' whose 'vile insidious onslaught strangles initiative in Councils, stratifies thought, sets fellow citizens at each other's throats, directing their attentions from the welfare of the home town towards the welfare of the bickering, snarling denizens of the Westminster snakepit'.[5]

In the election the Ratepayers' candidate was defeated, and the greatest indignity was that he came bottom out of three. In 1955 Birch was due to stand for re-election. In late 1954 he told the Society that he had decided to stand as a Conservative. 'Let me say that I know I can serve the inhabitants of Penn equally as well in either capacity and in view of the poor support given to your candidate at the last election it seems the best course to take.'[6] He said that 'except for the Party Tag my position would not be altered'.[7] The Secretary asked for his resignation as the official candidate and decided to run a Ratepayer candidate against him.[8] In the election Birch, the former Ratepayer who had once resolutely stood out against party politics, was the official Conservative candidate. He came top and the Ratepayers' candidate was again pushed into third place.

Baker next deserted the Society. He said he had accepted the Conservative nomination for the May elections in 1956. He said he would still serve the Ratepayers as he had done in the past[9] and he hoped good relations would continue.[10] The Society put up no candidate at the election. It was defunct.

[1] Letter from the Society to J. Beattie, 14.4.1954.
[2] Letter from Beattie to the Society, 15.4.1954.
[3] *E. & S.*, 20.4.1954.   [4] *E. & S.*, 22.4.1954.
[5] *E. & S.*, 26.4.1954.   [6] *M.R.S.*, 8.11.1954.
[7] *M.R.S.*, 16.12.1954.   [8] *E. & S.*, 13.11.1954.
[9] *M.R.S.*, 6.3.1956.   [10] *M.R.S.*, 11.2.1956.

Thus an organisation which had been a genuine independent association, not attached to any party and solely devoted to looking after the interests of the ward of Penn, had been throttled by the Conservative Association, not for local advantages but simply for Parliamentary tactics. However, although the major cause of the death of the Society was Conservative opposition, other long-term factors were undermining its position. The young men of the 1930s, who then in their thirties and forties had run the Ratepayers' Society, by the 1950s were in their fifties and sixties; yet they still regarded Penn as an isolated poorly-served community on the outskirts of Wolverhampton. They had become out of touch. Penn was very well served now with amenities and with social facilities, and trolley buses could quickly take the inhabitants to the town centre.

The fight with the Conservatives and the departure of Birch eroded its strength, but even at the point of death the Society had its last moment of glory. It championed the interests of Penn in a burst of activity which brought to its meetings the 100s and 150s of the 1930s instead of the 20s and 30s of the 1950s.[1] In 1954 it was made public that the National Coal Board was going to set up trial boreholes in Penn in search for coal, which was suspected to lie beneath the surface. The residents became anxious about subsidence and feared a decrease in the value of their property.[2] The Ratepayers took up their cause, while Enoch Powell refused to attend a protest meeting, claiming that the compensation was adequate if subsidence did occur.[3] By 1956 the scare had passed and with it died the Ratepayers' Society. Its Treasurer since 1930 had resigned after the defeat in 1954; the Society suffered financially, and only seven members paid their subscriptions.[4] Its candidates were trounced at the polls in 1954 and 1955. It had revived temporarily with the mining controversy, but, with Baker's desertion, the Society collapsed. The last entry in the minute books of the Society is a copy of an untypically ill-typed letter sent in May 1956 to an inquirer who wished to know how to appeal against the raising of his assessment from £14 to £24. He was told to get a form from the Valuation

[1] *M.R.S.*, 6.9.1955.
[2] *E. & S.*, 4.9.1954.
[3] *M.R.S.*, 5.10.1955. *Birmingham Post*, 7.9.1955.   [4] *M.R.S.*, 8.3.1955.

Officer. The Society could give no further help. The letter ended on a pathetic note with the statement that the subscription to the Society was 2*s* 6*d*.[1] Thus the last act of the Society was to deal with a problem which had initially brought it into being, assessments.

The Penn Ratepayers' Society was the first Ratepayers' Society in the town, and it lasted the longest. Two other wards, St Philip's and Bushbury, also possessed Ratepayers' Societies from the middle 1930s to the late 1940s. These two areas, like Penn, were recent acquisitions of the borough, but were not part of the Parliamentary constituencies of the town until 1948. Thus the Wolverhampton Conservative Associations until 1948 had no real interest in these wards. The Ratepayers' Societies here were not so flourishing as the one at Penn, since they were not so deep-rooted in the needs of the ward. They had been formed as electoral organisations to get representatives on to the Council. Indeed they only came into being around election time, and never met continuously to advance the interests of their wards. The Penn Society tried to link up with these Societies in 1934 and 1936, after demands for a Society for the whole town had been voiced at the Annual General Meetings.[2] In 1936 a scheme of federation was drawn up, providing for a central committee composed of three delegates from each ward society. It was to have little power, since the final clause stated that 'no action of this committee is to interfere with the liberty of individual societies'.[3] The plan came to nothing. The Societies preferred to cultivate their own wards; no other Societies sprang up in other wards. Indeed the aims of the Societies were different, although the names were identical. Bushbury and St Philip's were mere electoral organisations; Penn, however, fulfilled other functions, acting as the spokesman of the ward and providing some social and community services. There was therefore no common ground for unification.

The St Philip's Society was more successful than that at Bushbury; the former returned all the Councillors for the ward from 1933 to 1949, while the latter was unable to break the Labour hold on Bushbury. In 1948 these two Societies were transformed into ward branches of the Conservative Associations in the town,

[1] *M.R.S.*, May 1956.
[2] *M.R.S.*, 27.2.1934, 11.2.1936.   [3] *M.R.S.*, 14.7.1936.

when the areas were incorporated in the Parliamentary constituencies of South-West and North-East Wolverhampton. The change was peaceful; no one resisted or retired sulkily – again evidence that the Ratepayers' Societies here were not so thriving as at Penn and that they were basically anti-Labour electoral organisations formed in the absence of a strong Conservative Association. J. C. Homer, who had been a Ratepayer Councillor for St Philip's Ward since 1944, typifies the ease with which the transition was made. He announced that in 1949 he would stand as a Conservative and 'in accordance with Conservative principles I retain the right to say and do what I consider to be in the best interests of the borough and ward I represent.[1]

CONSERVATIVE FELLOW-TRAVELLERS

Thus those Councillors who sported the title Ratepayer were of two types: those whose loyalty was to Penn and those who were concealed Conservatives. Conservatives were reluctant on many occasions to fight elections openly as Conservatives, particularly in wards where there was strong Labour or Liberal support. They adopted many labels, both to attract Labour or Liberal votes and because of their belief that national parties were inappropriate in municipal affairs. In 1913 a Conservative in a strong Labour seat called himself the Friendly Societies' candidate.[2] The Friendly Societies condemned his presumption and stated that they were not running an official candidate.[3] Independent was a favourite label for the Conservatives in the inter-war years in such wards as Dunstall and St Mary's. In 1925 and 1927 some Conservative business and professional men styled themselves the 'Businessman's' candidates,[4] but their election addresses were identical with those of other members of the anti-Socialist alliance.[5] In 1945 the anti-Socialist Caucus ran its candidates as Progressives. The Conservatives feared that if they stood openly as Conservatives they would suffer as big a defeat as they had sustained at the General Election: the Secretary of the Progressives was, however, forthright in saying that it was not merely a subterfuge

[1] *W.C.*, 29.4.1949.   [2] *E. & S.*, 23.10.1913.   [3] *E. & S.*, 27.10.1913.
[4] *E. & S.*, 2.11.1925, 1.3.1927.   [5] *E. & S.*, 14.3.1927.

to disguise Conservatives but it was a genuine attempt to keep party politics out of the Council. Their election address proclaimed that over the last twenty-five years Wolverhampton had been very progressive; its achievements were listed as regards housing, health, sewage disposal, electricity, social welfare, education, highways and finance. This progress was not due to party political influence as such; and it could continue without any drastic alteration in the composition of the Council. The address made no definite proposals for the future, save that in a general way by pursuing the present programme 'we shall maintain full employment and the prosperity of the town'. Each member would stand for the town's good and 'their National Politics shall not be carried into the chamber'. Under this banner were united not merely Conservatives, but all candidates who were not Labour save the Communists.[1] It was the anti-Socialist alliance of 1927 resurrected.

The victory of the Labour Party in 1945 killed this group. The first reaction to the defeat came from one of the Progressives, Councillor L. R. Guy, who proposed the establishment of a Civic Association, which was to be the Progressive Association put on a permanent basis. It was to consist of 'all those citizens who have a definite stake in the country, those who have an asset to safeguard'. It was to embrace 'all industrialists, commercial men, tradesmen, shopkeepers, house-owners (in particular owner-occupiers and ratepayers)'. Guy devised a constitution, which revealed that the Association was to be an organisation to fight elections and to promote on the Council the interests of the supporting elements. It was to be a locally based party to fight the Labour Party, although Guy said, 'I am not against the Labour Party as such. I am against any one Political Party having a monopolistic control of the Council.' The Conservative Associations destroyed this scheme, since they regarded it as an unnecessary duplication of their own efforts. From 1948 they pressed that all non-Labour candidates should wear the Conservative label. After this there were no more plans for a local party to fight the Labour Party.

[1] *E. & S.*, 4.10.1945.

LIBERALS

The Liberals before 1914 fought local elections without official party support, although the loyalties of candidates were known and they were assisted informally by their political colleagues. In the early 1900s a group of Radical Liberals formed the Progressive Association to 'sweep away the Education Act' of 1902[1] and to curb the municipal extravagance. It was dead by 1910 when the controversy over education had subsided and when the Council was not engaged on any major projects. This Association was mainly an electoral organisation to find and sustain Nonconformist candidates against the supporters of the Education Act. On other Council matters it did not act formally to concert the voting of its members; unofficially and informally it did so. In the inter-war years the Liberals made an anti-Socialist pact with the Conservatives, participated in the anti-Socialist Caucus and stood for the Council not as Liberals, but as Independents, though their national allegiances were well known. By 1946 they had no members of the Council. They gave up fighting municipal elections in a systematic way. Up to 1962 occasional candidates would fight as Liberals, but rarely in the same ward each time.[2] Their backing in terms of organisation and votes was meagre. They merely made individual gestures, which hardly indicated that the party as such was thriving. The eastern part of Wolverhampton was the old stronghold of Liberalism, whose inspiration and strength came from the Mount Zion Primitive Methodist Chapel. But in the 1950s the East was barren ground for the Liberals. The candidates who did stand there lived in the South-West division and they gained few votes. No Liberal organisation existed in the North-East constituency after its formation in 1948.

In 1962 and 1963, however, a mild Liberal revival occurred in the safe Conservative seats in the west of the town, where Labour candidates were pushed into third place behind the Liberals, who ran the Conservatives a close second. During the early 1960s the South-West Wolverhampton Liberal Association flourished, so much so that it acquired a headquarters in the town. The majority of its membership and votes was concentrated in Merridale,

[1] *W.C.*, 8.7.1903.
[2] They fought no wards between 1950 and 1956.

Oxbarn and Penn, middle-class and owner-occupier areas, very different from the eastern part of the town. Two links, however, connected this new Liberal Party with the old. Its President, R. Lewis, was the son of the prominent Liberal leader at the turn of the century, Price Lewis, and a Methodist Chapel, Beckminster, provided the party with many of its leaders. One Conservative Councillor saw the 1964 election in Merridale Ward as a clash between the Conservative church party and the Liberal chapel party. The officers of the party were Nonconformists; the Chairman was a lay preacher.

The occupations of the officers were in the 'superior white-collar' category: a sales manager, a scheduling manager and a director of a small firm of heating engineers. No shopkeepers and no working men made up the leadership, which consisted of that occupational group, which formed only a small proportion of the two major parties' members of the Council. The Liberal Party of the 1960s was a party of 'new men', those not previously active in great numbers in municipal politics.

Although each ward had its own committee, the Executive Committee of the Constituency Party gave leadership to the party, deciding which wards would be fought and who would stand. It consisted of the officers, all close friends with similar occupations.

The party called for changes in the conduct of Council affairs. It urged that committee meetings be open to the press and public and that party discipline over voting be relaxed. It pressed for better treatment of the car-owner, more car parks and wider streets in the town centre, and it protested on behalf of ratepayers against waste, for example the purchase of an expensive computer and the construction of a costly ring road.[1] These policies reflected the interests of the owner-occupier car-owners of the west of Wolverhampton. The 1964 election blighted Liberal hopes of having a Councillor, for its share of the vote fell. The Liberal revival of 1962 and 1963 was only temporary.

EX-SERVICE MEN

The Council had a handful of members bearing less well-known titles. In 1919 two Councillors were elected who had stood as the

[1] *Liberal election addresses 1964.*

candidates of the National Federation of the Discharged and Demobilised Sailors and Soldiers.[1] One, William Morgan, was the organising Secretary of the local branch; he had been an engineer before the war, had been wounded, could find no employment after demobilisation and collected together the unemployed ex-soldiers of the town. The first point of his election address was that 'I will do all in my power to obtain increased Separation Allowances to Wives, Children and Otherwise, and Dependants of Serving Soldiers, as I think the Grants made under the present cost of living are totally inadequate. I also want to see Increased Pensions for the Widows and Dependants'. He then referred to the need for better housing and sanitation; he stood against the excessive expenditure of ratepayers' money and called for a greater Wolverhampton. His colleague, an ex-fitter, also pressed for the same; in addition, he sought free or penny fares on Corporation transport for ex-soldiers. He said he would fight Bolshevism as well as Capitalism.[2] They were elected in 1919 chiefly, says the ex-Councillor whom Morgan defeated, because they presented themselves as war heroes.[3] On the Council they made little impact. They concerned themselves only with trying to advance the ex-serviceman's cause, as for example in 1920 when they pressed for the setting up of a distress fund to help the ex-servicemen, their wives and dependants.[4] Otherwise they were insignificant on the Council and soon vanished.

I.L.A., FASCISTS AND COMMUNISTS

In the 1930s members of the Independent Labour Association were represented on the Council by four Councillors. This was the breakaway organisation from the official Labour Party, financed by W. J. Brown as the machine to fight his Parliamentary campaigns in the town. It was used, however, by W. Lawley to return himself and three allies to the Council, where to all intents they acted with the official Labour Party. One of these four, E. T. Bradley, while a member of the Council became the

[1] *E. & S.*, 3.11.1919.   [2] *E. & S.*, 29.10.1919.
[3] Morgan in his campaign made much of the fact that he had been wounded three times. *E. & S.*, 29.10.1919.
[4] *C.M.*, 11.10.1920. *W.C.*, 13.10.1920.

organising Secretary of the local branch of the British Union of Fascists. He had been a miner before the war; he had served in the war and afterwards as a regular soldier. Unemployed after leaving the army, he was in turn a Communist, involved in the Unemployed Workers' Movement, a Socialist, a member of the I.L.A. and then a Fascist. While on the Council he always spoke and voted with his I.L.A. allies, but after he became a Fascist he ignored the Council. Indeed he said that he joined the Fascists because he found he could achieve nothing on the Council.[1]

The same ward, St James', which sent to the Council Morgan the ex-soldier's candidate and Bradley the I.L.A. and then Fascist, also sent K. M. Brutton the Communist in 1945. The Labour Party had refused to fight this ward in 1945, when the Progressive Mayor for the year 1944–5 was seeking re-election.[2] He was T. W. Phillipson, a tobacconist, who faced opposition only from the Communist sheet-metal worker who defeated him.[3] There was little difference between the Communist and Labour addresses; indeed in Park Ward the Communist candidate stated that if elected she would work with the Labour Party and she endorsed Labour's programme.[4] On the Council Brutton made little impact. He voted up to 1948 with the Labour Party and made speeches to the effect that Labour was not going far enough. But in 1948 and 1949 he became a regular voter with the anti-Socialist Caucus, opposing the Labour Group's demand for a closed shop for all Corporation employees; supporting the Conservatives' traffic plans for the town; attacking the Labour proposals to grant to the Co-operative Society leases of shops on new housing estates; and advocating at the last Council meeting he attended, that contracts should be put out to tender and not granted to the Direct Building Department. Many in the Labour Party claim that he became a member of the Conservative Party. The reason for his switch is supposed to be the attention paid to him by some leading Conservatives, particularly Sir Charles Mander, who is said to have helped to find work for him. They are said by some to have been amusing themselves by getting him to give up his old position

[1] Bradley appears as 'Badly' in J. Yates, *Lifting Timber for the King*, London, 1939, p. 50.
[2] *E. & S.*, 3.11.1945.
[3] Ibid.   [4] *Election address of Miss D. Bootman.*

and adopt theirs. He retired from the Council in 1949 and emigrated.

Before 1945 the Communists were not very active in municipal politics. They first fought a ward in 1928 and again in 1932; both were safe Labour seats and they made little impact. Except for 1945–7 they rarely fought an election, but in the late 1950s and early 1960s they became much more active, running candidates at every election, most often in safe Labour seats, occasionally in a safe Conservative, but never in a marginal ward. They always came bottom of the poll with rarely over 150 votes, except once in 1961 when their candidate had the same surname as the Labour candidate.

The party before 1945 was very ramshackle, composed mainly of the unemployed who were organised also in the front organisation of the National Unemployed Workers' Movement, whose members flirted with Fascism too. In the inter-war years it was frequently reorganised, six times in twelve years.[1] Its main policy was to champion the interests of the unemployed. The party of the 1960s was quite different. It was firmly led by a school teacher and a café proprietor, whose close colleagues were white-collar workers, like a laboratory technician, and skilled men, like engineers and electricians. The Party had no ward organisation; its members joined constituency branches and they were led by a Borough Committee of nine. This body decided which wards would be fought and who would be the candidates. The party also had a branch for Indians and a branch in an aircraft factory. The total membership was around 120, mainly coming from the Council house estates of the east.

Its policy was to goad the Labour Party,[2] urging it to be more extreme and more sensitive to the needs of the working class, especially to reduce the rents of Council houses. It pressed for more Council houses, complete comprehensive education, health centres, reduced fares, higher wages and pensions, abolition of nuclear weapons and the dismantling of N.A.T.O. 'Peace and Socialism' was its slogan.

It fought those wards where its membership was concentrated, and did not fight in marginal wards for fear it might jeopardise

[1] J. Yates, op. cit., pp. 48–9.
[2] It accused the Labour Party of being 'Tory fellow travellers'. *E. & S.*, 6.5.1958.

Labour's majority and let the Conservatives take over. The leaders of the party were on very friendly terms with many leading members of the Labour Party, and especially with the M.P., John Baird, whose meetings they supported and whose election campaigns they assisted.

It was only from the middle 1950s that the members of the Wolverhampton Town Council became drawn exclusively from the two major parties. The Labour and Conservative Parties dominated all. They fought each other at elections, and on the Council their Groups were ranged against each other. In 1900 there was no concept of the majority party forming the government of the town, facing the minority party as an opposition, which would seek to reverse the position at the next election. In 1960 this was the pattern of politics. Between these two dates minor parties and small groups were squeezed out by the two leading parties. The vanishing of the small parties and Independents cannot be laid wholly at the door of the parties. The electorate bears the ultimate responsibility, since they were faced over the years with other candidates than Labour or Conservative. That only two parties count is because the electorate has willed it so.

11 The Chairmen

THE key figures on the Council in 1900 were the Chairmen of the Council committees. In 1964 they were still very influential, but were restrained by some limiting factors not experienced in 1900.

The relationship of a committee to the full Council did not change significantly over the period. In Wolverhampton the Council always granted wide powers to its committees. In 1911 the powers of the various committees were consolidated in a 'Delegation Book' kept in the Town Clerk's Department; it was periodically brought up to date and was still in use in 1964. Wolverhampton delegated powers to its committees long before the Local Government Act, 1933, allowed Councils to do so. The Delegation Book shows that the Council delegated to its committees the power 'to carry out and execute the statutory and other duties and powers of the Council'. As a new statute laid new powers on the Council these specific duties were then laid on the appropriate committee. But certain provisos were always observed. The power to make a rate or to borrow money was never delegated, nor the power to make by-laws, or to acquire or to dispose of land and buildings.[1] The Council left itself with the right to a 'concurrent and overriding exercise' of its functions and had the right 'to make or to amend' the delegations at any time. The committees had also to seek Council approval for any resolutions involving any important matter of policy, or which authorised the provision of any new service or the discontinuance of any existing service. Although wide powers were delegated to the committees, the full Council kept its hands on the reins; changes in policy and the spending of money[2] came within the Council's prerogative, and

[1] Statutory limitations.
[2] In 1900 a committee could spend up to £50 without seeking Council approval; in 1962 the amount was £300.

it had the power to supervise any action by any committee if it so required, down to detail.[1]

The committees therefore over the period were 'the workshops of the Council'. In 1897 a Chairman said that 'the very ABC of Council work was to, especially in great transactions, do the work in committee, and then have it ratified by the Council'.[2] This position was true over the period. Some committees resented the Council overlooking their activities, particularly if their Chairmen were imperious, like F. D. Gibbons. When he was Chairman of Sewage Committee in 1899 he moved a resolution that the Council give his committee permission to buy some land. He said 'it was the cheapest piece of land the committee had ever bought'.

A COUNCILLOR: 'Do I understand the land is already bought?'
'Certainly.'
'There is no use our discussing it.'
'No.' – loud laughter.
'I don't object to the committee buying this land; what I do object to is their method of doing it.'[3]

In 1905 Gibbons was Chairman of Watch Committee, and he told the Council: 'If there was a disturbance tonight I could go to the Chief Constable and give him orders, without you or anyone else interfering.'[4] Thus the situation was that committees were relatively independent of the Council; they had the monopoly of information about a project; they knew the snags of the administration of a service and they were thus in a more influential position than the rest of the Council. Further, since the Chairman was apt to be the dominant element in the committee, he assumed in the full Council the leading role on behalf of his committee. Chairmen were inclined to run their committees as petty empires and to resent interference with their proposals by the Council.[5]

---

[1] Exceptional in 1964 were the Housing and Town Planning Committees. The former had very wide powers to construct houses, and the latter to make planning decisions. They were both bound to report their actions to each Council meeting. The other committees had to report only when appropriate.
[2] *W.C.*, 24.2.1897.   [3] *W.C.*, 14.6.1899.   [4] *W.C.*, 15.2.1905.
[5] 'Committeeitis' affects not only Chairmen, but the ordinary members of the committee, who became utterly devoted to the work of the committees on which they served.

H   J.B.P.

Numerous were the complaints against the 'dictatorship' of the Chairmen over their committees and over the Council. In 1903 the proceedings of the Finance Committee were described as 'a complete farce'. 'You sit round the table and the work is done by the Chairman, and the other members say yes.'[1]

POWERS OF THE CHAIRMAN

A Chairman has formally no powers beyond those of the Aldermen and Councillors who are not Chairmen, save that the Chairman presides at the meeting of his committee and has a casting vote. Formally also a Chairman is appointed by his committee annually at the start of each municipal year; his election is announced to the next meeting of the full Council, which has to approve the choice.[2] In practice, however, his powers were greater, and the annual election a mere formality. Before 1945 a Chairman, once chosen, was constantly re-elected until he was removed by death, compelled to retire by senility or illness, defeated at an election, promoted from a minor to a major committee, driven to resign over a disagreement with the majority of the committee,[3] or disgraced publicly by incompetence or a scandal.[4] Thus a Chairman usually remained at the head of his committee for a long time. Joseph Jones was Chairman of the Free Library Committee for twenty-nine years from 1883 to 1912, J. Marston of Waterworks Committee for twenty-five years (1892–1917), Sir Charles T. Mander of Tramways Committee for twenty-four years (1896–1920) and T. A. Henn of Health Committee for twenty-one years (1915–36). Since 1945 such longevity has been curtailed because party became more significant. As one party gained control at the expense of the other, the Chairmen of the former controlling party were either ousted or retired. Between 1949 and 1952 no Labour members held Chairmanships and after 1955 no Conservatives. Apart from this change, the older tendencies continue; for instance, in 1945 Labour members H. E. Lane and C. B. V. Taylor became

[1] *W.C.*, 22.4.1903.
[2] Between 1888 and 1964 the Council never refused its consent.
[3] In 1918 the Chairman of Education Committee resigned in protest against the decision to appoint a Director of Education. *Minutes of the General Purposes Committee*, 25.6.1918.
[4] e.g., the Chairman of Education and Finance Committees in 1917.

Chairmen of Housing Committee and Parks and Baths Committee respectively; in 1962 they were still Chairmen of these committees and had been continuously except during the period of Conservative control from 1949 to 1952.

Over the period it was common for a Chairman to be the Chairman of only one Standing Committee at a time. Before 1917 there was no firm rule on this, only an 'unwritten law'[1] broken by two exceptional cases. Sir Charles T. Mander was Chairman of both Lighting (1893–1902) and Tramways (1896–1920) Committees; a combination justified on the grounds that electricity was a common factor of both, and that Mander's interest and expertise in electricity qualified him as the most suitable Chairman for both. Levi Johnson was Chairman of Finance (1898–1917) and Education (1905–17). He undertook the latter responsibility only after it had been vacant for six months and only after the Mayor had urged him to take it on, since no one else was prepared to.[2] His dual role put 'too much on his plate';[3] he was unable to fulfil either office effectively, and during his term an accountant clerk in the Education Department embezzled £84,000. As a result of this scandal it was definitely decided that no one should be a Chairman of more than one Standing Committee at a time.[4]

The length of the Chairman's term of office and his concentration on one committee meant that he became closely bound up with his committee and its projects; so much so that the Council chamber became to a large extent a battleground where each Chairman sought to promote the proposals of his particular committee, to obtain for his schemes the necessary amount of scarce resources and to prevent other Chairmen from pursuing any plans which might eat up the resources and leave none or little for him. Particular Chairmen were identified with their committees' objectives. F. Evans, Chairman of Markets Committee (1899–1912), 'practically built up the Wolverhampton Markets,' and was the driving force behind the construction of the new Wholesale Market, Cold Stores and Abattoir.[5] T. V. Jackson,

---

[1] *W.C.*, 15.3.1899.   [2] *W.C.*, 5.12.1917.   [3] *W.C.*, 11.7.1917.
[4] *Standing Orders* of the Council. In 1962 the exceptions were Civil Defence, Sanitation, Tenders, Special Purchases, Rating and Payments and General Purposes Committees.
[5] *W.C.*, 13.11.1907.

Chairman of Public Works Committee (1887–1901), 'initiated the
idea of a new Post Office. He was the prime mover and the main
spring in the whole of the negotiations.'[1] A. B. Bantock was
responsible for the laying out as a public garden of some wasteground on the west front of St Peter's, and for achieving improvements in Worcester Street. 'He had the confidence of the Public
Works Committee so entirely in his hands that practically he
carried the whole of the negotiations in that matter.'[2]

A few Chairmen, however, did not restrict their enthusiasm to
the cause of a single committee. S. Craddock was Chairman of
Parks and Baths Committee (1897–1917) and was instrumental in
getting St George's Churchyard laid out as a public park.[3] He
was Vice-Chairman of Tramways Committee, and was regarded
as the 'Butty',[4] the working partner of Mander; and like him was
thought to have 'tramways on the brain'.[5] Craddock followed
Mander as Chairman of the committee (1920–5). He was known as
the 'father of the Free Library' and the power behind the town's
Floral Fête; once when it was under discussion and he was absent,
one Councillor remarked that it was 'like playing Hamlet without
the Prince of Denmark'.[6] His tentacles were resented. In 1903 a
Labour Councillor commented that 'he had noticed for some time
past that in every new scheme that was born in that Chamber
Alderman Craddock always desired to have the first hand in
rocking the cradle . . . now he wanted to finish the lot to have a
hand in bringing into existence their new education baby'.[7] Sir
Charles T. Mander was also not limited to one committee. He was
especially renowned for bringing electric light to the town, for
electrifying the trams, for promoting the Lorain system and for
urging the abolition of the pan method of excrement removal. In
the 1920s and 1930s Aldermen Bantock and Myatt were regarded
as the two leading Chairmen (of Finance and Public Works
respectively), who kept an overview on all the other committees.
Such Chairmen, however, with a range of concern wider than the
particular committees over which they presided, were exceptional.

---

[1] *W.C.*, 10.11.1897.   [2] *W.C.*, 13.2.1903.
[3] *W.C.*, 13.1.1897. This was in the ward he represented and where his boot
factory was situated.
[4] *E. & S.*, 10.4.1929.
[5] *W.C.*, 13.1.1897.   [6] *W.C.*, 21.4.1909.   [7] *W.C.*, 11.2.1903.

Most often a Chairman devoted himself to promoting the interests of a single committee.

The Chairman around 1900, through his long concentration on one committee, would be the most knowledgeable member of the Council about the activities and problems of that committee. His continual involvement in the administration of his committee would make him often more experienced in its difficulties than even the permanent chief official. At this time the work of the committee was not so complex or technical as in the 1960s, and thus an 'amateur' Chairman was not so dependent for advice on an official. The Chairmen were deeply involved in administrative and technical minutiae, which today would be regarded as the sphere of the officials. The Chairman of Markets Committee 'had almost lived at the Town Hall on weekdays'.[1] The Chairman of Finance and Education Committees 'had given practically 3 days a week to Corporation work for many years'.[2] This situation began to change after the First World War. A Director of Education was appointed in 1918 because 'it was not a right principle that the Chairman of the Education Committee should be placed in the position of an expert' and because 'it was not fair to Alderman Richards or any other Chairman that they should have to devote so much time to details'.[3] Often the officials at the turn of the century were not full-time Corporation employees, but were engaged in private practice as well. The officials were not so professionalised as they later became, not having had to undergo a rigorous specialised training, nor served by professional associations and technical journals which kept them up to date on the latest developments. In expertise therefore the Chairman could overshadow his official, particularly when the Chairman was the better informed about the local context. Sir Charles T. Mander was most skilled in electricity, having introduced it into his house and works[4] and having experimented with it by models;[5] he could easily therefore face his official as an equal in technical knowledge. One official, R. E. W. Berrington, the Borough Engineer (1886–95), resigned as a Corporation employee, was elected to the Council and was made Chairman of Health and then of Sewerage Committees. In these positions he found that he could make more

[1] *W.C.*, 11.11.1908.   [2] *W.C.*, 15.9.1915.
[3] *W.C.*, 12.6.1918.   [4] *W.C.*, 16.11.1892.   [5] *W.C.*, 12.2.1902.

headway in achieving his goal of sanitary reform, particularly in having a 'destructor' erected and the water-carriage system substituted for the pan system, than he could as a mere official.[1] Thus the Chairman was in a more influential position than the official.

A further factor elevating the Chairman above the official around 1900 to an extent not possible in the 1950s and 1960s was the superior social status of the Chairman. The official was a mere Corporation employee, not entitled to any social deference, but the Chairmen were some of the leading social figures, not just in the Council but in the town also. Tables XXVIII and XXIX show that the Chairmen in 1888–9 and in 1903–4 were drawn from the élite of the Council; they were the leading manufacturers, commercial and professional men of the town, owners of substantial enterprises, wealthy, and inhabiting large houses in the attractive and salubrious west end of the borough. Few officials could overshadow such prestige. The highest salary paid to an official, excepting the Town Clerk, in 1900 was £450 a year. The same tables show that the occupational range of the Chairmen did not widen until the Labour Party gained Chairmanships, and that the Chairmen were most representative of the occupations of the members of the Council in 1953–4, when the Labour and Conservative Parties still shared the Chairmanships. But after Labour embarked in 1955 on the policy of taking all the Chairmanships, the occupational range of the Chairmen narrowed, to comprise an élite in reverse, working men, women and the lower middle class, on a lower social level than the officials. Thus the Chairmen of the 1950s and 1960s were not as socially superior as their counterparts in 1900; nor had they the education, or the experience of the technical problems faced by the committees, of the Chairmen of 1900. Further the work of the committees became more dependent on the expertise of the official, now highly trained, and backed by his professional associations and journals. Also in 1964 the salaries of the leading chief officials excepting the Town Clerk, were £3650 a year; much more than that earned by any Labour Chairman. In 1900 the Chairman was the senior partner; in 1964 the official was the senior partner.

[1] For his career see *W.C.*, 16.11.1904, *Wolverhampton Journal*, Nov. 1904, *E. & S.*, 25.1.1915.

ATTEMPTS TO LIMIT COMMITTEES

The possessiveness of the Chairmen and their jealous concern for their committees' independence can be illustrated by the stiff opposition they put up against proposals made from time to time to limit the autonomy of the committees. Since the late 1890s the story of the development of committees was largely that of attempts to check the independence of the spending committees, the vertical committees, by means of strengthening existing horizontal committees or by establishing new ones. In 1900 the Chairmen of the spending committees were very little restrained by the horizontal committees; in 1964 they were greatly limited by them.

In 1896 the Finance Committee proposed that its control over the expenditure of the spending committees should be increased. At that time if a committee wished to spend more than £50 it had to send an estimate of the item to the Finance Committee for examination, eight days before it was submitted to the full Council. The annual estimates were subject to the same procedure. In 1896 the Chairman of the Finance Committee proposed that the estimates be sent to the Finance Committee one month in advance, that the Finance Committee should attach its own report to the committee's report for the guidance of the Council, and that a special Council meeting should be called to consider the estimates. Only three voted in favour, the Chairman and two members of his committee, not Chairmen themselves. 'The Council generally objected to the report, which was received by laughter and sarcastic comment.'[1] In 1902[2] the Finance Committee again tried to assert itself, by moving that it be granted fourteen days to consider the estimates, that it should have the power to ask for further explanations from any committee about any estimate, and that in its report to Council it should be able to draw attention to any item or items of proposed expenditure which it considered unnecessary or undesirable. The proposers said that the Council and the Finance Committee had no control over expenditure of the committee. The Finance Committee simply received the estimates and handed

[1] *W.C.*, 16.9.1896. *C.M.*, 14.9.1896.
[2] *C.M.*, 12.5.1902, 8.12.1902. *W.C.*, 14.5.1902, 10.12.1902.

them to the Council. Neither had enough time to examine them
in detail; the Council lacked information and its attention was not
concentrated on any particular point. They did not intend the
Finance Committee to veto expenditure or to interfere in the work
of a committee, 'save and except that of making suggestions in regard
to any items of expenditure which in their opinion might be cut
down'.[1] The other Chairmen objected to 'the veteran leaders of
the Council being called to the bar of the Finance Committee,
composed as it was for the most part of junior members of the
Council'.[2] The Finance Committee could in its reports draw the
Council's attention to particular items of policy; there was no good
reason to justify the proposed change and they opposed the view
that 'the Finance Committee ought to be the strongest, as it
certainly was the most important Committee of the Council'.[3] Only
the proposal allowing the committee fourteen instead of eight
days to consider the estimates was adopted. But little change
occurred.

THE GENERAL PURPOSES COMMITTEE

Since the Finance Committee had proved feeble, those who
wanted to restrict the freedom of the spending committees turned
to the General Purposes Committee. One of the main points of
the Chairmen was that the Finance Committee did not consist of
the senior members of the Council; but the General Purposes
Committee did. It comprised all the Aldermen, the Chairmen of
the Standing Committees and the senior Councillor from each
ward; the Chairman was the Mayor *ex officio*. It was the largest
committee, around thirty in all; over half the Council. Its functions
were manifold. It was responsible for overseeing the Parliamentary
activities of the Corporation, the preparation of by-laws, litigation
in which the Corporation was involved, the conduct of the chief
officials, the staffing, salaries, and honoraria of the senior grades,
appointments of Council representatives to public bodies, the
mode of conducting Corporation business and any duty or power
not specifically delegated to any other committee. It was also to

[1] *W.C.*, 14.5.1902.   [2] *W.C.*, 10.12.1902.   [3] Ibid.

act as the consulting or advisory committee of every other committee.[1] Its main job was to act as a filter through which the
proposals of committees passed before coming before the Council.
Since it was largely made up of the Chairmen, it was a bargaining
ground, where each Chairman sought to obtain support for his
proposals and to ease their way through the full Council. If
support could be obtained then the measure was likely to pass
through, with the possibility of opposition from junior members
only; if agreement could not be reached, which happened most
often on big proposals, then the matter was transferred to the full
Council for its final verdict. Thus it was not an effective control
on the Chairmen; they used it to bid for support or to obstruct
the plans of others. If their own plans were opposed they would
deal directly with the Council. S. Craddock complained that the
committee was in reality ineffective and not able to carry out
its responsibilities.[2] In 1936 it was called a 'ladies' sewing
meeting'.[3]

In 1903, however, some had hopes strengthening it. A proposal
was made that if a committee planned to spend over £1000 on a
scheme, it should go to the General Purposes Committee, not to
be vetoed, but for the committee to call attention to any items it felt
unnecessary. This would stop the hurried consideration of
proposals and would give time for a full investigation of all aspects
of their implications. The General Purposes Committee was
preferred to the Finance Committee, since it was 'distinctly
representative of every part and section of the Council'. Craddock
opposed. Committees, he claimed, did not 'rush' into things: everything was well thought out before coming to the Council. 'Committees should be left to take the responsibility for their own
work.'[4] Though the proposal was approved, it did little to curb
seriously the autonomy of the committees, and other devices were
sought.

Following the elections in 1903, when a number of Progressives
entered the Council committed to reducing municipal expenditure,
T. Reade proposed the establishment of a special committee to
co-ordinate all the spending committees to achieve economies in

[1] *Council Standing Orders* and the *Delegation Book.*
[2] *W.C.*, 22.4.1903.
[3] *E. & S.*, 10.2.1936.   [4] *W.C.*, 22.4.1903.

the purchase of stores, stationery, 'and in other directions'.[1] He
said that 'the time had arrived, when the Finance or some other
Committee should have powers to check the expenditure of the
borough'.[2] The Chairmen were reluctantly prepared to co-ordinate
the stores and stationery aspects, but they objected to the 'in other
directions', which for Reade was essential since he wanted 'a strong
Committee of inquiry' of 'wide scope'.[3] By 1908 Reade admitted
that it had been a failure, since the only man capable of making it
work effectively, Bantock, had been made Mayor and a Chairman
of a spending committee,[4] and because of the hostility and non-
co-operation of men like Craddock, who, Reade said, 'should look
at their work as a whole and not regard each committee as an
independent committee acting by itself'.[5]

The General Purposes Committee was resorted to again in 1907
when it was proposed that it should have the power to supervise
any increase in the number and salaries of staff.[6] At that time each
committee had control over the number and salary of the staff
they employed, if their salaries were below £120 per annum.
Craddock opposed the suggestion. 'The respective committees
were better able to judge of the worth of the staffs they employed
than a committee who really knew very little about the matter.'[7]
But he was overruled.

The issue arose again in 1915 after the Local Government Board
had circularised Councils to set up a committee to obtain economy.
One group wanted an independent special committee composed of
non-Chairmen, to watch the Chairmen, who 'need watching most'.[8]
The others objected to a 'ferreting' committee, staffed by junior
members who would censure Chairmen. They wanted it to be
composed of the leading Chairmen, which in fact it was when it
emerged.[9]

THE VARLEY AFFAIR

Up to 1917 the Chairmen of the spending committees had fought
strenuously to preserve their independence against attempts to

[1] *C.M.*, 12.2.1904.   [2] *W.C.*, 14.2.1904.
[3] Ibid.   [4] *W.C.*, 11.11.1908.
[5] *W.C.*, 11.4.1906.   [6] *W.C.*, 24.7.1907. *C.M.*, 22.7.1907.
[7] *W.C.*, 16.10.1907.   [8] *W.C.*, 11.8.1915.
[9] *C.M.*, 9.8.1915. *W.C.*, 11.8.1915.

strengthen the powers of the Finance and General Purposes Committees and to create new committees to limit their autonomy. They had had to make minor concessions, but none really impeded them. In 1917, however, the revelations about Jesse Varley's embezzlement of £84,000 from the Corporation served as an incentive to establish tighter financial control over the individual committees. Varley was an accountant clerk to the Education Committee, who between 1905 and 1917 defrauded the Corporation of £84,335 4s 7d by drawing money for the salaries of non-existent teachers. He forged receipts, falsified entries, kept two sets of accounts and had bogus pages stitched into the minute books.[1] Both the Borough Treasurer and Levi Johnson, the Chairman of Finance and Education Committees, had had complete trust in Varley and let him have free rein in the Education Department. The judge at Varley's trial said that 'if proper supervision had been exercised',[2] the money would never have been lost. With his gains Varley had bought a huge house and grounds on the outskirts of the town and ran three cars. He had said that he could live in such a luxurious style, while drawing his salary of only £325 a year, because his wife had been left a fortune. This was one of his 'fairy tales', in which so many had had such 'childlike faith'.[3] In fact his wife was the daughter of an Irish peasant and her relatives lived in the poorest of circumstances. Varley received five years' penal servitude. After his release, he floated a bogus company, used the money for his own purposes and was sentenced to another three years. The judge noted that Varley had sought to 'gain a place in good society'.[4]

The repercussions of the case were far-reaching. Johnson was never to be allowed again to be in a position of responsibility as far as finances were concerned; the Treasurer and the Town Clerk were severely censured; a Director of Education was appointed; and it was decided that no one could be a Chairman of more than one Standing Committee at a time.[5] But, most important of all, the

---

[1] Details of Varley's techniques are found in the Report on the affair by Sir H. E. Haward presented to W. H. Fisher, 22.10.1917, and in a report of a special committee of inquiry of the Wolverhampton Council, 22.12.1917, and in *E. & S.*, 6.7.1917, 11.7.1917.

[2] *E. & S.*, 11.7.1917.   [3] *E. & S.*, 19.11.1917.

[4] *E. & S.*, 12.5.1924.

[5] *W.C.*, 7.11.1917, 12.12.1917. *E. & S.*, 24.1.1918, 18.6.1918.

Finance Committee elected as Chairman the man whom Reade
in 1908 had regarded as the only one able to make his economy
committee work. A. B. Bantock was acknowledged as the most able
and outstanding man on the Council. His appointment ushered in
a new era for the Finance Committee. He forged it into an effective
committee to control the other committees, although it was
achieved not so much by devising new formal controls as through
Bantock's own personal influence and persuasion.

THE ROLE OF BANTOCK

Before Bantock, the Chairman of Finance Committee had not
been the leading man on the Council. E. H. Thorne (1884–91),
J. Marston (1891–2), J. Saunders (1892–8) and L. Johnson (1898–
1917) were either not men in the top rank or else moved on to other
committees to make a positive contribution to the town. Their
terms of office were not long, save for Johnson's; and that he held
the Chairmanship in conjunction with that of Education is
evidence again of the lack of importance attached to the Finance
Committee. But after Bantock, the Chairmanship of Finance was
regarded as a position for the leading men in the Council. It was
not merely an accounting committee which co-ordinated the
expenditure of various committees and arranged the rate for the
year. It was a supervising and interfering committee, which
involved itself in the workings of each committee. The change
came during Bantock's twenty-one years' tenure of the Chairmanship of Finance Committee.

Bantock was remembered by the Town Clerk of 1919–29 as
being 'keen on finance'.[1] He would ask of every proposal, 'where
is the money to come from?' and 'if this were your money, would
you spend it?' At almost every Council meeting during his term
of office he was opposing some committee's plans to spend money,
for what he regarded as extravagance, Turkish baths, branch
libraries, milk for expectant mothers, or land for playing fields.
He extolled the virtues of 'sound finance' and 'economy'; by

[1] Others regarded him as mean. He would not give tips to his dustman;
and if he saw a member of the Town Hall staff carrying tea cups, he would
inquire if he was paid to do so.

cutting expenditure and reducing rates, trade could revive and the town prosper again. His views tallied well with the orthodoxy of economists and businessmen in the town, who faced the depression of the inter-war years. Thus it was not merely the personality of Bantock which raised the importance of the Finance Committee; the times were propitious, and enabled its role to be elevated to a new significance. In fulfilling his function Bantock introduced a new Standing Order which laid down that, if a committee wished to spend over £5000 on a scheme, the Chairman of Finance had to be consulted. This gave him an opportunity, through informal talks with the individual Chairmen and members of the committees concerned, to try and persuade them to cut down the estimates before presenting the matter to the full Council. Bantock's main influence was exercised in these informal, pre-natal consultations with Chairmen. He also took the lead in the Salaries and Wages Sub-Committee of the General Purposes Committee. The spending committees resented the way in which it cut down their salary recommendations. In 1920 the Health Committee complained of the Salaries and Wages Sub-Committee sitting 'in judgement' over the other committees.[1] In 1927 the Chairman of the Education Committee attacked 'the deliberate interference or a deliberate refusal to recognise the authority and knowledge of the Education Committee'.[2] Bantock retorted against such attitudes that Chairmen and committees could no longer act as 'freelances'; they had to look at the work of the Council as a whole.[3]

BANTOCK'S SUCCESSORS

The two Chairmen of Finance Committee who followed Bantock were also regarded as the leading and most able men in the Council, Sir Charles A. Mander (1938–50) and J. Beattie (1950–5); each of whom the Labour Party allowed to remain Chairman of Finance when it was in a majority (1945–9 and 1952–5), since it had no one to match their financial ability, experience and acumen. Each made a contribution to strengthening the influence of the Finance Committee over the other committees. Mander advocated

[1] *W.C.*, 13.10.1920. [2] *E. & S.*, 12.7.1927. [3] *E. & S.*, 30.9.1929.

considering the Corporation's financial policy over a five-year period;[1] and in 1939 he introduced his first five-year report,[2] which was dashed by the war. In 1946 a call was made for a five- to ten-year plan, providing background information against which to judge finance proposals, since 'financial matters were usually rushed through the Council partly because Councillors did not understand them, and partly because they knew they would be audited and were above suspicion'.[3] In the 1950s Beattie established a Priority Sub-Committee of the Finance Committee to recommend which projects of the Council should have priority, given the scarcity of resources, and to enable the Council to plan a long-term policy.[4] He was backed in this task by the Labour member G. Rastall, who also attempted within the Labour Group to set up a committee of Chairmen to plot out future financial commitments of the Corporation and to co-ordinate the plans of the individual committees. But his hopes were frustrated.

In 1955 the Labour Group replaced Beattie by D. A. Birch, a young but most able member of the Labour Group, though not its leader. He was very much in agreement with Beattie and Rastall about the need for the Finance Committee to control the expenditure of the other committees. During the 1950s costs had soared as the Council undertook new responsibilities and improved services; wages and salaries shot up; the credit squeeze and higher interest rates increased the cost of borrowing and of servicing the Corporation's debt. Fewer people bore the growing burden since the population of the town declined as areas were cleared and the population was rehoused beyond the boundaries. Changes in the grants system, the introduction of the Block Grant and a decline in the amount from the Rate Deficiency Grant further increased the financial difficulties of the Council. To stop rising costs was 'like trying to catch hold of a bouncing rubber ball in pitch blackness'.[5]

In opposition, Beattie complained that 'the method of controlling finance was out of date'. He noted the surprise that came when the estimates were produced, and the last-minute attempts at pruning which followed. He advocated that 'there should be places on the

[1] *E. & S.*, 9.11.1938.　　　　　[2] *E. & S.*, 10.1.1939.
[3] *E. & S.*, 1.8.1946.　　　　　　[4] *E. & S.*, 23.11.1954.
[5] *E. & S.*, 28.2.1956.

Finance Committee for the chairmen of other committees'. They would be able to discuss wage trends and overspending, so that 'the build-up of the rate would then be the result of a carefully discussed policy, instead of being handled late in the financial year, hurriedly and without time for manœuvres'.[1] Although Birch had the same long-term objectives as Beattie, his methods were different. Instead of bringing the Chairmen of the committees to the Finance Committee he wanted to take the Finance Committee to the committees, and involve it in the actual process of making the estimate. His aim was for a more permanent and continuous influence, a tighter and earlier control over the estimates, to stop last-minute panic steps to cut them down. He tried to get his way at first by voluntary methods and informal consultation, but some Chairmen objected. For instance H. E. Lane, Chairman of Housing Committee,[2] opposed Birch's proposals to introduce a differential rent scheme. Birch wanted to explain his ideas to the Housing Committee and to bring along the Borough Treasurer. Lane objected, saying that the Housing Committee had its own officials, and he blocked Birch's request. In 1959 Birch thanked 'most committees', who had 'voluntarily allowed a finance sub-committee [Priority] to exercise control over capital expenditure'.[3] It was clear that stronger devices were required. Birch wanted the sub-committee to be able to veto capital expenditure but the Group would not agree. What it did agree to was embodied in the revised *Council Standing Orders* of 1962. These form a most telling comparison with the position in 1900, when the Finance Committee was weak and the spending committees were almost autonomous.

After 1962 the process of making the rate began in December or January when each committee approved the estimates of both its income and expenditure for the coming year. The form of the estimates was determined by the Finance Committee. When the committee discussed the estimates, the Chairman of Finance or his nominee was entitled to attend and join in the discussion, although he could not vote. When later the Finance Committee itself considered the estimates from a committee it could invite

---

[1] *E. & S.*, 28.2.1956.
[2] A rival of Birch's for the Chairmanship of Finance.
[3] *E. & S.*, 23.2.1959.

the Chairman of the committee, or his nominee, and the chief official of the committee to attend. The Finance Committee could refer an item back to the committee with comment for its reconsideration. No committee was allowed to seek a supplementary estimate from the Council until it had been submitted to the Finance Committee; and if it disapproved, the committee was only allowed to proceed with the plan on the express approval of the whole Council. Just before 1962 if a committee wished to undertake capital expenditure it had to report the matter to the Finance Committee, which had the opportunity to make comments to the full Council on the scheme. Birch wanted the power to veto such plans, but obtained only the rule that no capital expenditure was to be recommended to the Council until the Finance Committee had been informed, and either the Finance Committee had no objection or else two meetings of the Council had taken place after the Finance Committee had been informed. Thus it had the power to delay for two months any committee's recommendations for capital expenditure. This gave the Chairman of Finance and the Treasurer time to bring pressure to bear on the Chairman of the spending committee and his officials if the expenditure was regarded as inappropriate or inopportune. Birch stressed the importance of such behind-the-scenes consultations, while members of the spending committees objected to what they regarded as the 'dictation' of the Finance Committee in the negotiations. Birch said that he realised that many members of the Council thought that 'the Finance Committee in general and its Chairman in particular too often stand in the way of progress'.[1]

This history shows that the spending committees and their Chairmen had, over the period, had their independence and autonomy severely curtailed. The most important area they lost was finance; thus they had taken away their power to decide what large projects they would advocate. In other fields, too, they were limited. Control over their staff, their wages and conditions, went largely to national negotiating machinery and to a separate Establishment Committee set up in 1961. Control over goods and services used by all departments was co-ordinated under a Tenders Committee set up in 1935. Rules were devised laying down the procedure to be followed by the committees in many

[1] *E. & S.*, 22.2.1960.

of their activities, for instance in awarding Corporation contracts. But these were pinpricks compared to the increase in the power of the Finance Committee and its Chairman over sixty years.

PARTY LIMITATIONS

In addition to the limitations imposed on the Chairmen of Council committees by the horizontal committees and particularly by the Finance Committee, the Chairmen of the 1950s and 1960s were further limited by their political parties to an extent which their counterparts in 1900 were not. The Chairmen of 1900 did not owe their seats on the Council to a political party, nor had they been made Chairmen because of their party's support.[1] Elections were not fought officially between parties, nor did the parties plan the voting of their members inside the Council. The Chairmen did not have to attend Group meetings nor be bound by Group decisions. They could advocate in their committees and in Council whatever policy they liked without fear of reprisal because they had deviated from a party programme. Their loyalty was to their committees rather than to their party.

In the 1960s, however, all Councillors owed their seats to party backing; if they failed to follow the party's policy, they endangered their position, since their party could refuse to readopt them as official candidates. They were bound to attend Group meetings and to abide by Group decisions. Each Chairman had to fit his committee's plans into the framework set by his party and his Group. His loyalty was to his party rather than to his committee. In addition, the majority party in the Council in the 1950s had proportionately the same majority in each committee; thus, although the Chairman had an automatic majority in his committee, these members of his party served to limit him in the sense of ensuring that he kept to the policy of the party. He could not overrule them, since they could appeal to the Group for a final decision.

[1] Committees were jealous of their right to select their own Chairmen; they even resented Council discussion of their choice. In 1899 a Chairman said: 'The Council had no right to go behind any Committee in reviewing its decision as to the appointment of its Chairman.' *W.C.*, 15.3.1899.

In 1900 the Chairmen were the dominant elements in their committees. Once they had the backing of the committee for a particular policy, they would meet together in the General Purposes Committee for horse-trading, and if they were dissatisfied, they could take the matter to the full Council. The party and its Group did not come into the process. In the 1950s and 1960s, however, the Group played a most significant part. It acted as the clearing house for the proposals of the committees; their plans went to the Group and it decided what the attitude of the party was to be and which way members were to vote in the Council.

Thus the Chairmen of 1960 were far more limited than the Chairmen of 1900. But they were not utterly subordinated to the Group. They held out successfully against Rastall's plan to set up a Group committee of the Chairmen, since they did not want to compromise their independence further by submitting their proposals to their colleagues, each seeking to press for his plan and to block theirs. They preferred to take their plans direct to the Group without having to go through a prior stage of supervision. A consequence of Rastall's failure was that, since the Chairmen would not submit to control over their committees' activities through their party, other means were sought inside the Corporation itself, through strengthening the Finance Committee.

The increase in the power of the Finance Committee and the important role of the Group detracted from the significance of the General Purposes Committee. Its composition remained the same over the period; namely, the senior members of the Council. It performed a moderately useful function of tidying up items before they went to the Council, acting like a second Chamber. It was no Cabinet, since its members belonged to different parties and it was too large, like a miniature Council. It could therefore give no political lead. The Town Clerk said that it did very little. It was overshadowed by the Finance Committee and the Groups. It was not an effective restricting element on the Chairmen in 1900; it was far less so in 1960.

THE CHOICE OF CHAIRMEN

In 1900 a member of the Council became a Chairman because his committee had chosen him as the most able member of that committee. His party affiliation was not a significant factor in his appointment. Chairmanships were allocated without regard to the strengths of parties in the Council as a whole. Labour members gained Chairmanships before they were made Mayors or reached the Aldermanic bench. T. Frost was the first Labour Chairman, of the Free Library Committee (1917–19); in 1925 J. Whittaker was made Chairman of the Care of the Mentally Defective Committee (to 1940) and A. Davies became the first Labour Chairman of a major committee, Transport, which he remained until 1949. By 1944 Labour had four Chairmanships: Allotments, Care of the Blind, Cleansing and Transport. On gaining its majority in 1945 it removed from the Aldermanic bench six non-Socialist Chairmen, ejected other Chairmen from their positions and took eleven Chairmanships, six major and five minor, leaving to the opposition also eleven, seven major and four minor. The Labour Group did not follow its party's model Standing Orders and take all the Chairmanships, since it had not enough experienced members available. The Conservatives and Independents bemoaned the loss of experienced Chairmen, but C. W. Hill, the Secretary of the Labour Group, said: 'I am not prepared to accept in all committees as in years gone by, the crumbs falling from the rich men's tables. We are able to pass the plate for a fair helping and we intend to do it.'[1] In 1949 when the Conservatives regained a majority they offered the Labour Party nine Chairmanships, six minor and three major. The Labour Group decided to refuse all; one of its members, A. A. Beach, Chairman of Watch Committee, refused to accept this decision. He thoroughly enjoyed being Chairman; it was the only part of the Council's work which interested him, meeting Home Secretaries, attending the Police Council and being saluted by the police. He resigned from the Group and said: 'I must retain my freedom to think, decide and vote for what in my opinion is right.'[2] In 1952 when the Labour Party regained its majority, it removed him from the Aldermanic

[1] *E. & S.*, 16.11.1945. [2] *E. & S.*, 28.5.1949.

bench. It did not at this point take all the Chairmanships: a
decision praised by the leader of the Conservatives as 'a sensible
arrangement whereby the Chairmanships would be held to some
degree by those best fitted by experience to take the responsibility.
I do most sincerely congratulate the Labour Party on their fairness
in this matter, and the Conservatives and Independents on their
good sense in accepting the suggestions put forward.'[1] Inside the
Labour Group the battle raged between those who felt that all
should have been taken and the majority who said that Labour
had not enough able men to replace certain very experienced and
not very partisan Conservatives. Gradually as Labour increased
its majority after 1952, it acquired more Chairmanships,[2] until in
1955 it decided to take all. J. Beattie protested at 'party politics
exhibited in their most futile and stupid form'. 'Since no one had
adversely criticised the work of the Conservative Chairmen in the
past, they must have been removed this year and last not because
they were inefficient, but merely because they were Conservatives.'[3]
The local paper said that the 'real evil' was the fact that 'men are
being given jobs for political not personal reasons, and that there
is a danger that if the Conservatives gained power they would
retaliate by throwing out the best of the Labour members'.[4] The
Labour Party claimed that a Conservative Chairman of a committee whose majority was Labour was in a difficult position in a
Council with a Labour majority, since he could not really speak for
his committee, nor take snap decisions, because he could not rely
on the loyalty of his committee, nor in open Council could he
wholeheartedly defend proposals with which he did not agree.[5]
The leader of the Labour Group said that it was nonsense to have
a Conservative Chancellor of the Exchequer (Chairman of Finance
Committee) in a Labour Government.

Closely connected with the choice of the Chairmen is the question
of the party composition of the committees. Before 1945 the actual

[1] *E. & S.*, 19.5.1952.
[2] e.g., Health Committee in 1953 when the Conservatives objected to the
removal, 'like an old shoe', of a Conservative doctor, who had been Chairman
for six years. *E. & S.*, 29.6.1953. Also Fire and Ambulance Committee in 1954.
E. & S., 4.6.1954.
[3] *E. & S.*, 27.6.1955.   [4] *E. & S.*, 28.6.1955.
[5] *E. & S.*, 27.6.1955. Similar arguments were used when Labour refused
to take Chairmanships while the Conservatives had a majority. *E. & S.*,
7.5.1951.

membership of committees was decided by the General Purposes Committee and immediately after 1945 by a special *ad hoc* committee of the leaders of the parties. In the late 1940s the majority party did not have a majority in every committee. In some it had, in others it was either equal or in a minority. In the 1960s the majority party had a majority in all committees, reflecting the strength of the parties in the Council. By 1964 the actual composition of the committees was arranged by the Secretary of the majority Group, who considered requests from his members, prepared a draft, and submitted it to the Group for a final verdict; the Secretary of the minority Group did the same for his members. After each election when the composition of the Council changed, the Secretaries conferred to redress the balance in the committees. The Conservatives complained that the Labour Group did not give them adequate representation.

Thus after 1955 the majority party Group took all the Chairmanships and had a majority in each committee. It also decided who should sit in which committee and who should be the Chairman of which committee. The Conservatives objected to 'the injection of permanent party politics' into the running of the Council. They rejected the analogy of Parliament, claiming that although it might be run on this system, the Town Council should not follow that example.[1] The Conservative leader said that 'practically all Council work was non-political',[2] and that therefore there was no need to select the Chairmen and decide the composition of committees in this way. By 1962, however, the Conservatives came to accept the Labour view of how the Council should be run. If it had gained a majority in either 1961 or 1962 it would have taken all the Chairmanships, replacing the Labour members with their 'Shadow' Chairmen. Thus both parties accepted the need for one party to assume the responsibility for running the Council; and that entailed that one party should have a majority on all committees and should take all the Chairmanships.

One objection to this system was voiced by the Conservative leader when in 1951 he asked the Labour Party to accept some Chairmanships. 'There are not enough people of experience and ability on one side of this Council to take all Chairmanships. We want to pick the brains and ability from all sides of the Council.'[3]

[1] *E. & S.*, 28.6.1955.   [2] *E. & S.*, 27.6.1955.   [3] *E. & S.*, 7.5.1951.

Labour refused, and it is acknowledged that some of the Conservative Chairmen were of very poor calibre. Labour, too, faced this problem, although the leader said that though some of Labour's Chairmen did not 'shine', they never had such 'duds' as the Conservatives had. In Wolverhampton this difficulty was particularly acute, since the parties were so evenly balanced, and, when the parties stood at 30:30, over two-thirds of the Labour members of the Council were Chairmen. While the majority party had 'to scrape the barrel', able men in opposition, deprived of a Chairmanship, retired from the Council and the Corporation as a whole suffered a loss. The outstanding example of this trend was James Beattie, who retired in 1956 after being removed from the Chairmanship of Finance Committee.

THE FUNCTION OF THE CHAIRMAN

The actual role of the Chairman varies according to a number of factors. It depends on the personality, temperament, ambition and ability of the Chairman, and how he conceives his job, and how much time he can devote to it. It depends on the work of the committee, whether it is largely technical or whether it is highly political. It depends again on the members of the committee, on their personalities, temperaments, ambitions and abilities, how they conceive their function and that of their Chairman and what time they have available. It depends also on similar factors in the make-up of the officials, particularly the chief official. It depends on the traditions of the Council regarding the role of the Chairman. The role therefore differs according to a host of fluctuating variables, so that it is impossible to generalise about the functions of the Chairman. Nowhere is it laid down what they should be, and practice is diverse.

Some Chairmen led and guided their committees in discussion; others let the meetings ramble without direction. Some were speedy in expediting business; others were slow. Some informed their committees fully; others were reticent. Some allowed the officials full freedom to take part in the proceedings of the committee; others let the officials speak only when requested. The relationship between the Chairman and his chief official is crucial, and it varies tremendously. Some Chairmen hardly every saw their chief officials save at the committee meetings or for a few minutes before when they talked over the agenda together. Some Chairmen let the officials alone 'to get on with the job they are paid for'. Their own role they regarded as being to provide the official with whatever services he needed to carry out his functions effectively. Others distrusted their officials, sought to know everything that they did, swooped down on the departments for inspections and to seek out complaints. Some were very close to their officials, in touch with them often three to four times a week, always available to each other at any hour of the day or night; such could be regarded as a team of two equals, feeding each other with ideas and plans. Some of these 'duets' took their committees into their confidence; others tried to rush their proposals through without much consultation. The time when they entered their positions was important. A new Chairman faced with an experienced official who has been in the department for a long time will not be able to assert himself so much as an experienced Chairman facing a new official, recently arrived from another authority. The official's ability to assert himself will depend also on whether the topic under consideration is politically contentious. In some of the committees like Water political issues rarely arose, but in Housing, Town Planning, Public Works or Education the official had to tread warily lest he became identified as the supporter of a particular party. In Wolverhampton the official was regarded as the servant to his committee or to his Council as a whole and not to a particular party, even if it had a majority. Thus the role of the Chairman in relation both to his committee and to his official varied according to an immeasurable number of factors.

In the Labour Party some members advocated that Chairmen should not stay indefinitely in office but should be limited to, say, a three-year term. In the 1960s some felt that the Chairman got 'into a rut', became the mouthpiece of his official, lacked a critical approach to the work of his committee, resented criticism as a personal attack and generally ran his committee as a personal show. To bring fresh ideas and new blood into the committee while ensuring that Chairmen were experienced in the work of a committee, they suggested that after one year's service as Vice-Chairman, a member should then be a Chairman for three years and then move on to another committee. In this way also Chairmen would be forced to see the work of the Council as a whole and not from the viewpoint of one committee. The opponents of this argument said that if such proposals were adopted, the influence of the official would be likely to increase, since it took about three years for a Chairman to learn the work of his committee thoroughly. Until then the official with his expertise and superior technical knowledge would be the driving force behind the Chairman. Popular control of the administration would thus be relaxed by the institution of a scheme for Chairmen to hold their offices by rotation. This latter view was expressed invariably by Chairmen, the former by relative newcomers, itching for a Chairmanship themselves. Once they attained the office, they rarely returned to their old cause.

In 1900 the key men on the Council were the Chairmen; in the 1960s to a great extent they still were. They were the dominant element in their committees, and in the Council spoke for their committees, explaining and defending their proposals. The successful achievement of a project still owed much to the ability and energy of a Chairman. A leading official singled out the work of some Chairmen as being vital for the attainment of the objects of their committees, such as Mrs R. F. Ilsley at Health Committee and H. Bagley at Cultural and Entertainments. G. Rastall at Public Works was the power behind the Direct Building Department; S. R. Swain in the Markets Committee was behind the construction of the new Retail Market, H. E. Lane behind the house-building and rent policy of the Housing Committee and D. A. Birch behind the increase in the powers of the Finance Committee. Most of the other Chairmen, however, had not the force, the ability or the ideas of the above. They were more led by their officials. In the 1960s there were more of this kind than in 1900, a change produced by the decline in the occupational and social status of the Chairmen and by the increasing complexity and technicality of the work of the committees, which exalted the official. In the 1960s the Chairmen, although still the key figures on the Council, suffered from a number of limitations on their autonomy, which their counterparts in 1900 never had to undergo. In the 1960s they had to work within the framework of a party policy and to accept Group decisions as binding on them and their committees. Also horizontal committees restricted their freedom; particularly, the Finance Committee encroached on to their preserves. The Chairmen resisted strenuously these limitations, and had at that time not completely capitulated, but no longer did they rule with virtual autonomy over their petty empires.

12 Mayors and Aldermen

THE MAYORS

The one individual in local government whose office is known to most people is the Mayor. His position is also the most sought-after by Councillors and Aldermen. And once it has been attained it remains the high peak of a Councillor's career, that part of his life about which he is most proud and most eager to talk. The mementoes of his period of office are carefully preserved; often the only press cuttings kept by a Councillor are those connected with his Mayoralty. Over sixty years the Mayor's legal position has not changed but in practice his functions have. The Mayor of the 1890s had a quite different role to perform from the Mayor of the 1960s.

The powers and potential powers of the Mayor can be seen as threefold. He can be a constitutional monarch, ceremonially representing the Corporation; a kind of Speaker of the Council, presiding at Council meetings; and a political leader of the Council, a kind of Prime Minister, promoting his own policy. The last function was less performed after the 1930s than at the turn of the century; the performance of the second depended on the individual capabilities of the Mayor, and the performance of the first altered significantly since 1900.

The Mayor is the most often recognised and is the best-known individual in a local authority because of his ceremonial activities. And it is these which make his office so attractive for aspirants. During his term of office the Mayor personifies the Corporation, the Council and the town. He is for a time 'Mr Wolverhampton', representing the Corporation at functions inside and outside the borough. Wearing his chain, the symbol of his office, he is the leading personality at school prize days, at banquets of associations, at functions of all kinds. In 1929 it was said that 'the calls upon a

Mayor are heavy'. He has to 'attend dinners, bazaars, football matches, dog shows, and all manner of meetings, and make speeches on a bewildering diversity of subjects'.[1] In the year 1929–30 he attended 228 functions.[2] In 1957–8 the Mayor attended 550 meetings in her term of office, including 400 outside functions.[3] No wonder that a former Mayor said that 'social duties abound'.[4]

Around the turn of the century the Mayor had no Mayoral allowance provided by the Corporation to enable him to maintain the dignity of his office. He had to finance himself during his term of office, which would leave him little time to earn a living, and he had to provide the money for the entertaining. Up to 1898 the Mayor had always been picked from the leading social figures of the town, men of substance and wealth, able to dispense patronage to the poor and unemployed in the form of food and clothing, to donate handsomely to the town's charities, to dispense patronage to various associations and to regale the borough with Mayoral receptions, balls and feasts. To be a Mayor was expensive. When a man was found who had the high social status and the means to indulge the town, he would be called to have more than one annual term of office. The outstanding example of this was Sir Charles T. Mander, the varnish manufacturer, who was Mayor for four terms, from 1892 to 1896, the record number of years of office of any Mayor in the town. John Jones, the japanner, was Mayor for three terms (1878–81) and A. B. Bantock, the carrier, also for three terms (1905–7, 1914–15). Between 1919 and 1939 it became less common for a Mayor to have more than one term of office.[5] The last was the son of Sir Charles T. Mander, Sir Charles A. Mander (1932–3, 1936–7), who was asked to become Mayor for a second term when it was known that Royalty was to visit the town. It was felt that he would be a more dignified representative of the town than a butcher who was next on the list for the office.

In 1898 a departure from traditional lines was recognised when he first 'democratic'[6] Mayor was selected, Price Lewis, the Radical

---

[1] *E. & S.*, 9.11.1929.

[2] *E. & S.*, 10.11.1930.   [3] *E. & S.*, 19.5.1958.

[4] One said that he attended functions from those at 'working men's clubs to those of the best people'.

[5] J. Thompson, Mayor 1920–2, the head of a firm constructing boilers, was given a second term because he spent money lavishly on the town.

[6] *E. & S.*, 8.10.1898.

Liberal tailor. He said that he was 'unequal to the pecuniary obligations which custom rather than necessity has attached to the office'.[1] He said that he would not follow out the lavish expenditure of the past; yet he would accept no money payment or salary to enable him to follow in the lines of his predecessors.[2] One of his first economy measures was to cut out the luncheon at the Town Hall after his ceremony of inauguration as Mayor.[3] Also, since he was a teetotaller, alcohol did not flow so freely as in the past. This change prompted a poem in the local press.

> Mourn, Aldermanic gourmands
> Who love the festive glass,
> For hock, champagne and cognac
> The new Mayor will not pass.
>
> No more you'll sip the eau de vie
> Your inner man to cheer,
> But Corporation water's cheap
> If alcohol is dear.[4]

Lewis was an exception; traditional types were selected until T. Frost, a carpenter, the first Labour Mayor, was chosen in 1922. To meet 'the essential disbursements incidental to the Mayoralty' a Mayoral allowance of £250 was instituted.[5] Fears were again expressed as to whether a working man could uphold the dignity of the office. When the second Labour Mayor, A. Davies, a railwayman, was chosen in 1930, the allowance was raised to £500.[6] In 1935 during the third Labour Mayor's term of office (J. Whittaker, a retired plumber and trade union official), a car and chauffeur were provided;[7] and following the Labour victory of 1945, the allowance was raised to £750.[8] In 1954, at the end of the first Labour Mayor's term of office since 1949, an entertainment allowance of £500 was granted in addition to the existing £750.[9]

Objections were raised against these increases in 1945. 'In the past the Mayor's position was looked upon as a job of honour and

[1] *Midland Evening News*, 4.10.1898.
[2] *E. & S.*, 4.10.1898.
[3] *E. & S.*, 8.10.1898.
[4] *E. & S.*, 4.10.1898.
[5] *E. & S.*, 12.12.1922.
[6] *E. & S.*, 27.10.1930.
[7] *E. & S.*, 7.8.1935.
[8] *E. & S.*, 4.1.1946. It was raised to £1250 in 1964 to help a Labour Mayor in financial difficulties. *E. & S.*, 4.5.1964.
[9] *E. & S.*, 25.10.1954.

a pleasure to serve the town without any salary whatever.'[1] Others argued that 'it gave the opportunity to be Mayor to able men from the working class' and that 'it would give to those over-burdened with money and spare time the opportunity to show their honourable desire to serve the community for nothing by refusing to accept payment'.[2] The early Labour Mayors found it impossible to maintain the expense associated with being a Mayor; A. A. Beach and W. Lawley both stressed that they were besieged by requests from various bodies for financial patronage. They were unable to equal the gifts given by such Mayors as Luce and Probert; the latter is said to have spent £3000 during his term of office. The largest expense for a Mayor in the 1960s lay in the cost of clothes for himself and his wife. It was felt that they should uphold the dignity of the town by being turned out at their best on every occasion. The Conservative Mayors in the 1950s also spent money in donating sets of cutlery and plate to the Corporation.

The rise of the Labour Party and its demand for the Mayoralty caused the office to become to all intents and purposes a full-time salaried job, financed out of the rates, since Labour members could not afford to be Mayors without pay. Where in the past the Mayor dispensed largesse from his own pocket, after 1945 he acted as a servant of the Council. Since the office became salaried and full-time it was no longer feasible for it to be held longer than for one term. Few individuals could be granted time off their work for a longer period than a year; and objections would have been vociferous against continually employing the same man out of the rates to enjoy himself. In addition, the competition for the office was so intense that one term was the maximum that was politically possible.

An important function of the Mayor is to act as Chairman of the Council. He presides at the Council meeting, keeps order in the Chamber, controls the debate, picks speakers and interprets the Standing Orders. At his left hand sits the Town Clerk, continually whispering advice about what points to make and when to close a debate and call for a division. In this role the Mayor is regarded as above party, as the impartial servant of all the Council. We have seen above, however, that the Mayor in 1936 managed to prevent

[1] *E. & S.*, 10.1.1945.
[2] Ibid.

a debate on the financial interests of some members, much to the annoyance of the Labour Party.[1] In 1936 Labour members Lane and Lawley objected to the powers of the Mayor to disallow supplementary questions, to remove a member who interrupted the proceedings and to clear the public gallery. They felt that these powers would be used to restrict the Labour Party's protests against Chairmen who did not give truthful answers to questions.[2] But it was in the early 1960s, when the Council was evenly divided, that this aspect of the Mayor's functions became of decisive political importance. This story is told in Chapter 16.

A function of the Mayor which has been swamped by his ceremonial duties is as the potential political leader of the Council. This role was not performed by the Mayor to any extent after the First World War. Before then, however, the Mayoralty was not merely a ceremonial office; it was an office of influence, conferring upon the holder unique opportunities to advance a particular scheme of his for the town. Indeed many Chairmen of committees used their terms of office as Mayor to press forward plans of their own or of their committees'. They could do this in their speeches to the Council outlining the year's future at the start of their terms of office. In their addresses to the numerous functions they attended, they could stress their pet plans. At these functions they could make many contacts and collect further support for their proposals. As Chairmen of the Council, as *ex officio* members of all committees and as Chairmen still of their own committees, they were in key vantage points from which to urge other Councillors to follow their lead. A particularly important position held by the Mayor *ex officio* was the Chairmanship of the General Purposes Committee. It met before the full Council meeting to discuss the agenda of the Council meeting. Here the Chairmen sought to promote the causes of their committees; here the horse-trading occurred and here the Mayor as Chairman was in an exceptionally advantageous position to advance the proposals of his own committee.

Sir Charles T. Mander during his four years of office continually urged a wider use of electricity, for lighting and for the tramways. In 1893 the first electric light works was erected in the town and

---

[1] See above, Chapter 6, p. 133.
[2] *E. & S.*, 2.10.1936.

mains were laid in the public streets. This had received 'a large share of the attention of the Mayor, who had worked zealously on behalf of it'.[1] An outstanding example of a Mayor at action as the leader of the Council comes from the term of office of Stephen Craddock, Mayor 1896–7. He had pressed for some time for a new Free Library, but to no avail, since agreement could not be reached on a site He cut through the obstructions by buying personally a plot of land and offering it to the Council. 'I have purchased it in my private capacity and if the Council do not ratify my action I shall not take it amiss. It required me to perform this act without delay; otherwise I consider a good bargain might have been lost.'[2] The site was accepted and the town built a new Free Library to commemorate Victoria's Golden Jubilee. Craddock was renowned as the 'father of the Free Library'.[3]

The Mayors were not such leaders after the 1920s. Their role became increasingly ceremonial. Each year a Mayor made the same sort of speeches at the same kind of functions as the Mayor of the previous year. Little distinguished one Mayoralty from another. Since 1945 only one term of office stood out from the general run, that of James Beattie, the Conservative leader, in 1951–2. He is remembered as making a tour of all the departments of the Corporation to see for himself what exactly was going on. These reviews were not merely ceremonial; as he went round he made criticisms and suggestions for improvement. The ultimate point in the Mayor's becoming purely a ceremonial figure was reached in the term of the Conservative leader, M. P. Birch (1962–3), when he promised the Labour Party that if he was made Mayor he would not use his vote in the Council to support the Conservative Party but would always allow the Labour Party to have a majority. Indeed the Conservatives agreed that if Labour members were absent from a division, sufficient Conservatives would leave in order to enable the Labour Party to keep a majority of one. Many Labour members were amused that the Conservatives were prepared to forgo political power in order to get Labour

[1] *W.C.*, 14.11.1894. He had installed electricity in his house and works. *W.C.*, 16.11.1892.
[2] *W.C.*, 10.2.1897.
[3] *W.C.*, 17.4.1912.

support for their nominee as Mayor, who would shake hands with the Queen when she visited the Grammar School during his term of office.

There were many reasons why the Mayor of the 1950s and 1960s did not act the part of a leader of the Council as was done by the Mayors of the 1890s and 1900s. It is true that his ceremonial functions had increased and had left him with little time to do anything else. But the main reason for the change lay in the growing importance of party. The Mayor of the 1950s and 1960s owed his position on the Council to the support of his party, and even his position as Mayor was attained by the backing of his party. As a party member he could advocate no policy at variance with a decision of the Group, and the Group had its own leaders. The Chairmen of the two party Groups were the leaders of the two parties on the Council. The Group of the majority party replaced the General Purposes Committee as the place where the Chairmen tried to promote the causes of their committees over those of other Chairmen. Since the Mayor was not the Chairman of the Group, his influence therefore correspondingly declined. The Group selected the Mayor for the performance of ceremonial not political functions; he was expected to be non-political during his term of office. Indeed he did not attend Group meetings during his term as Mayor. When Mansell, the leader of the Labour Group, was Mayor (1955–6), he resigned as leader and attended no Group meetings.[1] The only time a Mayor attended Group meetings was during C. H. Davies's term in the exceptional period of 1961–2. The Mayor of the 1890s and 1900s did not owe his position to any party; he was not limited by any party policy and could thus, with more freedom, act as a leader of the Council. In the 1960s, however, the Councillors regarded the Mayoralty as a ceremonial office, without political power save in abnormal circumstances. Leadership was not the function of the Mayor.

Before 1947 the Mayor was chosen initially by the Mayoral Committee, on which sat all ex-Mayors of the borough, who made a recommendation to the Council, which always accepted the advice of the committee. The committee would meet, deliberate and send two or three of its members to ask the chosen one if he would accept. The criteria by which a man was assessed, said

[1] As did the Conservative leader Birch when Mayor in 1962–3.

ex-members of this committee, were his length of service on the Council, his work for the Council, his character, his religion, his speaking ability, whether or not he had a wife and the qualities of his wife. The health of the man and his wife were considered, since the strain of the term of office was a killer. Not all those who were asked accepted. Some would cry off because of ill health or because their wives were ill, or did not want the trouble, or because the term of office would cause their business or professional activities to suffer. Before the First World War the main qualification for Mayor was whether the individual had the wealth to maintain Mayoral hospitality, save for Lewis's case in 1898. Afterwards, up to 1945, seniority was the leading criterion for a request to be made, except that some Labour members, though senior to many non-Labour members, were not asked.

The Labour Party objected to this method of selection; it suggested that the choice should emerge spontaneously from the Council and not be fixed beforehand.[1] It opposed the 'self-elected' committee, which even announced its choice to the press before the whole Council had had a chance to consider the matter.[2] In 1947 the Labour Group decided to take the Mayoralty for the year and chose H. E. Lane; the Mayoral Committee did not agree, but Lane became Mayor through Labour's control of the full Council. From then, whenever Labour decided to take the Mayoralty, the individual picked was selected at the Group meeting. The Conservatives, however, adhered to the Mayoral Committee, so that whenever the Labour Group decided to let the Conservatives nominate for Mayor, their members on the Mayoral Committee would remain silent while the Conservatives chose their own man. In 1958 the Conservative members on the committee differed from the majority of the Conservative Group. Although the former prevailed, the Conservatives decided to scrap the old Mayoral Committee and to follow Labour practice. In 1960 the Council decided that 'in future mayors be nominated at a private meeting of the whole Council and not in the first instance by a special committee of all ex-mayors of the borough'.[3] In practice the process was that the majority Group decided whether

[1] *E. & S.*, 10.11.1924.
[2] *E. & S.*, 14.3.1932, 12.4.1932. *C.M.*, 11.4.1932.
[3] *C.M.*, 26.1.1960.

J.B.P.

it would take the Mayor for the year; if it decided to do so then it elected one of its members and got it through the Council; if it decided to allow the minority Group to nominate, then the choice was left to the Group of that party. Conservatives tried to obtain an agreement with the Labour Party about allocating the Mayoralty on a rota, but the Labour Party was always reluctant to yield its freedom of manoeuvre.

The leader of the Labour Group, Mansell, said in public that the main qualification for being a Mayor was 'a record of public service to the town irrespective of financial ability or party affiliation'.[1] The main qualification in practice, as considered by both parties, was seniority within the Group on the Council. Concentration on that factor eliminated much wearisome and fruitless debate about the quality of a candidate. It made the choice easy, except that in the Labour Party many Councillors entered for the first time in November 1945 and therefore within the Group the problem arose as to who was the senior. The issue was settled by voting.

Once the Group selected the candidate, then it was expected that he would be supported by both parties. Indeed he was usually nominated in the full Council by a member of his own party and seconded by a member of the other; often the leaders of the Groups performed this function. It was also expected that throughout his term of office the Mayor would be backed by both parties, since he was regarded as above politics, representing the Council as a whole. The only complaints ever made that a Mayor was not being supported by the party opposed to his, came during C. H. Davies's term of office, when some Labour members complained that the Conservatives were boycotting functions attended by Davies.[2] This accusation the Conservatives strenuously denied.[3]

The growth of party inside the Council caused the Mayor to be more of a ceremonial than a 'political' leader of the Council. The advent of the Labour Party caused the Mayor to become a salaried official of the Council, and made the occupational range of the Mayors less restricted than it was at the turn of the century when the office was the preserve of the manufacturers, professional men

[1] *E. & S.*, 24.5.1954.   [2] *E. & S.*, 21.8.1961.   [3] *E. & S.*, 22.8.1961.

and substantial shopkeepers. The Labour Party gave the Mayoralty to working men, women and old-age pensioners.[1] The Mayors in the 1960s were older and served a longer period on the Council before becoming Mayor than at the turn of the century. The average age of the Mayors of 1888 to 1903 was 47·2 years: from 1954 to 1962 it was 60·4.[2] The Mayors of 1888–1903 had served on an average 10·8 years on the Council; those of 1954–62 an average of 14·8.[3] These increases arose from the concentration on the factor of seniority as the main qualification for the Mayoralty.

All the Mayors of Wolverhampton from 1848 were chosen from existing members of the Council. Never was a prominent outsider asked to fill the position. The reason for this was that not only was there competition for the office from within the Council, but also it was felt that for an individual to perform effectively the functions of the ceremonial head of the Council and of the Chairman of the Council, actual experience of the working of the local authority was a vital prerequisite. Only once was the Mayor neither a Councillor nor an Alderman. In 1961 the Council elected C. H. Davies as Mayor, but did not re-elect him to the Aldermanic bench.

THE ALDERMEN

A position which is also eagerly sought by Councillors is a seat on the Aldermanic bench. Although an Alderman has no more powers than a Councillor, the very title of Alderman is prized. To be an Alderman is regarded as a high honour. In 1955 a Conservative Alderman claimed that the Labour plan to abolish Aldermen as undemocratic was a personal insult, since he had been elected in recognition of his service to the Council.[4] The Aldermen's robes were more splendid than those of the Councillors', and they sat apart from the Councillors on an elevated bench looking down upon the body of the Council Chamber. In 1960 a proposal was made that their seats should be occupied by the Chairmen of Council committees so that the Chairmen could be closer to the

[1] See Tables XXX and XXXI.
[2] See Table XXIV.
[3] See Table XXV.   [4] *E. & S.*, 28.11.1955.

Council officials who sat behind the Aldermanic bench. This was to enable the officials to avoid an unseemly move through the Aldermen to brief Chairmen, who as Councillors sat in the lower part of the Chamber. The plan was dropped, and the Aldermen retained their superior position.[1]

The Aldermen form a quarter of the Council, and are elected to the bench by the Councillors for a period of six years, when they retire or seek re-eleetion. Half of them retire every three years. Thus every third year the Councillors elect half the Aldermen. They could have chosen as an Alderman anyone qualified to be a Councillor, but from 1882 to 1964 they have selected members of the Council, except in 1927 when W. M. Furniss, who was not a Councillor, was elected to the bench. He had been a member of a Parish Council, whose area had just been taken into the borough, and thus his seat on the bench was not so much in recognition of his personal qualities as a peace offering to the area recently acquired. The office of Alderman was, therefore, not used to bring on to the Council experts or people with special qualifications who for some reason were unable to involve themselves in elections. The bench was reserved for Councillors.

Around the turn of the century the main qualification for becoming an Alderman was to have been a Mayor. Before 1890 it was said, 'it had never happened that a Councillor had been elected to the position of Mayor without his having been appointed an Alderman before his retirement.'[2] As late as 1924 it was said that it was the invariable rule to elect to the bench 'those members of the Council who had gone through the Mayoral chair'.[3] Between 1878 and 1964 only three Mayors had never been Aldermen: E. L. Cullwick, Mayor 1908–9, who died during his term of office; J. Grout, Mayor 1909–10, who retired immediately after his Mayoralty; and J. Beattie, Mayor 1951–2, who never became an Alderman because the Labour Party took all the vacancies while he remained on the Council.

Another factor was length of service on the Council. The claims of E. Bagaley were urged in 1891 on the grounds that he had been a member for twenty-eight years.[4] In 1904 the senior Councillor,

---

[1] *M.L.G.*, 25.3.1960, 25.11.1960.
[2] *W.C.*, 30.7.1890.
[3] *E. & S.*, 29.9.1924.   [4] *W.C.*, 15.7.1891.

J. Mason, was elected to the bench after twenty-seven years on the Council, although he had been neither a Mayor nor a Chairman, nor had he spoken much in the Council. The senior Councillor, although never a Mayor, was likely to be elected an Alderman if no ex-Mayor was still a Councillor.

Party, too, was a factor which must have been considered, since usually a Conservative took the place of a Conservative, and a Liberal that of a Liberal. As is shown in Table VI, the ratio on the bench during the 1890s up to 1904 was six Conservatives and six Liberals; but after the education controversy the Conservatives took an extra seat to make the ratio 7:5, which lasted until after the First World War.

Although all the Councillors voted for the Aldermen, the name submitted to the Council was decided in the General Purposes Committee, 'the inner circle'[1] of the Council. Here the 'trading' was done, so that contests for the seats were rare in open Council and only arose if the committee had failed to agree.

In the 1920s and 1930s Labour gained its first representation on the bench; the pattern was for the Labour Mayors to be given a seat after their Mayoralty when one was vacant. Thus the first Labour Mayor, T. Frost, was the first Labour Alderman in 1925; Davies, Whittaker and Beach, the next Labour Mayors, also became the next Labour Aldermen. The Labour Party argued, however, that they were not given adequate representation on the bench in proportion to their Councillors' seats, and that regard was not paid to the long service of some of their members. They also claimed that Davies, who had been Mayor in 1929–30, should have filled an Aldermanic vacancy in 1930, which instead was taken by a Liberal who had never been Mayor, but who had served on the Council eight years longer than Davies. Davies was, however, made an Alderman in 1931 at the next vacancy. Thus it was difficult to balance the many criteria for an Aldermanic seat in the 1920s and 1930s without upsetting somebody's feelings; by following one rule, another would be broken. Yet up to 1945 a balance was roughly kept between the Mayoral qualification, promoting the senior Councillor and sharing the seats in some relaiton to party strength on the Council. The only exceptions to

[1] *E. & S.*, 5.10.1898.

these qualifications occurred after Wolverhampton had extended her boundaries in 1927, when some newly elected Councillors from the recently acquired areas were made Aldermen at once.

Up to 1945 a seat on the Aldermanic bench was secure. Between 1888 and 1945 only one Alderman who sought re-election was rejected by his colleagues, and that was H. C. Owen in 1898, an unpopular and inefficient Chairman of the Markets Committee. Once an Alderman, the individual stayed on until death, illness or his own desire caused him to vacate the seat. However, between 1945 and 1964 twelve Aldermen seeking re-election were not chosen by their colleagues and were thus thrown out of the Council never to return, because none ever stood again for the Council. In 1945 Labour won a victory in the Council elections which gave them a majority of Councillors; at the ensuing Aldermanic elections they failed to vote for the six retiring Conservative Aldermen, and in their place put the six senior Labour Councillors, which gave them a majority of the whole Council. The majority was further increased, because these new Aldermen vacated safe Labour wards which at the following by-elections duly returned more Labour members. The Conservatives who were removed had been Chairmen; all but two had been Mayors and they were recognised as some of the leading figures on the Council. Their departure was bitterly resented by Conservatives, who dated the influence of party politics on the Council from this event.[1] None of the new Labour members had been Chairmen; none had been Mayors and three of them made little impression ever on the Council.

In 1949 the Conservatives regained a majority, and in the following Aldermanic elections threw off the bench the eighty-six-year-old Labour Alderman, T. Frost, who had first entered the Council in 1901. The Labour Party claimed that he had been given the 'dirty kick-out' as retaliation for 1945. But the circumstances were different then. Labour had 26 and the anti-Labour forces had 34. It was necessary if they were to have a majority to displace six Aldermen. However, if Frost had been re-elected, the anti-Labour

---

[1] The *Express and Star* commented: 'Town Councils ought not to be the cockpits of party politics. Nor should party considerations be the sole reason for depriving the community of the services of men who were fitted to continue the administration of local affairs.' 10.11.1945.

Group would still have had a majority of six. As the next Aldermanic elections came round in 1952 it was felt that 'if the anti-
Socialists maintain or increase their majority of one on the Council,
it may be assumed that the five retiring Labour Aldermen seeking
re-election will be replaced from among the anti-Socialist
Councillors'.[1] Labour, however, gained a majority, and turned off
the two anti-Socialist Aldermen seeking re-election. From then
until the notorious days of 1961 no Alderman seeking re-election
was removed. The Labour Group in 1955 and 1958 re-elected the
retiring Aldermen *en bloc*.

The history of the Aldermanic bench from 1945 to 1952, and in
1961–2, shows that an Alderman was in a more insecure position
than when he was a Councillor, since to qualify for an Aldermanic
seat he would have to have been a Councillor for a long time, which
presupposed that he had held a safe seat. Thus in Wolverhampton
where the parties were so evenly balanced and control of the
Council was liable to go either way, a Councillor who gave up a
safe ward to become an Alderman was not gaining security from
the whims of the electorate but was putting himself in a more
insecure position. Since the parties were so close, the number of
Aldermen possessed by a party was of decisive importance in
determining which side would be in control. It was for that reason
that the Conservative Group imposed discipline on its members
with regard to voting for Aldermen. Where the control of the
Council by the Group was at stake, a majority decision of the
Group was binding on all members.

From 1952 to 1961 controversy about Aldermen centred on
whether the Labour Group would allow a casual vacancy in a
seat previously held by a Conservative to be filled again by a
Conservative. The Conservatives constantly sought an agreement
with the Labour Group about filling the vacancies, on the basis of
the bench reflecting the proportion of Councillors possessed by
each party. The Labour Group was divided. Some advocated that
every seat should be taken by the majority party, while others
pressed for an agreement. The way out of the dilemma was for
each case to be considered on its merits. The year 1957 illustrates
a typical situation. In June following the resignation of the Conservative, T. W. Phillipson, the Labour Group filled his seat with

[1] *W.C.*, 24.4.1952.

C. H. Davies, while the Conservatives voted for their senior Councillor, W. J. Foster. In July, after the death of the Conservative J. Haddock, the Labour Group allowed the Conservatives to fill the vacancy with W. J. Foster. One Labour Councillor, J. K. Woodward, walked out of the Chamber as the vote was taking place in protest against the Labour Group's decision not to take the seat. He was the main spokesman of those who wanted the party to take all the seats. During these years Labour increased its proportion of members on the Aldermanic bench from 8:7 in 1952 to 10:5 in 1957.

After 1945 the effective choice of the Aldermen took place not in the General Purposes Committee, but in the Groups of the two parties. The ultimate decision lay with the Group of the majority party. If it decided to take the seat, then it nominated and its majority ensured victory for its choice. If it decided to let the minority party nominate, then it stayed silent and did not vote in the Council when the minority Group brought forward its candidate. Inside the Groups the criterion for choosing an Alderman was length of service on the Council; the senior Councillor in the Group was granted the seat. If there was doubt about who was senior – for instance as in the Labour Group when many entered at the same time in 1945 a vote of the Group decided the winner.[1]

Length of service was a convenient objective test on which to base a decision. To try to appoint Aldermen on the subjective test of merit would have caused much controversy since opinions as to merit differ. Promotion by seniority helped to remove a large number of possible conflicts. A result of choosing Aldermen on length of service was an increase in the average age of the Aldermen. The average age of those appointed to the Aldermanic bench in 1888 to 1903 was 50 years; those elected between 1953 and 1962 averaged 65·1. The average age of the Aldermen in the Council of 1903–4 was 58·5; in that of 1962–3 it was 68·2.[2] The length of service on the Council before election to the bench increased from 11·6 years for those chosen in 1888–1903 to 15·8 years for those

---

[1] In March 1964 the Labour Group dropped the criterion of seniority, when it nominated as Alderman the Secretary of the Group, F. S. Smith, 'for services to the Group'. He won the ballot by one vote. Five Labour Councillors had longer periods of service than his.

[2] See Table XXIV.

chosen in 1953–62.[1] Although the average age of the Aldermen rose, there is no evidence that there were more useless and ineffective members on the bench than sixty years ago. If one takes any date over the period 1888 to 1960 one will find on the bench one or two, rarely more, who are too old to be efficient. Almost every decade has one Alderman who once gave good service to the Council, but in his eighties dutifully turns up to each Council meeting, is propped up in his chair, covered with a rug and sits staring to the front while business is conducted. Often his only movement comes when it is time to vote; and the way to vote is shouted down his ear trumpet or else a colleague lifts his hand or answers the roll call for him when his vote is called for. At the end of the meeting he will be carried out by a friend to a waiting wheelchair.[2] These individuals were once the leading figures in the Council, and members did not have the heart to remove them from the bench, since they realised that the disappointment would be fatal. These shadows of once effective men lived only for the Council.

The Aldermen over the period were the leading men of the Council, occupying the Chairmanships. Between 1888 and 1964 only four Aldermen never held a Chairmanship. They became Aldermen through seniority and two of them were made Aldermen in 1945 by the Labour Party when the six Conservatives were replaced. The majority of Aldermen had been Chairmen on being elected to the bench or else became Chairmen within a year. Only a few were not Chairmen and only became Chairmen some years later.[3] In the 1950s, of course, the Conservative Aldermen did not hold Chairmanships since the majority Labour Party took them all. In 1962–3 all the Labour Aldermen were

---

[1] See Table XXV.

[2] e.g., B. F. Williams, Alderman 1896–1911, aged 82 when out of office.

J. Marston,	Alderman	1891–1918,	aged 82	when out of office			
F. D. Gibbons,	,,	1882–1925,	,, 87	,,	,,	,,	,,
L. Johnson,	,,	1900–37,	,, 87	,,	,,	,,	,,
T. W. Dickinson	,,	1914–42,	,, 84	,,	,,	,,	,,
T. Frost,	,,	1925–49,	,, 86	,,	,,	,,	,,
J. Haddock,	,,	1931–57,	,, 83	,,	,,	,,	,,
J. H. Coleman,	,,	1933–61,	,, 88	,,	,,	,,	,,
J. Cahill,	,,	1938–64,	,, 89	,,	,,	,,	,,

[3] A notable example is L. J. Woolridge, elected to the Council in 1935; an Alderman from 1945, who became a Chairman only in 1960 of the new Civic Catering Committee because no one else was available to take it.

Chairmen. The leaders of the Labour and Conservative Groups were Aldermen. Some leading Chairmen, however, did not have Aldermanic seats, the Chairmen of Finance and of Education Committees for example, since they were not qualified through long service. Holding a Chairmanship is not proof of ability, but the holding of a key committee is. In 1962–3 Aldermen held the Chairs of Children's, Health, Housing, Transport, Parks and Cemeteries, and Civic Catering Committees, and if the judgment of the High Court had gone in favour of the Labour Party the bench would also have contained the Chairmen of Town Planning, Welfare Services, Watch, Cleansing, and Fire and Ambulance Committees. Thus the Aldermanic bench was not merely dignified; it supported members of the Council who had leading positions of responsibility, save for the one or two who once held such positions but whom old age had overtaken. Such a picture was accurate over the whole period.

The occupational composition of the Aldermanic bench changed since the turn of the century. Around 1900 the Aldermen were the leading social figures in the Council and in the town, the big manufacturers, professional men and merchants. With the rise of the Labour Party the 1940s and 1950s saw as Aldermen working men and women. Labour brought new groups to the bench.[1]

In Wolverhampton, despite the fact that the Conservatives suffered most from the Labour Party's use of the Aldermanic bench to reinforce or to obtain a majority, they defended the office of Alderman against Labour's attempts to abolish it. In 1955 the Council debated a Labour motion that the existence of the office was no longer justified either on grounds of principle or practical advantage, and that the Association of Municipal Corporations should be asked to make representations to the Minister to introduce legislation to abolish Aldermen. Labour members said that 'Aldermen were elected to suit the whims and fancies of the controlling political parties'; they were 'pawns in the political game': 'The office had been abused up and down the country': 'All power should come direct from the people and not second-hand': 'The Aldermanic bench represented the past and not the future.' The Conservatives defended the office as being a reward for long service and ability. 'It was good to have a group of elder

[1] Tables XXXII and XXXIII.

statesmen not looking over their shoulders all the time to the electorate for votes.' It was 'a haven of rest from the hurly-burly of electioneering'.[1] The motion was carried, referred to the A.M.C. whose General Purposes Committee rejected it.[2] Labour again called for the abolition of Aldermen during the crisis in 1961–2, but the office continued, still eagerly eyed by ambitious Councillors and still to be used as a 'pawn in the political game'.

The elected members were very keen to become Mayors and Aldermen. These were the top jobs in the Council. Competition was keen between individuals and between parties. But the conflicts were not simply about patronage for its own sake; they were about power, since the political control of the Council could turn on the Aldermen and even on the single figure, the Mayor. Personal and party ambitions combined to produce exceptionally bitter fights over these positions. The most bitter is described in Chapter 16.

[1] *E. & S.*, 28.11.1955. *C.M.*, 28.11.1955.
[2] *E. & S.*, 28.1.1956.

13 The Town Clerks

THE chief permanent official of the Corporation is the Town Clerk. He is its legal adviser, the head of the Corporation's administration and he is responsible for the secretarial work of the Council and its committees, e.g. providing clerks to record committee minutes. He also has various other duties to perform like drawing up the electoral roll. Legally he is the servant of the Council, but his permanency in office and his professional expertise give him in practice a more powerful role.[1] The potentialities of his office are great, since he surveys the work of the Council as a whole and is in touch with all departments and committees. But the use he makes of these potentialities depends on his personality, temperament and skill. If he so desires, he can become the leader of the Council, directing and energising all its activities, or he can be its servant in the background, confined strictly to his legal duties. Only the office of Treasurer has similar potentialities, since he, too, is concerned with the work of every committee; but his impingement on other committees is confined to one field, finance, and is thus not so extensive as the Town Clerk's. If the Clerk is exceptionally retiring and the Treasurer exceptionally forward, then the latter may be more powerful than the former. In Wolverhampton this situation occurred only for a very few years, and for this reason this study concentrates on the Town Clerks[2] without examining very deeply the role of the other officers.

Between 1900 and 1964 there were five Town Clerks of Wolverhampton, each differing in personality, temperament, skill and style of working. These personal differences were an important

[1] See T. Headrick, *The Town Clerk in English Local Government*, London, 1963.
[2] It would require another book to deal with the administrative history of the Corporation.

explanation for the comparative decline in the prominence of the office of Town Clerk over the period, and for this reason the first part of this chapter considers each Town Clerk individually. But other factors, too, reduced the freedom of action, independence and autonomy of the Clerks, namely the growing functions of the Council, the increase in administrative staff, the rising importance of other officials of the Corporation and the impact of the party system on the Council. These will be examined after the personal sketches of the Clerks.

SIR HORATIO BREVITT, 1882–1919

In 1900 the Town Clerk of Wolverhampton was Horatio Brevitt, knighted in 1915.[1] He had been appointed Town Clerk in 1882 at the age of thirty-five. He was the town's first full-time Clerk, since his predecessors had performed their Corporation duties while still remaining in private practice as solicitors. His immediate predecessor was Henry Underhill, to whom he had been articled. Before 1882 Brevitt's work had been in Wolverhampton only, as a solicitor, holding such offices as solicitor to the Wolverhampton Tradesmen's Association, clerk to the county magistrates of the Wolverhampton Division and Deputy Coroner for Wolverhampton. He had experience of no other town and had not been to university.[2]

He was a very tall and imposing man, with a large head, prominent features and a military moustache. He dressed in clothes which accentuated his impressive figure, a top hat and tail coat with a fur collar. He liked to convey to people that he was a man of power. He regarded himself and expected others to regard him as the 'Town Governor' and the 'leading man in the town'. He counted himself as on the same social level as the manufacturers and professional men, who were members of the Council and held the Chairmanships. When dealing with them, when arguing with them over a scheme, he would treat them as equals. Indeed he had been one of them when he had been a private solicitor, and he still met them socially and at church. He differed

---

[1] *W.C.*, 13.1.1915.
[2] *Wolverhampton Journal*, April 1902. *E. & S.*, 26.4.1933.

from the Chairmen only in that he was paid for his Council work and surveyed all committees and not just a few.

He did not regard himself as a mere servant of the Council. In debates he would intervene at will to expound his views and to explain his policy, much to the annoyance of those who were interrupted or attacked. In July 1905 Bantock was interrupted by Brevitt, who accused Bantock of making 'mis-statements', and of knowing nothing about the subject. Bantock demanded a withdrawal of the insult; he would not submit to such impertinence from the Town Clerk, who was the servant of the Council. Brevitt replied, 'I beg to say that I am not the servant of the Council.' Bantock: 'You are paid by the Council at any rate.' Brevitt: 'I am a public official of the Council.'[1] The Town Clerk was determined to press his opinion, whatever the Council might think, and to act independently of it. 'We have a Town Clerk who does not always obey his orders',[2] said the Chairman of Parks and Baths Committee in 1910. Complaints were made against his 'dictation',[3] that he was an 'autocratic boss',[4] 'on the high horse as usual'[5]. And it was said that 'any criticism of his actions amounted almost to a case of *lèse majesté*.'[6] On Brevitt's retirement in 1919, the Mayor spoke of him as being 'Napoleonic in manner and method',[7] but 'he had such a happy knack of being right: of suggesting the finest remedy, of clearly handling each knotty problem that the town and his colleagues had suffered him gladly'.

His work for the Council can be divided into three periods: the first from 1882 to the early 1890s, when he was learning his job; the second from the early 1890s to the early 1900s, when he was vigorously engaged in promoting numerous projects of various committees; and the third from the mid-1900s to his retirement in 1919, when he 'slowed down'. In the second period, that of his great creative activity, he helped to promote the Wolverhampton Corporation Act of 1887, the Wolverhampton Improvement Act of 1891, and the Wolverhampton Tramways Act of 1899, which

---

[1] *W.C.*, 12.7.1905. In 1903 the Chairman of Education Committee objected to Brevitt's interventions. *W.C.*, 18.3.1903.

[2] *W.C.*, 13.4.1910. [3] *W.C.*, 15.3.1893.

[4] *W.C.*, 11.11.1908. [5] *W.C.*, 10.10.1900.

[6] *W.C.*, 9.12.1903. [7] *E. & S.*, 14.7.1919.

enabled the town to build an Art Gallery, School of Art and a new Free Library, to extend its sewage works, to buy out the old tramway company and construct a new electric system. He helped to initiate and extend the Corporation's electricity undertaking, to build the new Wholesale Market and Cold Stores and Borough Hospital, and to obtain for the town the East Park. He helped to pilot the Bills through Parliament, he represented the Corporation in litigation over the acquisition of the tramways, the disposal of the town's sewage, and its water supply, and he negotiated with businessmen and landowners for land for the Corporation's undertakings.[1] In all these schemes Brevitt did not work alone, nor initiate the projects by himself. He worked with the Chairmen of the committees, assisting, guiding and at times dictating. It was not a one-man show; he was in partnership with the great social figures in the town, who were Chairmen of committees whose fortunes they were eager to forward.

Brevitt took great pride in being responsible for increasing in the Local Government Act of 1888 the number of County Boroughs from ten to sixty-one, thus including Wolverhampton. He claimed that when he saw that Wolverhampton was not to be a County Borough, he rushed to London to see H. H. Fowler, one of Wolverhampton's M.P.s, to whom he complained that Wolverhampton would become a second-rate borough. Fowler took him to see Ritchie, the President of the Local Government Board, whom they told that if he adhered to ten places only, he might count upon agitation. Fowler later told Brevitt that 'it was the immediate action he took which led to those good results',[2] i.e. of extending the number of County Boroughs to include Wolverhampton.

In the mid-1900s he sought no more great activity. In 1907 he was sixty, and growing older inhibited him from undertaking any more large projects. Seeking to avoid extra work, he argued against those who wanted the town to extend its boundaries, or to widen the streets in the town centre, or to demolish the old Retail Market Hall and to construct a new one, or to build a Public Hall for the town. He stressed the difficulties involved, the powerful resistance of vested interests, whether neighbouring authorities, Market Hall

[1] *W.C.*, 10.7.1907. *E. & S.*, 26.4.1933.
[2] *E. & S.*, 15.7.1919.

tenants, landowners, shopkeepers and ratepayers. He became a pessimistic 'stick in the mud'. The eager Chairmen like Bantock, Craddock and Myatt wished that Brevitt would retire,[1] since he was a stumbling block to their plans for the town. But Brevitt's age, his long service and experience, the respect in which he was held by the majority of the Council and the town, all contributed to his survival. What finally brought him down was the Varley scandal, which revealed that Brevitt had been lax about his duties, in that he had not adequately supervised the Education Committee and that he had disobeyed Council Standing Orders by not informing the Council that Varley as a Company Director had a remunerative appointment in addition to his position as an employee of the Corporation. Bantock, Craddock and Myatt hoped to use this episode to disgrace Brevitt and force him out. He was severely censured by the committees of investigation, and he told the Council that 'I have gone through enough to kill any man'.[2] But he stayed on as Town Clerk for eighteen months longer, until the end of the war. Although he had been 'ruined', he was still held in great respect, especially for his previous services to the Council. In 1919 at the age of seventy-two he retired; yet he did not sever all connections with the corporation, for he was retained as a 'consulting solicitor' for another six years at £500 per annum,[3] very much to the anger of some of his opponents. He was not consulted, however, by the new Town Clerk, who had no respect for Brevitt's abilities and regarded him as having neglected Wolverhampton's potential through his negative and obstructionist attitude.

F. W. HOWELL, 1919–29

Brevitt's successor was F. W. Howell, aged thirty-five, in 1919.[4] He had been articled to the Town Clerk of Birmingham, where he rose to be an Assistant Solicitor. In 1915 he was appointed Deputy Town Clerk of Wolverhampton. He was not a university graduate. Like Brevitt, he was tall, with a handsome, impressive figure and a forceful personality. He was as autocratic as Brevitt, 'a man of iron, with steel in him', but unlike Brevitt he was an adept flatterer,

---

[1] There was no formal retiring age of sixty-five then.
[2] *W.C.*, 5.12.1917.
[3] *W.C.*, 12.3.1919.   [4] *W.C.*, 18.6.1919.

who knew how to insinuate his ideas into the minds of the Chairmen so that they would enthusiastically advocate his proposals while regarding them as their own. He was regarded as more able than Brevitt, more competent and on top of his job; he was 'ultra-efficient', 'austere and dedicated to his work'. He was a young man in a hurry, out to make a name for himself and thus rise to higher office. In Wolverhampton he had full scope to make a reputation, since Brevitt's neglect of the town provided ample opportunities for him to display his talents. And to achieve his ends, he 'worked all hours'.

Howell had his own opinions about the policy the Council should pursue and he sought to get the Council to follow where he led. He complained that Brevitt had had no breadth of vision about the future of the town. Wolverhampton, to Howell, was in a 'superb position' to attract industry, situated as it was on the edge of the Black Country close to a densely populated urban area which would provide a good market, and yet close to an attractive rural area which would provide charming residences for businessmen. Howell's aim was 'to polish the apple to make it sell'. His objectives were to rebuild the town centre, particularly to widen the streets to make the shopping area more accessible to traffic, and to improve the shop frontages. This development would increase the rateable value of the property and attract more custom to the town. He wanted to demolish the old Market Hall, use the site as a parking area near the centre and rebuild the Market elsewhere. He wanted to expand the transport enterprise, to take the trams and then trolley buses further into the suburbs so that more people would find the town centre more accessible. He wanted to extend the boundaries of the town to produce a 'Greater Wolverhampton', with more resources to pay for its projects, and he particularly wanted to join to Wolverhampton the industrial areas to the east and north of the town to diversify the economy of Wolverhampton as a guarantee against slump in the metal industry. For this end also he sought to bring new industry into the town. His aims tallied well with those of such leading members of the Council as Bantock, Myatt and Craddock.

In the ten years of Howell's Town Clerkship of Wolverhampton most of his aims were realised. In 1926 the boundaries of the borough were extended for the first time in its history. Goodyear's

and Courtauld's established big factories in the town. An Improvement Act of 1925 enabled the Corporation to widen and improve
the streets of the centre and to expand the transport services.
The only parts of his projects which he had not fulfilled by 1929
were the demolition of the old Market Hall and the provision of
parking space near the centre. This was not achieved until the
late 1950s. Howell's departure in 1929 delayed his plan for thirty
years. Howell was in the thick of achieving these policies. He drew
up the Bills, piloted them through Parliament, was skilled in
putting his case, showed up well in cross-examination, and was
most astute in negotiating with businessmen to persuade them
to come to Wolverhampton.

Howell was not a dictator of the Council, he sought to carry
it with him; and he did this chiefly by convincing the two leading
Chairmen on the Council, Bantock and Myatt, of the value of his
schemes. To those two he devoted much time, and once he had
their support, he could rely on the Council following their lead.
In debate also he would speak, explaining his policy and persuading the Council to back him. When later in Manchester he tried
to speak for the same purpose in a debate, he found his action
frowned upon. Howell claimed that Brevitt had tamed the Wolverhampton Council into accepting a lead of this kind from the Town
Clerk. Howell regarded himself not as a mere servant of the
Council or an adviser, but as a 'Managing Director' who was to
stimulate and co-ordinate its work, to initiate policies and to
create among the members of the Council enthusiasm for the
policies. He was the leader of a team.

Howell regarded himself as the Chief Officer of the Corporation,
to whom the other officials were subordinate. He 'ruled' the other
departments as the 'boss'. If he wanted to speak to another official,
the latter had to come to Howell's office. He would tell other
officials that they were incompetent and 'pull them over the
coals' if he was dissatisfied with their work. When a leading official,
whom Howell regarded as incompetent, heard that Howell was
leaving, 'he danced a jig'. Howell held regular meetings with his
chief officials, over whom he presided. He was not merely a *primus
inter pares* but a boss. He was forced to be this to a large extent by
the nature of his plans. To produce the Improvement Act, for instance, required the active co-operation of almost every department.

To advance his schemes for the town as a whole demanded that he had to run the Corporation as a whole. Howell said that he was able to do this in the Wolverhampton of the 1920s and not in the Manchester of the 1930s, because of the smaller size of Wolverhampton; its Corporation was small enough for him to be able to keep all departments under control.

Howell was an impressive Town Clerk. He was regarded as a 'man of vision', 'initiative', 'great resources' and 'tenacity of purpose'. He had been 'an unparalleled success' as the 'guiding star of the borough'.[1] The reputation he earned at Wolverhampton gained him the appointment as Town Clerk of Manchester in 1928. And in 1938 he was made Joint-General Manager of the Halifax Building Society. This appointment, too, was based to a great extent on the reputation he had made for himself in Wolverhampton.

J. BROCK ALLON, 1929–54

As if seeking a respite and relaxation, the Council appointed as Howell's successor a man of 'retiring disposition'.[2] J. Brock Allon was forty when he became Wolverhampton's Town Clerk in 1929. He was the town's first Town Clerk to have a degree, a B.A. from London. He had had experience of many towns: articled to the Town Clerk of South Shields, he then served as Assistant Solicitor at Exeter, Deputy Town Clerk at Middlesbrough and Town Clerk of Dudley. Thus, unlike his two predecessors, he came to Wolverhampton after considerable experience elsewhere, and unlike Howell he was not at the start of a career with a name to make. It is generally agreed that he felt that on coming to Wolverhampton he had come to the end of his career. He was therefore not anxious to undertake any striking ventures.

The descriptions of Allon are in great contrast to those of Brevitt and Howell; 'quiet', a 'nice gentleman', and an 'uncle type' and 'homely'; he early 'got into the groove' and sought a 'quiet life', playing safe by taking the line of least resistance. He did not take the initiative, but waited on events and for others, whether the chief officers of other departments or elected members.

[1] *E. & S.*, 29.12.1928. [2] *E. & S.*, 4.12.1928.

Once these had proposed some course of action, he would try to guide them and smooth over any difficulties, supporting them with his 'anonymous enthusiasm'. He had no broad plans of his own for the town. He wanted the machine to keep ticking over. He was praised for being good at delegating work. Others regarded the same trait as 'laziness', and thought that he was inclined to leave things alone and let them slide. Clerks in his department felt that Brock Allon's appointment marked the start of the decline of the Town Clerk's department, which under Brevitt and Howell had been the leading department of the Corporation, with the greatest prestige and most attractive for school-leavers. But from 1929 the reputation of the department fell. Other departments and their officials asserted their independence. The Treasurer's department under Jesse Boydell,[1] a keen and vigorous man, who 'worked all day and night', had a higher standing than Brock Allon's department.

When Brock Allon retired in 1954 after twenty-five years as Town Clerk, the list of his achievements was meagre compared to that of Howell after just ten years. The Council mentioned that he had successfully promoted a Bill in 1932 to extend Wolverhampton's boundaries, that he had encouraged the building of the Civic Hall in 1938, that he was the Civil Defence Controller, had prepared Wolverhampton's evidence for the abortive Boundary Commission, had been responsible for the preparations for various royal visits and had been in charge of the celebrations of the centenary of the borough in 1948.[2] He was described as unassuming, a genial and kindly man, of grace and charm.[3] His reply to these praises seemed an attempt to depict himself as far more significant than he had been. 'It had been said that while a Council formed and initiated policy, an official should not interfere in the formation of that policy. But he had always felt it his duty to suggest policy to committees and to Chairmen and to take part in private, and in committee, in policy discussions. He felt he should make available to a committee the fund of experience and intimate knowledge of the Council's affairs which he had acquired over the years.'[4] In 1949 he had said in an interview to the local newspaper

---

[1] 1926–32. He was appointed Treasurer of Nottingham in 1932.
[2] *C.M.*, 21.12.1953.
[3] *E. & S.*, 21.12.1953.   [4] Ibid.

that he was not 'simply a grand co-ordinator', but that he did take the initiative in matters of policy, suggesting various lines to pursue.[1] Yet even his own description of what taking the initiative meant was very pale and weak compared to what Howell meant by the same words.

A. G. DAWTRY, 1954–6

As if reacting to Allon's quiet regime, the Council chose as his successor the more dynamic A. G. Dawtry, aged thirty-nine. He was the town's first Town Clerk to have a law degree, from Sheffield University. He had been articled to the Town Clerk of Sheffield, Assistant Solicitor there too, and Deputy Town Clerk at Bolton and Leicester. He had been a lieutenant-colonel in the Royal Artillery,[2] and had been to Military Staff College. First and foremost he was a brisk administrator, concerned to run a well-oiled machine and to prevent snags. In his two years in Wolverhampton he was not able to make any contribution in the form of policy or any new project, and the reputation he earned was as an efficient administrator and manager of men in an organisation. He was not intimate enough with Wolverhampton nor interested enough in its problems to conceive any long-range plans for its future. Almost as soon as he arrived, he seemed keen to move on elsewhere. Within a year he was short-listed for the Clerkship of the L.C.C.,[3] and in two years he had been appointed Town Clerk of Westminster.[4] No positive achievements could be credited to his name on his retirement from Wolverhampton, and his own speech of farewell was largely a justification of his leaving so soon. He said that officials should move from place to place before settling down, to broaden their experience and to bring to local government as a whole the experience of other local authorities.[5] Dawtry's main achievement was perhaps to convince the Council that it did not want another unknown, using Wolverhampton as a stepping-stone to higher office.

---

[1] *E. & S.*, 16.11.1949. [2] *E. & S.*, 24.9.1953.
[3] *E. & S.*, 4.10.1955. [4] *E. & S.*, 9.3.1956.
[5] *E. & S.*, 23.7.1956.

R. J. MEDDINGS, 1956–

Dawtry's successor, R. J. Meddings, was well known to the whole Council. Aged thirty-nine in 1956, he had spent most of his working life in the Wolverhampton Corporation. He had been articled to the Town Clerk of Todmorden in Yorkshire and in 1947 arrived in Wolverhampton as third Assistant Solicitor. He rose through the grades until in 1954 he became Deputy Town Clerk, and in 1956 Town Clerk. Thus his only experience of the administration of a large town was in Wolverhampton itself. He was not a university graduate.

His outstanding characteristic to both Councillors and officials was his sociability; a 'hail-fellow-well-met-type', on Christian name terms with all. 'They call him Ronnie; he plays darts, bowls and cricket and drinks with his colleagues and Councillors.' He was a far cry from the unapproachability and disdainful aloofness of Brevitt, Howell and even Allon.

The Labour Group which was in a majority while he was Town Clerk found him a 'true servant'. One Labour Alderman regarded Allon as a 'big stinker, hand in glove with the Tories', but Meddings he described as 'a true white man'. The Labour Group admired Meddings and listened most attentively to his advice. Officials within his department thought highly of him too, regarding as first-class his abilities as a co-ordinator of the administration and as an adviser of the Council.

So far the Town Clerk's position has been considered in terms of the personality of the individual holder of the office. The great divide has been seen as 1929 when the somewhat ineffectual Brock Allon replaced the dynamic Warbreck Howell. The decline of the Town Clerk, however, cannot be completely explained away by personalities. Other trends were at work which would have limited even Howell if he had remained in Wolverhampton. The 1930s and 1940s witnessed the rise in the importance and independence of the chief officials of other Town Hall departments, and the rise and growing significance of the party Groups. Whatever the temperament and attitude of the Town Clerk to his job, he could not fail to be severely restricted by these two processes.

OTHER CHIEF OFFICIALS

In 1900 there was no other official to rival Brevitt. Many were part-timers like the Treasurer and the Medical Officer of Health. Others had not the social standing nor the professional qualifications of the Town Clerk. During the 1920s and 1930s as the work of the Corporation increased in amount and technicality, part-timers were removed and their jobs became full-time, while new officials were appointed to new departments. A single solicitor could not have all the activities of the Corporation at his finger-tips.

These chief officials were members of their professional associations, skilled in the mysteries of their professions, jealous, too, of their skills against interference by the unqualified; one of whom would be the Town Clerk. The coming of Brock Allon, who was not of the temperament to assert his department's authority, coincided with an increase in the self-consciousness of the other officials, who were eager to assert the independence of their departments against the subjection which Howell had maintained over them. They would stress that they were directly responsible to their committees and ultimately to the Council as a whole and not to them through the Town Clerk, nor to the Town Clerk himself. Some idea of the standing of the Town Clerk's official colleagues can be gauged from a consideration of the offices held in their professional associations by the chief officers of the Corporation in 1954 on Brock Allon's retirement. The Chief Constable had been President of the Association of Chief Police Officers; the Medical Officer of Health, President of the Society of Medical Officers of Health; the Manager of the Sewage Disposal Department, the President of the Institute of Sewage Purification; the Water Engineer, the President of the Institute of Water Engineers; The Treasurer, the President of the Institute of Municipal Treasurers and Accountants; the Transport Manager, the President of the Municipal Passenger Transport Association; the Borough Engineer, Vice-President of the Institute of Municipal Engineers, and the Inspector of Weights and Measures, the Vice-President of the Institute of Weights and Measures.[1]

[1] *E. & S.*, 18.11.1954.

That they held these positions indicates that they were men of some standing in their professions and were unlikely to allow themselves to be dominated by the Town Clerk. They were experts in their own fields. Brevitt and Howell never had to face such qualified colleagues, conscious of their own professional standing. Meddings was limited by such men. He did not hold regular meetings with the chief officers, but if he was involved in any project which required their assistance, then they would assemble to talk it over. It was purely an *ad hoc* affair and implied no subordination of the officers to the Town Clerk. In Wolverhampton as the committees and the Chairmen were very independent, so were the chief officials. Meddings regarded his job as one of co-ordination, to ensure that all the officials were pulling in the same general direction, and that the administrative machine was working smoothly. He saw the Council as a 'confederation', of largely independent departments and committees, subordinate only in a broad way to his department and the Council as a whole.

Another indication of the change in the relationship of the Town Clerk with the other chief officials can be seen from a comparison of the salaries paid to the Corporation officials in 1900 and 1963. In 1900 the Town Clerk received £900 a year; the other chief officials received £450. In 1963 the Town Clerk received £4300 and five other officials received £3650. The narrowing gap between the salaries is symbolic of the decline of the supremacy of the Town Clerk in relation to his colleagues.

THE PARTY GROUPS

Neither Brevitt not Howell had to face party Groups on the Council. The Conservative and Liberal Parties then had no municipal programmes to implement, and the Labour Party, which had, never numbered more than thirteen until 1933. Policy-making was effectively left to the committees of the Council and particularly to the Chairmen, assisted by their chief officers. In this context there was ample scope for the Town Clerk to intervene with policies of his own, and to act as a broker between the competing Chairmen and committees. During the 1930s the Labour numbers increased, and after 1945 the Group system became common to both sides. The parties therefore set the framework of policy, within which the Town Clerk was expected to operate. For him to press his own line would be taken as an intrusion into the sphere of the elected members. Thus the Town Clerk no longer intervened in debate to advocate his own plans, nor could he be recognised as having a policy of his own. He was regarded by the Labour Chairmen of Finance as an 'administrative leader', concerned with the overall efficiency of the Town Hall machine, and as the legal adviser to the Council. He was not viewed as the policy or political leader. That function was for the party Group. In 1900 only the Town Clerk had an overall view of the work of the Council. In 1960 the party Groups performed the function also.

Meddings, then, was not associated with any particular policy. He did not initiate. Most of the initiatives in the Corporation originated from the departments and especially from the chief officials. They then tried to encourage the elected members to take them up, chiefly through persuading the Chairmen, who then tried to persuade the leaders of the Group and then the Group itself. The Town Clerk pointed out the difficulties involved in the adoption of the proposals and gave assistance to his officials in smoothing away the snags. He was very close to the leader of the Labour Group, whom he could ring up at any time and with whom informally he had many talks about the problems of the Council. He was on similar easy terms with the leader of the Conservative Group too. The Town Clerk, then, acted as a co-ordinator between the officials themselves, and between the officials and the party Groups through the leaders of the Groups. He thus tried to promote a consensus between the various elements which were concerned with policy, and in the process of working out compromises and arrangements between these elements he could, if he was skilful, press home a particular line of his own, perhaps to produce a shift of emphasis. But he could not impose a particular policy of his own.

Brevitt did not operate in the context of party Groups or face powerful chief officers of Corporation departments. He was imperious and autocratic, regarding himself as on a par with the Chairmen. He had no overall thought-out plans for Wolverhampton, but reacted to initiatives of the Chairmen; in the 1890s he responded enthusiastically and assisted them to promote some great projects. In the 1900s he responded negatively and sought to obstruct the schemes of the Chairmen. Howell also did not come up against party Groups or rival officials. He was imperious, but able to flatter the Chairmen into following his guidance, and he had plans for Wolverhampton as a whole which covered a wide range of Council activities. Brock Allon was retiring, not eager to assert himself against the growing influence of other officials in the Corporation. Also during his term of office the elected members organised themselves into party Groups, which regarded themselves as the source and final arbiter of policy. Dawtry was concerned with administrative efficiency only. Meddings had to come to terms with the party Groups and with the chief officers of the Council departments. He was thus far more limited in his freedom of action and in his scope for promoting his own plans for Wolverhampton.

14 Pressures and Controversies – the traditional system

THE majority of the items dealt with by the Council over the whole period were non-controversial: routine administrative matters or policy decisions which had been worked out thoroughly in the departments by the officials, and in the Council's committees and sub-committees by the elected members. After scrutiny by the Finance and General Purposes Committees and then by the Groups, they passed quickly through the Council with little comment and no opposition. Over the whole period it would have been most exceptional for a single Council meeting to have witnessed divisions or more than four issues. At least 95 per cent of Council business was non-contentious. However, over sixty years there was a slight decline in the number of divisions and a large change in the types of issue which resulted in a division. Around the turn of the century there were more divisions on a wider range of issues but provoking less intense reactions than fifty or sixty years later.

During the 1950s and 1960s each Council meeting usually divided about twice, over issues which the speakers claimed involved the basic principles of their parties. Set debates took place between two disciplined parties over items which had been selected at the Group meetings. Each party justified its policy: the majority party defended its proposals, while the minority party criticised and suggested alternatives. When the vote was taken, the members of each party voted together. But around the turn of the century, when the officials were not so prominent, when the Finance Committee was not so significant and when there were no Groups, each Council meeting saw raised a hotch potch of issues. Chairmen and their committees would advocate projects which would meet opposition from other Chairmen and their committees, and conflicts would arise over priorities, the allocation of scarce resources and the prestige of individual Chairmen. Councillors would bring forward measures to benefit their wards, meeting opposition from those who wanted their wards to receive the benefits instead, or from those who claimed to look at the welfare of the town as a whole. Members representing certain interests – economic, social and religious – would urge benefits for their groups or seek to prevent injury befalling them, while rivals would object to preferential treatment for them and try to channel the benefits to their own groups. Some individuals would advocate their personal and idiosyncratic proposals and oppose those of others. Since neither the Conservative nor Liberal Parties had municipal programmes to implement, the Council did not divide along party lines, except when the Labour representatives, who had a policy of their own, brought forward their schemes. But even then, although the Labour Councillors voted together, they would sometimes attract some Conservatives and Liberals, so that it was only rarely that the Labour Party faced the united opposition of all the other non-Labour members of the Council. The party conflict therefore was not the dominant divisive factor in the proceedings of the Council which it became fifty years later.

In the 1960s non-party conflict was rare: only occasionally were party lines broken. The Chairmen and their committees might rebel against other Chairmen, particularly against the Chairman of Finance Committee, as when he opposed the Water Committee's proposal to provide extra parking space at the Water Department's offices.[1] Councillors of a particular ward might rebel against a policy which they feared would harm their ward, as when the Councillors of Graiseley Ward objected to the prohibition on children playing games on an open space in the ward.[2] Members connected with a particular group might rebel when they felt that its interests were in jeopardy, as when the allotment-holders objected to their plots being turned back into public parks.[3] Individual eccentricities might be allowed full scope, as over the question whether fluoride should be added to the drinking-

[1] *E. & S.*, 26.1.1960. *C.M.*, 25.1.1960.
[2] *C.M.*, 26.11.1962.
[3] *C.M.*, 28.9.1953. This was also a conflict between the Chairmen of the Small Holdings and Allotments Committee and of the Parks and Physical Recreation Committee.

water of the town.[1] These kinds of conflicts, the common stuff of Council meetings at the turn of the century, became in the 1960s very few and far between, deviations from the norm of party strife.

In earlier chapters we have looked at the conflicts between the Chairmen, between the spokesmen of wards, between the representatives of religious groups and between those who were linked to various social and economic interests. In this chapter we shall examine more closely the latter, and what they sought to obtain from the Council. They can be regarded as contestants for the prizes which the Council had to offer. Before 1945 they were somewhat disparate and diffuse in activity, each seeking to promote its particular objective, but since 1945 they had to operate within a framework set by the two parties. This development tamed and neutralised them to some extent, since the parties, in order to appeal to a wide electorate, were unable to be merely mouthpieces for narrow sectional interests, and thus they forced the interests to take account of a wider public than their own immediate supporters.

Working within and through parties forced together many interests which previously had fought each other. Those most alike in aims had to sink their differences to combine against what was regarded as the greater evil. Where at the turn of the century they manifested themselves spasmodically in an *ad hoc* fashion, competing against each other whenever their interests were touched, by the 1950s they were forced to support one of two parties. Thus around each party coalesced certain groups: the parties could be regarded as coalitions of these groups, but although the groups helped shape the style, ethos and policies of the parties to a great extent, the parties were not the mere spokesmen of the groups. Because the groups came to act within the parties, the conflicts between the parties at local level over the policies of the Council were not artificial. The division between the Conservative and Labour Parties in local government in Wolverhampton was not merely a reflection of a national and Parliamentary conflict which had no relevance at local level. The contest locally was a genuine clash between local interests and pressures which found their homes within two parties. Each party on the Wolverhampton Town Council represented a distinctive

[1] *C.M.*, 23.12.1963.

set of interests, which had its own series of principles and its own policy, and sought to obtain its aims in its own particular style and ethos, and through its own way of conducting its own affairs and those of the Council. Party politics were therefore not inappropriate in local government in Wolverhampton.

It must not be thought, however, that the parties in some blind determinist way merely repeated the economic and social demands of their constituent elements. In bringing them together in one party, the party had to impose on them certain limitations as to their objectives. Since the primary objective of the party was to win votes from as many people as possible, it could not allow itself to appear too closely identified with a particular sectional interest. It had to cast its proposals to benefit the whole community and it had to proclaim its concern with the general public welfare of the town. Also for many members the party itself assumed a greater importance than the sectional interests to which they were also attached. It became an entity in its own right, and was regarded not just as a channel or device through which other groups achieved their aims; it had its own policies which conflicted with those of the sectional groups. The party had its own set of loyalties, which were stronger than those linking members to their interest groups.

Further, those members of a party who became Councillors did so not merely because they wanted to promote the aims of a particular sectional group to which they belonged. Although this factor was a significant motive for their desire to enter the Council, it was not the only one, nor was it always likely to be dominant. It is well-nigh impossible to explain why one individual becomes a Councillor. Some have a deliberate intention. They are interested in local government, in the welfare of the town or in the problems of a particular service. Some might want to implement the policy of their party; others to further the interests of some group they are associated with. Some are out for personal gain. Besides tangible rewards, the intangible may be equally powerful. Some may want to be at the centre of events in the town and involved in the making of decisions which will affect them and the town; some may want to enjoy the exercise of power; others might be satisfied with the limelight of being a Councillor and the deference paid by the public to a member of the Council. Some might enjoy just being in contact with those who exercise power and have the distinction of being regarded as the town's leading citizens. Some may have a dull and unsatisfying job and they may find their talents and abilities satisfied through Council work. Some have ideas about public duty and seek to serve the community, or the movement, or their party, or people like themselves. Some have become Councillors through no deliberate intention of their own. Fortuitous events combined and they just drifted in, perhaps asked to stand by a neighbour, or a business colleague or a friend at a club, or because their party asked them to stand, either as a reward for long service to the cause or because their abilities were regarded as suitable for the Council, or because a Councillor thought the individual would support him once elected.

Once the individual is on the Council he is apt to stay on as he learns about the work, and appreciates the comradeship of the members. Some people who have joined the Council with no real interest or understanding have gradually gained an insight and an interest, and ultimately become effective members. Others, however, have stayed only for the three-year term and then voluntarily resigned, because they were not interested, or because they had no opportunity to make a mark immediately, or because they had other more satisfying demands made upon their time from business, clubs, family, friends and hobbies. Poor health or failure to get on with colleagues are also explanations for wastage, as is the feeling that there was nothing significant for the individual to achieve, a feeling which particularly affected the Conservative members when in opposition. Thus it is hard to isolate a single motive or explanation as the reason why a particular individual entered the Council. Motives are often mixed, and even the individual himself may not be aware of why he wants to be a Councillor. What is certain is that men do not become Councillors simply to promote their own advantage or that of their economic group, nor do they leave the Council when they fail to achieve these objectives.

With these qualifications and conditions in mind it is possible now to examine what the various groups sought to get from the Council.

THE MANUFACTURERS

At the turn of the century the largest element among the manufacturers on the Council was that connected to the metalware industry, who also provided most of the Chairmen of the Council committees. We have seen that they were keen for money to be spent on the schemes of their own committees, but that they were reluctant for other Chairmen to have the money for their projects. Rates had to be kept low, save where one of their own committees' plans was involved.

The plight of the metal-goods industry in the Black Country gave a special force to their argument to keep rates down. Since the late 1870s Continental and American competition had hit hard their exports to Europe, the Empire, the world generally and even their home market. These relative newcomers to industrialisation, with ready supplies of raw materials and possessed of up-to-date technical knowledge, industrial plant and equipment, were able to steal the march on the Midland ironmasters and metalware manufacturers, whose enterprises had once led the industrial revolution, but whose equipment was now obsolete. Further, they were losing their easy supply of local raw materials. The coal and iron seams, on which the Black Country was founded, were exhausted or else their few remaining sources were hard to tap because of flooding and subsidence. Consequently these resources had to be transported from other parts of the country. Freight charges were therefore an additional burden, but they were imposed not only on the carriage of raw materials, but also on the finished articles, which had to be taken to the ports for export. It is little wonder that Wolverhampton was to the fore in the campaign to lower railway rates.[1] All parties protested: the Conservative M.P. for West Wolverhampton, Sir Alfred Hickman, urged a reduction time and again in Parliament; the Labour Party bemoaned the ill-effects of high railway rates,[2] and Liberal manufacturers in the Chamber of Commerce supported the cause.[3]

[1] i.e., freight charges.

[2] In 1913 its newspaper criticised a 4 per cent increase in the rates. 'We have already seen the once prosperous district of Horseley Fields ruined by railway rates, previous to the latest imposition. We have seen works dismantled and removed to the seaboard: we have seen the district depopulated by the removal of its best skilled workers: we have seen prosperity give place to abject poverty. We have seen the small shopkeepers struggle on for years in a vain and pathetic attempt to keep the wolf from the door and the unskilled labourer has been thrown out of work because he could not be taken with the other skilled.' *Wolverhampton Worker*, June 1913.

[3] See V. B. Beaumont, *Record of the Wolverhampton Chamber of Commerce, 1856–1956*, 1956, pp. 61–74.

Since industry was thus burdened there was a great incentive for the manufacturers to keep municipal expenditure low, so as not to raise the rates they would be called upon to pay. High rates were blamed for the closing down and migration of Wolverhampton businesses like Thorneycroft's in the late 1870s, or Lysaght's, which moved to Newport in the 1890s, or the Jones galvanised-iron factory which moved to Ellesmere in the 1900s. High rates, it was argued, had driven the bicycle, motor-cycle and motor-car industries from Wolverhampton to Coventry, where rates were lower.[1] But high rates was not the only factor encouraging businessmen to move their enterprises. In 1903 E. P. Jones gave four other reasons why he was moving to Ellesmere. He would be nearer the ports and thus gain advantages in the export trade. He could evade heavy railway charges, increase his competitive power against newer firms, and make use of a new type of steel, which could not be made in the Black Country.[2] Thus the complaint of 'high rates' was merely one factor among many, and perhaps not the fundamental one, which impelled factories to move out. Yet it was always a potent argument for manufacturers to use against those who wished to increase municipal expenditure.

Lysaght's also claimed that they had taken their firm from Wolverhampton to escape the policy of the Council's Sewerage Committee. During the 1880s and 1890s the Corporation was involved in litigation with the owners of land which bordered on those watercourses into which was poured the treated sewage effluent of the borough.[3] The riparian owners successfully complained that the effluent had not been adequately processed and that it had polluted the water and fouled their land, thus depriving

---

[1] *W.C.*, 1.4.1903.

[2] *W.C.*, 13.5.1903.

[3] (a) *The Annual Report of the Sewerage Committee*, Nov. 1890, tells the story of the litigation against Squire Giffard.

(b) A Committee Report of March 1893 describes the controversy between A. Crosbie and the Sewerage Committee.

(c) In December 1896 the Committee published its correspondence with Lysaght's from February 1891.

(d) A series of articles in the *Wolverhampton Chronicle*, 20.11.1895, 27.11.1895, 4.12.1895, 11.12.1895, described the problems faced by Wolverhampton in the disposal of her sewerage.

These sources provide information about the difficulties besetting the industrialists, the Corporation and the riparian owners.

them of good fishing and fertile soil. After paying out heavy compensation the Council, to prevent a recurrence of the contamin-
ation, decided to control more strictly the measures taken by the
metal trades of the town to treat their industrial waste, the chemicals and acids which they used in the manufacture of their products. The Council claimed that this waste was the cause of the
defilement of the watercourses. It built a new sewage works to
treat the effluent and imposed on the industrialists the obligation
to treat their own waste more effectively before discharging it
into the public sewers. Those industrialists whose waste was found
to be above the strength laid down were prosecuted. Lysaght's felt
that this policy was too oppressive; and one industrialist, A.
Crosbie, sought election to the Council in 1893 to protest against
what he regarded as a discriminatory policy. He wanted the Council
to build a sewage-disposal unit capable of treating all waste and
not to impose restrictions on business.[1]

Another limitation which the industrialists sought to avoid was
any control on the amount of smoke they emitted from their
chimneys. In 1898 they argued that control would hinder trade,[2]
and in 1929 they opposed the Chairman of Health Committee
when, anxious about the unhealthy effects of the thick smoke
which covered the east end of the town, he proposed to limit
the emission of industrial fumes to three minutes within a period
of thirty minutes. They claimed that such a policy would assist
foreign competitors who were not so shackled; trade would
therefore suffer and unemployment increase; and since it did not
apply to houses the by-law was unfair.[3]

Manufacturers were eager not only to prevent injury to their
interests but also to obtain positive advantages. In 1931 during
the depression, the Chillington Tool Company, whose Managing
Director was Councillor B. E. Hunt, requested a reduction in the
charges levied by the Corporation for electricity supplied to the
firm. In opposition the Chairman of Electricity Committee said
that factories taking bulk supply were obtaining electricity cheaper

[1] *W.C.*, 31.10.1893. In a letter to the Town Clerk, Crosbie said: 'My object
in seeking a seat on the Council is to endeavour to assist, in however small a
degree, a satisfactory solution of this sewage difficulty.' *Report of the Sewerage
Committee*, 20.3.1893.

[2] *E. & S.*, 12.12.1898.

[3] *C.M.*, 13.5.1929. *E. & S.*, 14.5.1929.

than domestic consumers and even the Corporation itself. His objections were overruled, mainly on the grounds that the Council had a duty to help local manufacturers in a depression.[1] This latter argument was most often used when tenders for contracts were being considered. Even if the tenders of Wolverhampton firms were higher than those from outside the town, it was said that the contracts should be granted to the local enterprises to encourage trade and employment in the town. The opponents of this view argued that trade would recover only if municipal expenditure was kept low and that therefore the lowest tender should always be accepted. For example in 1932 a Manchester company tendered to supply electrical switchgear at £42,470, but the committee advised acceptance of a local firm's tender of £43,813. The Chairman of Finance Committee exclaimed that 'we need to buy everything as cheaply as possible'.[2]

So valuable were these contracts to local industry that at times, especially in the depression, devious means were used to influence the Council's decision. For instance after the debate on the contracts for the switchgear, it was revealed that two local firms had canvassed Councillors to vote for their tenders.[3] Officials, too, were vulnerable; for example in 1933 one official approached a firm tendering for the supply of machinery oil and paraffin and suggested the following course. The corks of bottles containing the firm's products were to be marked with a groove so that when he came to sample the oils he would be able to identify those submitted by that firm. When accused of this deceit he pleaded that he felt strongly that a local firm should have been awarded the contract.[4]

The terms of contracts were of great importance for the businessmen and one aspect made them anxious over a long period of time. At the turn of the century they had been hostile to the demands of trade union members to include within the contracts a 'fair wages clause'. In 1891 one ironmaster on the Council said that if such a clause were embodied in contracts, employers would tell the Corporation to mind its own business,[5] and in 1894

---

[1] *C.M.*, 8.6.1931. *E. & S.*, 8.6.1931. See also *C.M.*, 11.4.1932 and 30.10.1933, and *E. & S.*, 11.4.1932 and 30.10.1933.
[2] *C.M.*, 3.8.1932. *E. & S.*, 3.8.1932.
[3] *E. & S.*, 31.10.1932. [4] *E. & S.*, 30.10.1933. [5] *W.C.*, 16.9.1891.

another ironmaster said that if the Corporation interfered with the contractor and his men work would stop.[1] When the clause had been adopted, the contractors found that the Labour members were always keen to denounce breaches of it; as in 1904 when the low wage rates paid by a firm constructing a steam dynamo were exposed,[2] or in 1939 when a firm supplying electrical equipment was accused.[3] Labour members were anxious to impose severe penalties on errant firms, as when in 1924 they sought to prevent two building contractors from ever again executing a contract for the Corporation.[4] The manufacturers had to yield over the fair wages clause, but they made every effort to resist Labour's demands for penalties for breaches of it. They were successful also in opposing Labour pressure that Corporation contractors should employ trade union labour only.[5]

Manufacturers therefore had many incentives to become Councillors both to prevent the Council from harming their interests and to use the Council to promote them. In 1930 one businessman-Councillor said that 'the interests of business should be made the paramount deciding factor in municipal and national matters. Manufacturers ought to get together, form an organisation on a non-political basis and be prepared to give it proper financial backing with the object of putting forward their own candidates at municipal elections.'[6] He clearly recognised that there were prizes to be won from membership of the Council. But, as we have seen, from this time the number of manufacturers on the Council fell. The disadvantages of membership for the businessmen had become greater than the incentives.

THE PROFESSIONAL MEN

Sharing the Chairmanships at the turn of the century with the manufacturers were the professional men, solicitors and doctors. Two jobs within the patronage of the Corporation attracted the solicitors to the Council, the offices of Borough Coroner and Clerk to the Borough Magistrates. Election to the first was by the

---

[1] *W.C.*, 15.8.1894.
[2] *C.M.*, 8.8.1904.
[3] *C.M.*, 25.9.1939.
[4] *C.M.*, 11.2.1924. *E. & S.*, 11.2.1924.
[5] *C.M.*, 9.3.1914.
[6] *E. & S.*, 23.12.1930.

Council as a whole, and to the second by the borough J.P.s, most of whom, around 1900, were members of the Council.[1] In open Council the merits of competitors for the office were debated. In 1899 R. A. Willcock, Chairman of Markets Committee (1881–99), was chosen Coroner, but only after his colleagues had weighed his qualifications against those of the Deputy Coroner.[2] On Willcock's death in 1911 two Councillors sought his office, W. G. Allen, Chairman of Lighting Committee (1903–11), and J. Grout, Mayor (1909–10). The latter, however, promoted his own candidature so ineptly that one Councillor objected that 'he had canvassed him personally and other members and had used his position as a member of the committees of the Town Council in such a way as should rightly debar him.'[3] Again in 1924, when the office fell vacant, Councillor A. C. Skidmore, Chairman of the Care of the Blind Committee (1921–4), obtained this office. The Clerkship to the Borough Magistrates was gained in 1891 by Councillor E. H. Thorne, Chairman of Finance Committee (1884–91). He was succeeded in 1901 by Councillor T. F. Waterhouse, who had competed against Councillor W. G. Allen for the position. Thus over a period of thirty-three years six members of the Council sought to use the Council as a stepping-stone to legal positions in the gift of the Council.[4] Through their membership of the Council they had the opportunity to gain a good reputation among their colleagues who would ultimately decide who was to be appointed.[5]

Another inducement for solicitors to enter the Council was that here they could further the interests of their clients, and, having won esteem as an effective defender of their interests, they could attract even more clients. Publicity gained from being a member of the Council would tend to raise the status and spread the name of the individual. R. A. Willcock by the time he left the Council in 1899 was the solicitor for many local trade associations: the Licensed Victuallers' Association, the Wholesale Grocers' Trading Associa-

---

[1] In 1903–4, 13 out of 48 members of the Council were J.P.s. In 1962–3, 5 out of 60 members of the Council were J.P.s.

[2] *C.M.*, 11.9.1899. *W.C.*, 13.9.1899.

[3] *C.M.*, 10.7.1911. *W.C.*, 12.7.1911.

[4] Councillor J. A. Wolverson (1916–20) was appointed surgeon to the borough police. *E. & S.*, 4.10.1932.

[5] Since one could not by law be both a member and an employee of the Council, a contestant for one of these offices would resign from the Council just before selection was made.

tion, the Coal Dealers' Association, the Butchers' Association and the Fruit and Poulterers' Trading Association.[1] As Chairman of Markets Committee he was well placed to assist their objectives. And in Council he was vociferous in defending their interests, as in 1898 when he led the opposition against a proposal to erect 'kiosks' in the streets to sell stationery, sweets and tobacco in competition with local shopkeepers.[2]

The Labour Party was for a long time suspicious of solicitors and their connections with particular groups interested in land. In the 1930s Councillor H. H. Kendrick, a solicitor, was a director of a local building society. His efforts for the landowners could be seen for example in 1934, when he successfully persuaded the Council to reverse a previous decision that the owners of frontages should pay the cost of widening certain streets in the town centre. He claimed that it was a double hardship for the owners to give up their land and to pay for the widening. The opposition claimed that it was unfair for the Council to improve roads for the advantage of the landowners, without their being required to pay for the improvement. Kendrick's victory, said a Labour Councillor, was a concession to 'vested interests'.[3]

Labour members also alleged privately that some members of the Planning Committee informed private developers about the Council's development proposals, thus enabling them to purchase land cheaply and then sell it dear to the Corporation. They were also accused of influencing committees' decisions to favour their friends. An estate agent on the Council, who in 1958 proposed a motion to allow private enterprise to redevelop slum clearance areas, was accused by Labour members of being the spokesman of private developers trying to get a stranglehold on some of the best land in the town.[4] He further angered some Labour members when he acted on behalf of people appealing against the Council's slum clearance purchase orders and on behalf of the Retail Market Tenants objecting to the terms imposed on them by the Council.[5]

[1] *Wolverhampton Journal*, June 1902.
[2] *W.C.*, 20.4.1898.
[3] *C.M.*, 10.7.1933 and 8.1.1934. *E. & S.*, 10.7.1933 and 8.1.1934.
[4] *C.M.*, 28.7.1958 and 22.9.1958. *E. & S.*, 29.7.1958 and 24.11.1958.
[5] *C.M.*, 28.9.1959 and *E. & S.*, 29.9.1959.

Solicitors always aroused suspicion on the Council. In 1888 a Councillor objected to the large number of lawyers on the Council,[1] and the first Labour candidate ever to contest a municipal election in Wolverhampton complained that 'the other side were bolstered up with help by clerks and members of the legal fraternity'.[2]

The large proportion of medical men on the Council at the start of the century can be explained by the inducements offered with regard to the running of the hospitals of the town. Most of the doctors were not mere general practitioners but surgeons holding positions in the town's hospitals. The *Directories* of the town between 1900 and 1920 show that serving the hospitals were such members of the Council as T. V. Jackson, E. Deanesely, T. H. Galbraith, F. Edge and J. Wolverson. With the removal of hospitals from the care of town councils to the regional hospital boards, there was no longer incentive for medical men, concerned about the work of their hospitals, to enter the Council.[3] Now they sat on the regional hospital boards.[4] No longer did the Council contain a man like Alderman J. W. Hamp, a doctor, who 'made the work of the Health Committee particularly his own' and took 'especial interest in the Borough Hospital'.[5]

At the turn of the century medical men took a keen interest in sanitary reform, which they sought to promote on the Council. In the 1890s Councillor C. R. Smith, a doctor, displayed a 'lively interest in sanitation'[6] and helped to inaugurate the campaign to substitute the water closet for the pan-and-earth closet, which he felt accounted for the high sickness and mortality figures in the east end of the town.[7] Another doctor on the Council, T. V. Jackson, urged the Council to inform the Local Government Board of the large number of unvaccinated people in the town, and to ask the Board to take immediate action, since there was

[1] *W.C.*, 21.10.1888.
[2] *E. & S.*, 3.11.1890.
[3] One way in which the doctors could promote hospital reform occurred in 1890, when they pressed that two, not one, extensions be made to the Borough Infectious Diseases Hospital. *C.M.*, 10.11.1890.
[4] A statutory provision.
[5] *W.C.*, 14.11.1900.
[6] *W.C.*, 27.4.1892.
[7] *C.M.*, 13.5.1895, 18.11.1895. *W.C.*, 15.5.1895, 21.5.1895, 20.11.1895.

serious danger of smallpox.[1] He was a champion of compulsory vaccination against a group of Radical Liberals, who regarded compulsion to be healthy as an invasion of personal liberty.

Thus professional men at the turn of the century had many incentives to encourage them to enter the Council. Since then, however, the incentives for medical men declined, as regional hospital boards took over the hospitals and as sanitary reform advanced and public health improved, while the incentives for solicitors and estate agents increased as the planning powers of local authorities grew.

THE SHOPKEEPERS

Throughout the whole period shopkeepers formed a constant, sizeable section of the Council. One explanation why they were so closely linked to the Council is that the Council had many prizes which they were anxious to obtain. As with the manufacturers, Corporation contracts were eagerly sought by traders. In 1891 Councillor W. Shepherd, a coal merchant, proposed that tenders for supplying coal to the Corporation should be thrown open for public competition. His opponents stated that coal of the desired kind could be obtained direct from the collieries, and that the Council should not be put at the mercy of the coal dealers.[2] In the 1950s a contract of considerable importance was that of supplying milk to schools. When it was revealed that all tenders had been identical, Councillor P. Morrell, the managing director of a dairy, offered more favourable terms, which were accepted.[3]

The Council's power over the licensing of certain trades encouraged interest from the shopkeepers. In 1927 a candidate sought election as 'the voice of the fish frying trade', 'the most discouraged and restricted trade in Wolverhampton'. He looked forward to 'a new helpful and friendly policy towards this honest ratepaying and food-supplying trade'.[4] The objections against the trade were that nuisance was created by the smell. A similar

[1] *C.M.*, 11.10.1897. *W.C.*, 13.10.1897.
[2] *C.M.*, 10.8.1891, 14.9.1891. *E. & S.*, 12.8.1891, 16.9.1891.
[3] *E. & S.*, 23.1.1956.
[4] *E. & S.*, 15.3.1927.

complaint was made against private slaughter-houses and knackers' yards. Those who wished to limit their numbers deprecated the smell and the screams, and wished that the butchers would use the municipal abattoir. The butchers disapproved of the 'persecution of small traders'.[1] In 1929 the Chairman of Health Committee said that it had been his committee's policy for over twenty years to close private slaughter-houses; they had been reduced from 80 to 12,[2] but the pace had been so slow because of opposition from the butchers. The butchers also protested against the proposal to impose the use of the humane killer. The champions of this method were worried about the cruelty inflicted on the animals by the inexpert use of the pole-axe, but Councillor R. E. Probert, a butcher, denied that there was cruelty in Wolverhampton: 'no one would take more care of an animal than the man to whom it belonged.'[3] He again supported the cheap traditional methods, when it was proposed to introduce a mechanical killer for sheep. He said it was suitable for pigs but not for sheep, and if it was introduced the cost of slaughtering would increase.[4] One other form of licensing caused conflict in the Council in the 1920s when some traders objected to a committee's refusal to let shopkeepers erect petrol pumps on the pavement in front of their shops.[5]

The shopkeepers were united on the Council in 1898 against a scheme to erect 'kiosks' in the streets to sell newspapers, magazines, tobacco, cigars, sweets and fruit. Anger was intense against the 'syndicate of strangers' who would compete with the town's own traders, who would have to pay higher rates than the owners of the small kiosks.[6] But they were not as united just before the First World War over the Early Closing Movement. In early 1912 some butchers petitioned the Watch Committee to suppress Sunday trading by butchers and meat salesmen: other traders followed suit against Sunday trading in their wares. The committee decided to instruct the Town Clerk to issue a notice of caution

---

[1] *C.M.*, 14.12.1896, 13.12.1909, 10.1.1910. *W.C.*, 16.12.1896, 15.12.1909, 12.1.1910.
[2] *C.M.*, 9.12.1929. *E. & S.*, 9.12.1929.
[3] *C.M.*, 10.3.1930. *E. & S.*, 10.3.1930.
[4] *C.M.*, 11.6.1934. *E. & S.*, 12.6.1934.
[5] *C.M.*, 9.10.1922, 12.2.1923. *E. & S.*, 12.2.1923.
[6] *C.M.*, 18.4.1898. *W.C.*, 20.4.1898.

J.B.P.

to tradesmen that legal proceedings would be taken against breakers of the law. A group of smaller shopkeepers then organised themselves into the Small Tradesmen's Protection Association to protest against the reinforcement of an obsolete Act. They claimed that they conducted their Sunday trading in a quiet, steady and orderly way, and that if they were closed, great hardship would befall many widows, cripples and old people, who earned a meagre living out of shopkeeping. The committee then reversed its decision, and the other traders then protested. During the Council debate on the topic the opponents of Sunday trading said that Sunday should be set aside for 'something higher than shopping', and that poorer tradesmen should not be forced to work long hours. The Chairman of Watch Committee explained that it was difficult to enforce Sunday closing, since the Act of the reign of Charles II was 'rusty, musty and fusty', and in many towns magistrates had refused to apply it: it did not cover publicans and refreshment-house keepers, who could open and dispose of articles which others were not permitted to sell. His solution was to petition Parliament for a modern Act, which the Council did.[1]

After the Shops Act of 1912 a similar division occurred over early closing on Thursdays. It was proposed to enforce a weekly half-holiday on Thursdays, and again the Small Tradesmens' Association protested against the injustice to small shopkeepers.[2] When they lost, their spokesman on the Council, R. L. Clarkson, a furniture dealer, then sought to have various trades exempted from the ban, including his own, but, as before, he was defeated.[3]

One group of traders which over the period was most concerned with the Council was the traders in the Wolverhampton Market, both the retailers in the Market Hall and the open market, and the wholesalers in the Wholesale Market. The users of the town's cattle market were also active whenever their interests were at stake. For instance in 1890 the Markets Committee proposed to

[1] *C.M.*, 1.8.1912. *W.C.*, 3.8.1912, 11.9.1912.
[2] *C.M.*, 10.3.1913. *W.C.*, 12.3.1913.
[3] *C.M.*, 12.1.1914, *W.C.*, 14.1.1914. The Council's liberal attitude to early closing was at variance with its policy in 1907 and 1909, when it had rejected the requests of the sub-postmasters to close their post offices on Thursday afternoons. The business and professional men did not want to be inconvenienced by finding no post offices open on Thursday afternoons. *C.M.*, 11.3.1907, 13.12.1909. *W.C.*, 13.3.1907, 15.12.1909.

end the privileges of the only two auctioneers allowed to conduct their business inside the cattle yards and to open them to all auctioneers. The market-users protested[1] and it was not until 1907 that another auctioneering firm was admitted.[2] In 1891 the stall-holders in the Retail Market condemned a scheme to increase the hours of sale in the Wholesale Market, on the grounds that their own trade would be reduced, the wholesalers would strengthen their monopoly, and they would have advantages over the stall-holders who had higher rents, while ultimately the public would face higher costs. The wholesalers argued that the increase would bring more purchasers into the borough, which would help the trade of everyone.[3] The retailers and wholesalers, however, were more often in alliance than opposed, as in 1923 when they objected to amusement fairs which visited the town and set up their stalls on the market patch. Councillor T. W. Dickinson, a wholesale fruit and potato merchant, complained that the fairs caused grave inconvenience to the market people.[4]

The market traders were not merely negative, opposing projects harmful to their interests; they also promoted certain schemes to benefit their trade. They pressed for the acquisition of an extra and heavier weighing machine in 1891,[5] and in 1960 were urging the Council to devise a plan for large-scale car-parking facilities, off-street and multi-storey.[6] Their greatest positive achievement was the construction in the early 1900s of a new covered Wholesale Market, Cold Stores and Abattoirs, under the Chairmanship of the Markets Committee of F. Evans, himself a fruit, vegetable and fish merchant. In the 1890s the law against the use of borax and boracic acid as food preservatives was being strictly enforced, and butchers, poultry dealers and greengrocers required new means to keep perishable commodities. They also sought more extensive wholesale facilities, particularly a roof to protect them and their goods from bad weather. Evans and his committee persuaded the Council to grant their wishes.[7] A minority objected

[1] *C.M.*, 10.3.1890.
[2] *C.M.*, 13.5.1907. *W.C.*, 15.5.1907.
[3] *C.M.*, 25.3.1891. *W.C.*, 1.4.1891.
[4] *E. & S.*, 11.6.1923.
[5] *C.M.*, 12.1.1891. *W.C.*, 14.1.1891.
[6] *C.M.*, 25.1.1960. *E. & S.*, 26.1.1960.
[7] *C.M.*, 27.2.1899, 14.5.1900. *W.C.*, 16.5.1900.

strenuously that the Corporation had been landed with a 'white elephant' to satisfy the market men, and they attacked Evans for causing the rates to rise so much.[1]

If this project was the market traders' greatest positive achievement, then their greatest negative achievement was to delay for over fifty years the construction of a new Market Hall for the retail traders. In 1905 Horatio Brevitt, the Town Clerk, considered the removal of the Market Hall from opposite the Town Hall and his office to another site, but dropped the scheme when it became evident that some of the traders would oppose moving away from the centre and from proximity to the Wholesale Market. In the 1930s Brock Allon, the Town Clerk, again considered the matter, and again the traders objected. Their spokesman was W. H. Farmer, a stationer with a stall in the market, whose vigour on behalf of the traders brought him to the attention of the Conservative Party, which asked him to stand for the Council. He was elected in 1934. By 1940 positive proposals were made to demolish the old Market Hall and to construct a new one in the Brick-kiln Croft area. The traders, however, protested that this site was far from the traditional shopping flow of the public; putting the new market there would dislocate established shopping habits; shopkeepers near the existing market would be ruined; the town would lose revenue and trade would fall.[2] Twelve years later Farmer was still criticising the 'indecent haste' with which the Markets Committee was planning the 'rash move' to rebuild the market on the same 'outlandish site'.[3] Not until 1957 did the Market Hall Tenants' Association call off its opposition and decide to co-operate in the establishment of the new Market Hall, since 'opposition now serves no useful purpose'.[4] Peace did not descend at once, however, for a new quarrel arose over the terms on which the traders were to hold their stalls; they felt that the Corporation was charging too much.[5]

Shopkeepers and traders of various kinds had many incentives to enter the Council, since it had the power to influence their livelihood in many ways, through contracts, licensing, controls

[1] *E. & S.*, 2.11.1903.
[2] *C.M.*, 8.4.1940. *E. & S.*, 8.4.1940.
[3] *C.M.*, 29.12.1952. *E. & S.*, 29.12.1952.
[4] *E. & S.*, 28.1.1957.
[5] *C.M.*, 28.9.1957. *E. & S.*, 29.9.1957.

over certain trades, controls over hours and through its responsibility for the markets of the town. By becoming members of the Council shopkeepers and traders were in an advantageous position to promote their interests and to oppose schemes which might injure their interests.

THE 'DRINK' INTEREST

One particular kind of trade demands special consideration, the 'drink' interest, licensed victuallers, wine and spirit merchants and brewers. Up to the 1940s they were a significant proportion of the Council. We have seen that they entered the Council, around the turn of the century, as a defensive move against the temperance reformers, and in the Council conflict between the drink interest and the teetotallers often flared up, sometimes on the most unlikely occasions. In 1892 when a motion was before the Council to erect a footbridge over a canal to link a housing estate with some near-by works, an advocate of the bridge complained of the dangers of the long walk along the towpath to the road. He told the story of a man who fell in. 'Was he drunk?' cried an Alderman who opposed the bridge, 'I don't know,' said Councillor Lewis, who was a temperance reformer, 'and if he was why should you grumble when you give a man plenty of opportunity to get drunk.'[1] The reformers were eager to prosecute any breach of the law by publicans, as in 1890 when they proposed that the Council should tell the Chief Constable to take proceedings against specific publicans who had served drinks after hours.[2] Lewis was keen to prosecute men who got others drunk.[3] They tried a more constructive approach in 1900 by proposing that the lease of the Squirrel Inn should be granted for seven years at a rental of £120 per annum to the People's Refreshment House Association.[4] This tavern was the last remaining in the Corporation's hands of those which it had acquired when improving the town centre in the 1880s. The reformers wished Wolverhampton to set an example to other towns by establishing a temperance refreshment house, which

[1] *C.M.*, 12.12.1892. *W.C.*, 14.12.1892.
[2] *C.M.*, 14.7.1890.
[3] *W.C.*, 15.7.1891.
[4] *C.M.*, 12.3.1900, 14.5.1900. *W.C.*, 14.3.1900, 16.5.1900.

might influence future legislation on public house management.[1] Opponents of the idea denounced it as a 'fad', and complained that it would be unjust to the sitting tenant who was paying £130 per annum, and to the ratepayers who would have to bear the loss of £10 per annum.[2]

After the turn of the century the temperance reform movement declined, but well into the 1920s individual teetotallers sought to impede the publicans and brewers in various ways; objecting in 1920 to permission being granted the Springfield brewery to reconstruct its bottling stores[3] and then its boilerhouse,[4] or objecting to licensed premises being erected on new Corporation housing estates without a referendum among the inhabitants first. A retired brewer, Councillor J. Cahill, attacked the teetotallers who wanted to deprive the people on the new estates of the rights and privileges enjoyed by others. He saw the plan for a referendum as 'the thin end of the wedge to provide a test case for local option'.[5] This occasion was the last time the drink interest had to defend itself against the reformers in the Wolverhampton Council. Thus the drink interest was on the Council largely to protect itself. Of course being a Councillor could help attract custom to one's establishment and generally give the trade a good reputation for public service. By the 1960s only two members of the Council had connections with a brewery.

At the turn of the century the interests considered above – the manufacturers, professional men and traders – formed the bulk of the Council membership. Each occupational group sought to promote its own interests and to prevent harm to them. These objectives were not the sole reasons why individuals entered the Council but they were important ones, and for that reason are stressed in this chapter. Because concentrating on this aspect gives the impression that the members only sought to further their own interests, it is important to remember that this was not their sole motive for entering the Council and that it did not occupy all their time on the Council. As we have seen, other motives operated and

[1] *W.C.*, 16.5.1900.
[2] *E. & S.*, 12.3.1900, 15.5.1900.
[3] *C.M.*, 14.6.1920. *W.C.*, 16.6.1920.
[4] *C.M.*, 13.9.1920. *W.C.*, 15.9.1920.
[5] *C.M.*, 10.1.1927, 3.8.1927. *E. & S.*, 10.1.1927, 3.8.1927.

members had to busy themselves with many functions of the Council which did not touch their immediate personal or group interests. Other objectives which they sought to advance were the projects of their own committees and the welfare of their wards. Regard for these interests often cut across their economic interests, and it is impossible to propound a general law about which won.

In a Council which witnessed divisions over such various topics it was impossible to have a constantly recurring cleavage along a single line. On each issue there was a new grouping of the Council members. Party politics was therefore inappropriate. The parties did not have distinctive municipal policies; their concern was with Parliament and national politics, with electing an M.P. not with running the Town Council. What did eventually push the groups together was the rise of the Labour Party, representing a different set of interests opposed to those of the traditional groups on the Council. The latter found that they had a common cause in resisting the Labour Party and its policies. The objectives of the Labour Party, and the nature of the party conflict in the Council after 1945, are considered in the next chapter.

15 Pressures and Controversies—the Labour initiative and the Conservative response

THE Labour Party in Wolverhampton was founded by the Trades Council and financed by trade unions; its Councillors were often unpaid part-time branch officers and some were even full-time district officials of their unions. In its early years the policies of the party reflected the interests of the trade unions, and it acted in the Council to promote some specific trade union objectives. The bulk of the Labour Party's votes and membership came from the working class, and its policies reflected their interests too. Through the whole period of its existence it sought to improve the social conditions of the working class, an aim which remained constant, even though its role as a trade union pressure group declined. Council house tenants and the Co-operative Society were two particular groups which gave support to the party; and its policies consistently advanced their interests, particularly those of the former. In pursuing the causes of these groups the party came into conflict with those groups examined in the last chapter. As a defensive move against growing Labour pressure they united their forces, which before had been divided, under the aegis of the Conservative Party.

The prime purpose of the Labour Representation Committee was to get its members elected to the Council. Direct Labour representation was demanded not just on the doctrinaire grounds of political equality, that working men had a right to be represented by their own kind, but also because it was felt that the social position of the working man could be improved only if Councillors had first-hand experience of the problems of working men.[1] This argument was rebutted by many businessmen, who claimed that

[1] *E. & S.*, 3.11.1890.

as large employers, concerned to keep the wheels of trade and industry humming, and with the time, experience and knowledge to serve on the Council, they were best fitted to protect the interests of their workmen.[1]

To enable working men more easily to be Councillors, the L.R.C. advocated that the Council should meet, not in the afternoons, but in the evenings.[2] At the turn of the century no allowances for loss of earnings were paid, and thus even if a working man could find an employer who would let him have time off work to serve on the Council, he could still suffer financial hardship. Labour members said that it would be easier for the businessman to give up the evening than for the working man to give up the afternoon. 'Should the sacrifice be made by those members of the Council who had to work hard every day for their daily bread, or should it be made by those to whom the matter was simply a matter of personal convenience.[3] Businessmen expressed amazement that trade unionists who campaigned for shorter hours were urging longer hours for Council work.[4] 'Businessmen and tradesmen would come at 6.00 thoroughly fagged out and unable to give that attention they should do to the various important questions that had to be considered.'[5] The timing of the Council meeting was thus arranged to suit the habits of the economic groups dominant in the Council. The payment for loss of earnings, first by the L.R.C. and then by the Council,[6] reduced the demand for evening meetings. It arose for the last time in 1946, when a minority of the Labour Group pressed for it against the majority. The latter argued that able officials would not serve the Corporation if they had to attend in the evenings; such a move would reduce the status of the authority to that of a district council; and in any case committees, where the real work was done, could meet at all times.[7]

---

[1] Ibid.   [2] *C.M.*, 8.5.1893, 13.12.1897, 10.10.1904.
[3] *W.C.*, 10.5.1893.   [4] Ibid.   [5] *W.C.*, 15.12.1897.
[6] It was impossible to penetrate the secrecy which surrounded the expenses paid to members in Wolverhampton. The variety of local authority practices is shown in the *Report of the Inter-Departmental Committee on Expenses of Members of Local Authorities*, Cmd 7126, H.M.S.O. 1947. Expenses were put on a more regular basis by the Local Government Act 1948.
[7] *E. & S.*, 15.1.1946. *C.M.*, 14.1.1946.

TRADE UNIONS

Once on the Council the Labour representatives acted in concert with those trade unions who were seeking higher wages and better conditions for Corporation employees. For example in 1904 they called for a minimum 'living wage of 6*d* per hour'[1] and by 1912 of 25*s* per week;[2] they proposed pensions and longer holidays for Council employees,[3] and higher wages and improved conditions for tramway workers,[4] road sweepers and menders.[5] But the businessmen replied that 'the price of Labour ought to fix itself as any other commodity did'. They should not run the Corporation as 'a philanthropic institution', with 'soft hearts and soft heads', but they should look at the issue from a 'business standpoint'.[6]

The Labour members retaliated by opposing salary increases for Corporation officials. Scarcely a year passed between 1894 and 1929 without Labour representatives objecting to such increases. They argued that since the workmen were in greater need, the increases should be refused until a minimum wage was granted.[7] In 1906 a Labour Councillor said: 'they looked through one end of the telescope at the higher officials' salaries, and reversed it when they looked at the wages of the rank and file.'[8] During the 1920s the majority of the Labour members dropped their blanket opposition to salary increases, accepting the argument that an able official, who would ultimately save the town money, deserved a high salary.[9] But there were still a vocal minority who protested that a salary of over £1000 was too large for anyone[10] and that those at the bottom who did the work should be lifted up first.[11]

Conflicts in the Council over the pay of Corporation employees

---

[1] *W.C.*, 14.9.1904. *C.M.*, 12.9.1904.
[2] *W.C.*, 12.6.1912. *C.M.*, 10.6.1912.
[3] *E. & S.*, 1.11.1894.
[4] *W.C.*, 27.10.1897.
[5] *W.C.*, 15.6.1910.
[6] *W.C.*, 15.6.1910, 12.6.1912.
[7] *W.C.*, 15.8.1894, 13.7.1898.
[8] *W.C.*, 8.8.1906. In the First World War they complained that war bonuses and honoraria granted to the officials were excessive compared to those for the workmen. *W.C.*, 10.5.1916, 13.6.1917, 10.9.1919.
[9] *W.C.*, 13.10.1920.
[10] *W.C.*, 12.1.1925.
[11] *E. & S.*, 13.7.1936.

declined from the 1920s, as national negotiating machinery removed from the Council the responsibility of deciding the wages of its servants. This development was not accepted immediately with good grace. In 1920 the Council refused to implement an agreement negotiated by the National Joint Board of Employers and Members of Staff (Electricity Supply Industry). Labour members urged acceptance because the Council was under a moral obligation to honour the decision of a Whitley Council; if they dishonoured their pledge, the Ministry of Labour was likely to intervene; refusal might lead to a strike and a loss of power in the town. Their opponents claimed that the award was excessive; 'electric rises', which would set other employees an example; it was inopportune, when works were closing down for lack of trade and when tradesmen could hardly make both ends meet. The Council 'was in the cart' through granting plenary powers to the negotiating body. After the rejection of the award, union representatives and officials from the Ministry met members of the Council; a strike was threatened; special meetings of the Council were called and finally the award was adopted by a slim majority.[1] Both sides then accepted the machinery of negotiation, and no further conflict arose over this issue until 1941, when the Labour Party tried to alter an award, but in an upward direction. The majority now argued that the Council was not competent to deal with such matters, while the Labour Party said that it was not throwing over the negotiating machinery by paying wages above the minimum.[2] From the 1920s, therefore, the trade unions did not have to deal directly with the Council to advance the claims of their members, so that they had less need of the assistance of Labour Councillors to support their objectives. In addition they were stronger than in 1900, more able to stand on their own feet and negotiate without assistance from Councillors.

Controversy over the salaries of officials continued a little longer, into the 1930s. In 1930, in an attempt to stop the wrangles which occurred whenever an increase was proposed for an individual official, a comprehensive grading scheme was devised

[1] *W.C.*, 15.12.1920. *E. & S.*, 27.1.1921, 1.2.1921. *C.M.*, 13.12.1920, 26.1.1921, 14.2.1921.

[2] *E. & S.*, 28.10.1941, 9.12.1941. *C.M.*, 27.10.1941, 8.12.1941.

which fixed the minima and maxima for all officials, the increments and dates, so that each could know his exact position in the scale.[1] This system produced no dissension until 1936 when the scales were increased. Labour members objected.[2] The controversy resulted in the delegation of decisions on salaries to the General Purposes Committee. An attempt in 1947 to return this power to the full Council was heavily defeated. It was felt that such a topic should be discussed in secret to avoid the vituperation of earlier years, and to prevent bad relations between Councillors and the officials, who were unable to reply to debate in open Council.[3] Thus an issue which had once bitterly divided the Council was no longer contentious, owing to the transfer of discussion to committee, the growth of the officials' trade union (N.A.L.G.O.) and their professional associations, and the establishment of national negotiating machinery.

Labour members were also eager to advance the interests of those employed by Corporation contractors, particularly to expose any breach of the fair wages clause and to prevent an employer condemned for such a breach from executing any future contract. They also sought, but in vain, to impose on the contractors the obligation to employ trade union labour only.[4] Although not able to enforce this rule officially, the Labour Group exercised unofficial discrimination. In 1959, for instance, the Public Works Committee withdrew a proposal to purchase an air compressor from a company, because it refused to employ trade union labour.[5] Such efforts on behalf of trade unions were more necessary in 1900 than they were in 1964, since in 1964 unions were stronger and more able to negotiate directly with the employers with more effect.

The only specifically trade union objective which Labour members tried to achieve after 1945 was the 'closed shop'. In 1947 the Council resolved that all manual labourers employed by the Corporation should be members of a trade union.[6] Labour members said that there were times when the general principle of

---

[1] *E. & S.*, 1.10.1929. *C.M.*, 13.1.1930.
[2] *E. & S.*, 8.6.1936. *C.M.*, 8.6.1936.
[3] *E. & S.*, 10.3.1947. *C.M.*, 10.3.1947.
[4] *C.M.*, 9.3.1914, 11.5.1914.
[5] *M.L.G.*, 19.6.1959.   [6] *C.M.*, 10.2.1947.

the liberty of the subject had to be subordinated to the benefit and the interests of the whole of the inhabitants: therefore those workmen who accepted benefits won by trade unions should pay for them through union membership. If the proposal was not adopted, it was feared that the Corporation's workforce would be disrupted, since unionists would not work with non-unionists. The Conservatives saw the plan as 'the thin end of the wedge towards dictatorship'. They regarded unions as 'political machines for the Labour Party' and therefore opposed forcing a man to join a political group in order to earn his living.[1] Later they complained that an army of snoopers was wasting man-hours discovering if men were union members.[2] One of the first reversals of Labour policy by the Conservatives when they regained their majority in 1949 was to rescind the resolution of 1947,[3] in order to clear away the spirit of compulsion which was against 'all the finer principles of a free democracy'. The Labour Party said that the Conservatives Group was 'getting its own back' and was prejudicing the smooth operation of the Corporation departments.[4] Although Labour regained its majority in 1952, there was no return to the closed shop. In 1959 the Trades Council asked the Group to readopt the policy;[5] advice was sought from Transport House which replied that it was illegal to compel employees to join a trade union.[6] A deputation from the Trades Council pointed to other authorities which had made union membership compulsory for all manual workers, but the Group followed the advice of their party headquarters and let the matter drop.[7]

Labour members were concerned with the interests of men not merely at work but also when they were unemployed, particularly in the depression of the inter-war years. Their objectives were twofold: to persuade the Council to provide work, and to ensure that adequate relief was paid. The undertaking of public work was, claimed the Labour members, a constructive approach to the unemployment problem, since work could be provided for the men and the town could be improved; a new road built, streets

[1] *E. & S.*, 11.2.1947.
[2] *E. & S.*, 9.11.1948.
[3] *C.M.*, 28.11.1949.
[4] *E. & S.*, 28.11.1949.
[5] *M.L.G.*, 10.11.1959.
[6] *M.L.G.*, 17.12.1959.
[7] *M.L.G.*, 4.11.1960.

and property repaired and the pan system finally abolished. But their opponents argued that their first requirement was 'to get industry on its legs' and that meant reducing taxation and public expenditure. If the rates rose, industry would be further crippled, the unemployed would grow and more people would be unable to pay their rates. Public works and public expenditure would not break the vicious circle.

In the 1930s the Labour Party in Wolverhampton took the lead in opposing the rates of relief which the Ministry ordered the Public Assistance Committee to pay to the unemployed. Those given by the committee were more generous than those laid down by the Ministry. The Labour members convinced a majority of the Council to make a stand against the Government. Again and again the Council voted to defy the Minister, arguing that the inadequate benefit and the means test were demoralising the nation; family life was being broken up and the casual wards were overflowing with young men, who were being turned into habitual vagrants. When the Minister threatened to establish a Commission to administer the relief if the Council remained obdurate,[1] the majority capitulated; Labour members accused them of having 'the backbone of a jelly fish'. One Labour Councillor refused to sit down despite repeated requests from the Mayor. Another jumped up, shouting, 'I have no time for any of you people'. Cries of 'dirty dogs' were heard from the public gallery. Police were brought in and the two Councillors were 'forcibly removed from the Council chamber still shouting and struggling'.[2]

Labour members tried to get the Council to oppose the Unemployment Assistance Act of 1934, on the grounds that it was inhuman, injuring family life and the physical well-being of the people. To compel a man to receive training as a condition of receiving benefit was a renewal of chattel slavery. But the Council congratulated the Government on its prompt action to reduce hardship;[3] they were very pleased that no longer would they bear the odium of administering the relief. The Act may not have taken unemployment out of politics, but by transferring the responsi-

[1] *E. & S.*, 10.5.1932, 27.9.1932, 10.1.1933. *C.M.*, 9.5.1932, 26.9.1932, 9.1.1933.

[2] *E. & S.*, 13.3.1933.

[3] *E. & S.*, 12.2.1935. *C.M.*, 11.2.1935.

bility of administering relief from local authorities to the Unemployment Assistance Board, it removed from the Council of Wolverhampton a topic which had caused bitter conflict.

Thus the Labour Party from its foundation in the 1890s to the late 1940s promoted the interests of trade unionists. But this aspect of Labour policy declined in importance as many of the topics with which the unions were concerned were taken from the purview of the Council, as the unions grew stronger and less dependent on Councillors to assist their campaigns, and as the Labour Party became the majority and the governing party on the Council with responsibilities to a wider electorate and not just to the trade unions. This trend is exemplified in Labour's refusal in 1959 to advocate a closed shop for the Corporation's employees.

THE CO-OPERATIVE MOVEMENT

The Co-operative Society supported the Labour Party in Wolverhampton in a spasmodic fashion. It was interested in the Council in order to obtain contracts and sites for shops on new housing estates. In the 1930s the Labour Party claimed that the Co-op was refused permission to open shops in some areas because of prejudice against the Society. But the non-Labour members said, as in 1935, that the sites suggested were not zoned for shops; ribbon development had to be curtailed and the amenities of the area preserved.[1] In the 1940s and 1950s the Conservatives alleged that the Co-op was given preferential treatment by the Labour Group in the allocation of shops on new Council estates. In one case a Conservative said that 'it was obvious that pressure had been brought to bear on Socialist members of the Council to ensure that the Co-operative Society would get the site'. The Labour Party was making 'a goodwill offering for services rendered'. Other shopkeepers should be given a chance, ex-servicemen or small traders from the slum clearance areas. Labour members said that they would support 'co-operative enterprise in the interests of the people as a whole', against 'private enterprise'. The housing estates contained many members of the Society, who, if there was not a full range of Co-operative shops on their estate, would have

[1] *E. & S.*, 12.2.1935. *C.M.*, 11.2.1935.

to travel to town to purchase their goods. And since the rents of the new shops were too high for small traders, it was better that they should go to the Co-op than to a large private concern.[1]

The Labour Group was not always united over assisting the Co-op. In 1957 when it was proposed at a Group meeting to lease a shop site to the Co-op at the valuation of the District Valuer, two private grocers moved an amendment that the lease be put out to tender and awarded to the highest tenderer. Eleven were in favour and the same number against: the casting vote of the Chairman was for the original motion.[2] Members of the Group also attacked the Co-op for not allowing its employees sufficient time off work to pursue Council business,[3] and for taking part in a price ring for supplying milk to schools. (Five tenders had been submitted, all the same.)[4] So strained were relations between the Group and the Co-op, that the National Organiser of the Co-operative Party asked the Group to meet a Co-op delegation to clear up misunderstandings and to effect a closer relationship of mutual benefit.[5] After the meeting a Liaison Committee was set up to 'discuss all matters of principle that coexist between the Co-operative Party and the Labour movement'.[6] Relations became more congenial; the Co-op financed the election campaigns of three candidates, gave money to the general funds of the party and allowed the party and the Group to hold meetings at its central premises. But in the 1960s there was little contact. No more elections were financed, and only one Labour member of the Council was active in the Co-operative Movement and she was over eighty. By 1964 the Co-op was not much in evidence as a pressure group on the Labour Party.

COUNCIL TENANTS

Council house tenants gave consistent support to the Labour Party, in votes, for the safe Labour wards were those where

---

[1] *E. & S.*, 30.9.1947, 14.2.1949, 23.9.1958. *C.M.*, 14.2.1949, 29.9.1957, 22.9.1958.
[2] *M.L.G.*, 19.7.1957.　　　　[3] *M.L.G.*, 23.9.1959.
[4] *M.L.G.*, 25.1.1957.
[5] *M.L.G.*, 28.12.1956.　　　　[6] *M.L.G.*, 25.1.1957.

Council houses predominated, and in members, for a large proportion of the Labour members of the Council were tenants themselves. In return the Labour Group looked after the interests of the tenants assiduously. Municipal housing was a bone of contention between the Labour and the non-Labour forces on the Council from the 1890s to the 1960s, when it remained one of the major items of conflict between the parties.

At the end of the nineteenth century Labour members urged that the Council should build houses with the latest sanitary improvements at a low rent for the working class.[1] It would not give 'the private speculator and small property owner anything to fear', since the object was 'to build a class of house to let at a rental to meet the incomes of small wage earners, which it would not pay the property speculators to erect'.[2] The Labour Party pressed for a permanent Housing Committee to be set up to build low-rent houses.[3] Their opponents – shopkeepers and builders particularly – objected to subsidising rents out of rates, since this would really mean subsidising wages. If these were higher then the working man could afford economic rents. In addition, the builders feared municipal competition subsidised by their rates.[4] One builder who was a Councillor said that 'private enterprise would come along and solve the difficulty, if only speculators were allowed to get a fair remuneration on their outlay.'[5] Progress was slow before 1919: an *ad hoc* committee had built fifty cottage tenements by 1906, an expensive and disappointing venture:[6] in 1913 a permanent Housing Committee was established when the Health Committee found that its plans to clear away unfit houses were held up because it was unable to find accommodation for tenants at rents comparable to what they had been paying.[7] The war prevented it from achieving anything significant, and only after the war, with generous government subsidies, did regular and large-scale construction of Council houses begin.[8]

[1] *W.C.*, 31.10.1894, 27.10.1898. *E. & S.*, 16.10.1908. *Wolverhampton Worker*, November 1913.

[2] *W.C.*, 3.7.1901.   [3] *W.C.*, 14.11.1906.

[4] *E. & S.*, 21.3.1900. *W.C.*, 15.7.1914.

[5] *W.C.*, 11.2.1914.

[6] *Wolverhampton Journal*, October 1906.

[7] *W.C.*, 6.8.1913, 12.11.1913, 10.12.1913.

[8] *E. & S.*, 14.7.1919. *C.M.*, 14.7.1919.

Labour members then pressed that the houses should be built not by contractors, but by a special Corporation department. In 1924 the Labour Party for the first time suggested the establishment of a direct building department which would build houses more cheaply and quickly than private enterprise. But their opponents said that the Corporation should not pretend to teach the builders how to do their own business.[1] On gaining a majority in 1945 the Labour Group speedily set up such a department. It was, they claimed, 'not based on any political fetish', nor would the contractors be cut out, for they would continue to exist side by side with the department. The Conservatives said that 'this extravagant scheme' would not build houses better, more cheaply or more quickly, and the engineer would be inconvenienced by additional duties. The Labour Party retorted that such arguments were invalid and that the town as a whole would benefit, for builders would have to cut their costs in the face of competition for the first time.[2] The Conservatives were very hostile to the department: they removed Sir Charles Mander from the Presidency of the South-West Wolverhampton Conservative Association after he had praised the department. Yet when they regained their majority in 1949 they did not dismantle it. The Conservative Chairman of the Housing Committee, who had previously been a bitter opponent, defended the department against many in his own party. It had made good progress; the men in the department had to be given work and if all contracts were sent out these men would be out of a job and house-building would be delayed.[3] When they returned to opposition, however, they resumed their whole-hearted criticism, advocating that all work should go out to tender, since 'private enterprise would do the job better,' and that the lowest tender should be accepted. They objected to the department being given any work, whether building and repairing houses or constructing a sports stadium.[4] Labour members alleged that the opposition represented private

---

[1] *E. & S.*, 14.4.1924. *C.M.*, 14.4.1924. It was raised again in 1926 (*W.C.*, 10.2.1926. *C.M.*, 8.2.1926) and 1935 (*E. & S.*, 12.3.1935. *C.M.*, 11.3.1935).

[2] *E. & S.*, 12.3.1946, 29.10.1946. *C.M.*, 12.3.1946.

[3] *E. & S.*, 26.7.1949. *C.M.*, 25.7.1949.

[4] *E. & S.*, 28.7.1953, 27.7.1954, 28.6.1955, 23.7.1956, 7.5.1957. *C.M.*, 27.7.1953, 26.7.1954, 27.6.1955, 23.7.1956, 6.5.1957.

builders only, who feared the department because it had kept their profits low.[1] It had saved the ratepayers many thousands of pounds.[2]

The Labour Party always took a special interest in the welfare of the Council tenants, particularly trying to keep their rents as low as possible. Since 1919 the Labour Party complained against rent increases, while their opponents said that if rents were subsidised from the rates, Council tenants would benefit at the expense of those having to subsidise them. In the 1950s and 1960s much conflict raged around the Conservatives' proposals to introduce a rent rebate scheme, varying the rent according to need. Councillor Farmer, its leading advocate, claimed that it would 'ensure that people are not subsidising those better off than themselves';[3] 'the rates would be reduced, while relief would go to those people who genuinely could not afford to pay an economic rent.[4] In the Labour Group a sizeable minority was in favour of his proposal, but the majority remained firmly opposed. Labour spokesmen said that the Conservatives had no workable scheme; it was liable to be so complex that no working man would understand it; it would be expensive to administer and there would be 'prying and snooping'[5] into the financial circumstances of the tenants: a means test again. The present rents charged were high because of the Conservative policy of high interest rates. The Labour Party called on private landlords to set an example by applying a differential-rent scheme for their tenants.[6] The Labour Group feared that such a differential-rent scheme would raise the rents for the majority of the tenants, who might then refuse to support the Labour Party.

In other ways the Labour Party sought to protect the tenants. In the 1920s it proposed that the £2 deposit paid by tenants on occupying a Council house should be abolished. Labour members said that it caused hardship, forced many to the money-lender to borrow it and was a barrier to many against applying for a house. Their opponents saw it as a useful safeguard against bad tenants; it enabled broken windows and lights to be paid for; there was no evidence of hardship and tenants appreciated receiving back the

[1] *E. & S.*, 29.10.1957.   [2] *E. & S.*, 23.12.1958.
[3] *E. & S.*, 23.7.1956.
[4] Ibid. and *E. & S.*, 24.3.1959.
[5] *E. & S.*, 24.11.1959.   [6] *E. & S.*, 25.6.1957.

lump sum when they moved elsewhere.[1] Labour members were keen to expose evidence of the poor quality of repair or the building of the houses,[2] complaining in 1950 of a reduction in standards, especially in size,[3] and producing crumbling bricks to demonstrate inferior materials.[4]

As a service to the tenants the Labour Party advocated extending municipal enterprise into two fields, which provoked stiff opposition. In the 1930s it urged that Council house rents should be collected by the Housing Department and not by estate agents. It was wrong in principle that the collection of the rents of publicly owned properties should be done by private individuals. Corporation employees would be more humane and less inconsiderate to the tenants than the estate agents, and they could act as a bridge between the tenant and the housing manager. But their opponents argued that they should let well alone; the agents were effective, lenient and reasonable in cost.[5]

In 1938[6] and 1956[7] the Labour Party advocated that the Corporation should sell second-hand furniture to its tenants. If it provided garden sheds, why not essential articles of furniture?[8] People who moved from slums required decent furniture on entering a new Council house, but the terms offered by private traders were excessive. The Corporation could offer better and fairer terms; the scheme would be self-supporting without any free gifts. The Conservatives, supported by the Credit Traders' District Council and by associations of retail furnishers and shopkeepers, called on the Council to leave trading to those whose job it was. The Town Hall staff would be burdened by extra work; their time and the ratepayers' money would be wasted on buying furniture from dealers and auctioneers. Tenants could afford furniture and any rare cases of genuine hardship could obtain assistance elsewhere.[9] The local paper saw the plan as a 'step towards despotism', where people were 'units of population,

[1] *E. & S.*, 20.4.1925, 12.7.1927.   [2] *C.M.*, 13.4.1930.
[3] *C.M.*, 27.11.1950. *E. & S.*, 28.11.1950.
[4] *E. & S.*, 10.1.1949.
[5] *E. & S.*, 9.12.1930, 14.1.1933, 11.7.1933, *C.M.*, 8.12.1930, 13.1.1933, 10.7.1933.
[6] *C.M.*, 31.10.1938.   [7] *C.M.*, 22.10.1956.
[8] *E. & S.*, 1.11.1938.   [9] *E. & S.*, 22.10.1956.

directed, fed, clothed, and owned body and soul by officialdom'.[1]
The door would be open to 'the ultimate Socialist Utopia in which
the local Soviet will be the fountain from which all blessings
flow'.[2]

The anti-Labour forces, who had been reluctant to allow the
Council to build houses, occasionally sought to persuade the
Council to sell its stock of houses. This suggestion was first mooted
in 1925, in a proposal to offer the houses to the sitting tenants.
The Council had a duty to provide houses and not merely to
remain landlords, claimed the advocates of the plan. They wanted
every man in England to be, not a tenant, but his own landlord.
Labour members objected that no working man had enough
money to be a purchaser, and that it would hinder mobility if a
man had to take a job a hundred miles away and he found himself
tied to his own landlordship.[3] The scheme was introduced in
1928, and an Alderman claimed that 'every Corporation house sold
meant more capital for the Corporation to build more houses'.[4]
But, as the Labour Party had predicted, there was scant demand
for purchase by the tenants, and the scheme petered out. The topic
remained dormant until in 1952 the Conservatives urged the
Labour Group to make a 'Coronation gesture' by allowing tenants
to purchase their own houses.[5] They could now afford to do so.
It was unfair that people who could afford to buy their own houses
or pay economic rents were subsidised by ratepayers who often
earned less than the tenants. Ownership brought a sense of
responsibility and it was the Conservatives' objective that we
should not 'become a nation of municipal tenants bossed around
by little men with small minds and big heads, who cling to the
delusion that they know best what flowers should be grown, how
tall your hedge should be and what colour your front door'.[6]
The Labour Group replied that few had applied to buy; if they
had the money they could buy through private enterprise; it
was the Corporation's responsibility to provide houses for those
who could not afford to buy them; and since the waiting list was
not decreasing significantly, the Council needed as large a pool

[1] Ibid. [2] *E. & S.*, 23.10.1956.
[3] *E. & S.*, 14.7.1925.
[4] *E. & S.*, 13.2.1928. *C.M.*, 13.2.1928.
[5] *E. & S.*, 27.10.1952. *C.M.*, 27.10.1952. [6] *E. & S.*, 26.10.1954.

of housing for letting as possible. To devise a scheme would be difficult, since the houses were built under different Acts and qualified for different subsidies. In any case it would be a poor gesture to sell many of them since the new owners, especially of the older property, would face big repair bills. One Councillor alleged that the Conservatives were acting for the building societies, who wished to get their hands on the 'golden plums'.[1]

MUNICIPAL ENTERPRISE

During the various controversies over housing policies, one particular item of the Labour proposals excited exceptionally fierce opposition, the expansion of municipal enterprise, whether in the building of houses, the collecting of rents or the selling of furniture. In the 1890s the question of municipal enterprise, ownership and trading did not divide the Council on political lines. Both Conservatives and Liberals advocated and opposed the municipal acquisition of the tramways and the gasworks, and these matters were discussed on their technical merits without any overtones of political ideology. But the Labour Party from its earliest years made municipal enterprise an article of political faith and principle, identifying it as a specifically Labour policy. In 1897 a Labour candidate based his platform on the principles of 'municipal ownership and collective management'.[2] In time the anti-Labour forces united in opposition to this policy, so that two polarities existed whenever this topic arose, and debates were conducted less on the technical merits of the proposals and more on the ideological case for public as against private enterprise.

In the 1890s the Labour Party, together with members of other parties, urged the municipalisation of the gas company and the tramways,[3] but the party made one cause in particular its own,

---

[1] For debates on this topic see *E. & S.*, 27.10.1952, 26.10.1953, 24.11.1953, 3.1.1956, 24.3.1959, 24.11.1959. *C.M.*, 27.10.1952, 25.10.1953, 23.11.1953, 2.1.1956, 23.3.1959, 24.11.1959.
The Conservatives also pressed the Labour Group in vain to sell land and give assistance to Housing Associations to build houses. *C.M.*, 25.2.1963, 25.3.1963, 27.1.1964.
[2] *W.C.*, 3.11.1897.
[3] *W.C.*, 31.10.1894, 27.10.1897, 3.11.1897.

the municipalisation of the cemetery. Labour members complained that the charges imposed by the Cemetery Company for interments, grave spaces, tombstones and monuments were too high; that the common grave was a mere pit into which too many bodies were put with too little soil covering each body; that the graves were inadequately numbered and cared for and that accommodation at the Chapel was unsatisfactory.[1] Not until 1936 was the company purchased by the Corporation and not until 1946 was a new Municipal Cemetery and Crematorium established. The delays occurred because many objected to the idea of a municipal cemetery competing against a private one and to the penny rate required to finance it; others objected to paying £20,000 demanded by the directors for buying them out; and there was always the difficulty of finding a suitable site.[2] During the investigations and arguments the Labour Party inveighed against 'the revolting idea of making commercial profit out of the disposal of the dead'.[3] On gaining power the party was determined to have a municipal cemetery which should be a 'work of beauty', and they engaged a landscape gardener at a fee of 500 guineas and sent him on a tour of Continental cemeteries with all expenses paid. The Conservatives attacked the Labour Group for 'thinking more of the dead than the living', but the party which had waited so long for a municipal cemetery was resolute to make it a first-class enterprise.[4]

After the First World War Labour members called for the municipalisation of milk retailing, to get cleaner and cheaper supplies. The opposition argued that municipal trading lost money and that prices would rise further.[5] After the Second World War civic catering was a battleground for the rival factions. After 1945 the Conservatives sought to reduce the number of British Restaurants, claiming that the wartime need had gone; less overtime was worked and women had returned to their homes. Since many of the restaurants were running at a loss, they should be shut. In 1950 the Conservative majority closed two. The Labour Group argued that the service should be considered as a whole and not each

[1] *Report of the General Purposes Committee*, 26.9.1898.
[2] *Reports of the Cemetery Committee*, 10.10.1910, 2.12.1912.
[3] *W.C.*, 12.10.1890.
[4] *E. & S.*, 12.2.1946.   [5] *W.C.*, 15.6.1921. *C.M.*, 13.6.1921.

restaurant separately. Profitable ones should subsidise those running at a loss, which yet provided a vital public service, especially in those areas where numerous small firms were unable to provide canteens for their employees. Conservative policy was driving men at lunch time into public houses in search of sandwiches.[1] In 1960 the Council set up a municipal catering department to provide meals at the new municipal restaurant in the new Market Hall and at the Civic Hall. The Conservatives proposed that all the catering should be put out to tender, so that private enterprise, those who had made it their life's work, should have the catering privileges and not the inexperienced Corporation. Business risks were the responsibility of businessmen minding their own money and not of local authorities using the money of ratepayers. The Labour scheme was a piece of empire-building and an attempt to introduce public ownership by the back door.[2] In these controversies the traders of the town disliked their rates being used to finance an enterprise which would compete against them, and they felt that they were the most competent people to provide the services.

Two further aspects of municipal enterprise were attacked by the Conservatives in the 1950s and 1960s. They urged that private enterprise should be allowed to redevelop clearance areas, which, it was argued, would speed up development, reduce the housing shortage and reduce the overspill problem. The Labour Group maintained the Corporation's right to develop the land, alleging that the Conservatives were making a 'snatch and grab' attempt to get a 'stranglehold on some of the town's best land, in order to gratify the profit motives of the estate agents and builders who ran the Conservative Party'.[3] Secondly the Conservatives opposed the use of the municipal farm as a means of disposing of sewage after treatment at the sewage works. They claimed that the farm always made a loss and that therefore it should be turned over to men who made farming their occupation. The Labour Group tried to blame the losses on such contingent factors as the weather, or to blame industrialists for so polluting the effluent that it destroyed

[1] *E. & S.*, 13.3.1945, 15.5.1945, 27.3.1950. *C.M.*, 12.3.1945, 14.5.1945, 27.3.1950.
[2] *E. & S.*, 28.3.1960, 29.3.1960. *C.M.*, 28.3.1960.
[3] *E. & S.*, 29.7.1958, 22.9.1958. *C.M.*, 28.7.1958, 22.9.1958, 24.11.1958, 25.11.1963.

the fertility of the soil, and in vain they asked the Conservatives to suggest another means of disposing of the waste.[1]

Both parties in Wolverhampton explained that they were bitterly divided over the place of municipal enterprise in the town, and another divisive issue was the provision of social services financed by the rates. Labour members were keen to use the Council to improve the social conditions of the working class, which meant using the rates to finance services whose main benefits flowed to the working class. Conservatives usually opposed their proposals on the grounds that the money of ratepayers should not be used for services which people were able to afford for themselves. They disliked their rates being used to finance for others services which very often they had provided for themselves independently. When such cases arose, the Conservatives stressed their role as guardians of the rate and as proponents of the principle that people should be self-reliant and not dependent on public authorities. Labour members stressed the inability of people with low incomes to obtain these services privately and they welcomed the redistributive effects of using the rates from the richer groups to finance services for the poorer.

Such controversies arose over the whole period. Labour in 1908 was urging the implementation of the Feeding of Necessitous School Children Act and the introduction of medical inspection of school children, against a majority who argued that voluntary effort would suffice.[2] In 1931, following the Government's advice to make economy cuts, it was resolved to charge 3*d* a tin for dried milk for nursing mothers; Labour members objected that it would bring hardship to the poor and unemployed. 'Do not let us pursue this murderous policy of robbing little kiddies of their milk.' But the majority said that economy was vital and that voluntary workers would relieve genuine hardship.[3] Nurseries provided a

---

[1] *E. & S.*, 5.5.1964. *C.M.*, 25.9.1961, 24.6.1963. The Conservatives also opposed the Labour proposal to remove the Workshops for the Blind from a voluntary institution and to run them as a Corporation enterprise. *E. & S.*, 23.12.1957. *C.M.*, 23.12.1957.

[2] *E. & S.*, 16.10.1908.   [3] *E. & S.*, 9.11.1931. *C.M.*, 9.11.1931.

battleground in the 1950s. In 1951 the Conservative majority resolved to close the Birmingham Road Day Nursery, since the one at the Woodlands was sufficient. They complained that too many women were putting their children into nurseries in order to earn pin money, while their husbands were earning big sums too. They should be at home caring for their children. Labour members said that the production drive depended on women at work; if the nursery was closed they would have to get up at 5 a.m. to take their children to the nursery at the other side of the town; and the extra money was very often what held their homes and families together.[1] Although the Conservative motion was carried,[2] when the Labour Group regained its majority in 1952, the nursery was reopened.[3]

Education provided another arena of conflict between the parties, not along sectarian lines as at the turn of the century, but over the position of the Grammar School. This school always excited the wrath of the Labour Party. In 1896 in a debate on the disposal of the proceeds of the Local Taxation Act of 1890, Labour members opposed the proposal to give £250 to the Wolverhampton Grammar School to erect science buildings, because it was a 'class school', not open to the children of the poor.[4] In 1905 they proposed that it be made a free school, open to merit without any barrier because of poverty.[5] In 1914 they opposed an increase in the grant to the school because they argued that each scholar assisted by the Council cost them £22, while the others were admitted at £15.[6] In 1920 the Labour Party said that 'the principle of giving grants to schools over which the Council did not have control was wrong'. The Council should run the school and make it open to all boys.[7] The opponents asked them not to injure 'an asset to the town',[8] and claimed it would be injured if it were swamped with free-place scholars.[9] Not until 1945 was its status settled in a way acceptable to most Labour members, when the Council was granted a third of the governors, control over the admissions policy and

---

[1] *E. & S.*, 1.1.1952.		[2] *C.M.*, 31.12.1951.
[3] *C.M.*, 23.6.1952. *E. & S.*, 24.6.1952.
[4] *W.C.*, 12.2.1896. *C.M.*, 10.2.1896.		[5] *W.C.*, 14.5.1905.
[6] *W.C.*, 14.1.1914. *C.M.*, 12.1.1914.
[7] *W.C.*, 13.10.1920. *C.M.*, 11.10.1920. They had attacked the establishment of the Girls' High School for similar reasons. *W.C.*, 7.10.1908. *C.M.*, 5.10.1908.
[8] *W.C.*, 14.1.1914.		[9] *W.C.*, 12.10.1920.

scope to carry out a 'wide open door policy', and fees were abolished.[1] By the late 1950s some Labour members wanted to submerge the school in a comprehensive system for the town as a whole. The Conservatives opposed, defending the Grammar School against abolition. The Labour Group itself was divided and draft plans for comprehensive education excluded the Grammar School.[2] Still a sizeable minority in the Labour Group wanted to transform it into a comprehensive school.

THE CONFLICT ON THE COUNCIL

The Labour Party first entered the Council to promote specific trade union objectives, but over the period this aspect of its work declined. It also sought to advance in a more general way the social conditions of the working class, using the Corporation to undertake certain enterprises and to provide certain services. This aspect of its work remained constant. Its championship of these aims brought it into conflict with those groups who had previously held sway in the Council. Their main concerns had been to improve the amenities of their particular wards, to protect the interests of their occupational and social groups and to further the causes of their particular committees. They found their interests attacked by the Labour Party. They objected to paying higher rates for better wages and conditions for Corporation employees and they opposed the growth of trade unions, which were limiting their freedom of action in their private concerns too. They objected to paying rates to finance municipal services which they had provided for themselves, and municipal enterprises which would compete against their own businesses. As the Labour Party grew, and as it organised itself into a united block on the Council, its opponents found that if they wished to defend their interests, they would have to follow suit and organise themselves in a similar fashion. Thus by the 1950s two parties faced each other. Behind each group was a different set of forces. Quite distinct sets of occupational and social groups provided the voters and the membership of each party and each Group. And each party was out to provide benefits for its voters and supporters.

[1] *E. & S.*, 25.9.1945. *C.M.*, 24.9.1945.
[2] *E. & S.*, 25.1.1960, 23.2.1960. *C.M.*, 25.1.1960, 23.3.1960.

Before the First World War, and to a lesser extent in the inter-war years, the voting in the Council was not along strict party lines. Some Conservatives and some Liberals supported some of the Labour proposals and at times the Council adopted Labour schemes. Sometimes an occasional Labour member would object to a particular plan of his party. But on the whole the Labour members took the initiative in bringing forward the kinds of proposals examined in this chapter, and on the whole the majority of Labour members supported them; those from other parties who joined the Labour members on such items did not do so consistently, but only occasionally. And on the whole the opponents of the Labour schemes were those groups who belonged to other parties. The deviant from the party on either side was an eccentric odd man out. After 1945 it was very rare for a member of one Group to vote against his Group. Voting was more strictly on party lines.

The conflict between the parties over local government in Wolverhampton was not artificial. It was relevant to the local context, for both parties represented distinct sets of supporters, whose interests they were trying to promote. The division was not imposed on the town by the political parties thinking only of their national and Parliamentary prospects. The division over local politics was the same as that over national politics; the same parties competed, the same people argued, and the same people fought both municipal and Parliamentary elections. The voters, too, were the same; but fewer of them turned out for the Council elections, although the share of the vote which each party obtained at the municipal elections was very similar to what it got at the Parliamentary elections. There was no meaningful antithesis between the parties' activities in local and national politics; the two skirmishes were part of one battle fought by the same armies.

16 Crisis in Wolverhampton 1961-2

IN 1961 and 1962 Wolverhampton became notorious for displaying the evil effects of party politics in local government. The national and local press pointed to Wolverhampton as an example of the way in which the conflict between parties abused the institution of the Aldermanic bench. The crisis of these years shows the political system on the Wolverhampton Council under exceptional strain.

In February 1961 the Labour Group unanimously decided to take the Mayoralty for the coming municipal year and to nominate for the office Alderman C. H. Davies, the Chairman since 1954 of the Fire and Ambulance Committee.[1] Protests came from Conservatives, who objected to the way in which the decision was reached. They claimed that the Labour Party was 'inviting public conflict over who should be the chief citizen of the town', because it had not sought 'any private and friendly discussions between past Mayors or senior members of both parties', in an attempt 'to present a united recommendation'.[2] Further, Labour's choice was announced to the press immediately after its Group meeting, and before the full Council, in private session, had had an opportunity to discuss the matter. Such precipitate action, claimed the Conservatives, was an insult to the Council. But their main objection was that they had not been allowed to take the Mayoralty. At the private Council meeting when Davies was adopted as Mayor-elect, the Conservative nominee, Councillor M. P. Birch, the leader of the Conservative Group, said, 'my group put me up because we have had the mayoralty only once in the last eight years. We feel it is time we had it again.'[2] Two Conservative Councillors, who had not been Mayors, had each served on the Council a year

[1] *M.L.G.*, 24.2.1961.   [2] *E. & S.*, 29.5.1961.   [3] *E. & S.*, 27.2.1961.

longer than Davies.[1] Birch claimed, 'I am senior to Alderman Davies . . . and these things up to a point, should go on seniority.'[2] Some Conservatives also had private misgivings about Davies's competence. It was feared that he would not maintain the dignity of the office, because he was an old-age pensioner who had never signed a four-figure cheque, who lived in a Council house, who had often been on the dole and whose last job had been to open and close the gates of the gasworks. Davies was a Welshman who had lived in Wolverhampton since 1941; he was seventy-six years old, retired on his pension and living with his children, after many jobs as a miner, bus conductor, clerk, electrician's mate, and gasworker.[3]

It was expected that the coming municipal elections would prove unfavourable to Labour, producing a Council evenly divided with the Mayor holding the casting vote. He would therefore decide which party would be in control, and thus the Conservatives, in a minority since 1952, and without Chairmanships since 1955, felt that at last they were on the point of regaining a majority. The Labour Party naturally wanted to avoid this eventuality, and for this reason decided to take the Mayoralty, although some Labour members agreed that it should have been the Conservative's turn if there had been no prospect of Labour losing control. For the Labour Group it was important that the Mayor should follow Group instructions. Davies was 'a safe man, who would do as he was told'. He had never been a leading or controversial figure in the party, and he had always been loyal to Group decisions. Therefore he was the Labour choice for Mayor, not only because he was the senior Labour member of the Council who had never been Mayor and who was willing to take the office, but also because he would always give his casting vote to the Labour side in any controversy whatsoever.

Before the elections in May, Labour had twenty-five Councillors and the Conservatives twenty; of the Aldermen Labour had ten and the Conservatives four.[4] There was one Aldermanic vacancy,

---

[1] Davies was elected in 1945, while M. P. Birch and A. H. Windridge were co-opted in 1944.
[2] *E. & S.*, 27.2.1961.
[3] *E. & S.*, 27.2.1961, 24.5.1961. Council Yearbooks, 1945–61.
[4] Table VI.

because in March an eighty-eight-year-old Conservative Alderman, J. H. Coleman, had retired, and although the Labour Group had elected the eighty-year-old Labour Councillor, Mrs M. Dale, to the bench, she had not made the declaration of acceptance.[1] This episode embittered even more the relations between the parties, for the Conservatives felt that a Conservative should have replaced Coleman. Birch said: 'I have seen Mr Coleman several times recently, and he had hoped that he could have made way for someone on the Conservative side. I know it will hurt him when he sees in tonight's paper that a Socialist has taken his place.' Of the Aldermen due to retire in 1964, all eight were Labour, while, of the others due to retire in 1961, two were Labour, four were Conservatives and one seat was vacant. Thus control of the Council was going to depend on the results of the Aldermanic elections as well as on the results of the May municipal elections.

The municipal elections were a defeat for Labour, for Conservatives gained three seats in marginal wards, so that they had twenty-three Councillors to Labour's twenty-two.[2] The Labour Group faced a difficult situation. Only Councillors and the Mayor can vote in Aldermanic elections, and thus Labour could have a majority only if the Mayor gave both his Mayoral vote and his casting vote for the Labour candidates. It was important therefore that the Mayor should be a Labour supporter. But a snag arose because Davies was himself a retiring Alderman. The Town Clerk, whose legal advice the Labour leader sought, said that Davies would be able to give his vote as Mayor, but not his casting vote as the presiding officer of the meeting, since he would be acting against natural justice and common law if he presided over his own election. The prospect was of a tie without any means of reconciling it. The Labour leaders had many consultations with the Town Clerk about what they could do. They wanted a procedure which would allow them to retain control of the Council by taking all the Aldermanic seats. The plan which emerged out of these discussions was finally adopted by the Group.[3]

The plan was to go ahead with the election of Davies as Mayor.

[1] *E. & S.*, 27.3.1961.
[2] *E. & S.*, 12.5.1961.
[3] A reading of the *Labour Party's Local Government Handbook*, 1960, pp. 234–6, would have shown them a sounder way of achieving their objectives.

For the Aldermanic elections he would vacate the Mayoral chair and return to his old seat, while a non-retiring Alderman would be elected to the chair temporarily. When the vote was taken the Mayor could give his Mayoral vote, thus producing a tie, then the Alderman in the chair would give a casting vote in his capacity as Chairman of the meeting, thus giving the Labour candidates a majority of one. The Labour Group planned to replace all the Conservative Aldermen with Labour Councillors; by-elections would be held in the five safe Labour wards from which the new Aldermen had been taken, and five new Labour Councillors would be elected.[1] At the end of these events Labour would have all the fifteen Aldermen and twenty-two Councillors, while the Conservatives would have only twenty-three Councillors. Labour would have a majority of fourteen.[2]

The Labour Party was determined not to lose control. After the declaration of the poll in May, Councillor H. Bagley, Chairman of the Borough Labour Party, had said 'we shall take all the Aldermanic seats at the annual meeting, fight by-elections in Labour strongholds and so consolidate our position on the Council'.[3] The leader of the Group announced after the Group had decided its course of action that 'we shall take all steps to retain our majority on the Council'.[4] The Conservatives, however, claimed that the voice of the electorate had spoken in their favour, and that with a majority of the directly elected representatives they were morally entitled to choose not only the Mayor but the Aldermen. Since they believed that the Aldermanic bench should reflect the respective strengths of the parties' numbers of Councillors, they said that they were entitled to a larger number of Aldermen than they had at the moment.

The counter-plan of the Conservatives was largely the handiwork of a Councillor elected only that May, Stanley Brindley, a solicitor. The Conservatives were lucky in being able to draw on his legal knowledge. At his first Group meeting Brindley explained why he thought that the Labour plan, details of which had become known to the Conservatives, was illegal. He said that if a Mayor did not preside, he would have to leave the chamber, for the Mayor if

---

[1] *M.L.G.*, 16.5.1961. *E. & S.*, 17.5.1961.
[2] Table VI.   [3] *E. & S.*, 12.5.1961.   [4] *E. & S.*, 17.5.1961.

present had to take the chair. Brindley's advice was to let the Labour scheme take its course and then to challenge it in the courts. His stiffest battle in the Group was to convince the older members, who were eager to be Mayors, not to oppose Davies's nomination for Mayor. He said that opposition would serve no useful purpose, as the Labour Party had a majority of the whole Council which would enable them to make anyone Mayor. With so much at stake, they were unlikely to choose a Conservative. For the Conservative plan to work it was necessary that a Labour retiring Alderman seeking re-election should be made Mayor so that he would be unable to preside over the Aldermanic elections and have to leave the meeting. Brindley feared that the Labour Group might decide not to nominate Davies, the only one of the retiring Aldermen who had not been Mayor, and to choose instead a non-retiring Alderman, for example the sitting Mayor, for another term of office. He would then be able to give both his Mayoral and his casting vote for the Labour Aldermanic candidates. Then, since he was an epileptic, he could resign as Mayor on the grounds of ill-health and Davies could take his place.[1] Brindley's fears were in fact groundless, for the Labour Party were thoroughly convinced about the soundness of their plan. Brindley convinced the Conservative Group. Its plan was to let Davies be chosen as Mayor, and in the Aldermanic elections to vote for the four retiring Conservative Aldermen, to fill the vacancy with a Conservative, and to replace the two Labour Aldermen with Conservative Councillors from safe Conservative wards. The ensuing by-elections would return three new Conservative Councillors. This end might be achieved if any Labour member failed to attend the meeting. Otherwise the Conservatives hoped that the High Court would declare the Labour procedure illegal and thus validate the Conservative plan.[2] At the end of these events the final composition of the Council would be eight Labour and seven Conservative Aldermen, and twenty-two Labour and

---

[1] He outlined later another possible course of action. The Labour Party could have elected Davies as Mayor, but he need not have signed the declaration of acceptance, thus leaving the previous Mayor in the chair. 'Our party would have had no point of order to raise whatsoever.' *E. & S.*, 31.5.1961. Brindley enjoyed taunting the Labour Party with alternative legal means they might have adopted to gain their ends. *E. & S.*, 2.8.1961.

[2] *M.C.G.*, May 1961.

twenty-three Conservative Councillors, with the Labour Mayor tipping the balance in Labour's favour.[1]

The Labour Party then became anxious as to whether all their members would be able to attend the Council meeting. The Secretary of the Labour Group, Councillor F. S. Smith, was taken ill with gastric influenza. A photograph on the front page of the local paper showed him in bed, and the caption said, 'I'll crawl there if necessary'.[2] The leader of the Conservative Group announced that 'as far as I know, everyone is fit, no one is on holiday and all our members should be at the meeting to vote'.[3]

29 May was the day of the Council meeting and everything went as both Groups had planned. All members were present. Davies was elected Mayor by the Labour members, while the Conservatives abstained.[4] He made the declaration of acceptance and was enrobed. Then the leader of the Labour Group, the non-retiring Alderman F. Mansell, was voted temporarily into the chair and Davies returned to his old seat. The Aldermanic elections were then held. Davies gave his Mayoral vote for the Labour candidates. Mansell announced a tie of twenty-three votes for each slate, and gave his casting vote as Chairman of the meeting for the Labour candidates. Brindley, on behalf of the Conservatives, in his maiden speech objected. He said: 'If the Mayor vacates the chair, he must absent himself from the chamber immediately and remain absent until the completion of the elections.' The Town Clerk was asked as legal adviser to the Council to explain the legal position. He said, 'The Mayor as such is given a vote in the election of Aldermen. It has nothing to do with the question of whether he presides or not.' He could 'see no grounds for saying that merely because the Mayor had vacated the chair, he should forgo the right to vote. . . . If I am to be proved wrong, if the Council act on my advice and I prove to be wrong, it will have to be by taking High Court Action to get a ruling on this matter.' Brindley replied that the Conservatives reserved the right to present an election petition to the High Court.[5]

[1] Table VI.   [2] *E. & S.*, 25.5.1961.
[3] Ibid.
[4] A Conservative spokesman said: 'I am not putting up an alternative name because our party is not voting for or against the proposal.' *E. & S.*, 29.5.1961.
[5] *E. & S.*, 29.5.1961. *C.M.*, 29.5.1961.

Two of the ejected Conservative Aldermen instructed solicitors to present a petition to the High Court to declare void the election of 29 May and to declare the Conservative Aldermen duly elected, because the Mayor having vacated his seat was not entitled to vote in the election.[1] A public subscription fund was set up to meet the costs. Its Secretary was the Secretary of the Conservative Group, himself the son of one of the ejected Aldermen. The Vice-Chairman of the Group said that the Group was 'right behind these ex-Aldermen in the fight'.[2] The petition was presented on 11 June.[3]

The Conservatives objected to the Labour Party's manipulation on the grounds not only of illegality but also of immorality. It was 'a negation of democratic principles'.[4] They were attempting to remain in power for three years 'irrespective of the will of the people and contrary to the spirit of our local government law and tradition'.[5] There had been no need for them to turn off the Conservative Aldermen, for if they had re-elected the four Conservative Aldermen they would still have kept a majority, since the composition of the Council would have been thirty-three Labour and twenty-seven Conservative members, 'surely a large enough majority for effective control'.[6] Instead the Labour Group removed four long-serving Aldermen, who had all been Chairmen of Council committees. But in May neither party was in the mood for compromise; each was eager to do the utmost damage to the other. The Labour Party was not prepared to let the Conservatives remove two of their Aldermen, including their Mayor, while the Conservatives, strengthened by their electoral victory, resented Labour's stratagems to deprive them of the Mayoralty, to keep them out of office and to manipulate the Aldermanic elections so brazenly.

The Labour Party was convinced it had succeeded. The Mayor was confident. He said: 'storm clouds are good, because behind the clouds, the sun shines. I know that the sun is behind the clouds, so I am not perturbed about that side of the matter.'[7] Labour candidates were selected to stand in the five safe Labour seats, vacated by its new Aldermen. The Chairman of the Borough

[1] *E. & S.*, 31.5.1961.
[2] *E. & S.*, 1.6.1961.
[3] *E. & S.*, 13.6.1961.
[4] *E. & S.*, 6.8.1961.
[5] *E. & S.*, 31.5.1961.
[6] *E. & S.*, 2.6.1961.
[7] Ibid.

Labour Party said, 'we shall fight every inch to retain control of the seats.'[1] In one ward, Low Hill, a Communist candidate stood against the Labour candidate, while in Parkfield Ward an Independent Conservative stood. The other three Labour men faced no opposition. The Conservatives officially put up no candidates, since they argued that if the High Court upheld their petition, the elections would be void.[2] The agent for the North-East Conservative Association said: 'In the circumstances this association does not intend to take any steps which might involve the ratepayers or the association in unnecessary expense.'[3] This view was not accepted by one Conservative, a solicitor, R. J. Dallow, who had fought Parkfield Ward as official Conservative candidate in May. He argued that since the new Labour Aldermen had made the declaration of acceptance of Aldermanic office, they had vacated their seats as Councillors and therefore by-elections to fill these seats would be valid. He was convinced that even if the Conservatives did win the petition, the by-elections would be legal, otherwise it would have been a waste of time and money for him to stand.[4]

Labour won the five seats,[5] and the new members attended the Council meeting in July, when Labour had a majority of fourteen.[6] Four days later the High Court upheld the Conservatives' petition. Counsel for the Labour respondents argued that if Parliament had intended to disfranchise the Mayor when he happened to be a candidate for the Aldermanic bench, it would have done so in express language. The fact that the Mayor was a candidate did not take away his vote. He further argued that the statutory provision that the Mayor should preside, should be read as impliedly subject to any common-law rule, and that it was not mandatory but directive, and consequently the election was not invalidated by a breach. Their lordships rejected these arguments. The provision was mandatory. Mr Justice Glyn-Jones said: 'a Mayor unless presiding, cannot be present at a meeting and cannot vote. If he could not preside there was no other capacity in which he was capable of being present at that meeting.'[7]

---

[1] *E. & S.*, 30.5.1961.　　　　[2] *E. & S.*, 8.6.1961.
[3] *E. & S.*, 15.6.1961.　　　　[4] *W.C.*, 16.6.1961.
[5] *E. & S.*, 7.7.1961.　　　　[6] *C.M.*, 24.7.1961.
[7] Details of the case and the judgment can be found in 3 All E.R., [1961] 446–52 and 3 W.L.R. 1139–48, [1961]. See also *The Times*, 29.7.1961, and *Justice of the Peace*, 5.8.1961.

A similar case at Slough attracted press comment, but the procedure taken was sufficiently different to put it within the law. The Mayor, also a retiring Alderman, gave his Mayoral vote in the Aldermanic elections *from his Mayoral chair*, and then for the counting of the votes vacated his seat, which was taken temporarily by a non-retiring Alderman who gave his casting vote for the Labour list.[1] The advisers of the Labour Party at Slough were clearly more astute than those at Wolverhampton.

The successful petitioners were met on the station at Wolverhampton by 'a little group of people with a large-size Union Jack demonstrating their "faith in British justice" '.[2] The Town Clerk was shocked at the judgment. He felt that the judges had made a bad decision, making moral judgements on the political proposal to take all the Aldermen and not interpreting the intention of the law. The Borough Labour Party called a special meeting, instructed their solicitors to lodge an appeal and asked the National Executive Committee of the party for advice.[3] The Labour Party nationally examined the case, but gave little help, since it said that it found the case interesting and hoped it would be taken further to clarify the position once and for all.

The Conservative Party, though victorious, were uneasy, for they doubted whether their new Aldermen should make the declaration of acceptance. If the Labour appeal were successful, they might be deposed from their Aldermanic status, and if their old seats as Councillors had been filled at subsequent by-elections they might find themselves not members of the Council in any form. After some delay they signed,[4] but only after the Town Clerk, having taken legal advice, announced that the valid members of the Council were the deposed Labour ex-Aldermen not the newly elected Labour Councillors. He said that the opinion of Counsel was that 'the effect of the High Court decision is that none of the five persons was validly elected as an Alderman and that therefore no vacancy occurred in the office each held as Councillor. No one could therefore be elected to fill the vacancy which did not exist.'[5]

---

[1] *Justice of the Peace*, 28.10.1961, *Sunday Times*, 30.7.1961, and *The Observer*, 30.7.1961.

[2] *The Times*, 29.7.1961.   [3] *E. & S.*, 8.6.1961.

[4] *E. & S.*, 4.8.1961, 19.8.1961.   [5] *E. & S.*, 4.8.1961.

The Conservative Aldermen could thus sign the declaration, secure that they would not be deprived of Council membership if the Labour appeal were successful. Official Conservative candidates were selected for the three safe Conservative wards vacated by the new Aldermen. Two were returned unopposed, but in the third an Independent Socialist candidate stood, backed by 'six or seven members' of the Labour Party.[1] The Labour Party officially did not put forward candidates on the grounds that if their appeal were successful the elections would be superfluous. The Independent Socialist stood in order to propagate his views on the H-bomb: his campaign was concerned more to display the views of C.N.D. than to discuss the problems of Wolverhampton.[2] He lost.[3]

The Town Clerk's ruling provoked a bitter battle within the Labour Party. His advice was accepted by the majority of the Borough Party, including two of the five who had been elected to the Council in July and then removed, but three of the five said that only the High Court, not the Town Clerk, could declare by-elections invalid. They therefore instructed solicitors to challenge his ruling.[4] The Borough Party warned that 'if these persist in any legal action they will almost certainly be expelled'.[5] They were accused of 'going behind the backs of people'.[6] A motion for their expulsion was brought up at the Borough Party. 'I'm staggered,' said one of them, 'everybody is crying out for unity but this is not the way to get it.'[7] One ward party passed a resolution that 'the sooner we cut out the bickering that is going on inside the party the better'.[8] The plans for expulsion were dropped, chiefly through the influence of the West Midlands Regional Organiser of the Labour Party, who urged the party to concentrate on winning the next May elections.[9] Two of the five refused to sign a pledge of loyalty to the party and were consequently excluded from the panel of municipal candidates.

Plans to seek a High Court ruling as to who were the valid

---

[1] *E. & S.*, 29.8.1961.
[2] *E. & S.*, 2.9.1961, 7.9.1961, 11.9.1961.
[3] *E. & S.*, 15.9.1961.
[4] *E. & S.*, 17.10.1961. *The Times*, 17.10.1961.
[5] *E. & S.*, 17.10.1961.
[6] Interview with H. Bagley.　　　　[7] *E. & S.*, 10.11.1961.
[8] *E. & S.*, 27.11.1961.　　　　[9] *E. & S.*, 30.11.1961.

Councillors were dropped and the party decided not to appeal against the High Court's decision over the Aldermen. There was by now considerable doubt if it would win the appeal and most important of all it feared the cost. A bill of £329 for the costs of Counsel and solicitors was presented to the party. 'The organisation is broke',[1] said the Secretary of the Borough Party. A public appeal was launched to raise the money, and the party's funds set aside for a new headquarters were eaten into.[2]

The composition of the Council remained at 30:30 with the Labour Mayor's casting vote holding the balance until Christmas Day, when Alderman H. Mash, the epileptic, died.[3] The election of his successor almost lost the Labour Party control, but the Conservatives' blunders saved their opponents. It caused bitterness between the parties to flare up again after a few months of relative peace. A reconciliation between the two groups had been called for by the Rector of Wolverhampton[4] and the leading Baptist Minister. The December Group meetings of both parties discussed a pact. Two items were the centre of discussion, the Mayoralty and the Aldermanic vacancy caused by Mash's death. The Mayoralty for 1962–3 was particularly important, since three days after the Mayor-making ceremony the Queen was to visit the town. The Labour Group decided 'not to nominate because we do not want there to be any fight between ourselves and the Conservatives over who shall be Mayor-elect. We particularly did not want any acrimony in view of the Queen's visit.'[5] But there could be no compromise over the Aldermanic vacancy. Mansell said, 'we would like to see the office of Alderman abolished. Under these circumstances, the meeting felt that we could not start making an agreement when we don't believe there should be such an office.'[6] The Group would support the Mayor for the vacancy. The Conservative leader had stated that 'my group would welcome a peace pact',[7] but the Conservative Group felt that it was entitled to the vacancy on the principle of proportional representation. Birch said that if the Labour Party had been prepared to discuss a general policy on the allocation of Aldermanic seats, 'it is possible we

[1] *E. & S.*, 6.7.1962.
[2] *E. & S.*, 8.6.1962. [3] *E. & S.*, 27.12.1961.
[4] *E. & S.*, 5.9.1961. [5] *E. & S.*, 12.1.1962.
[6] Ibid. [7] *E. & S.*, 28.12.1961.

should have supported Mr Davies. . . . The Socialists have themselves to blame.'[1]

For the January meeting of the Council when the election to the Aldermanic vacancy was to take place, all members of the Council were present except the Mayor, who was very ill, just discharged from hospital and thought to be on the brink of death.[2] The appointment of a Chairman of the meeting was the first item of business. The Mayor from his hospital bed had chosen the Labour Alderman, C. B. V. Taylor, to be the Deputy-Mayor on the death of Mash. Taylor told the Council that he could not preside unless chosen by the Council. The Conservatives, realising that for the first time since 1952 they had a majority, elected to the chair, by thirty votes to twenty-nine, Alderman Dr A. Byrne-Quinn. Then followed the Aldermanic election. The twenty-two Labour votes were cast for the Mayor, while twenty-three Conservative votes were cast for Councillor A. H. Windridge.[3] Since he came from a safe Conservative seat, the Conservatives thought that they could hold a by-election quickly and then they would control the Council by thirty-one votes to twenty-nine, thus making nugatory the casting vote of the Mayor. As they began to seek a candidate, they found that they had miscalculated, for Windridge was due to retire in May 1962 and Section 67 of the Local Government Act, 1933, prevented them from filling the vacancy before the May elections, since it was laid down that if there is less than six months of the Councillor's term due to run before the May elections, then the vacancy must be filled along with the others at the annual elections. Thus the Mayor still held the balance between twenty-nine Labour and thirty Conservative members.[4]

The local paper, hitherto hostile to the Labour Group, condemned the Conservative Party for flinging down the political gage and reopening warfare[5] by not voting the Mayor to the bench. It called for an end to the 'wrangling and wangling'.[6] In the Labour Group a significant number wanted to repudiate the promise not to nominate for the Mayoralty in view of the Conservatives' action in taking the Aldermanic vacancy, but the

---

[1] *E. & S.*, 25.1.1962.
[3] *E. & S.*, 22.1.1962. *C.M.*, 22.1.1962.
[5] Ibid.

[2] He died eight months later.
[4] *E. & S.*, 23.1.1962.
[6] *E. & S.*, 1.2.1962.

original promise was reaffirmed by a small majority,[1] and M.P. Birch was chosen Mayor-elect at a private meeting of the Council in February.[2]

The May elections were awaited. It was expected that they would resolve the deadlock. In fact they produced the worst situation so far. The local paper said after the declaration of the poll that 'one of the biggest municipal rows in Wolverhampton's history is likely to follow'.[3] Labour gained one seat from the Conservatives, thus making the parties equal with thirty members of the Council apiece while the Mayor held the deciding vote.[4] Thus at the Mayor-making ceremony Davies would hold the deciding vote, and if Birch were then elected Mayor, the Conservatives would be in control. Labour claimed that the elections were a Labour victory and that 'it would seem contrary to Labour Party policy to allow a Conservative Mayor's casting vote to be used against the implementation of our policies.'[5] Some Labour members canvassed the idea that they should not let Birch be elected Mayor, but that they should choose one of their defeated candidates in the elections for the office. Some Conservatives suggested that one of their aged Aldermen should retire and make way for a Labour member to enable Labour to have a majority. 'Forward a Sir Galahad! A Conservative Alderman willing to give up his seat', cried the paper,[6] but none could be found. Others suggested that Birch himself should give up his Aldermanic seat, and be, like Davies, a Mayor who was neither a Councillor nor an Alderman.[7] The Young Liberals' Association stated that 'a public referendum should be held to elect a new Mayor'.[8]

The two Groups planned to meet on 14 May, a week before the Mayor-making ceremony. On 13 May the leading members of both Groups met at the house of a Conservative Alderman, H. T. Fullwood; the first time the leaders had come together officially to discuss the political situation in Wolverhampton since the crisis broke. They devised 'an unprecedented agreement', 'a triumph for reason', 'a compromise worthy of the wisdom of Solomon'.[9] A pact was drawn up by Birch and signed by both

[1] *E. & S.*, 23.2.1962.　　　　[2] *E. & S.*, 26.2.1962.
[3] *E. & S.*, 11.5.1962.　　　　[4] Ibid.
[5] Ibid.　　　　　　　　　　　[6] *E. & S.*, 14.5.1952.
[7] Ibid.　　　　　　　　　　　[8] Ibid.
[9] *E. & S.*, 15.5.1962.

sides. It provided that Birch was to be Mayor, but during his term of office he was to remain neutral and not to vote on any issue, even on Aldermanic elections. If a tie seemed likely when the Mayor would have to use his casting vote, a Conservative member would leave the Council chamber. 'The Mayor elect has readily given his solemn pledge to remain neutral and not at any time during his year of office to exercise his right to vote in the Council chamber. To obviate any embarrassment which might be caused by the Mayor being forced to give a casting vote, one of the Conservative members would refrain from voting should there be a danger of an equal vote.' Birch said 'I have always felt that the Mayor should be neutral, and in agreeing I am not going against any of my principles.'[1] Thus the Conservatives were to gain the Mayoralty and the Labour Party to maintain control.

The pact was not greeted with approval by all members of each Group. A number of the younger Conservatives objected to signing away the possibility of power in order that their leader might enjoy the delights of the Mayoralty. They argued that since Davies might be too ill to attend the Mayor-making ceremony they might win both the Mayoralty and control. But the pact was accepted by a majority. In the Labour Group the pact was adopted by only fifteen votes to thirteen. The minority contended that Conservatives could never be trusted: they would dishonour the pledge in order to take power. The Labour leaders must have been befuddled with Fullwood's drink to have agreed to such a proposition. The leadership claimed that the Labour Group was assured of control. The agreement was so public that the Conservatives would never dare abuse it: and by signing it the Conservatives had proclaimed that they were more interested in the honours of office than in implementing their principles and policies. At a crucial juncture a letter from Davies was read which moved the Group almost to tears. He begged them not to make a dying man give his casting vote for a Labour Mayor, but to let him enjoy his final meeting free from squabbling. It was so agreed.

Birch was elected Mayor. He shook hands with the Queen. He kept his pledge and remained neutral during his term of office.[2] Labour stayed in control. At the municipal elections of May 1963

---

[1] Ibid.   [2] e.g., *E. & S.*, 24.7.1962.

Labour gained four seats, thus having a majority of eight in the
Council.[1] The Mayor for the year was a Labour nominee.[2] During
the municipal year 1963–4 two Conservative Aldermen died and
were replaced, against Conservative opposition, by Labour
Councillors.[3] At the municipal elections of May 1964 there was
no change.[4] For the Aldermanic elections seven of the eight retiring
Aldermen were Labour. The Conservatives did not oppose them,
hoping that the Labour Group would support their single candidate.
But the Labour Group took all the seats, replacing Windridge
by a Labour Councillor,[5] whose former seat was filled at a
subsequent by-election by another Labour member.[6] The Labour
Party also took the Mayoralty again.[7] The composition of the
Council at the end of June 1964 was that Labour had 10 Aldermen
and 27 Councillors, while the Conservatives had 5 Aldermen and
18 Councillors, giving Labour a majority of 14.

1961 and 1962 were a time of great strain for the chief officials
of the Corporation, especially for the Town Clerk. He said that
he found his position very difficult. He preferred to work with a
Council in which one party had a working majority. In the balanced
situation each party was waiting to take up anything for its
advantage against the other. If, for example, an official objected to
the policy of one party, the other took up his point and used it to
score off the other. His major objection was that business was not
dispatched with speed and consistency. An example was the story
of the Health Committee's proposal for a compulsory purchase
order for some houses in a clearance and redevelopment area. This
recommendation came before the second January 1962 Council
meeting.[8] The Mayor was absent, sick in hospital, and the Conservatives elected Dr Byrne-Quinn to the chair. They proposed
that there should be no compulsory purchase order, but a clearance
order instead, which would allow the individual owners to retain
the ownership of the land and to develop it themselves. The debate
was a battle between the Labour advocates of municipal enterprise

[1] *E. & S.*, 10.5.1963.   [2] *E. & S.*, 21.5.1963.
[3] *C.M.*, 24.2.1964, 23.3.1964.
[4] *E. & S.*, 8.5.1964.
[5] *C.M.*, 25.5.1964. *E. & S.*, 25.5.1964.
[6] *E. & S.*, 26.6.1964.   [7] *E. & S.*, 25.5.1964.
[8] *C.M.*, 22.1.1962.

and the Conservative advocates of private enterprise. The officials had advised a compulsory purchase order for technical reasons, because the individual owners were often unknown, and the area could be cleared and developed in one piece only if a compulsory purchase order was made. The Conservative Chairman of the meeting gave his casting vote for the Conservative amendment.[1] The committee reconsidered the matter and at the next Council meeting, which the Labour Mayor was able to attend, the original Labour motion was passed.[2]

The way in which party conflict in an evenly balanced Council disrupted the business of the Council is seen also from the adventures which befell the motion of a Conservative Councillor, P. T. W. Farmer, that all Council houses should be offered for sale to the tenants. He had moved a similar motion for years and the latest one was due to be discussed again at the November 1961 Council meeting. It was the last item on the agenda.[3] About 4 p.m. some Labour members realised that they could embarrass the Conservatives by rushing through the agenda and reaching his motion while he was out of the chamber taking tea. The paper commented that 'all thirteen items on the agenda had been disposed of with surprising speed'.[4] No. 14 was Farmer's motion. A Labour Councillor moved that it be struck from the agenda in view of Farmer's absence, which he said was a discourtesy to the Mayor and members. At 4.24 p.m. the meeting came to an 'abrupt end'. Farmer later said, 'I went out for a cup of tea. We had such a lot of items on the agenda I did not expect my motion to be reached so quickly'. The 'cuppa controversy' raged in the correspondence columns of the press. Labour members condemned tea-tippling Tories for their absences while such items as old people's welfare, water supply and slum clearance were being discussed. 'Catching these gentlemen out is quite easy. The difficulty is in catching them in.' Conservatives attacked the Labour Party for 'rattling through the agenda', working a 'childish stratagem' and for conducting 'the slickest Council meeting I've ever known'.[5]

The motion came up again at the first meeting in the new year.[6]

[1] *E. & S.*, 23.1.1962.   [2] *C.M.*, 19.2.1962.   [3] *C.M.*, 27.11.1961.
[4] *E. & S.*, 28.11.1961.
[5] *E. & S.*, 30.11.1961, 2.12.1961, 5.12.1961.
[6] *C.M.*, 1.1.1962.

It missed being passed by the slightest accident. The Mayor was absent, ill again. The Labour Group proposed its leader, Mansell, to act as Chairman; the Conservatives proposed Alderman Homer. Mansell was elected by 27 votes to 26. Homer himself did not vote and a few seconds after the voting another Conservative arrived, too late to vote. The Labour members moved an amendment to Farmer's motion that a detailed report should be made on the full implications of the scheme to the tenants and the local authority. Twenty-eight voted for and 28 against. Mansell gave his casting vote for the Labour amendment.[1] The report came before the March Council meeting and the Labour Party moved that there be no sale. A Conservative amendment to sell was lost by 30 votes to 29, with the Mayor's vote again decisive.[2] Davies had managed to attend this meeting.

Council house rents were another topic of party conflict at this time. The Minister of Housing and Local Government had until February 1962 granted a dispensation to members of the Council who were Council house tenants, enabling them to speak and vote on questions concerning Council houses. But since he felt that the Conservatives had a majority on the Council he granted the dispensation in February only to allow the tenants to speak but not to vote, thus disfranchising fifteen Labour members.[3] The Conservatives thus were able easily to pass a resolution that a differential rent scheme be formulated.[4] The Labour Party escaped from this predicament by reforming the membership of the Housing Committee, replacing all Council house tenants by non-Council house tenants, thus ensuring that their members could vote in committee. In this way they could prevent any differential rent scheme from emerging from the committee.[5] Subsequently the Minister granted the dispensations, but only after great Labour protests.

[1] Ibid. and *E. & S.*, 1.1.1962.

[2] *E. & S.*, 27.3.1962.

[3] The Minister's policy on such dispensations was outlined in Circular 30/56 of the Ministry of Housing and Local Government, May 1956, *Voting by Councillor Tenants on Rent Policy*. He would grant a dispensation, if a policy was likely to be adopted 'to which the majority of the Council were opposed'. *The Guardian* reported: 'Normally the Minister grants a dispensation where it seems likely that without it the view of a majority of members will not be carried.' 3.6.1964.

[4] *C.M.*, 26.2.1962.   [5] *E. & S.*, 16.5.1962, 30.5.1962.

Bitterness between the parties during this period was more intense than for some years. In June 1961 Councillor Farmer referred to the Aldermanic bench as 'once a seat of merit and now a bench of dishonour'. A Labour member said: 'He is an ignorant devil.' Cries for apologies and withdrawals were uttered.[1] In the debate on compulsory purchase in January, a Labour Alderman shouted at the Conservatives, 'For years now you have had your pound of flesh, you Shylocks.' Objections were immediate.[2] The Labour Party complained that the Conservatives were boycotting the Mayor, being conspicuously absent from Mayoral functions. 'Nothing short of disgraceful', claimed the Chairman of the Borough Labour Party.[3] The Mayor described himself as 'hung, drawn and quartered', but 'in my heart, there is no bitterness towards anyone'.[4] The Conservatives accused Labour Councillors, especially the married women, of claiming excessive expenses,[5] and alleged that a Labour Councillor had received preferential treatment in the allocation of a new Council flat.[6] Both charges were disproved, and condemned as unfair by the local press, but they left a nasty taste and did not contribute to any reconciliation between the parties.

The Labour M.P. for North-East Wolverhampton, John Baird, became involved in the controversy. In March 1962 on an adjournment motion in the House of Commons he criticised the Minister of Housing and Local Government for refusing to grant a dispensation to the members of the Council who were Council house tenants, and he accused Enoch Powell, M.P. for South-West Wolverhampton and Minister of Health, of putting pressure on his colleague to refuse the dispensation.[7] Earlier in the year, when the Conservatives had voted Windridge and not the Mayor to the Aldermanic bench, he said that Davies 'should have been treated with more consideration and respect by these little squirts who call themselves Conservatives'.[8] The latter replied that 'we do not wish to enter into a slanging match with Mr Baird, who is too well

[1] *E. & S.*, 27.6.1961.   [2] *E. & S.*, 23.1.1962.
[3] *E. & S.*, 21.8.1961.   [4] *E. & S.*, 27.3.1962.
[5] *E. & S.*, 5.6.1961, 6.6.1961, 7.6.1961, 8.6.1961, 10.6.1961.
[6] *E. & S.*, 27.3.1962.   [7] *E. & S.*, 29.3.1962.
[8] *E. & S.*, 29.1.1962.

known for his habit of resorting to such language before fully acquainting himself with the facts. Therefore we treat his personal remarks with the contempt they deserve and without further comment.'[1]

The controversy over the Aldermen stimulated a debate on the merits of the institution of Aldermen. The Labour Group, as in 1955, called for their abolition. At the October 1961 Council meeting Labour members argued that the alleged advantages of Aldermen, their wisdom, experience and special aptitudes, had disappeared with the coming of party politics into local government. The system was not democratic and the office was used to give a political advantage to one side or the other.[2] The local paper agreed: 'The office of Alderman had outlived its usefulness'; it was being used 'solely in perpetuating a political ascendancy'.[3] The paper had complained that the original non-political objectives of the Aldermen had disappeared. Elder statesmen, instead of being guaranteed a more secure place than Councillors, were liable to be cast out to make room for men of less experience in order to give one party the upper hand.[4] But a defence of the Aldermen was provided by the Conservatives. Brindley said that they had lasted for more than a thousand years, and they gave to the Councils great practical advantages from their experience and they were a means of recognising and rewarding service.[5] The Labour motion calling for their abolition was passed by the Council[6] and sent to the Association of Municipal Corporations, whose Council, as in 1956, rejected it.[7]

The events from about February 1961 to May 1962 provoked more sustained interest in the work of the Council than ever before. More space was taken up in the press, particularly on the front page, with the crises which followed one after the other. The correspondence columns were full of letters about the Council. Some justified the positions of their respective parties; some called for reconciliation between the parties; some urged the removal of party politics from local government and one said: 'Some Sergeant-Major type, preferably a Communist, should get them into two lines and bang their heads together.'[8] But once Birch as Mayor had

---

[1] *E. & S.*, 30.1.1962.   [2] *E. & S.*, 24.10.1961.   [3] Ibid.
[4] *E. & S.*, 12.5.1961.   [5] *E. & S.*, 24.10.1961.   [6] Ibid.
[7] *E. & S.*, 25.1.1962.   [8] *E. & S.*, 1.2.1962.

shown that he was adhering to the peace pact, the reporting of and
the attention given to local government affairs subsided to the
previous minor proportion of the newspaper's coverage of events.
The press and the majority of its readers were concerned primarily
with scandals and rows. The normal routine of Council work
commanded few readers.

The Council in 1961 and 1962 seemed similar in many respects
to the House of Commons in 1950, 1951, 1964 and 1965, when
Labour, too, held on to power by a handful of votes. But in Wolverhampton the Conservatives felt that they had won an electoral
victory in May 1961, and were deprived of control by a Labour
trick. The original bitterness of the Conservatives stemmed from
Labour's refusal to join in an agreement about the sharing of the
Mayoralty and the Aldermanic seats. It was intensified by Labour's
refusal to discuss these matters with them and then by its illegal
manipulation in the Aldermanic elections. The Labour Party, on
the other hand, was desperate to remain in control and to keep the
Conservatives in opposition. It was shaken by the High Court
judgment, which also shattered its faith in the Town Clerk. For
over a year each side sought to score off the other whenever an
opportunity arose. What ended the conflict were the elections in
May 1962, which, far from resolving the deadlock, offered the
prospect of further bitterness. To avoid another year of dissension
was the motive behind the reconciliation between the parties. It
would be wrong to judge the effect of party politics in local
government from these events alone. They were crisis times, a
purely temporary phenomenon, which could affect central government too. Indeed the crisis showed just how similar to the Parliamentary system was the Council system in Wolverhampton. Two
parties faced each other: the one the majority party holding all
the positions of responsibility, the other the minority, the opposition
party, whose function was to embarrass the governing party. Each
party had its own committee to decide on policy and tactics in the
Council. The chief officials of the Council, although striving to be
neutral and to serve both parties, came to be the advisers of the
majority party. But in central government there were no institutions corresponding to the Mayor or the Aldermen, and the crisis
in Wolverhampton was intensified by the anomalous position of
these two institutions. The Mayor found it hard to be a political

figure, a speaker of the house and a constitutional monarch. In the end he was reduced to a constitutional monarch and an emasculated Chairman. The Aldermanic bench was revealed as anachronistic, able to be manipulated so that one party could escape the consequences of electoral defeat. The crisis did not make the parties change their ways. In 1962, 1963 and 1964 they carried on in their previous ways. No agreements were made about the Mayoralty or the Aldermen.

Conclusion

In April 1966 a new Wolverhampton County Borough came into existence, formed from an amalgamation of the old one with neighbouring authorities. Labour held a majority during its first year, but in May 1967 lost control to the Conservatives, who became the majority party in Wolverhampton for the first time in fifteen years. In a clean sweep of all positions of responsibility they took all the Chairmanships and Vice-Chairmanships, the Mayoralty and all the Aldermanic vacancies, ejecting five Labour Aldermen, including one first elected to the Wolverhampton Council in 1927 and another first elected in 1937. It appears that the new Council is like the old; no one party has a firm majority, and the margin between them is so narrow that patronage to the offices of Mayor or Alderman will be bitterly fought. The Conservative Group will be resorting to the same techniques of government as the Labour Group when in a majority.

The Conservative take-over was not simply a matter of a change of personnel at the top. Policies changed radically. Within twelve months of taking office the Conservatives reversed many Labour policies. They dismantled the Corporation's civic catering department and its direct-labour building department. They ran down the Corporation's experimental estate agency and decided to close the municipal sewage farm. Council houses were offered for sale to tenants, Council house rents were raised, a rent rebate scheme introduced, and tenants were allowed to build porches at their front doors. Corporation land was sold to housing associations for building. Labour's proposals for comprehensive education were revised to save the main Grammar Schools, and a selective system of education was introduced into one area which had had comprehensive schools for twelve years. These events showed clearly that the battles between the parties locally were significant and that a change of party control meant important changes of policy.

The main conflicts on the Council were between the parties, but more traditional clashes occurred, between wards and between Chairmen of competing Committees. In the wards comprising the former borough of Bilston, Council house tenants fiercely objected to the imposition on them of Wolverhampton's ban on pets in Council houses, and their Councillors spoke out on their behalf. The Chairman of the Cultural and Entertainments Committee complained that the Corporation spent too little on the arts. Economic interest groups continued to press their claims. The stall-holders in the Retail Market criticised conditions there and the way the market was run. Immigrant groups urged their demands, particularly that the Transport Committee should amend its rules to allow Sikh bus conductors to wear beards and turbans. Thus the patterns of conflict on the old Council are reproduced on the new.

There was also considerable continuity in personnel between the old and the new authorities. The present chief officials served the old Corporation, and the leading elected members were prominent on both. The former leader of the Conservative Opposition, W. G. Morrison, who had replaced M. P. Birch on his death, is the leader of the Council, while the former Labour leader of the Council, F. Mansell, is Deputy Leader of the Labour Group, having been defeated for the leadership by D. A. Birch, the former Chairman of Finance Committee, after the Conservatives gained the majority in May 1967.

It appears as if the political process of the new Wolverhampton Council will be similar to that of the old. However, it is too early to assess whether the areas recently added to the town will modify the process in any major way.

THE SIGNIFICANCE OF THIS STUDY

This book has shown the close connection between the physical, economic and social structure of the town and the political structure and processes of its Council. The environment posed the problems and influenced the way the Councillors looked at them and the solutions which emerged. Above all, the decisive factors shaping the political process were the elected members and the officials.

Each Town Council is unique; it has its own environment, its own problems and evolves its own conventions to enable a bare legal structure to operate and produce solutions. Most of all each town throws up its own unique individuals. No other town could have had characters identical to Sir Horatio Brevitt, Sir Charles T. Mander, Warbreck Howell, Baldwin Bantock, Frank Myatt, Ted Lane, Will Lawley, Sir Charles A. Mander, James Beattie, Brock Allon, Denis Birch or Ron Meddings and the host of others whom this book is about. They were the dynamic element in the political framework.

But these people were a very small proportion of the town's population. The majority have no continuing and deep interest in local government. Even the few who vote at local elections seem influenced more by national than local events. In all about 900 at most out of a population of 150,000 had an active interest in local politics, and that is a rather generous estimate. Very few people keep the system going. The apathy of the majority perhaps reflects their satisfaction. If things went wrong and services broke down, they would protest, agitate, organise and vote in strength. That they have never done so in Wolverhampton is a tribute to the responsiveness of the Council to the needs of the people of the town. One does not have to be actively involved and interested in local government to know when things have gone wrong at the Town Hall. The people of Wolverhampton have displayed a common-sense realism and sense of proportion about local politics and government. They have paid attention to the important things of life: their jobs, homes, families, loved ones and pleasures, leaving politics to those few who are fascinated by it and prepared to engage in it. But the majority know that with the ballot box they have the ultimate power to express dissatisfaction, and so they leave politics to their representatives. And the Councillors have been close enough to the majority never to get seriously out of line with what they want. This is surely the essence of local representative democracy.

Finally the most important conclusion of this book is that on balance the growing involvement of parties in local government has had good results. Parties have made the Council more democratic and less oligarchic. More people vote, stand for and are elected to the Council now than before the days of party, and they come from a wider range of occupations. Parties have enabled individuals to devise a programme of policies and to implement it, and they have presented these programmes to the public in a dramatic and comprehensible way, enabling the public to judge a team of men and measures; thus the accountability of government to the electorate has been strengthened. Further, the organisation of parties, both inside and outside the Council, has enabled the humblest member of the rank and file to exercise influence on the party leaders, and to reject them and their policies if necessary. Although public participation in local government is small, it is more than it was in the days before political parties became actively involved, and for that increase parties deserve the credit.

Appendix

The basic source for the occupations of the members of the Council is the annual *Council Diary and Yearbook*. But it is not a completely trustworthy or useful source for three main reasons:

(i) The descriptions of the members in it are based on the members' own descriptions, which they put on their nomination papers. No one has lied in Wolverhampton about his occupation, but many have tended to raise the status of their jobs by giving them more flamboyant titles than one would normally; e.g. hotel proprietor or maltster for licensed victualler; a millinery specialist for a hat-seller.

(ii) The descriptions become out of date when members change their occupations or rise in their jobs. Often the member's original description stays with him, e.g. an 'engineer' is really a chief buyer; a 'carpenter' is the head of a firm of shop-fitters.

(iii) Many descriptions are too vague to be useful, e.g. 'engineer', 'manufacturer', 'merchant', 'company director', 'secretary', 'housewife', 'gentleman', and such terms as 'solicitor' or 'grocer' give no indication of the size, status or success of the concern.

Therefore the information in the *Council Yearbooks* must be supplemented by newspaper reports and interviews if a more accurate picture of the occupations of the Council members is to be obtained.

TABLE I

Population of Wolverhampton

1750	7454
1801	12,565
1811	14,836
1821	18,380
1831	24,732
1841	36,382
1851	49,985
1861	60,860
1871	68,291
1881	75,766
1891	82,662
1901	94,187
1911	95,328
1921	102,342
1931	133,190
1933	138,600[1]
1951	162,672
1961	150,385
1967	267,000[1]

[1] Includes extended area

TABLE II

Results of Wolverhampton's Parliamentary Elections, 1885–1966

East Division		West Division	
	Nov 1885		*Nov 1885*
H. H. Fowler (Lib.)	3935	A. Hickman (Con.)	3722
W. Bird (Con.)	2648	W. C. Plowden (Lib.)	3569
	July 1886		*July 1886*
H. H. Fowler (Lib.)	3752	Sir W. C. Plowden (Lib.)	3706
J. Underhill (Con.)	2629	A. Hickman (Con.)	3583
	July 1892		*July 1892*
H. H. Fowler (Lib.)	No opp.	Sir A. Hickman (Con.)	4772
		Sir W. C. Plowden (Lib.)	3656
	July 1895		*July 1895*
Sir H. H. Fowler (Lib.)	4011	Sir A. Hickman (Con.)	4770
R. E. C. Kettle (Lib. Un.)	2977	G. R. Thorne (Lib.)	3947
	Oct 1900		*Oct 1900*
Sir H. H. Fowler (Lib.)	No opp.	Sir A. Hickman (Con.)	No opp.
	Jan 1906		*Jan 1906*
Sir H. H. Fowler (Lib.)	5610	T. F. Richards (Lab.)	5756
L. S. Amery (Con.)	2745	Sir A. Hickman (Con.)	5588
	Jan 1908		
G. R. Thorne (Lib.)	4514		
L. S. Amery (Un.)	4506		
	Jan 1910		*Jan 1910*
G. R. Thorne (Lib.)	5276	A. Bird (Un.)	6382
L. S. Amery (Un.)	4462	T. F. Richards (Lab.)	5790
	Dec 1910		*Dec 1910*
G. R. Thorne (Lib.)	5072	A. Bird (Un.)	5925
R. B. Whiteside (Un.)	3881	P. Lewis (Lib.)	5631
	Dec 1918		*Dec 1918*
G. R. Thorne (Ind. Lib.)	7660	A. Bird (Un.)	13,329
Rev. J. A. Shaw (Coal. Lab.)	7138	A. G. Walkden (Lab.)	10,158
			Mar 1922
		Sir R. Bird (Con.)	16,790
		A. G. Walkden (Lab.)	13,799
	Nov 1922		*Nov 1922*
G. R. Thorne (Lib.)	11,577	Sir R. Bird (Con.)	17,738
C. H. Pinson (Con.)	9410	A. G. Walkden (Lab.)	15,190
W. T. A. Foot (Lab.)	3076		
Rev. J. A. Shaw (Lloyd George Lib.)	1169		
	Nov 1923		*Nov 1923*
G. R. Thorne (Lib.)	No opp.	Sir R. Bird (Con.)	15,990
		W. J. Brown (Lab.)	15,749

TABLE II (*continued*)

East Division		West Division	
	Oct 1924		*Oct 1924*
G. R. Thorne (Lib.)	11,066	Sir R. Bird (Con.)	17,866
Sir T. Strangeman (Con.)	10,013	W. J. Brown (Lab.)	17,046
D. R. Williams (Lab.)	5188		
	May 1929		*May 1929*
G. le M. Mander (Lib.)	15,391	W. J. Brown (Lab.)	21,103
P. G. T. Buchan-Hepburn		Sir R. Bird (Con.)	17,237
(Con.)	10,163	G. H. Roberts (Lib.)	4580
D. R. Williams (Lab.)	8840		
	Oct 1931		*Oct 1931*
G. le M. Mander (Lib.)	14,945	Sir R. Bird (Con.)	26,181
A. W. Taylor (Con.)	12,628	W. J. Brown (I.L.A.)	17,090
J. Smith (Lab.)	6340		
	Nov 1935		*Nov 1935*
G. le M. Mander (Lib.)	15,935	Sir R. Bird (Con.)	19,697
J. Brockhouse (Con.)	11,935	W. J. Brown (Ind.)	14,867
H. E. Lane (Lab.)	4985	Rev. R. Lee (Lab.)	1325
	July 1945		*July 1945*
J. Baird (Lab.)	17,763	H. D. Hughes (Lab.)	21,186
Sir G. le M. Mander (Lib.)	11,206	J. Beattie (Con.)	14,176
W. F. C. Garthwaite			
(Con.)	8266		

North-East Division		South-West Division	
	Feb 1950		*Feb 1950*
J. Baird (Lab.)	29,235	J. E. Powell (Con.)	20,239
A. W. G. Holland (Con.)	14,592	H. D. Hughes (Lab.)	19,549
A. Brown (Lib.)	5482	W. F. H. Rollason (Lib.)	4229
	Oct 1951		*Oct 1951*
J. Baird (Lab.)	30,643	J. E. Powell (Con.)	23,660
J. P. J. Ellis (Con. & Nat.		Mrs P. L. Davies (Lab.)	20,464
Lib.)	18,563		
	May 1955		*May 1955*
J. Baird (Lab.)	23,596	J. E. Powell (Con.)	25,318
F. Hardman (Con.)	14,387	L. H. Burgess (Lab.)	16,898
	Oct 1959		*Oct 1959*
J. Baird (Lab.)	20,436	J. E. Powell (Con.)	25,696
O. A. Pomeroy (Con.)	16,639	E. L. J. Thorne (Lab.)	14,529
	Oct 1964		*Oct 1964*
Mrs R. Short (Lab.)	18,997	J. E. Powell (Con.)	21,736
Mrs M. M. M. Greenaway		A. J. Gardner (Lab.)	11,880
(Con.)	14,914	N. G. Lloyd (Lib.)	4233
	Mar 1966		*Mar 1966*
Mrs R. Short (Lab.)	21,067	J. E. Powell (Con.)	21,466
G. I. Wright (Con.)	12,965	A. S. Collier (Lab.)	14,881

Borough Politics

TABLE III

Standing Committees of the Council, 1900–1

Title	Number of elected members	Number of co-opted members	Meetings
Art	8	4	monthly
1 Sub.			monthly
Finance	13	0	monthly
Free Library	8	5	monthly
2 Subs.			each monthly
General Purposes	varies	0	monthly
Health	13	0	2 per month
2 Subs.			(i) monthly
			(ii) when required
			2 per month
Lighting	13	0	when required
1 Sub.			monthly
Markets	13	0	when required
1 Sub.			monthly
Parks & Baths	13	0	when required
1 Sub.			2 per month
Public Works	13	0	when required
1 Sub.			2 per month
Sewerage	13	0	monthly
1 Sub.			2 per month
Streets	13	0	when required
1 Sub.			2 per month
Team	12	0	monthly
1 Sub.			2 per month
Tramway	13	0	2 per month
1 Sub.			2 per month
Watch	17	0	3 per year
1 Sub.			monthly
Water	13	0	when required
1 Sub.			

Total	15 Committees
	15 Sub-Committees
	+ 2 Special Committees

	Elected Members	Co-opted Members	Meetings
Housing of the Working Classes	14	0	2 per month
Public Improvement, Queen Square	9	0	when required

Source: Council Year Book and Wolverhampton Red Book.

TABLE IV

Standing Committees of the Council, *1963–4*

Title	Number of elected members	Number of co-opted members	Meetings
Children	8	2	monthly
Civic Catering	10	0	alternate months
Civil Defence	10	2	alternate months
Cultural & Entertainments	10	0	monthly
1 Sub.			monthly
Education	19	3 + 7 nominated	monthly
6 Subs.			⎧ 3 monthly ⎨ 2 alternate months ⎩ 1 quarterly
Establishment	9	0	monthly
Finance	14	0	monthly
2 Subs.			when required
Fire & Ambulance	10	0	alternate months
General Purposes	varies		monthly
5 Subs.			when required
Health	15	6	monthly
3 Sub.			monthly
Housing	10	0	monthly
Markets	10	0	monthly
1 Sub.			when required
Parks & Physical Recreation	10	0	monthly
Public Works & Estates	10	0	monthly
1 Sub.			when required
Rating and Payments	6	0	monthly
Sanitation	8	3	monthly
Sewage Disposal	10	0	monthly
Smallholdings	10	3	every 3 months
1 Sub.			every 3 months
Special Purchases	4	0	when required
Tenders	9	0	when required
Town Planning	10	0	monthly
1 Sub.			monthly
Traffic and Highways	10	0	monthly
Transport	10	0	alternate months
1 Sub.			alternate months
Watch	12	0	monthly
Water	10	2	monthly
Welfare Services	11	4	monthly
1 Sub.			monthly
Total	26 Committees 23 Sub-Committees		

Source: Council Year Book and *Council Minutes,* May 1963

TABLE VA

Corporation Officers, 1900–1

Town Clerk's Department
Town Clerk
Assistant Town Clerk
Chief Committee Clerk
Second Committee Clerk
3 Clerks

Finance Department
Borough Accountant
Chief Clerk
6 Clerks
Borough Treasurer

Improvement Rate Department
2 Collectors
Cashier
Clerk

Water Department
Water Engineer
Draughtsman
2 Clerks
3 Foremen at Pumping Station

Water Rate Department
Cashier
3 Collectors
2 Clerks

Electrical Engineer's Department
Electrical Engineer
Draughtsman
Collector
Junior Assistant
Foreman Engineer

Borough Engineer's and Surveyor's Department
Borough Surveyor
Assistant Surveyor
General Assistant
Draughtsman
2 Clerks
Manager, Sewage Outfall Works
Foreman, Sewage Outfall Works
Manager, Sewage Farm
Foreman, Sewage Farm

Parks Superintendent
East Park Keeper
Manager of Baths
Highways Foreman
Highways Inspector
2 Building Inspectors
New Street Inspector

Health Department
Medical Officer of Health
Chief Inspector of Nuisances
Assistant Inspector of Nuisances
Borough Analyst
2 Clerks
Matron, Borough Hospital

Free Library Department
Librarian
Assistant Librarian
Science Master
Hall Keeper

Art Gallery and School of Art
Curator and Headmaster
2nd Master
Science Master
Assistant Secretary
Hall Keeper

Team Department
Manager
Collector
Clerk

Markets
Superintendent
Cattle Market Superintendent

Police Force
Chief Constable and Director of Fire Brigade
Superintendent
91 other ranks
Inspector of Weights and Measures
Hall Keeper
Mace Bearer

Source: Wolverhampton Red Book and Council Year Book.

TABLE VB

Corporation Officers, 1963

Town Clerk's Department
  Town Clerk
  Deputy Town Clerk
  Senior Assistant Solicitor
  3 Assistant Solicitors
  Chief Clerk
  Organisation and Methods Officer
  Mayor's Secretary
  Mayor's Sergeant

Treasurer's Department
  Borough Treasurer
  Deputy Borough Treasurer
  Principal Assistant
  Chief Audit Assistant

Engineer's and Surveyor's Department
  Borough Engineer and Surveyor
  Deputy Borough Engineer and
    Surveyor
  Deputy Borough Architect
  Deputy Planning Officer
  Chief Engineering Assistant
  Chief Clerk
  Park Superintendent
  Cemeteries and Crematorium
    Superintendent
  Aldersley Stadium Organiser

Education Department
  Director of Education
  Deputy Director of Education
  Principal School Medical Officer
  Senior School Medical Officer
  Principal Dental Officer
  Chief Inspector of Schools
  School Meal Organiser
  Chief Clerk
  Superintendent, Educational Wel-
    fare Service
  Youth Employment Officer

Transport Department
  General Manager
  Engineer and Deputy General
    Manager
  Traffic Superintendent
  Chief Clerk

Water Undertaking
  Water Engineer
  Deputy Water Engineer
  Chief Assistant Engineer
  3 Assistant Engineers
  Chemist and Bacteriologist
  Chief Clerk

Health Department
  Medical Officer of Health
  Deputy Medical Officer of Health
  Senior Assistant Medical Officer of
    Health
  2 Assistant Medical Officers of
    Health
  Chief Public Health Inspector
  4 Authorised Officers (Mental
    Health)
  Superintendent Health Visitors
  Supervisor of Midwives
  Superintendent District Nurses
  Supervisor of Home Helps
  Supervisor of Occupation Centre
  Chief Clerk

Welfare Services Department
  Chief Welfare Officer
  Deputy Chief Welfare Officer
  7 Superintendents of Centres

Children's Department
  Children's Officer
  Assistant Children's Officer
  3 Superintendents of Homes

Housing Department
  Housing Manager
  Deputy Housing Manager

Civic Catering Department
  Manager

Civic Hall
  Manager
  Assistant Manager

Public Library
  Chief Librarian

Art Gallery
  Curator

College of Art
  Principal
  Registrar

Municipal Baths
  Superintendent

Civil Defence
  Civil Defence Officer

Cleansing Department
  Superintendent of Cleansing and
    Salvage
  Chief Assistant

Markets
  General Manager of Markets
  Chief Assistant

TABLE VB (*continued*)

Weights and Measures Department
  Chief Inspector
  Public Analyst

Sewage Disposal Department
  Manager
  Chief Technical Assistant
  Engineer Assistant
  Farm Manager

Smallholdings
  Supervisor

Registration Department
  Superintendent Registrar

Police Force
  Chief Constable
  Police Surgeon
  Deputy Chief Constable
  3 Superintendents
  258 all ranks

Fire and Ambulance Service
  Chief Fire and Ambulance Officer
  Deputy Chief Fire Officer
  Fire Prevention Officer
  Ambulance and Transport Officer

Source: Council Year Book

TABLE VI

Political Composition of the Town Council, 1887–1964

Total 1888–1926:
- Aldermen 12
- Councillors 36
- Total 48

Date		Lab.	Con.	Ind.	Lib.
1887–8	A*	—	4	—	8
	C*	—	19	4	13
	T*	—	23	4	21
1888–9	A	—	5	—	7
	C	—	18	4	14
	T	—	23	4	21
1890–1	A	—	5	—	7
	C	—	19	3	14
	T	—	24	3	21
1891–2	A	—	4	—	8
	C	1	20	4	11
	T	1	24	4	19
1892–3	A	—	5	—	7
	C	1	24	4	7
	T	1	29	4	14
1893–4	A	—	6	—	6
	C	1	23	4	8
	T	1	29	4	14
1894–5	A	—	6	—	6
	C	1	23	3	9
	T	1	29	3	15
1895–6	A	—	6	—	6
	C	1	24	4	7
	T	1	30	4	13
1896–7	A	—	6	—	6
	C	2	24	5	5
	T	2	30	5	11
1897–8	A	—	6	—	6
	C	3	22	4	7
	T	3	28	4	13
1898–9	A	—	6	—	6
	C	5	20	4	7
	T	5	26	4	13
1899–1900	A	—	5	—	7
	C	5	20	5	6
	T	5	25	5	13
1900–1	A	—	6	—	6
	C	4	19	4	9
	T	4	25	4	15
1901–2	A	—	6	—	6
	C	5	18	3	10
	T	5	24	3	16
1902–3	A	—	6	—	6
	C	4	19	3	10
	T	4	25	3	16
1903–4	A	—	6	—	6
	C	4	19	2	11
	T	4	25	2	17
1904–5	A	—	7	—	5
	C	4	15	2	15
	T	4	22	2	20
1905–6	A	—	7	—	5
	C	5	12	2	17
	T	5	19	2	22
1906–7	A	—	7	—	5
	C	5	12	2	17
	T	5	19	2	22
1907–8	A	—	7	—	5
	C	4	13	2	17
	T	4	20	2	22
1908–9	A	—	7	—	5
	C	2	16	2	16
	T	2	23	2	21
1909–10	A	—	7	—	5
	C	2	17	2	15
	T	2	24	2	20
1910–11	A	—	7	—	5
	C	3	18	2	13
	T	3	25	2	18

* Abbreviations: A = Aldermen   C = Councillors   *T = Total*

TABLE VI (*continued*)

Date		Lab.	Con.	Ind.	Lib.
1911–12	A	—	7	—	5
	C	4	15	3	14
	T	4	22	3	19
1912–13	A	—	7	—	5
	C	3	17	3	13
	T	3	24	3	18
1913–14	A	—	7	—	5
	C	3	18	3	12
	T	3	25	3	17
1914–15	A	—	7	—	5
	C	3	18	4	11
	T	3	25	4	16

War – No elections

Date		Lab.	Con.	Ind.	Lib.
1919–20	A	—	7	—	5
	C	6	18	6	6
	T	6	25	6	11
1920–21	A	—	8	—	4
	C	7	17	7	5
	T	7	25	7	9
1921–2	A	—	8	—	4
	C	10	15	5	6
	T	10	23	5	10
1922–3	A	—	8	—	4
	C	9	17	4	6
	T	9	25	4	10
1923–4	A	—	7	—	5
	C	10	16	4	6
	T	10	23	4	11
1924–5	A	—	6	—	6
	C	11	16	3	6
	T	11	22	3	12
1925–6	A	1	4	1	6
	C	12	17	2	5
	T	13	21	3	11

Total 1927–33:
Aldermen 13
Councillors 39
Total 52

Date		Lab.	Con.	Ind.	Lib.
1927–8	A	1	5	2	5
	C	12	16	5	6
	T	13	21	7	11
1928–9	A	1	4	3	5
	C	11	17	5	6
	T	12	21	8	11
1929–30	A	1	5	2	5
	C	12	16	5	6
	T	13	21	7	11
1930–1	A	1	4	2	6
	C	9	16	9	5
	T	10	20	11	11
1931–2	A	2	4	3	4
	C	9	17	8	5
	T	11	21	11	9
1932–3	A	2	5	3	3
	C	10	16	9	4
	T	12	21	12	7

Total 1933–65:
Aldermen 15
Councillors 45
Total 60

Date		Lab.	Con.	Ind.	Lib.
1933–4	A	2	5	4	4
	C	12	16	13	4
	T	14	21	17	8
1934–5	A	2	5	4	4
	C	13	16	13	3
	T	15	21	17	7
1935–6	A	2	5	4	4
	C	11	17	12	5
	T	13	22	16	9
1936–7	A	2	5	4	4
	C	13	17	11	4
	T	15	22	15	8
1937–8	A	3	3	4	5
	C	13	17	11	4
	T	16	20	15	9

Date		Lab.	Con.	Ind.	Lib.
1938–9	A	3	3	5	4
	C	14	17	10	4
	T	17	20	15	8
1939–40	A	3	2	5	5
	C	16	16	10	3
	T	19	18	15	8

War – No elections

Date		Lab.	Con.	Ind.	Lib.
1945–6	A	9	1	5	—
	C	23	22	10	—
	T	32	13	15	—
1946–7	A	9	1	5	—
	C	26	11	8	—
	T	35	12	13	—
1947–9	A	9	1	5	—
	C	22	15	8	—
	T	31	16	13	—
1949–50	A	7	1	7	—
	C	19	17	9	—
	T	26	18	16	—
1950–1	A	7	1	7	—
	C	19	19	7	—
	T	26	20	14	—
1951–2	A	6	1	8	—
	C	22	18	5	—
	T	28	19	13	—
1952–3	A	8	7	—	—
	C	27	18	—	—
	T	35	25	—	—
1953–4	A	8	7	—	—
	C	27	18	—	—
	T	35	25	—	—
1954–5	A	8	7	—	—
	C	28	17	—	—
	T	36	24	—	—
1955–6	A	9	6	—	—
	C	25	20	—	—
	T	34	26	—	—

Date		Lab.	Con.	Ind.	Lib.
1956–7	A	9	6	—	—
	C	26	19	—	—
	T	35	25	—	—
1957–8	A	10	5	—	—
	C	27	18	—	—
	T	37	23	—	—
1958–9	A	10	5	—	—
	C	29	16	—	—
	T	39	21	—	—
1959–60	A	10	5	—	—
	C	29	16	—	—
	T	39	21	—	—
1960–1	A	10	5	—	—
	C	25	20	—	—
	T	35	25	—	—

May 1961, Position before Aldermanic election

	Lab.	Con.
A	10	4 (1 vacancy)
C	22	23
T	32	27

Labour solution after Aldermanic election

	Lab.	Con.
A	15	0
C	22	23
T	37	23

Conservative solution after High Court decision

	Lab.	Con.
A	8	7
C	22	23
T	30	30

Labour Mayor, not Alderman or Councillor, has casting vote

January 1962, After death of Labour Alderman

	Lab.	Con.
A	7	8
C¹	22	22
T	29	30

(1 vacancy, not filled until May)
Labour Mayor still has casting vote

TABLE VI (*continued*)

		May 1962				Date		Lab.	Con.	Ind.	Lib.
		Lab.	Con.			1963–4	A	7	8	—	—
	A	7	8				C	27	18	—	—
	C	23	22				T	34	26	—	—
	T	30	30								

Tory Mayor agrees not to vote at all

Date		Lab.	Con.	Ind.	Lib.			Lab.	Con.	Ind.	Lib.
1962–3	A	7	8	—	—	1964–5	A	10	5	—	—
	C	23	22	—	—		C	27	18	—	—
	T	30	30	—	—		T	37	23	—	—

NOTES
Sources: Newspapers, interviews and Party minutes.

To about 1914 the political labels really denote national party affiliation.

The term 'Independent' up to 1914 really denotes those whose affiliation cannot be discovered. Later it refers to those who did not stand openly under a party label at elections.

TABLE VII

Participation in Local Elections – The Town Council

(*a*) *1894* (*Wolverhampton Chronicle*, 31.10.1894)

> 2 contests
> 64% of those eligible in the 2 wards voted
> 21% „ „ „ „ „ town „
> 3% of the population of the town voted
> 17% of the population eligible to vote

(*b*) *1897* (*W.C.*, 27.10.1897)

> 4 contests
> 76% of those eligible in the 4 wards voted
> 27% „ „ „ „ „ town „
> 4% of the population of the town voted
> 15% of the population eligible to vote

(*c*) *1900* (*W.C.*, 7.11.1900).

> 1 contest
> 69% of those eligible in the ward voted
> 6% „ „ „ „ „ town „
> 1% of the population of the town voted
> 17% of the population eligible to vote

(*d*) *1903* (*W.C.*, 4.11.1903)

> 9 contests
> 71% of those eligible in the 9 wards voted
> 53% „ „ „ „ „ town „
> 10% of the population of the town voted
> 18% of the population eligible to vote

(*e*) *1912* (*E. & S.*, 2.11.1912)

> 3 contests
> 69% of those eligible in the 3 wards voted
> 18% „ „ „ „ „ town „
> 3% of the population of the town voted
> 19% of the population eligible to vote

(*f*) *1921* (*E. & S.*, 2.11.1921)

> 5 contests
> 64% of those eligible in the 5 wards voted
> 26% „ „ „ „ „ town „
> 10% of the population of the town voted
> 38% of the population eligible to vote

TABLE VII (*continued*)

(*g*) *1932* (*E. & S.*, 2.11.1932)

    8 contests
    37% of those eligible in the 8 wards voted
    23% ,, ,,　　　,, ,, ,,　town　,,
    10% of the population of the town voted
    46% of the population eligible to vote

(*h*) *1952* (*E. & S.*, 9.5.1952)

    14 contests
    49% of those eligible in the 14 wards voted
    43% ,, ,,　　　,, ,, ,,　town　,,
    29% of the population of the town voted
    68% of the population eligible to vote

(*i*) *1960* (*E. & S.*, 13.5.1960)

    15 contests
    33% of those eligible in the 15 wards (town) voted
    22% of the population of the town voted
    68% of the population eligible to vote

TABLE VIII

Participation in Local Elections – The School Board

(a) *1894* (*W.C.*, 21.11.1894)

        58% of those eligible in the town voted
        10% of the population of the town voted
        17% of the population eligible to vote

(b) *1897* (*W.C.*, 24.11.1897)

        59% of those eligible in the town voted
        10% of the population of the town voted
        16% of the population eligible to vote

(c) *1900* (*W.C.*, 28.11.1900)

        59% of those eligible in the town voted
        10% of the population of the town voted
        17% of the population eligible to vote

TABLE IX

Comparison of Local and Parliamentary Elections

West Wolverhampton
1945 November Municipal results

Ward	Con. %	Lab. %	Poll %
Graiseley	42	58	45
St George's	12	88	37
St Matthew's	40	60	43
Blakenhall and St John's	41	59	40
St Mark's and Merridale	64	36	39
Park	64	36	54
Dunstall	39	61	45
Average	43	57	43
Parliamentary result 1945	40	60	75

1951 May Municipal results

North-East Ward	Con. %	Lab. %	Poll %	South-West Ward	Con. %	Lab. %	Poll %
St Peter's	55	45	43	Graiseley	63	37	50
St James'	40	60	25	St Matthew's	44	56	31
Dunstall	49	51	46	St George's	46	54	39
Park[1]	71	29	47	Blakenhall & St John's	53	47	41
Heath Town	51	49	33	St Mark's & Merridale	70	30	48
Bushbury	34	66	20	Penn	75	25	40
Low Hill	22	78	23	St Philip's[1]	80	20	59
St Mary's	45	55	34	*Average*	61	39	44
Average	46	54	34				

Parliamentary results

	Con. %	Lab. %	Lib. %	Poll %		Con. %	Lab. %	Lib. %	Poll %
1950	29	60	11	83	1950	46	44	10	88
1951	37	63	..	81	1951	54	46	..	86

[1] 1952 figures

1955 May Municipal Results

North-East Ward	Con.	Lab.	Poll	South-West Ward	Con.	Lab.	Poll
	%	%	%		%	%	%
St Peter's	56	44	44	Graiseley	60	40	54
St James'	36	64	38	St Matthew's	29	71	28
Dunstall	47	53	44	St George's	28	72[1]	27
Park	79	21	43	Blakenhall & St John's	52	48	45
Heath Town	45	55	31	St Mark's & Merridale[2]	80	20	36
Bushbury	37	63	29	Penn	77[3]	23	41
Low Hill	25	75	27	St Philip's[2]	87	13	41
St Mary's	32	68	27	*Average*	59	41	40
Average	45	55	35				

Parliamentary results

	%	%	%		%	%	%
1955	37	63	71	1955	60	40	78

[1] Included 3 Communist
[2] 1954 figures
[3] Included 20 Ratepayer

1960 May Municipal Results

North-East Ward	Con.	Lab.	Poll	South-West Ward	Lib.	Con.	Lab.	Poll
	%	%	%		%	%	%	%
St Peter's	53	47	34	Blakenhall		59	41	47
Oxley	58	42	46					
Low Hill	24	76[1]	25	East Park	14	23	63[2]	24
Heath Town	48	52	29	Graiseley		66	34	43
Eastfield	39	61	16	Merridale		88	12	39
Dunstall	51	49	35	Oxbarn		74	26	40
Bushbury	45	55	25	Parkfield		27	73[3]	25
Average	45	55	30	West Park		90	10	33
				Penn		90	10	37
				Average	2	64	34	36

Parliamentary results

	%	%	%		%	%	%
1959	45	55	73	1959	64	36	79

[1] Included 6 Communist
[2] Included 3 Communist
[3] Included 6 Communist

TABLE X

Occupational Composition of the Council – Specific Councils
(Figures are percentages)

Occupation	1888–9	1903–4	1919–20	1929–30	1945–6	1953–4	1962–3
Manufacturer	38	33	35	21	12	12	7
Shopkeeper	19	23	21	19	18	23·5	27
Drink	10	10	10	8	7	3	2
Professional	21	17	19	8	7	5	8
Administrator (R.)[1]	6	4	4	6	5	5	10
Administrator (N.R.)[2]	0	0	4	8	8	8	10
Worker	0	9	13	13	25	23·5	15
Woman	0	0	0	4	5	10	13
Retired	6	4	4	13	13	10	8

[1] Administrators, Managers – white-collar workers holding positions of responsibility and status.

[2] Administrators, clerical workers – white-collar workers holding positions of no responsibility and low status.

TABLE XI

Occupational Composition of the Council – New Entrants
(Figures are percentages)

Occupation	1888–1903	1903–19	1919–29	1929–45	1945–53	1953–62
Manufacturer	27	24	27	8·5	15·5	9
Shopkeeper	26	22	9	20	20	26
Drink	9	6	2	2	0	0
Professional	12	30	8	10	2·5	13
Administrator (R.)	5	2	5·5	8·5	2·5	9
Administrator (N.R.)	2	4	11	10	13	11
Worker	15	8	23	24	31	15
Woman	0	0	5·5	8·5	11	11
Retired	4	4	9	8·5	4·5	6

TABLE XII

Occupational Composition of the Council – in specific periods
(Figures are percentages)

Occupation	1888–1900	1900–10	1910–19	1919–30	1930–40	1940–50	1950–60
Manufacturer	33	27	27	25·2	16	18	13
Shopkeeper	23	20	23	18·1	22	23	25
Drink	11	8	7	7·1	11	8	3
Professional	16	21	27	13·1	8	8	7
Administrator (R.)	6	6	5	4·1	6	8	9
Administrator (N.R.)	0	1	0	6·1	4	3	5
Worker	6	10	10	16·1	17	17	18
Woman	0	0	0	4·1	4	4	10
Retired	5	7	1	6·1	12	11	10

TABLE XIII

Occupation and Political Allegiance
New Entrants

Occupation	Con.	Lib.	Lab.	Others
(a) 1888–1919				
Manufacturer	14	9	0	4
Shopkeeper	8	13	1	4
Drink	7	0	0	1
Professional	16	5	0	1
Administrator (R)	3	1	0	0
Administrator (N.R.)	2	0	1	0
Worker	2	0	11	0
Woman	0	0	0	0
Retired	0	4	0	0
(b) 1919–45				
Manufacturer	14	2	0	2
Shopkeeper	11	1	1	2
Drink	0	0	1	1
Professional	5	0	1	3
Administrator (R)	4	3	0	1
Administrator (N.R.)	1	3	4	2
Worker	1	0	21	2
Woman	0	1	6	0
Retired	3	1	4	1
(c) 1945–62				
Manufacturer	7	N	3	1
Shopkeeper	15	O	3	3
Drink	0	N	0	0
Professional	7	E	0	0
Administrator (R)	4		1	0
Administrator (N.R.)	1		10	0
Worker	0		21	0
Woman	2		7	1
Retired	1		4	0

TABLE XIV

Occupation and Political Allegiance – Specific Councils

(a) *Council 1903–4*

Occupation	Con.	Lib.	Lab.	Ind.	Total
Manufacturer	9	6	0	1	16
Shopkeeper	2	7	1	1	11
Drink	5	0	0	0	5
Professional	7	1	0	0	8
Administrator (R.)	1	1	0	0	2
Administrator (N.R.)	0	0	0	0	0
Worker	1	0	3	0	4
Woman	0	0	0	0	0
Retired	0	2	0	0	2
Total	25	17	4	2	48

(b) *Council 1962–3*

Occupation	Con.	Lab.	Total
Manufacturer	4	0	4
Shopkeeper	13	3	16
Drink	0	1	1
Professional	5	0	5
Administrator (R.)	3	3	6
Administrator (N.R.)	1	5	6
Worker	0	9	9
Woman	1	7	8
Retired	3	2	5
Total	30	30	60

TABLE XV

Attachment to the Town

	1888–9	1903–4	1919–20	1929–30	1945–6	1953–4	1962–3
Total	48	48	48	52	60	60	60
Unknown	19	18	17	20	14	12	10
Natives	15	16	18	19	30	31	31
Residence in the town over 10 years	11	11	9	9	13	16	15
Residence under 10 years	3	3	4	4	3	1	4
Therefore							
Rooted	26	27	27	28	43	47	46
Unrooted	3	3	4	4	3	1	4

TABLE XVI

*Council Members being members
of the Chamber of Commerce*

Council	Con.	Lib.	Lab.	Total
1888–9	6	5	0	11
1903–4	5	4	0	9
1919–20	4	1	0	5
1929–30	3	1	0	4
1945–6	1	0	0	1
1953–4	3	0	0	3
1962–3	1	0	0	1

TABLE XVII

Council members being directors of local building societies

Building Socs	1903–4				1919–20				1929–30			
	Con.	Lib.	Lab.	Total	Con.	Lib.	Lab.	Total	Con.	Lib.	Lab.	Total
(1) South Staffs.	1	1	0	2	1	1	0	2	3	2	0	5
(2) Freeholders	2	0	0	2	2	0	0	2	6	0	0	6
(3) Permanent	0	3	0	3	1	1	0	2	4	2	0	6
Total	3	4	0	7	4	2	0	6	13	4	0	17

Building Socs	1945–6				1953–4				1962–3			
	Con.	Lib.	Lab.	Total	Con.	Lib.	Lab.	Total	Con.	Lib.	Lab.	Total
(1) South Staffs.	1	0	0	1	0	0	0	0	0	0	0	0
(2) Freeholders	1	0	0	1	1	0	0	1	1	0	0	1
(3) Permanent	1	0	0	1	1	0	0	1	0	0	0	0
Total	3	0	0	3	2	0	0	2	1	0	0	1

TABLE XVIII

*Council Members being members
of Rotary and Round Table*

Council	Con.	Lib.	Lab.	Total
1929–30	7	5	0	12
1945–6	11	0	0	11
1953–4	10	0	0	10
1962–3	11	0	0	11

TABLE XIX

Religion and Party Affiliation – Specific Councils

Denomination	1888-9 Con.	Lib.	Total	1903-4 Con.	Lib.	Lab.	Total	1919-20 Con.	Lib.	Lab.	Total
Anglican	14	3	17	17	0	1	18	11	0	2	13
Methodist	1	5	6	1	5	1	7	2	4	0	6
Congregationalist	0	9	9	0	8	0	8	1	4	0	5
Baptist	0	1	1	0	2	0	2	0	1	1	2
Presbyterian	0	1	1	0	0	0	0	0	0	0	0
Quaker	0	0	0	0	0	0	0	0	0	0	0
R.C.	2	2	4	2	2	0	4	2	2	1	5
Unknown	10			9				17			
Total	48			48				48			

Denomination	1929-30 Con.	Lib.	Lab.	Total	1945-6 Con.	Lib.	Lab.	Total	1953-4 Con.	Lab.	Total	1962-3 Con.	Lab.	Total
Anglican	10	0	3	13	12	0	5	17	10	7	17	19	14	33
Methodist	1	7	2	10	2	0	7	9	3	6	9	0	4	4
Congregationalist	1	4	1	6	2	0	0	2	2	0	2	0	0	0
Baptist	0	1	0	1	0	0	1	1	0	1	1	0	0	0
Presbyterian	1	0	0	1	0	0	0	0	0	0	0	0	0	0
Quaker	0	0	0	0	0	0	1	1	0	1	1	0	0	0
R.C.	4	0	1	5	3	0	2	5	3	3	6	3	2	5
Unknown	16				25				24			18		
Total	52				60				60			60		

TABLE XX

*Members of the Council being related
to other Council Members*

Council	Con.	Lib.	Lab.	Total
1888–9	7	7	0	14
1903–4	7	5	1	13
1919–20	6	5	1	12
1929–30	7	7	2	16
1945–6	9	0	6	15
1953–4	7	0	6	13
1962–3	8	0	4	12

TABLE XXI

Quality of Council Members correlated with occupation (A)

Occupation	1888–9					1903–4					1919–20				
	A	B	C	D	Total	A	B	C	D	Total	A	B	C	D	Total
Manufacturer	4	6	3	5	18	3	4	1	8	16	2	2	4	4	12
Shopkeeper	—	1	—	8	9	—	2	5	4	11	—	2	5	3	10
Drink	1	—	—	4	5	1	—	1	3	5	2	—	1	2	5
Professional	—	5	3	2	10	—	3	3	2	8	—	3	3	3	9
Administrator (R.)	—	1	2	—	3	1	—	—	1	2	1	—	—	1	2
Administrator (N.R.)	—	—	—	—	—	—	—	—	—	—	1	—	1	1	2
Worker	—	—	—	—	—	—	3	1	—	4	1	1	1	3	6
Woman	—	—	—	—	—	—	—	—	—	—	—	—	—	—	—
Retired	—	1	—	2	3	—	1	—	1	2	—	1	—	1	2
Total	5	14	8	21	48	5	13	11	19	48	6	9	15	18	48

Occupation	1929–30					1945–6				
	A	B	C	D	Total	A	B	C	D	Total
Manufacturer	1	4	3	3	11	1	1	3	2	7
Shopkeeper	—	3	3	4	10	—	—	7	4	11
Drink	1	1	—	2	4	—	—	1	3	4
Professional	—	1	2	1	4	—	2	1	1	4
Administrator (R.)	1	—	1	1	3	2	—	—	1	3
Administrator (N.R.)	—	—	3	1	4	—	1	2	2	5
Worker	1	2	1	3	7	—	5	2	8	15
Woman	—	—	1	1	2	—	2	—	1	3
Retired	—	1	3	3	7	2	—	2	4	8
Total	4	12	17	19	52	5	11	18	26	60

Occupation	1953–4					1962–3				
	A	B	C	D	Total	A	B	C	D	Total
Manufacturer	—	2	3	2	7	—	—	2	2	4
Shopkeeper	—	2	7	5	14	—	2	7	7	16
Drink	—	—	1	1	2	—	—	—	1	1
Professional	—	2	—	1	3	—	4	1	—	5
Administrator (R.)	2	—	1	—	3	1	3	1	1	6
Administrator (N.R.)	—	2	—	2	4	—	1	1	4	6
Worker	—	5	5	5	15	—	4	1	4	9
Woman	—	2	1	3	6	—	2	—	6	8
Retired	1	—	2	3	6	—	1	3	1	5
Total	3	15	20	22	60	1	17	16	26	60

TABLE XXII

Quality of Council Members correlated with
occupation (B)

Occupation	(i) Absolute figures					(ii) Percentages				
	A	B	C	D	Total	A	B	C	D	Total
Manufacturer	11	19	19	26	75	15	25	25	35	100
Shopkeeper	0	12	34	35	81	0	15	42	43	100
Drink	5	1	4	16	26	19	4	15	62	100
Professional	0	20	13	10	43	0	47	30	23	100
Administrator (R.)	8	4	5	5	22	36	18	23	23	100
Administrator (N.R.)	0	4	7	10	21	0	19	33	48	100
Worker	2	20	11	23	56	4	36	20	40	100
Woman	0	6	2	11	19	0	32	10	58	100
Retired	3	5	10	15	33	9	15	30	46	100

TABLE XXIII

Education and Party Affiliation – Specific Councils

Education	1888–9			1903–4				1919–20			
	Con.	Lib.	Total	Con.	Lib.	Lab.	Total	Con.	Lib.	Lab.	Total
Elementary	5	1	6	1	4	1	6	2	3	6	11
Secondary	0	0	0	0	0	0	0	0	0	0	0
Grammar School	1	3	4	2	2	0	4	7	1	0	8
Higher Grade Sc.	0	0	0	0	0	0	0	0	0	0	0
Public School	1	2	3	1	3	0	4	1	2	0	3
College	1	2	3	1	0	0	1	0	0	0	0
University	2	1	3	4	0	0	4	2	1	0	3
Unknown			29				29				23
Total			48				48				48

Education	1929–30				1945–6			1953–4			1962–3		
	Con.	Lib.	Lab.	Total	Con.	Lab.	Total	Con.	Lab.	Total	Con.	Lab.	Total
Elementary	3	4	5	12	3	17	20	6	16	22	3	18	21
Secondary	0	1	0	1	2	0	2	1	3	4	6	5	11
Grammar School	2	1	0	3	1	1	2	5	2	7	10	1	11
Higher Grade Sc.	0	0	0	0	3	2	5	2	3	5	2	2	4
Public School	0	1	0	1	2	0	2	2	0	2	2	0	2
College	0	0	0	0	0	0	0	0	0	0	0	0	0
University	1	0	0	1	2	1	3	1	1	2	3	0	3
Unknown				34			26			18			8
Total				52			60			60			60

TABLE XXIV

Average Ages of Council Members

	1888–9	1903–4	1919–20	1929–30	1945–6	1953–4	1962–3
Councillors							
Lib.	49·1	52·1	54·4	56	—	—	—
Con.	43·7	54·7	49·8	54·1	58·9	53·9	47·2
Lab.	—	43·6	54·5	50·6	46·5	51·4	53·3
Rest	71	57·5	39·3	62	—	—	—
All Councillors	48·1	52·7	50·5	53·7	53·2	52·4	50·3
Aldermen							
Lib.	59·2	61·3	63·2	61·6	—	—	—
Con.	54·6	55·6	65·7	62	68	69·4	71·8
Lab.	—	—	—	66	57·9	59·8	64·1
All Aldermen	57·9	58·5	64·6	62·1	61·2	64·3	68·2
Whole Council							
Lib.	54·6	55·3	58	58·6	—	—	—
Con.	45·6	55	54·6	56	59·5	58·2	53·8
Lab.	—	43·6	54·5	51·6	51·5	53·4	55·8
Rest	71	57·5	39·3	62	—	—	—
Whole Council	50·5	54·4	54·5	57·8	53·5	55·4	54·8
Chairmen							
Lib.	54·1	53·4	58	62	—	—	—
Con.	54·6	53·1	57·4	61·1	64·8	58·5	—
Lab.	—	—	—	58·5	55·9	57·1	57
All Chairmen	54·3	53·2	53·2	60·8	59·9	53·1	57

	1873–87	1888–1903	1904–18	1919–30	1931–44	1945–53	1954–62
Mayors							
Lib.	50·2	48·2	50·8	51·2	65	—	—
Con.	47·1	46·5	48·8	61	51·5	51·5	69·5
Lab.	—	—	—	55	62	52	57·8
All Mayors	49·4	47·2	49·8	54·6	52·6	51·7	60·4

	1888–1903	1903–19	1919–29	1929–45	1945–53	1953–62
New Entrants						
Lib.	42·8	43·9	48·8	48	—	—
Con.	42·2	43·4	47	47·2	45·7	42·6
Lab.	39·6	32·5	39·9	48·1	45·4	46·1
Rest	52	44·5	46	—	—	—
All New Entrants	43·1	43·3	44·6	47·5	45·5	44

	1873–88	1888–1903	1903–19	1919–29	1929–45	1945–53	1953–62
New Aldermen							
Lib.	50·5	50·6	54·6	57·5	63·3	—	—
Con.	48	49·6	58·5	54·6	63·9	56	70·1
Lab.	—	—	—	62	61·6	54·9	59·2
All New Aldermen	49·8	50	57·1	56·6	65·1	55·2	65·1

TABLE XXV

Average Years of Service of Council Members

	1888–9	1903–4	1919–20	1929–30	1945–6	1953–4	1962–3
Councillors							
Lib.	7·2	4·7	13·2	8·1	—	—	—
Con.	5·1	6·9	6·8	6·3	9·6	7·9	3·8
Lab.	—	2·7	7	4·9	2·2	4·6	8·6
Rest	7·5	4·5	6·5	1·5	—	—	—
All Councillors	6·3	5·6	7·7	5·9	5·6	7·6	6·2
Aldermen							
Lib.	16·7	19·8	23·4	22·8	—	—	—
Con.	12·4	19	28·4	17·5	26·2	29·5	24·2
Lab.	—	—	—	28	19	19·6	24·8
All Aldermen	14·9	19·4	26·3	20·7	21·4	20·2	24·5
Whole Council							
Lib.	10·1	9·7	17·5	14·9	—	—	—
Con.	6·9	9·9	12·6	9·1	12·8	14	9·3
Lab.	—	2·7	7	6·6	7·1	8	12·4
Rest	7·5	4·5	6·5	1·5	—	—	—
Whole Council	9·9	9	12·3	9·6	9·6	10·5	12·5
Chairmen							
Lib.	15	14	19·6	23·1	—	—	—
Con.	11·4	13·6	12·4	14	17·2	17·4	—
Lab.	—	—	—	14	11·9	12	13·6
All Chairmen	13·9	13·7	15	17·3	14·4	14·3	13·6

Service on Appointment							
	1873–87	1888–1903	1904–18	1919–30	1931–44	1945–53	1954–62
Mayors							
Lib.	7·1	12·5	8·6	10·5	12·7	—	—
Con.	5·7	9·8	7·3	13	9·1	14·7	16
Lab.	—	—	—	15·5	19·5	16·2	14·5
All Mayors	6·6	10·8	7·9	12·3	11·8	15·5	14·8

Service on Appointment							
	1873–88	1888–1903	1903–19	1919–30	1930–45	1945–53	1953–62
New Aldermen							
Lib.	7·3	13·1	11·3	14·4	14·6	—	—
Con.	6·5	10·6	13·7	8	16·7	19·2	19·1
Lab.	—	—	—	24	18	12·8	11·8
All New Aldermen	7	11·6	12·7	12·3	16·4	14·5	15·8

TABLE XXVI

Quality of Specific Councils

Type of Councillor	1888–9 %	1903–4 %	1919–20 %	1929–30 %	1945–6 %	1953–4 %	1962–3 %
A	10	10	12	8	8	5	2
B	29	27	19	23	18	25	28
C	17	23	31	32	30	33	26
D	44	40	38	37	44	37	44

TABLE XXVII

Quality of Council Members and Party Allegiance

Absolute figures

Specific Council	TYPE A					TYPE B					TYPE C					TYPE D					Grand Total
	Con.	Lib.	Lab.	Ind.	Total	Con.	Lib.	Lab.	Ind.	Total	Con.	Lib.	Lab.	Ind.	Total	Con.	Lib.	Lab.	Ind.	Total	
1888–9	3	2	0	0	5	7	7	0	0	14	4	3	0	0	7	9	9	0	4	22	48
1903–4	3	2	0	0	5	5	6	2	0	13	5	4	2	0	11	11	7	0	1	19	48
1919–20	3	2	1	0	6	4	4	1	0	9	7	5	2	0	14	12	1	2	4	19	48
1929–30	2	1	1	0	4	6	4	2	0	12	7	5	5	0	17	11	3	5	0	19	52
1945–6	2	0	3	0	5	3	0	8	0	11	10	1	7	0	18	8	2	14	2	26	60
1953–4	1	0	2	0	3	5	0	10	0	15	11	0	9	0	20	8	0	14	0	22	60
1962–3	0	0	1	0	1	6	0	11	0	17	12	0	4	0	16	12	0	14	0	26	60

TABLE XXVIII

Occupational Composition of the Chairmen

Occupation	1888–9	1903–4	1919–20	1929–30	1945–6	1953–4	1962–3
Manufacturer	8	6	5	4	3	2	0
Shopkeeper	0	3	4	4	3	7	3
Drink	0	2	2	2	1	1	1
Professional	3	4	3	1	2	1	0
Administrator (R.)	1	1	2	1	1	2	2
Administrator (N.R.)	0	0	0	1	2	0	3
Worker	0	0	0	3	3	5	6
Woman	0	0	0	0	1	3	5
Retired	0	0	1[1]	3[2]	6[3]	1[4]	1[5]
Total	12	16	17	19	22	22	21

[1] Retired Shopkeeper.
[2] Retired Shopkeeper, Commercial Traveller, Insurance Agent.
[3] Retired Manufacturer, Brewer, Worker, 3 Railwaymen.
[4] Retired Worker.
[5] Retired Worker.

TABLE XXIX

Occupational Composition of the Chairmen and Party Allegiance

Occupation	1888–9			1903–4			1919–20			1929–30		
	Con.	Lib.	Lab.	Con.	Lib.	Lab.	Con.	Lib.	Lab.	Con.	Lib.	Lab.
Manufacturer	2	6	0	4	2	0	3	2	0	1	2	1
Shopkeeper	0	0	0	1	2	0	2	2	0	1	3	0
Drink	0	0	0	2	0	0	2	0	0	2	0	0
Professional	3	0	0	3	1	0	3	0	0	1	0	0
Administrator (R.)	0	1	0	1	0	0	1	1	0	0	1	0
Administrator (N.R.)	0	0	0	0	0	0	0	0	0	0	1	0
Worker	0	0	0	0	0	0	0	0	0	0	0	3
Woman	0	0	0	0	0	0	0	0	0	0	0	0
Retired	0	0	0	0	0	0	0	1	0	3	0	0
Total	5	7	0	11	5	0	11	6	0	8	7	4

Occupation	1945–6			1953–4			1962–3	
	Con.	Lib.	Lab.	Con.	Lib.	Lab.	Con.	Lab.
Manufacturer	3	0	0	1	0	1	0	0
Shopkeeper	2	0	1	5	0	2	0	3
Drink	1	0	0	1	0	0	0	1
Professional	2	0	0	1	0	0	0	0
Administrator (R.)	0	0	1	1	0	1	0	2
Administrator (N.R.)	0	0	2	0	0	0	0	3
Worker	0	0	3	0	0	5	0	6
Woman	0	0	1	0	0	3	0	5
Retired	2	1	3	0	0	1	0	1
Total	10	1	11	9	0	13	0	21

Source: newspapers, *Council Minutes* and *Yearbooks.*

J.B.P.

TABLE XXX

Occupational Composition of the Mayors

Occupation	1848–68	1868–88	1888–1900	1900–10	1910–19	1919–30	1930–40	1940–50	1950–61
Manufacturer	7	9	4	0	0	2	4	2	0
Shopkeeper	5	1	1	2	3	2	1	3	2
Drink	0	0	0	2	1	0	1	1	1
Professional	4	2	1	4	2	0	1	1	0
Administrator (R.)	2	2	2	1	1	0	1	1	1
Administrator (N.R.)	0	0	0	0	0	0	0	1	0
Worker	0	0	0	0	0	1	1	0	4
Woman	0	0	0	0	0	0	0	0	2
Retired	0	0	0	0	0	2	0	1	2
Unknown	1	4	0	0	0	0	0	0	0

TABLE XXXI

Occupational Composition of the Mayors and Party Allegiance

Occupation	1888–1900			1900–10			1910–19			1919–30		
	Con.	Lib.	Lab.	Con.	Lib.	Lab.	Con.	Lib.	Lab.	Con.	Lib.	Lab.
Manufacturer	2	2	0	0	0	0	0	0	0	0	2	0
Shopkeeper	0	1	0	0	2	0	0	2	0	0	1	0
Drink	0	0	0	2	0	0	1	0	0	0	0	0
Professional	1	0	0	3	1	0	2	0	0	0	0	0
Administrator (R.)	2	0	0	0	1	0	1	1	0	0	0	0
Administrator (N.R.)	0	0	0	0	0	0	0	0	0	0	0	0
Worker	0	0	0	0	0	0	0	0	0	0	0	2
Woman	0	0	0	0	0	0	0	0	0	0	0	0
Retired	0	0	0	0	0	0	0	0	0	2	0	0
Total	5	3	0	5	4	0	4	3	0	2	3	2

Occupation	1930–40			1940–50			1950–64		
	Con.	Lib.	Lab.	Con.	Lib.	Lab.	Con.	Lib.	Lab.
Manufacturer	3	1	0	1	1	0	0	0	0
Shopkeeper	1	0	0	1	0	2	3	0	2
Drink	1	0	0	0	0	0	0	0	1
Professional	1	0	0	1	0	0	0	0	0
Administrator (R.)	0	1	0	0	0	1	1	0	0
Administrator (N.R.)	0	0	0	0	0	1	0	0	0
Worker	0	0	1	0	0	0	0	0	4
Woman	0	0	0	0	1	0	0	0	2
Retired	0	0	0	0	0	0	1	0	1
Total	6	2	1	3	2	4	5	0	10

TABLE XXXII

Occupational Composition of New Aldermen

Occupation	1848–68	1868–88	1888–99	1900–10	1910–19	1919–30	1930–40	1940–50	1950–60
Manufacturer	9	9	5	0	0	5	3	3	1
Shopkeeper	8	2	1	0	2	4	2	4	4
Drink	1	0	0	3	0	2	2	2	0
Professional	5	2	2	3	2	0	0	2	0
Administrator (R.)	4	1	2	0	1	0	1	1	0
Administrator (N.R.)	0	0	0	0	0	0	1	1	0
Worker	0	0	0	0	0	0	2	2	6
Woman	0	0	0	0	0	0	0	0	2
Retired	0	0	1	0	0	2	2	2	1
Unknown	12	4	0	0	0	0	0	0	0
Total	39	18	11	6	5	13	13	17	14

TABLE XXXIII

Occupational Composition of New Aldermen and Party Allegiance

Occupation	1888–99			1900–10			1910–19			1919–30		
	Con.	Lib.	Lab.	Con.	Lib.	Lab.	Con.	Lib.	Lab.	Con.	Lib.	Lab.
Manufacturer	2	3	0	0	0	0	0	0	0	2	3	0
Shopkeeper	0	1	0	0	0	0	0	2	0	2	2	0
Drink	0	0	0	3	0	0	0	0	0	1	0	0
Professional	2	0	0	2	1	0	2	0	0	0	0	0
Administrator (R.)	2	0	0	0	0	0	0	1	0	0	0	0
Administrator (N.R.)	0	0	0	0	0	0	0	0	0	0	0	0
Worker	0	0	0	0	0	0	0	0	0	0	0	1
Woman	0	0	0	0	0	0	0	0	0	0	0	0
Retired	1	0	0	0	0	0	0	0	0	2	0	0
Total	7	4	0	5	1	0	2	3	0	7	5	1

Occupation	1930–40			1940–50			1950–60		
	Con.	Lib.	Lab.	Con.	Lib.	Lab.	Con.	Lib.	Lab.
Manufacturer	1	2	0	3	0	0	1	0	0
Shopkeeper	2	0	0	2	0	2	4	0	0
Drink	2	0	0	1	0	1	0	0	0
Professional	0	1	0	2	0	0	0	0	0
Administrator (R.)	0	1	0	0	0	1	0	0	0
Administrator (N.R.)	0	0	0	0	0	1	0	0	0
Worker	0	0	2	0	0	2	0	0	6
Woman	0	0	0	0	1	0	0	0	2
Retired	2	0	0	0	0	1	0	0	1
Total	7	4	2	8	1	8	5	0	9

Sources

ECONOMIC AND SOCIAL DEVELOPMENT OF
WOLVERHAMPTON AND DISTRICT

Allen, G. C., *The Industrial Development of Birmingham and the Black Country 1860–1927*, London, 1929.

Beaumont, V. B., *Record of the Wolverhampton Chamber of Commerce, 1856–1956*, Wolverhampton, 1956.

Brennan, T., *Wolverhampton Social and Industrial Survey 1945–6*, Wolverhampton, 1948.

Briggs, A., *The History of Birmingham*, vol. ii, Oxford, 1952.

Brown, E. T., *The Book of the Clyno Car*, London, 1928.

Butter, F. J., *Locks and Lockmaking*, London, 1926, pp. 121–3.

Chiles, C. R., *Railways of the West Midlands 1808–1954*, London, 1954.

Chilton, C., & Stanford, J., *The Vintage Motor Car*, London, 1954.

Court, W. H. B., *The Rise of the Midland Industries 1600–1838*, 2nd ed., London, 1963.

Gill, C., *History of Birmingham*, vol. i, Oxford, 1952.

Griffiths, S., *Blast Furnaces of Great Britain*, 1862.

Holcroft, H., *The Armstrongs of the Great Western*, London, 1953.

Huffer, D. B. H., 'Economic and Social History of Wolverhampton, 1750–1850', Unpublished London M.A. thesis.

Jenks, A. E., *The Staffordshire and Worcestershire Canal*, Wolverhampton, 1907.

Johns, W. D., *Pontypool and Usk Japanned Wares*, Newport, 1953.

Jones, W. H., *The Story of the Japan, Tinplate Working and Iron Braziers' Trades, Bicycle and Galvanising Trades and Enamel Ware Manufacture in Wolverhampton and District*, London, 1900.

Loves, T. E., *A History of Mining in the Black Country*, Dudley, 1898.

Mander, G. le M., *The History of Mander Brothers*, Wolverhampton, 1955.

Montagu of Beaulieu, Lord, *Lost Causes of Motoring*, London, 1960.

Nickols, I., & Karslake, K., *Motoring Entente*, London, 1956.

Perkins, T. R., 'The Railways of Wolverhampton', *Railway Magazine*, July 1952, pp. 448–54 and August 1952, pp. 515–20.

Price, G., *A Treatise on Fire and Thief Proof Depositories and Keys*, London, 1856, pp. 845–92.

Sheldon, J. H., *The Social Medicine of Old Age*, London, 1948.

Timmins, S., *Birmingham and the Midland Hardware District*, London, 1866.

Toller, J., *Papier-mâché in Great Britain and America*, London, 1962, pp. 37–47.

MISCELLANEOUS

Census for 1901, 1911, 1921, 1931, 1951, 1961.

West Midland Group on Post-war Reconstruction and Planning, *Conurbation, a planning survey of Birmingham and the Black Country*, London, 1948.

British Association for the Advancement of Science, *Birmingham and its Regional Setting, a scientific survey*, Birmingham, 1950.

D.S.I.R. Memoirs of the Geological Survey of England and Wales, *The Country between Wolverhampton and Oakengates*, London, 1928.

The Story of the Tyre, Wolverhampton, 1952.

Hobson – a personal story of 50 years, Wolverhampton, 1953.

The History and Development of the Sunbeam Car 1899–1924, Wolverhampton, 1924.

A Brief History of Wolverhampton and one of its many flourishing industries, J. Thompson Ltd., Wolverhampton, 1927.

The Wolverhampton Reference Library has a collection of brochures issued by various firms in the town, describing their activities, and it has collected programmes from exhibitions which have been held in the town, which describe many of the trades of the area. The library also has some magazines issued by local enterprises, e.g. Manders', Chillington Tool, Courtaulds' and Butler's.

THE TOWN

(1) Directories and Guides

The Wolverhampton Red Book and Directory – almost annually published 1892–1960 in Wolverhampton, incorporated in *Kelly's*

Directory of Wolverhampton after 1960, published in Kingston upon Thames.

Official Handbook to the town, published by the Corporation, 1929, 1930, 1931, 1935, 1936, 1938, 1948, 1949–50, 1953, 1956, 1960, 1963.

Commercial Directory, Manchester, 1818, pp. 471–81.

Directory of Wolverhampton, Wolverhampton, 1827.

The Birmingham, Wolverhampton, Walsall, Dudley, Bilston and Willenhall Directory, London, 1831, pp. 71–90.

Bridgen's Directory of the Borough of Wolverhampton, Wolverhampton, 1833, 1838.

Wolverhampton Post Office Directory, Wolverhampton, 1847.

Wolverhampton Directory for 1849, Wolverhampton.

Melville's Directory of Wolverhampton, Worcester, 1851.

The Household and General Almanack and Strangers' Guide of Wolverhampton, Wolverhampton, 1854.

Wolverhampton Almanack and Strangers' Guide to South Staffordshire, Wolverhampton, 1855.

Wolverhampton and Staffordshire Almanack and Directory for 1856 and 1857, Wolverhampton.

Wolverhampton and South Staffordshire Almanack and Municipal Directory, Wolverhampton 1861 and 1862.

Trades Directory of Wolverhampton, London, 1862–3.

Steen and Blackett's Wolverhampton Guide, Wolverhampton, 1871.

Visitors' Guide to Wolverhampton, Wolverhampton, 1871.

Hurley's Directory of the Parliamentary Borough of Wolverhampton, Birmingham, 1873.

Hurley's Directory of the Hardware District, Birmingham, 1879–80.

Directory of Wolverhampton and Six Miles Round, London, 1879–1880.

Crocker's Post Office Wolverhampton and District Directory, Birmingham, 1884.

Barker's Wolverhampton Trade Directory and Guide, Wolverhampton, 1887.

Old King Coal's Guide to Wolverhampton, Wolverhampton, 1884.

Mansell's Family Almanack, Wolverhampton, 1885, 1886, 1887.

Hinde's District Almanack, Wolverhampton, 1886.

Handbook and Popular Guide to Wolverhampton, Wolverhampton, 1890.

Hinde's Household Almanack, Wolverhampton, 1890.

Peck's Circular Trades Directory, Birmingham, 1896–7.

The Prico Illustrated Descriptive Guide to Wolverhampton, Cheltenham, 1906.

Hinde's Household Almanack, Wolverhampton, 1909.

Spennell's Wolverhampton Directory, Birmingham, 1921–2.

Classified Industrial Directory, Manchester, 1952.

G.P.O. Telephone Directory for West Midland Area (Northern), 1961.

(2) General

The Development Plan, Wolverhampton, March 1952 – comprising the written statement, report of the Town Planning Committee, report of the survey and proposals with maps.

Local Government Commission, *Final Report and Proposals for the West Midlands Special Review Area*, London, May 1961.

Report of the Inspectors appointed by the Ministry of Housing and Local Government to hear objections to the proposals of the Local Government Commission for England for a pattern of County Boroughs for the Black Country, London, 1962.

Adams, R. J., *Album of Wolverhampton*, Wolverhampton, 1884.

Adams, T., *The Story of a Midland Town*, Wolverhampton, 1908.

Allen, W. E., *The Black Country*, London, 1946.

Burrit, E., *Walks in the Black Country*, 1868.

Gordon, W. J., *Midland Sketches*, 1898, pp. 46–58.

Guy Motors Ltd., *Where Industry and Agriculture Meet*, Wolverhampton, 1953.

Hinde, A., *A Handy History of Wolverhampton and Guide to the District*, Wolverhampton, 1884.

Jeffcock, J. T., *Wolverhampton Guide*, 2nd ed., Wolverhampton, 1884.

Jones, J. P., *The Heart of the Midlands*, Wolverhampton, 1906.

Lawley, G. T., *The Bibliography of Wolverhampton*, Bilston, 1890.

Mander, G. P., & Tildesley, N. W., *A History of Wolverhampton to the early Nineteenth Century*, Wolverhampton, 1960.

Roper, J. S., *Historic Buildings of Wolverhampton*, Wolverhampton, 1957.

Shipman, J., *Holiday Letters of a Geologist*, Nottingham, 1887, pp. 106–41.

(1) The Council

Council Minutes, 1889–1964.
Committee Reports (printed in *Council Minutes*), 1889–1964.
Standing Orders of the Council, 1889–1964.
Delegation Book of the Council, 1911–64.
Council Diaries and Yearbooks, 1889–1964.

(2) Acts, Statutory Instruments, By-laws

The Wolverhampton Acts and Orders including the Charter of Incorporation, ed. C. Pritchard, 1908 – contains at back the Wolverhampton Corporation Acts, 1925, 1928, 1932 and 1950.
Alphabetical Index to the Wolverhampton local Acts and Orders 1908–41 and Table of Amendments and Repeals in the Wolverhampton local Acts and Orders 1869–1941 from 1904 to 1941, ed. J. B. Allon.
By-laws, County Borough of Wolverhampton, 1926–37, 1938–59.
Wolverhampton Local Acts:
Wolverhampton Improvement Act, 1869, 32 & 33 Vict. cxxxi.
—————— Corporation Loans Act, 1882, 45 & 46 Vict. ccxl.
—————— —————— Act, 1887, 50 & 51 Vict. clxxiv.
—————— —————— ——1891, 54 & 55 Vict. cxiv.
—————— —————— ——1899, 62 & 63 Vict. cclix.
—————— —————— ——1904, 4 Edw. VII, xcix.
—————— —————— ——1908, 8 Edw. VII, lxxv.
—————— —————— Water Act, 1915, 5 & 6 Geo. V, lxiv.
—————— —————— Act, 1920, 10 & 11 Geo. V, lxx.
—————— —————— ——1925, 15 & 16 Geo. V, cxxiii.
—————— —————— ——1926, 16 & 17 Geo. V, cvi.
—————— —————— ——1928, 18 & 19 Geo. V, cix.
—————— —————— ——1932, 22 & 23 Geo. V, xc.
—————— —————— ——1936, 26 Geo. V and 1 Edw. VIII, cxi.
—————— —————— ——1950, 14 Geo. VI, lviii.

(3) General

The Book of the Century 1848–1948, Wolverhampton, 1948.

A Report on the Growth of the Borough of Wolverhampton by J. B. Allon, The Town Clerk, in the *Council Minutes*, 20.5.1948.

The Public Parks of Wolverhampton, Historical Sketch, Wolverhampton, 1881.

Centenary of the Opening of the Retail Market Hall, 1853–1953, commemorative pamphlet, 1953.

Markets Handbook, 1961.

A Brief History of the Water Undertaking and description of new work, 1911.

A History of the Water Supply of Wolverhampton 1847–1947, Wolverhampton, 1947.

Barnes, J. P., *Sewage Disposal in Wolverhampton*, Typescript, 1963.

Berrington, R. E. W., *A short account of the Wolverhampton Sewage Works with some remarks on the Pan System*, Wolverhampton, 1891.

Bishop, R. A., *The Electric Trolley Bus*, London, 1931, pp. 19, 22, 46, 55, 91, 111.

Report of Sir H. E. Haward to W. H. Fisher on the *Defalcations of Jesse Varley*, London, October 1917.

Jones, J., *The Mayors of Wolverhampton*, vol. i, 1848–80; vol. ii, 1881–1909.

Jones, W. H., *The Story of the Municipal Life of Wolverhampton*, London, 1903.

Webb, J. S., *Tramways of the Black Country*, Bloxwich, 1954.

AUTOBIOGRAPHIES, BIOGRAPHIES, MEMOIRS

Amery, L. S., *My Political Life*, vol. i, London, 1953.

Bantock, A. B., *Memoirs of my Father's Retirement from Public Life*, Wolverhampton, 1893.

Brodhurst, J. P., *William Parke, a Sketch*, Wolverhampton, 1876.

Brown, W. J., *So far . . .*, London, 1943.

Dictionary of National Biography, vol. xx, *sub* 'Charles Pelham Villiers', London, 1909, pp. 318–23, and 2nd Supplement, *sub* 'Henry Hartley Fowler', London, 1912, pp. 49–52.

Drummond, J. S., *Charles A. Berry. A Memoir*, London, 1899.

Anon., *Reminiscences of the Reverend C. A. Berry*, 1899.

Fowler, E. H., *The Life of Henry Hartley Fowler*, London, 1912.

Henderson, W. O., 'Charles Pelham Villiers', *History*, 1952, pp. 25–39.

Husenbeth, F. C., *The Life of the Right Reverend John Milner*, Dublin, 1862.

Love, T., *Poke your own fire and burn your own lamp. The life of Councillor Joseph Devey*, Barnsley, 1884.

Owen, J. B., *G. B. Thorneycroft. A Memoir*, London, 1856.

Yates, J., *Lifting Timber for the King*, London, 1939.

VARIOUS TOPICS

Guide to the Church Congress, Wolverhampton, 1887.

A Record of the 900th Anniversary of the Collegiate Church of Wolverhampton, Wolverhampton, 1894.

SS. Mary and John, Wolverhampton, 1855–1955, West Bromwich, 1955.

Centenary of Darlington Street Methodist Church, 1825–1955, Wolverhampton, 1955.

Trinity Methodist Church, 1863–1963, Wolverhampton, 1963.

Wolverhampton and South Staffordshire Biographical and Commercial Sketches, London, 1899.

History of the Wolverhampton and Midland Counties Eye Infirmary, Wolverhampton, 1931.

West Midland Group on Post-War Reconstruction and Planning, *Local Government and Central Control*, London, 1956.

Anderson, J. S., *Presbyterian Church of England, Merridale Road 1862–1962*, Wolverhampton, 1962.

Barnett, T. J., *A History of the Lodge of Honour No. 526 holden at Wolverhampton 1846–96*, Wolverhampton, 1896.

Berry, C. A., *Municipal Patriotism* (a sermon), Wolverhampton, November 1896.

Corbett, G., *100 years at Heath Town*, Wolverhampton, n.d., but about 1952.

Express and Star supplement 'About Ourselves', 13.1.1958.

Jones, J., *Historical Sketch of the Art and Literary Institutions of Wolverhampton 1794–1897*, London, 1897.

Jones, J. C., *Quakerism in an Industrial Town 1704–1803*, type-script, n.d.

Jones, W. H., *History of the Congregational Church of Wolverhampton*, London, 1894.

Mander, G. P., *History of the Wolverhampton Grammar School*, Wolverhampton, 1913.

Matthews, A. G., *The Congregational Churches of Staffordshire*, London, 1924.

May, H. A., *Queen Street Congregational Church. The Story of 100 years 1809–1909*, Wolverhampton, 1909.

Pratt, A. C., *Black Country Methodism*, London, 1891.

Roper, J. S., *A History of St John's Church Wolverhampton*, Halesowen, 1958.

Small, H., & Farlan, J. M., *Mr Small's Book*, typescript of a BBC broadcast 11.3.1953 on the 60 years in Wolverhampton journalism of W. Small.

The Thorneycroft's Patents and Inventions with Tours, flights, trips, sports and pastimes and biographical sketches, Wolverhampton, 1891, Author not given.

Wells, H. G., *The New Machiavelli*, London, 1911.

Willmore, F. W., *A History of Freemasonry in the Province of Staffordshire*, Wolverhampton, 1905.

PARTIES

(1) Conservative

Minute book of the East Wolverhampton Conservative Association, 1918–1930s.

Minute book of the Wolverhampton Conservative Group, 1952–1961.

Minute books of the Management Committee of the West Wolverhampton Conservative Association, 1908–35.

Miscellaneous papers and minute books of the West and then the South-West Wolverhampton Conservative Association from the late 1930s to the early 1950s.

Model Rules No. 3, Conservative and Unionist Central Office, London, 1956.

Press Cutting Books of the West Wolverhampton Conservative Association, 1918–45.

Subscription Book of the West Wolverhampton Conservative Association, 1907–47.

Terms of Reference of the Wolverhampton Conservative Group, 1961.

(2) Labour

Local Government Handbook, The Labour Party, London, 1960.

Minute book of the N.U.R. No. 6 branch Wolverhampton, 1923–1926.

Minute books of the Wolverhampton Labour Party and its Executive Committee, 1907–48.

Minute books of the Wolverhampton Labour Group, 1945–61.

Minutes and miscellaneous papers of the Wolverhampton Central Labour Party, the Policy Committee and the Organising Committees, 1948–50.

Panel of Labour Party Municipal Candidates, November 1962 and November 1963.

Rules of the N.E., S.W. and Borough Labour Parties in Wolverhampton.

Wolverhampton, Bilston and District Trade Council Yearbooks, 1940s, 1950s, 1960s.

(3) Liberal

Minute books of the League of Young Liberals in Wolverhampton, 1923–9.

(4) Ratepayers

Minute books and papers of the Penn Ratepayers' Association, 1930–55.

The Pennman – journal of the Penn Ratepayers' Association. One issue only, in 1948.

(5) Communist

A statement on the future of Education in Wolverhampton, Wolverhampton Communist Party, 1963.

NEWSPAPERS AND JOURNALS

Express and Star, 1889–1964.
Wolverhampton Chronicle, 1889–1930, 1947–64.
——— *Journal*, 1902–9.
——— *Magazine*, 1963–4.
——— *Times*, 1930–1.
——— *Worker*, 1913–15.
Midland Evening News, 1889–1915.
Shaw's Monthly Home Journal and Advertising Medium, renamed
  Wolverhampton Free Journal, 1913–14.
The Congregationalist.
Birmingham Post.
The Times.
The Guardian.
Sunday Times.
Observer.
Justice of the Peace.
Municipal Journal.
Municipal Yearbook.
Whitaker's Almanack.
All England Law Reports.
Weekly Law Reports.

MISCELLANEOUS

Wolverhampton Rotary Club Yearbook 1961–62.
Annual Report of the Graiseley Tenants' Association, 1963.
Personal press-cuttings and scrapbooks of:
  A. A. Beach
  L. R. Guy
  J. C. Homer
  J. F. Myatt.
Notes for an autobiography by W. Lawley.
Letters to the author from:
  H. Brabin, Local Government Officer, Conservative Central
  Office.
  W. Lawley.
  S. C. Loweth, Secretary of Wolverhampton Rotary Club.

Gravestones in the Wolverhampton Cemetery, Jeffcock Road.
Maps:
(i) Alfred Hinde's Map of Wolverhampton with borough and ward boundaries marked by the Borough Engineer's Department.
(ii) Burrow's Pointer Guide Map of Wolverhampton, London, n.d., *circa* 1961.
(iii) Those in the various guides to the town.

Interviews with 105 past and present members of the Council, officials and party leaders. Questionnaires returned from 92 past and present members of the Council.

ELECTION ADDRESSES

1900   *Liberal* A. B. Bantock.
1919   *Discharged and Demobilised Sailors' and Soldiers'* W. Morgan.
1939   *Conservative* L. R. Guy.
1945   *Anti-Socialist* M. P. Birch, L. R. Guy, W. J. Rawlins.
        Labour H. E. Preece.
        Communist Miss D. E. Bootman.
        Independent A. E. Lacon.
1951   *Ratepayer* J. Ireland.
1960   *Conservative* T. J. Blest.
1961   *Labour* A. Morey, F. Henderson.
        Conservative F. C. Evans, D. Reynolds.
1962   *Conservative* H. Miller.
        Labour G. J. Costley.
1963   *Conservative* R. G. Gough.
        Labour A. Lusby.
1964   *Labour* H. Bagley, P. F. Bentley, D. A. Birch, S. E. Birt, L. Clutton, M. Collis, Mrs V. A. Costley, J. G. Davies, E. J. Foster, R. J. Garner, Mrs W. F. K. Reynolds, H. Turner.
        Conservative S. Brindley, H. J. Ebbon, F. C. Evans, F. E. C. Goatman, R. J. Greenly, G. A. Guy, W. G. Morrison, S. E. Nicholls.
        Liberal R. J. Beddow, R. J. Washbourne, A. H. Wright.
        Communist M. J. Bennett, K. Evans, W. F. Laws, K. H. Pearce.

Author attended meetings of:
  Wolverhampton Conservative Group.
  ——   Labour Group.
  ——   Borough Labour Party.
  South-West Wolverhampton Constituency Labour Party's General Management Committee.
  Blakenhall Ward Labour Party.
  Wolverhampton Fabian Society.
  North-East Wolverhampton Conservative Association, Young Conservatives.

STUDIES OF OTHER AREAS IN BRITAIN AND OF THE TOPICS
CONSIDERED IN THIS THESIS

Barker, B., *Labour in London*, London, 1964.
Bealey, F., & Bartholomew, D. J., 'The Local Elections in Newcastle under Lyme, May 1958', *British Journal of Sociology*, 1962, pp. 273–85 and 350–68.
Bealey, F., *et al.*, *Constituency Politics*, London, 1965.
Benham, H., *Two Cheers for the Town Hall*, London, 1946.
Bentley, B. R., 'Conventions in Local Government: a study of the party system in Coventry', Pnpublished Birmingham M.Comm. thesis, 1960.
Birch, A. H., 'The Habit of Voting', *Manchester School*, 1950, and *Small Town Politics*, Oxford, 1959.
Block, G., *Party Politics in Local Government*, London, 1962.
Blondel, J., 'The Conservative Association and the Labour Party in Reading', *Political Studies*, 1958, pp. 101–19.
Bonnor, J., 'Public Interest in Local Government', *Public Administration*, 1954, pp. 425–8.
Brennan, T., *et al.*, 'Party Politics and Local Government in Western South Wales', *Political Quarterly*, 1954, pp. 76–83, and *Social Change in S.W. Wales*, London, 1954, ch. 5.
Briggs, A., *Victorian Cities*, London, 1963.
Bulpitt, J. G., 'Party Systems in Local Government', *Political Studies*, 1963, pp. 11–35.
Bulpitt, J. G., *Party Politics in English Local Government*, London, 1967.

Butler, D. E., 'Local Government in Parliament', *Public Administration*, 1953, pp. 46–7.

Chester, D. N., 'Council and Committee Meetings in County Boroughs', *Public Administration*, 1954, pp. 429–31.

Cole, G. D. H., *Local and Regional Government*, London, 1947, ch. 13.

Cole, M., *Servant of the County*, London, 1956.

Davies, C. S., *A History of Macclesfield*, Manchester, 1961.

Donnison, D. V., & Plowman, D. E. G., 'The Functions of Local Labour Parties', *Political Studies*, 1954, pp. 154–67.

Garner, J. F., 'Administration in a Small Authority' (Andover), *Public Administration*, 1960, pp. 227–33.

Gowan, I., 'Role and Power of Political Parties in Local Government', *Local Government Today . . . and Tomorrow*, ed. Dudley Lofts, London, 1962.

Grundy, J., 'Non-Voting in an Urban District', *Manchester School*, 1950, pp. 83–99.

Hasluck, E. L., *Local Government in England*, Cambridge, 1948, pp. 32–7.

Headrick, T., *The Town Clerk in English Local Government*, London, 1962.

Howard, A., 'City Before Party' (Manchester), *New Statesman*, 1964, p. 202, and 'Power Behind the Throne' (Nottingham), *New Statesman*, 1964, p. 234.

Hutchison, P., 'Committee System in East Suffolk', *Public Administration*, 1959, pp. 393–402.

Jackson, R. M., *The Machinery of Local Government*, London, 1956, ch. iv.

Jennings, W. I., 'Corruption and the Public Service', *Political Quarterly*, 1938, pp. 31–46.

Keith-Lucas, B., 'A Note on the legal aspects of agreements between local political parties', *Political Studies*, 1957, p. 88, and 'Local Government in Parliament', *Public Administration*, 1955, pp. 207–10; and *The Mayor, Aldermen and Councillors*, Unservile State Papers No. 3, 1961, and *The Councils, the Press and the People*, Conservative Central Office, 1961.

Lee, J. M., *Social Leaders and Public Persons*, Oxford, 1963.

MacColl, J. E., 'The Party System in English Local Government', *Public Administration*, 1949, pp. 69–75.

Mackenzie, W. J. M., 'Local Government in Parliament', *Public*

Administration, 1954, pp. 409–23, and 'The Conventions of Local Government', *Public Administration*, 1951, pp. 345–56.

Maddick, H., & Pritchard, E. P., 'The Conventions of Local Authorities in the West Midlands', *Public Administration*, 1958, pp. 145–55 and 1959, pp. 135–43.

Morrison, H., *How Greater London is Governed*, London, 1935.

Ostrogorski, M., *Democracy and the Organization of Political Parties*, vol. i, London, 1902.

Powell, B. M., 'A study of the change in social origins, political affiliations and length of service of members of the Leeds City Council 1888–1953', Unpublished Leeds M.A. thesis, 1958.

Redford, A., *A History of Local Government in Manchester*, vols. i, ii, and iii, London, 1939–40.

Rees, A. M., & Smith, T., *Town Councillors*, London, 1964.

Robson, W. A., *The Government and Misgovernment of London*, London, 1954.

Sharpe, L. J., 'The Politics of Local Government in Greater London', *Public Administration*, 1960, pp. 157–72, and *A Metropolis Votes*, London, 1962; and 'Elected Representatives in Local Government', *British Journal of Sociology*, 1962, pp. 189–209.

Sharpe, L. J. (ed.), *Voting in Cities*, London, 1967. Contains a good bibliography, pp. 337–40.

Simon, E. D., *A City Council from Within*, London, 1926.

Simon, S. D., *A Century of City Government, Manchester 1838–1938*, London, 1938.

Stacey, M., *Tradition and Change – a study of Banbury*, Oxford, 1960.

Stanyer, J., *County Government in England and Wales*, London, 1967.

Swaffield, J. C., 'Greenfingers in the Council Chamber' (Blackpool), *Public Administration*, 1960, pp. 131–5.

Thornhill, W., 'Agreements between Local Parties in Local Government Matters', *Political Studies*, 1957, pp. 83–8.

Warren, J. H., 'The Party System in Local Government', *The British Party System*, ed. S. D. Bailey, London, 1952, and *Municipal Administration*, London, 1948, ch. xiv.

White, B. D., *A History of the Corporation of Liverpool*, Liverpool, 1951.

Williams, J. E., 'Paternalism in Local Government in the Nine-teenth Century', *Public Administration*, 1955, pp. 439–45.

Willson, F. M. G., *Administrators in Action*, London, 1961.

Wiseman, H. V., 'The Working of Local Government in Leeds', *Public Administration*, 1963, pp. 51–69, 137–55; 'Local Government in Leeds', Unpublished typescript; *Local Government at Work*, London, 1967.

'N.A.L.G.O. survey Interest in Local Government', *Public Administration*, Autumn 1957, pp. 305–9.

'Councils and Delegations to Committees' (a Brighton report), *Public Administration*, 1958, pp. 279–83.

'What's wrong with Local Government?', *The Economist*, 30.1.1960, pp. 401–13.

'The Machinery of Local Government', *Local Government Chronicle*, 29.4.1961, pp. 555–6; 6.5.1961, pp. 591–2; 13.5.1961, pp. 631–2.

Conference proceedings, Report of the Local Government Research Conference held at the University of Exeter, 25–27 September 1963.

Report of the Committee on the Management of Local Government, 5 vols., H.M.S.O., 1967.

AMERICAN STUDIES WHICH GIVE VALUABLE INSIGHTS INTO METHODS OF APPROACH TO THE STUDY OF URBAN POLITICS

Banfield, E. C., *Political Influence*, Glencoe, Illinois, 1961.

Banfield, E. C., & Wilson, J. Q., *City Politics*, Cambridge, Mass., 1963.

Dahl, R. A., *Who Governs?*, New Haven, 1961.

Kaufman, H., *Politics and Policies in State and Local Governments*, New Jersey, 1963.

Polsby, N. W., *Community Power and Political Theory*, New Haven, 1963.

Sayre, W. S., & Kaufman, H., *Governing New York City*, New York, 1960.

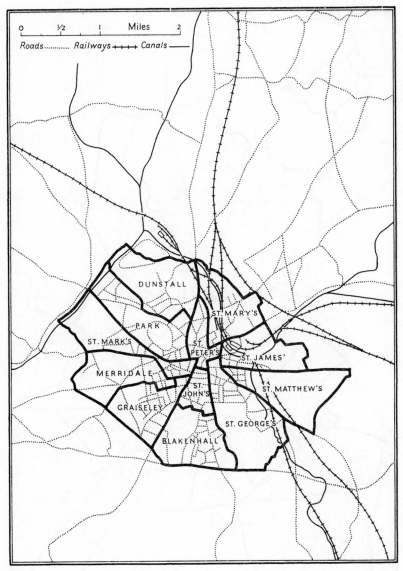

The wards of Wolverhampton, 1896–1926

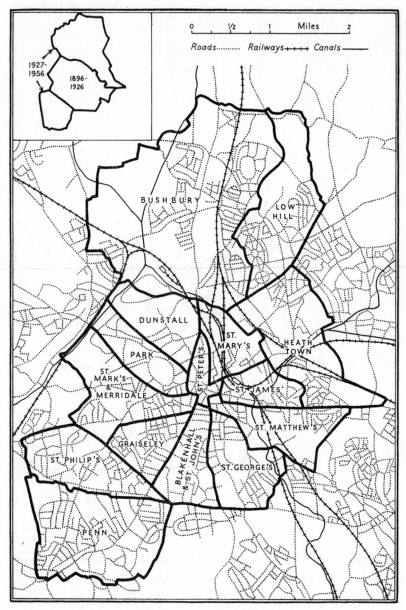

The wards of Wolverhampton, 1927–56

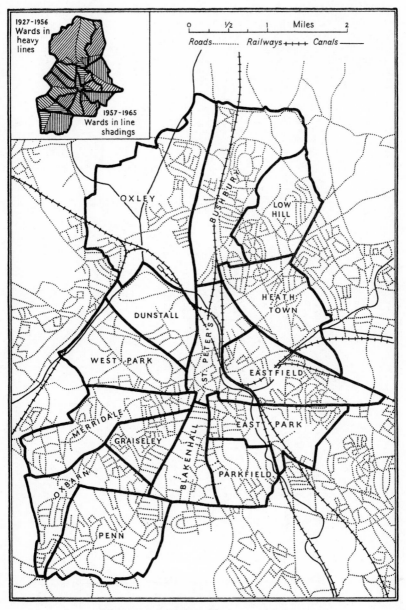

1927-1956 Wards in heavy lines

1957-1965 Wards in line shadings

0   ½   1   Miles   2

Roads............   Railways ++++   Canals ———

OXLEY

BUSHBURY

LOW HILL

DUNSTALL

HEATH TOWN

WEST PARK

ST. PETER'S

EASTFIELD

MERRIDALE

GRAISELEY

EAST PARK

BLAKENHALL

OXBARN

PARKFIELD

PENN

The wards of Wolverhampton, 1957–65

Index